"The message is clear: listen to what's going on with all your senses. Get your business associates and partners to do the same. Pay attention. Get agile."

—Robert H. Waterman
Co-Author of *In Search of Excellence* and Author of *The Renewal Factor*, *Adhocracy: The Power to Change* and *What America Does Right*

"The unfortunate reality is that agile transformations would be better called fragile transformations. It is too easy to unknowingly downplay a critical area that compromises, and often ends, your improvement journey. This book provides the vision, and more importantly the advice, to help get you and then keep you on the path to business agility."

—Scott Ambler
VP & Chief Scientist for Disciplined Agile,
Project Management Institute

"Navigating the contemporary business landscape requires organizations to consider not just market forces, rapidly changing regulatory contexts, fluctuating trade relations, pandemic-driven travel restrictions, huge environmental change and increased competition, but also radically innovative technologies (many driven or enabled by software) that are making obsolete things that seemed new only recently. It's no longer enough to merely follow the leading companies; to survive, organizations must anticipate the future trends using approaches like Wardley Mapping and Domain-driven design (DDD), combined with sense-making techniques like Cynefin® and Team Topologies. And only by explicitly enabling the organization to 'sense' its environment can leaders expect to achieve business agility. *Radical Business Agility* by Hans Amell is a timely book that provides context and actionable patterns for this new 'organizational sensing' that brings true business agility."

—Matthew Skelton
Director at Conflux and Co-Author of *Team Topologies*

"Effective leadership is one of the lynchpins of a successful and agile organization, but getting traditional executives to embrace agility can be tough. *Radical Business Agility* is a practical, pragmatic guide for leaders who understand the need for real, lasting agility but struggle to make it their reality."

—Andrea Fryrear
President and Co-Founder, AgileSherpas

"Hans Amell has written a really important book. For a couple of decades now we have seen a lot of volatility. This is unlikely to change in the foreseeable future. This book provides the reader with a sound intellectual framework for how to cope in different volatile situations using agility as a headline for different activities. It also gives practical advice coming from the vast experience of the author's long life in the corporate sector. It is a book I really recommend for anyone entrusted with leading companies in the next volatile decade."

—Leif Johansson
Chairman Ericsson & AstraZeneca

"Terrific opportunities! This book charts a clear course for your C-suite to consider for quickly and easily leading the business through the 'perfect storms' of uncertainty."

—Hans Levenbach MS, MA, Ph.D.
President Delphus Inc., Co-Author of *Demand Forecasting:*
Practice and Process for Demand Management

"Hans is the wisest person I know. This wisdom comes from thirty years of advising on leadership and agility. Hans has packed this book full of practical methods to improve on organizational agility. By making his valuable insight available to all, Hans created a lasting legacy."

—Martin Wade III
CEO Broadcaster, BOD Professional, Head of
Investment Banking in PriceWaterhouseCoopers

"Reading the book *Radical Business Agility* you cannot help but feel at the mercy against the forces changing the world in devastating directions at an ever-increasing pace. The quest for agility is made so clear that even a fifth grader would lay down his video game, which he or she has just learned to master with great agility. As CEO and majority owner, I have transformed F.E. Bording, a Danish Plc, from printing on paper to IT and communication services over the last 10 years. The authors make it evident that we do not have that long to succeed in the next agile transformation of the business model for my company. To be agile, as the book excellently stresses, it is mandatory to stay vigilant and predict the magnitudes of the disruptions happening when you least expect it. Read the book and your perceptions change, forcing you to think about your pertinent concerns."

—Hans Therp, Ph.D.
CEO F.E. Bording

"*Radical Business Agility* is a powerful book describing how excellence is no longer enough. Getting agile also must include how truly great leadership can and should create engagement, plus decisive execution by training in mastering the senses, mindsets and relationships between people. Kurt Larsson and Hans Amell provide great insights and deliver simple effective tools to address that important and growing field. Enjoyable reading and learning!"

—Remy Nilson
Senior Advisor and Former CEO of ATG, Sweden

"*Radical Business Agility* has captured lightning in a bottle—the elusive understandings of dynamic leadership that is required for success in a world of tectonic global business and economic transformations."

—Norman Friedland, JD
Non-Profit Attorney

"*Radical Business Agility* offers a timely look at some of the global political, economic, technological and social forces rocking today's corporate world and offers plenty of well-crafted advice for not only staying afloat but sailing ahead. It is a must-read for current and future business leaders who want to navigate the sea of changes taking place."

—Dr. John W. Graham, Ph.D.
Professor of Economics at Rutgers, The State University of New Jersey

"Today's problem is that change is speeding up. This book can help you better deal with that challenging fact."

—G. Chris Andersen
Investment Banker

"Anything that can save time and money and enhance quality for the healthcare system is mandatory. *Radical Business Agility* with its suggestions can do just that. A must-read for all leaders in healthcare and elsewhere. On a more personal note, I first met Hans some years ago feeding pigeons in 'pigeon park' in San Juan, Puerto Rico. After a start like that, how could things go wrong? We discovered many common interests; family, friends, golf and most of all our 'love' of lawyers and politicians. My friendship with Hans and his family has been a rewarding element in my life through good times and bad. I congratulate the author for this important, eye-opening and timely book."

—John Kirkpatrick, MD, MBA, FACS
Executive Director the Surgical Advisory Group, LLC

"*Radical Business Agility* is a very impressive guide to why corporate agility is an absolute required trait for corporations going forward. As important as a cup of coffee in the morning."

—Henrik Perlmutter, MBA, MSc.
Entrepreneur

RADICAL BUSINESS AGILITY

RADICAL BUSINESS AGILITY

Navigating through Uncertain Times

Hans Amell

with contributions from Kurt Larsson
and a foreword by Robert H. Waterman Jr.

BROWN BOOKS
PUBLISHING GROUP

We have neither asked for nor received any promotional money from any of the companies or people mentioned in this book. We offer them up only as examples we consider that illustrate well the content contained herein.

Radical Business Agility
Navigating through Uncertain Times

Brown Books Publishing Group
Dallas, TX / New York, NY
www.BrownBooks.com
(972) 381-0009

A New Era in Publishing®

Publisher's Cataloging-In-Publication Data

Names: Amell, Hans, author. | Larsson, Kurt, 1957- author.
Title: Radical business agility : navigating through uncertain times / Hans Amell, with Kurt Larsson.
Description: Dallas, TX ; New York, NY : Brown Books Publishing Group, [2022] | Includes bibliographical references and index.
Identifiers: ISBN 9781612545448 (hardback) | ISBN 9781612545660 (ebook)
Subjects: LCSH: Agile project management. | Organizational change. | Business planning.
Classification: LCC HD69.P75 A44 2022 (print) | LCC HD69.P75 (ebook) | DDC 658.404--dc23

ISBN 978-1-61254-544-8
LCCN 2021947767

Printed in the United States
10 9 8 7 6 5 4 3 2 1

For more information or to contact the author, please go to www.MasteringAgilityBlog.com.

CONTENTS

Foreword

I have known Hans for years. Long ago we both worked at McKinsey. During that time, we both skied together, and due to a certain agility in our skiing ability and thinking, we survived an avalanche that could have killed us both. We had ventured into some terrain that looked beautiful, but our senses said "wrong." We gave the snow a kick and a slab of snow, a meter thick and hundred meters wide broke from below us, gained momentum, picked up more snow, and crashed into the valley below.

Most skiers I know wouldn't have survived that avalanche. Hans and I, with years of skiing experience, could employ this book's idea of listening with all our senses (I'm told the Swedish word for this is *Lyhordhet*). The snow "sounded" wrong. We immediately knew what to do. As this book explains quite clearly, leaders in business must be able to sense avalanche-size change in their markets and react appropriately and quickly.

Throughout this book, the authors enumerate and elaborate the forces that could destabilize your business world or mine. Whether these forces or others combine to create the perfect storm for your business or mine, the authors don't pretend to know. But they do make a convincing case that the same or similar forces have, in recent years, decimated company after company and industry upon industry. The message is clear: listen to what's going on with all your senses. Get your business associates and partners to do the same. Pay attention. Get agile.

The last part of the book is full of suggestions on how to get agile. Full disclosure: one of the frameworks they use for ensuring agility is the 7S framework that Peters and I developed in our search for excellence. In my admittedly biased view, this framework is still one of the best tools that has come along for recognizing the complexity of change, for changing in ways that reinforce rather than confuse, and for changing in ways that yield strategic advantage.

—Robert H. Waterman
co-author of *In Search of Excellence* and author of *The Renewal Factor*,
Adhocracy: The Power to Change, and *What America Does Right*

Acknowledgments

We would very much like to thank our families and our wives, Barbara and BrittMarie, for trusting us to pursue this latest adventure. We would also like to thank our friends at the Stockholm International Rotary Club, our recently departed friend Carl Wilson and his lovely wife Art Kosol for providing us the opportunity to meet. We would also like to thank the Minerva Team in both Stockholm and Gothenburg, Sweden for their help and support, friends and colleagues from McKinsey, Ari Kienänen, Bob Waterman and Remy Nilsson for their friendship and encouragement. Special thanks also to Erik Obermeyer, Juliette Fairley, and Barbara Amell for the final run-through regarding grammar and spelling. Well done! A warm thank you to Veronica Gyllenstedt and especially Ricardo Acevedo for their patience and help on the graphics. And, a warm thank you to friends departed like Don McFarland, Patrick Collard, and all the other wonderful people we have come to know through them and their guidance in re-learning what it means to be physically, consciously and financially agile. We are all connected!

Finally, a huge thank you to Milli Brown and her team at Brown Books Publishing, who put together a stellar book in record time and with great quality. I could not have done it without you!

Preface

In Search of Excellence (Waterman, 1982) is still one of the most influential business books of all time. Written by two great McKinsey leaders, Thomas J. Peters and Robert H. Waterman, it was first published in 1982. When written, it was an adventure in the same vein as the book you now hold in your hands. It captured the essence of the exciting times that were just then emerging. Their message was simple, "Why does one corporation do extraordinarily well, while another, similar company just wallow in mediocrity?" The 1980s and even the 1990s were focused on being bigger, better, and faster than everyone else. And for those of you who remember, what a ride it was!

That worked—until it didn't.

We are now experiencing the backlash from this go-for-broke era as giant mega-corporations such as Google, Facebook, and even old behemoths such as General Motors suffer from the excesses of size, arrogance, and rapidly shifting customer needs and values. If companies of this size are having trouble coping with current market volatility, what are your chances?

You could almost say that this book is our attempt to practically respond to the excesses and turbulence of the mindset that *In Search of Excellence* helped to create. As with any powerful trend, excellence seems to have finally peaked. Somewhere between 2009 and now, excellence morphed into something more uncertain. With human nature and the pursuit of power and pleasure being what it is, those who prospered from excellence and got used to riding that wave of power chose to "party on," using any and every means of connection necessary. The focus switched to keeping the good times rolling, whatever the ultimate cost!

Fast-forward to 2021. After several market crashes and with the growing probability of another one of seismic proportions on the horizon, you would have to have been asleep to miss that many positive trends of expansion have now been pushed far beyond excellence. With the help of record levels of debt, historically and ridiculously low interest rates, hypercompetitive development, increasingly shorter product and service life-cycles, globalization and, lest we forget, the excessive printing of money, uncertainty is again back in style but now with a vengeance. The consequences of these trends are showing up as a string of so-called "dislocations" that are now biting harder and harder. Not only individuals, but now companies and, increasingly, even countries are suffering from the rapidly increasing damage. Incredible technologies and trends mixed with this avalanche of debt, fiscal mismanagement, geopolitical, health, and social upheavals are causing even more turbulence faster.

As early as 2016, *Harvard Business Review* published an article titled "Embracing Agile" in its experimentation column, citing ways to transform internal personal structure and culture in order to achieve agility. This was nearly fifteen years after I first presented to Fortune 100 companies the importance of agility and how it would make an impact of future earning, growth, and sustainability.

Further, *Harvard Business Review* has reported in May/June edition in 2020, in "The Agile CSuite," the key components of focusing on "individuals and interactions, not processes and tools." (Darrell Rigby, Sarah Elk, and Steve Barrez of Bain & Company, pp. 64–73)

As recent as May 2021, McKinsey published a study that urged organizations to become agile in their practices. Only 12 percent of companies surveyed considered their organization as inherently agile, with 44 percent in the midst of or having already completed an agile transformation. A small group of only 10 percent, considered "trailblazers" of those detailed, have transformed their entire organization. First in line of these are those within the sectors of consumer retail services, naturally, followed by telecom and financial services (see also pg. 264)[1].

So, you may still consider yourself excellent, but if you get caught up in your own hubris and are not agile nor present enough to avoid or tackle these uncertain economic seas, the chances of you and your excellent organization being swallowed whole by them grows daily.

The yacht metaphor

The deep ocean currents of societal and technological megatrends are so extremely potent that they can easily be perceived as both exciting and scary. Simultaneously, we seem to be experiencing a build up to a potentially perfect storm including geopolitical, financial, environmental, even health and social issues. These two major forces of megatrends and perfect storms contribute to one single big and unavoidable consequence: count on being continuously bombarded with larger, newer threats and greater opportunities at a rapidly increasing pace!

Sooner or later, this torrent of increasing and unforgiving change will force you to listen more closely and consciously adjust your way of doing business quickly, or you and your organization will perish. In short, it is high time to: get agile now!

As fellow stewards of and participants in our brave new world, each of us needs to understand the nuances of these major friction points. We need to practice being exceptionally agile in our ability to listen closely, respond decisively, then measure the result and learn and improve from it. Mastering this art and practice of business agility will allow us to transform our organizations while we simultaneously grow professionally and as responsible and compassionate human beings. What if from this point on, practicing agility in all you do will become the most important key factor in your bid for success?

Bear with us a moment as we explain why the expertise needed for sailing a crew-sized yacht may be the perfect metaphor to use to compare the running of a modern corporation, especially in an increasingly uncertain and turbulent world. As captain, you must be assured that you and your crew (management) can change direction quickly to survive and thrive. It is no longer remotely sufficient to take a year, or even six months, to react when economic, societal, legal, and customer demands are changing daily!

This book explains our reasoning about why consciously understanding these powerful megatrends, anticipating the perfect storm, and focusing primarily on what's ahead while avoiding getting bogged down with tradition and legacy inhibitors will define your ability to be agile. Understanding these traits will help, but practicing the mastery of the tools provided here will help you most. It will also help you to discover and understand other still undiscovered traits plus make your path to success increasingly more probable.

So now, please sit down comfortably in the captain's chair on your own eighty-five-foot Catamaran sailing yacht. Your friends and crew call you "El Capitan" and your corporate yacht is called *The CatAmar*. Under your command is an eight-person crew of competent and trusted colleagues and friends. The plan for your trip is to leave from the Connecticut, Indian Harbor Yacht Club in Greenwich and reach St. Thomas in the US Virgin Islands via Bermuda. On a normal eighty-five-foot single-hull vessel, such a trip would take about twelve days. However, you can easily do it in nine, including a well-deserved forty-eight-hour break in Bermuda. Whether it's your first trip or your twentieth, it promises to be quite an adventure. Although your destination is fixed, is it at all prudent to expect and prepare only for fair winds and easy sailing?

To avoid the worst of the hurricane season, you have decided to start the journey in mid-November. Even so, winds change, sails must be trimmed and adjusted very quickly for those shifts. Equipment will break, obstacles will appear and currents will change. Your crew must learn in detail about this particular yacht, its equipment, and their specific role. Mastering each role, as well as responsibly and optimally performing it, will dictate the fate of everyone's safety and success.

Figure 1. Smooth sailing, but for how long?

The engines and generators must work flawlessly while the yacht must be generously bunkered with fuel and provisions. Radar, sonar, weather fax, and plotter must all be perfectly calibrated for an accurate view of what lies ahead. This is especially important when your vision is limited and surprises appear seemingly from nowhere. Focusing behind your boat, on its wake, having your specialized crew placed in the wrong part of the boat, or someone not communicating an important command understandably almost guarantees trouble, maybe even disaster. Are you getting the picture?

Everything and everyone must be synchronized, communication must be clear and directed to the right people, and all must learn to trust their own keen senses, as well as each other's, at all times. Everyone on board must train to be open to sensing and anticipating oncoming opportunities and dangers, as well as be ready and able to change direction at a moment's notice. Finally, in order to respond effectively, you need presence, anticipation skills, and curiosity to stay on top of the constantly changing situation. This is agility.

If you think the oceans of market research and business development have changed society fast and hard in the past thirty years, then get ready. You ain't seen nothin' yet!

Hold on tight to your captain's hat. The next fifteen years will bring numbing and totally explosive threats and opportunities. Moreover, each and every situation, while potentially dangerous, can also be loaded with opportunity and transformational power!

By the time you finish this book, you will understand why this bold statement is truer now than ever before. It is also our intention that you will be much surer about what to do in order to survive and prosper! Listening more deeply, combined with a more decisive and effective ability to change, allows and encourages companies to respond quicker to threats and opportunities. Just like a sailboat crew on a stormy sea, business and market "sailing" allows increasingly less time for uncertainty. Product and business life cycles are shortening drastically and continuously. They are also completely unforgiving. Recent polls show that people feel more uncertain about their lives, jobs, and the future than they have in generations. Some studies also point to more mental illness and suicides. Yet this uncertainty creates both an increased threat to protect against and a greater opportunity for more and faster success than ever! Will you choose to die trying to avoid failure or to master and enjoy more agility and success?

More than 2,000 respondents in the May 2021 McKinsey survey reported the following as a result of their agile transformations: a 30 percent increase in customer service, a 30 percent improvement in core operational processes, a 10 percent increase in decision-making speed, a 30 percent increase in employee engagement, and 30 percent gains in efficiency[2].

To increase a corporation's capacity to survive and thrive in a time of shortening business cycles offers both the challenge and opportunity to develop a more agile organization.

Figure 2. The consequences of "business as usual"?

The time frames for development, production, distribution, sales, and services are not only continuing to shorten, but also this trend continues to accelerate! Your organization has to quickly respond to an ever-increasing number of external and internal forces, both within and out of your control. Many of these forces are potentially lethal to your business, especially if you do not have the ability to respond or adjust quickly.

A cellular metaphor for megatrends and perfect storms?

Research in the growing field of epigenetics (the study of genes and their surroundings) by Dr. Bruce Lipton[3] and now others, points to each cell in our bodies having two basic operating states: growth or protection.

- When a cell in your body perceives its environment as safe, it naturally opens up its cell walls to confidently take advantage of the positive surroundings, to attract and receive information, nutrition, and energy, moving toward this positive environment in order to grow and develop.
- When a cell in your body perceives a hostile or threatening environment, it does the opposite. The cell shuts down and protects itself by cutting off all contact with the surrounding environment—including nourishment—and moves away from the perceived threat.

What if this basic biological principle is also the basis of human behavior? What if we are always either leaning toward openness, trust, and a willingness to grow, or toward a closed, protective, and ready-to-defend state, or somewhere in between?

Let's be a bit creative and use this growth/protection spectrum as a metaphor for positive megatrends and negative perfect storms. For instance, don't you naturally open up for new innovations and development trends, while doing your best to minimize the risk of damage from approaching storms? These two processes can also occur simultaneously on different levels and toward different situations. Never has that possibility been more apparent than now.

Seasoned leaders know that both too much success and too much failure can be equally devastating. If this reality makes you feel a bit more challenged than usual, you are not alone. As all these issues converge, without taking on agility as a lifestyle, your chances of being chewed up and spit out—even by challenges you have successfully navigated in the past—drastically increase.

Turbulence, connection, and transformation

Even if you don't fully sense it yet, you should soon notice and understand what leaders in the field of quantum physics have been screaming about for quite some time: that we are all connected in many ways and on many levels. Moreover, wherever there is a conscious connection, transformation can take place more easily and effectively. From the cellular level in each of us, right up to the corporate boardroom, and to top levels of government, the need for recognizing these connections and for increased agility, transparency, cooperation, and openness is growing (as well as the consequences for not practicing these skills). Have you too noticed that a slick "all show, no go" slide presentation no longer works? People are now being forced to get better at sourcing the truth. Continuing to disregard this trend or resist it creates increasing peril.

Even though we are fundamentally creatures of habit, we still possess an incredible ability to adapt to and overcome new obstacles. To make it more fun though, each one of us has a different understanding and threshold of agility. You may have also noticed that your understanding is not always in harmony with that of your fellow workers. The more we become aware of these differences and realize the profit in connecting anyway, the more we can navigate and overcome challenges that we will inevitably face together. To hammer this point home, McKinsey conducted one of their *Global Surveys*[4] to find out "what, if anything" companies were doing to improve their business agility and what measurable impact it was having. Those companies that showed the most positive results created and optimized a full operating model across strategy, structures, processes, people, and technology by going after flat and fluid structures built around high-performing cross-functional teams. The results for these dedicated organizations were increases of up to 30 percent of business as usual. What if practicing to connect diverse disciplines in a way that is understood and appreciated by all parts is the way to ensure your form of agile transformation endures?

Distrust has reached critical mass

Everyone and everything from trusted leaders to ancient institutions are now being called into question—and with good reason. Corruption has infected virtually every type of organization, from local football clubs to organized religion. The result is personal frustration, societal anger, increasing resignation, and, for many leaders, an increasing sense that even more drastic change is coming. Whether we like it or not, business and society have become more volatile and predatory

Figure 3. Danger/opportunity

As with anything that changes, both threats and opportunities will arise. The more agile you become, the more you will anticipate and handle what lurks just over the horizon. Just as this Chinese symbol represents both danger and opportunity, so do the times in which we live.

In our effort to try to explain and give you the tools to handle this epic situation that is approaching, we will divide this book into four parts:

- Megatrends & Opportunities
- The Perfect Storm
- Get Agile Now!
- The Agility Toolbox

Part I: Megatrends & Opportunities

These are those deep, long-term, unavoidable, tectonic trends that are so large they can be hard to see and impossible to control. They can often only be recognized afterwards. If you are lucky enough to recognize them, they then have to be acknowledged, dealt with and/or exploited on their own terms. We will list some of the largest here, but this is in no way meant to be a comprehensive list. Our point is to increase your awareness of their existence, give you an idea of their properties, qualities, and texture, as well as point out the danger and the opportunity certain megatrends can provide.

Part II: The Perfect Storm

This section describes some of the most erratic and potentially dangerous trends that will sooner or later overwhelm business as usual and, like it or not, force change. Just as sailing obliviously into a hurricane, overlooking another vessel on a collision course with your ship, or walking blindly out on fresh, new shore before a tsunami hits, unconsciously ignoring or consciously avoiding danger is not a winning tactic. The more you can identify and prepare for these outcomes, the more agility you have.

The issues listed are those which are currently acknowledged and do not include the so-called 'black swans' that can suddenly appear from nowhere and wreak untold havoc (like the emergence of COVID-19). Yet keep in mind, where there is increased danger there is also increased opportunity.

Part III: Get Agile Now!

Success can overwhelm you as much as failure. Your ability to listen closely with all your senses and consciously master business agility will increase your ability to survive, and your chances to survive and even prosper. Indeed, in increasingly turbulent times, it may not be as much a question of being more successful as it is first a question of survival. Mark Twain said, "I am not so much interested in the return on my money as I am in the return of my money." Similarly, when asked how he went bankrupt, Ernest Hemingway quipped, "Two ways. Gradually, then suddenly."

The point of these two quotes is that failure can happen just as quickly as success to anyone. Even so, having the right tools available at the right time and knowing how to use them effectively will increase your agility and your ability to prosper. The point of this book is to introduce you to some tools that can make you and your crew more agile. This will increase both your chances for survival as well as asymmetrical success. Interested?

Part IV: The Agility Toolbox

This final section will help you with simple, practical, and useable tools to better weather these exciting and turbulent seas of change. This section describes what makes us tick, and how we can consciously choose to identify and tackle positive trends and negative storms, whether they are expected or not. It provides proven tools, methods, and training tips to become consciously business agile, thus benefitting you and everyone in your organization. If you already recognize and understand the need for agility and are in a hurry to get agile, you are welcome and encouraged to skip directly to this section.

In short, we can either continue to react habitually from years of training and conditioning to eventually suffer a similar result as Captain Smith, skipper of the *Titanic*, or we can instead increase our agility and consciously respond to the circumstances unfolding before us. This requires practice using our expanded toolbox in the most appropriate and effective way, which is in the here and now. Yet only one approach offers the best chance to survive and thrive in these increasingly uncertain times.

Asymmetrical returns still possible!

With uncertainty comes volatility, and with volatility comes the opportunity for asymmetrical returns. "Asymmetrical" in this context means disproportionate profit or loss. The purpose of this book is to awaken you to the need for business agility, create a background for understanding it, and to provide you with the tools and a source of expertise to avoid catastrophe and dramatically improve your future.

Beware, however, that to just think about becoming more agile is no longer enough!

It is important to act quickly, confidently, and decisively even if you turn out to be wrong! Mastering business agility means constantly absorbing new information, testing, measuring the change, adjusting to it, and learning from it. The more you master this process, the more opportunity you and your team have to create positive asymmetrical returns for yourself and your organization.

Most of all, wake up!

Start practicing by actively wetting your fingertip, sticking it up in the breeze and sensing which way the economic and social winds are blowing. Continue to marvel at the latest technological achievements, yet increase your vigilance for what they are being used for and by whom: "follow the money and follow the power." Most of all remain curious, vigilant, and a bit skeptical. Consciously, curiously, and tirelessly question everything and everyone. Then continue to learn.

Always strive to improve your position. However, we also challenge and encourage you to package it in a way that benefits everyone else! Practice living like we are all connected, even if you don't yet feel it. What if your increased agility ultimately depends upon increasing the agility of all those around you? Remember that "a smooth sea never made a skillful sailor." We only develop and improve our skills through experiencing unpredictable and, at times, perilous situations. This process usually occurs while being badgered with the questionable advice and help of others. The exponential growth of new exciting technologies is occurring with increasing ferocity. Many of them will fundamentally change everything we do. Welcome aboard and prepare to set sail!

PART I

Megatrends & Opportunities

Recognizing the corporate sea, climate, seasons, and weather

Let's start this journey of discovery by discussing a few trends we have been following that are so deep and potent that no amount of adjusting or long-term manipulation can change them. Like the Gulf Stream, the jet stream, or even a strong yet hidden undertow, trends are constantly there; but, you have to know what you are looking for to become aware of them.

Most megatrends start their development agonizingly, glacially slowly, too slowly to be noticed. Yet as they grow in size and importance, they begin moving quicker and eventually reach critical mass and velocity. If you are not prepared when they begin to matter, you risk catastrophic danger, or you may miss out on the incredible opportunities they provide. Just like knowing how to ride the currents, riding big trends will help you leverage their power and place the force of the wind, water, and/or markets at your back.

No matter what we do, the large trends we list here and others, both bigger and smaller, will continue. So, we all had better learn to ride them well. Hopefully, you already understand that there are many other trends not discussed in these pages, which are building and may become unavoidably obvious at any time. Our task here is not to scientifically prove, catalogue, and measure each trend, only to convince you that you will fare better if you train to notice them, then act decisively with increased agility. Whether or not you are aware of these trends, or others not discussed here, count on them affecting you and your crew.

CHAPTER 1

The Singularity

There is more evidence emerging every day that we are all connected, that these connections are becoming more obvious and are starting to merge together. This idea that things are starting to merge together is also known as the "singularity." The singularity started out as the term first used by Vernor Vinge to describe the moment when computers with superhuman intelligence overtake our ability to control them.

Below are the opening comments from Vernor Vinge's famous 1993 "Technological Singularity" speech:[1]

> Within thirty years, we will have the technological means to create superhuman intelligence. Shortly after, the human era will be ended.
>
> Is such progress avoidable? If not to be avoided, can events be guided so that we may survive? These questions are investigated. Some possible answers (and some further dangers) are presented.
>
> What is the singularity?
>
> The acceleration of technological progress has been the central feature of this century. I argue in this paper that we are on the edge of change comparable to the rise of human life on Earth. The precise cause of this change is the imminent creation by technology of entities with greater than human intelligence. There are several means by which science may achieve this breakthrough (and this is another reason for having confidence that the event will occur):
>
> - The development of computers that are "awake" and superhumanly intelligent. (To date, most controversy in the area of AI relates to whether we can create human

equivalence in a machine. But if the answer is "yes, we can," then there is little doubt that beings more intelligent can be constructed shortly thereafter.)

- Large computer networks (and their associated users) may "wake up" as a superhumanly intelligent entity.
- Computer/human interfaces may become so intimate that users may reasonably be considered superhumanly intelligent.
- Biological science may find ways to improve upon the natural human intellect.

Since this famous speech was presented, the term singularity has been broadened to include many socioeconomic factors that are also merging into Vinge's original race toward artificial intelligence. The term "transhumanism" comes to mind. Many argue that our future will develop into something dark like Skynet from the movie *Terminator*. Whereas others argue that the difference between intelligence (artificial or natural) and human feeling will naturally become more pronounced. They argue that computers are incapable of developing the capacity to become self-aware, especially in a destructive manner toward humans. It is worth noting that this rosy declaration excludes those psychopathic and even evil individuals who can easily program or pay for programming their cold-blooded behavior into such machines.

The trend of an explosion in computing power is now firmly in place. To paraphrase Peter Siljerud from his company, Future Wise[2], "soon everything that can be done with muscle will be done with robotics, and everything we can calculate with our brain will be done by computer." So far though, machines have been incapable of developing a heart, morals, or a conscience. In short, what machines and computers cannot replicate or reproduce is our ability to feel, and, therefore, cannot yet create meaningful relationships with us or each other.

Moving forward, your ability to feel, sense, and communicate effectively to emotionally move your listener into a desired action may well become one of your greatest tools or assets. As computers and machines take over more of life's mundane tasks and calculations, count on your ability to listen with all your senses, express yourself confidently, create mutual understanding, and make "agreements that stick" to become major factors in determining your value in the marketplace.

We also seem to be rapidly approaching the breaking point, where computer power will eclipse our ability to keep up with how it's used. If you think you are stressed now, how will this increase in computer power over your personal sovereignty affect your health, well-being, and prospects for a successful (and free) future?

Convergence of technologies

Anyone working in the IT and telecoms business recognizes that the technological differences between competing companies, as well as their solutions, are decreasing with each passing day. For instance, the distinction between telephones, computers, and televisions becomes blurrier every day. These three distinct technologies are rapidly fusing into one smartphone.

Within most technological areas, the differences between competing products is rapidly decreasing. For instance, if you trade in your iPhone for the latest Android, you will probably be up and running in no time because how much difference is there, really, between today's competing car models. Agile competitors have recognized this trend and have helped this fusion process along (often slitting their own throats in the process), by focusing on extras such as easy transference from one platform to another. The irony of this becomes that they also quickly make themselves irrelevant in the process.

Open sourcing

Open sourcing is where anyone can contribute to a program or the development of an operating system. This process lessens the need to purchase and be loyal to a proprietary standard, owned and controlled by a large firm. The Linux Operating System is one prime example. Open sourcing is indeed creating a revolution in software development as everyone can now contribute. This allows you and anyone else to take this code and develop it, add to it, customize it, or do whatever you wish.

Indeed, there is a growing slice of the population that hates being a subscription slave to a large corporate entity and warmly welcomes, supports, and encourages open-source solutions. Indeed, the relatively new blockchain industry could be said to have developed from and served such rebellious sources.

Another branch industry is now developing out of this open software boom. Companies such as Red Hat certify, customize, and support the open-source code of the Linux operating system. Their niche is making open-source software safe, stable, and secure for large companies to build their own infrastructures, thereby freeing themselves from what some now openly call the "tyranny of Microsoft."

A huge and unforeseen side effect that now contributes greatly to this open-source trend is the increasing amount of your personal data and behavior characteristics being gathered by large companies such as Microsoft, Apple, Google, Facebook, and others. It's been calculated that some of these tech giants can now create a frightfully good behavior profile on you from as little as eight posts! As open-source software is inherently transparent, you can easily see if someone has inserted questionable or even dark lines of code that may record, monitor, or do something you may not approve of or wish for. This is not true of proprietary code which is usually patented, concealed, mysterious, and may be (and now usually is) monitoring and tracking your behavior without your knowledge.

One of the most interesting and ironic effects of this data gathering process is that the more our lives and behavior patterns are being revealed, collected, and categorized over the web, the less we will blindly trust leaders, companies, and governments who promise that our personal information is indeed safe. There have now been too many examples of data-leaks from previously "trusted" institutions for even the most trusting or naive user to ignore.

The backlash of the data-collection is the rise of yet another branch industry: the privacy programs industry. These programs identify, distract, and thwart these increasingly intrusive data collection methods. The practice of using Virtual Private Networks (or VPNs), encryption, and even separate computers to hide or keep private your personal and professional data is rising rapidly, as is the increase in new and ever more devious ways to get around them. That is why one of the stated visions of most blockchain pioneers is for the user to retake control of their personal data. The user can then provide exactly what is needed (often anonymously) only when they choose or when they can make some money on it. We will need to remain vigilant for how long this noble crusade for a return personal privacy and freedom lasts.

Convergence of intelligence and machines

Back to the bright side: we now have the Internet of Things, or IOT. This provides driverless cars, refrigerators that can order groceries when you run out, and apps that can turn your home thermostat up or down remotely from your phone. You can now pay your bills from your smartphone, detect who is responsible for the music you are listening to, order tickets, etc. Using Siri or Alexa, for instance, you can receive an answer to a question or play your favorite music just by shouting out your favorite tune's name. All of these innovations do make our lives easier.

On the other side of the coin, each time you create a request or login, you are creating a data trail. This trail is being tracked, monitored, and saved by companies and organizations to get to "know and serve you better." This makes all these new-found conveniences a double-edged sword.

David Pogue's article, "Robots Rising," in the *Scientific American*[3], updates the discussion about how we will converge singularity with intelligent robots. In an interview with Max Tegmark, MIT professor and co-founder of the Future of Life Institute, he mentioned that artificial intelligence is even less forgiving. Professor Tegmark points out, "When we invented less powerful technology, like fire, we screwed up a bunch of times; then, we invented the fire extinguisher. Done. But with more powerful technologies like human-level artificial intelligence, we want to get things right the first time."

"The worry," writes Pogue, "is that once AI gets smart enough, it will be able to improve its own software, over and over again, every hour or minute. It will quickly become so much smarter than humans that—well, we don't actually know."

Tegmark concludes, "It could be wonderful or it could be pretty bad."

For instance, Pogue states, "Programming machines to obey us precisely can backfire in unexpected ways. If I tell your super AI-car to get to the airport as fast as possible, it'll get you there but you'll arrive chased by helicopters and covered in vomit."

There are now an increasing number of reports of people wishing for something with their Alexis system on and listening, only to have their "wish" delivered and billed to them a few days later. These are rather benign when compared to what AI weaponry could do in the hands of incompetent or unscrupulous members of the military—or even your local police.

Pogue also contributes a new, interesting slant about robotics replacing workers: he emphasizes, "So much of our sense of purpose comes from our jobs. We should think hard about the sort of jobs we would like to keep doing and getting our identity from." He concludes, "the loss of jobs will also mean the loss of human fulfillment."

We are already seeing the effects of this in the home. Traditional family roles have been destroyed, especially when it comes to immigrant families. Often, the father—who has been the traditional bread winner in their home country—is no longer employable (often due to a language barrier) and is reduced to relying on the mother or children to support the family economy. With the loss of his traditional role of breadwinner, the father's pride and confidence disappear, and destructive habits and abuse can further irritate the already tense situation at home. This is only one small illustration of how rapidly society and technology are changing. More on this in the "Perfect Storm" section.

What happens when this situation and others fully manifest themselves into the core workers of middle-class society? Already, AI and sophisticated shopping solutions, both online and off, are preying on employment opportunities in the restaurant and retail sector. Entire shopping malls are closing due to increased e-commerce. Yes, these are all exciting trends and they need to be seen in a larger, more connected context.

Now there is the virus, pandemic, and social distancing. Another book could be written on both its origins and the response to it. The point here is that a drastic, even catastrophic number of small businesses, especially main street mom-and-pop shops, are being forced out of business due to the threat of contagion and new rules regarding it. This has been a boon for those in online businesses and for home delivery, but the chaos it is causing on Main Street is immense. More on this also in the next section.

Now multiply these effects by as many industries as you can name.

Convergence of old industries

Depending upon the source, in the year 1900 there were between 300 and 800 different automobile manufacturing companies in Detroit alone. By the end of the depression, there were only a handful of them left. In the 1980s, there were a myriad of personal computer manufacturers ranging from IBM, Compaq, Olivetti, Ericsson, Philips, HP, Apple, etc. How many are still in the game? Right now, how many online gambling sites can you choose from?

As industries mature, Charles Darwin's law of the "survival of the fittest" (or is it the shrewdest?) becomes boldly apparent in the marketplace. As of this writing, bigger still seems perceived as better, but for how long? With recent losses due to COVID-19, for example, bigger (perhaps less agile) companies have suffered greater losses than smaller rivals. Yet, through bankruptcy, mergers and acquisitions, "easier" financing, and friendly and hostile takeovers, shrewd companies continue to consolidate and expand. Although there still is perceived safety in reaching a larger size, this advantage may quickly be going the way of the dinosaur. Bigger now seems to be better, but only to the point that Too Big To Fail (or TBTF) seems to be the ultimate goal. How long are you willing to bet your company's future that this trend can and will continue? This is at a time when even more international giants use lobbyists, legislators, and the mainstream media—plus an increasing array of obvious as well as underhanded tactics—to maintain or accelerate growth. The larger and more unmanageable these behemoths become, the more unstable, uncontrollable, and untrustworthy they seem to become also. With one look at the current problems of Facebook and its use/misuse of personal account information, the increasing number of questions and questioners surrounding "solutions" to the current pandemic may begin to sum up what seems to be a growing epidemic of misused blind trust. Apple's Siri app was recently revealed to be listening to couples when they were having sex "but only for the first few seconds." Ahem.

Have you ever actually read the fine print in even one of the terms of use contracts you agree to when you open a new app? Chances are you have just compromised your future right to privacy more than you could imagine! For instance, who now owns the rights to all those pictures you post? Just as a tree cannot grow to the moon, peak limits will appear and may be starting to already show. With history as a guide, those organizations and leaders found extending their reach past these limits of personal and professional integrity may suddenly (probably?) lose all former agility, and ultimately crash and burn.

At the same time, different processes are merging and many products are merging into one. For instance, look at the trend that started with the room-size Sperry Univac in 1947. Computers became smaller and more powerful just as cameras, televisions, and telephones did. All these technologies have now merged into smartphones and smarter tablets. Multitasking has become the rage. How many young people even wear a watch now, for other than a fashion statement? What's the point when you can just check your phone for the time? Yet even with this information as a background, sales of Rolex and other luxury watches as well as their prices have continued to break records . . . until recently.

Rockefeller combined all the processes from the discovery of oil to its final destination in the tank of your automobile into a company called Standard Oil. Big players understand that the more you control the entire process, the more you can set/dictate the rules. Want more proof? Look at the rise of subscription services. Customers can subscribe to everything from software, to eyeglasses, to tampons, to your morning coffee; thus locking you, the customer, into a complete process rather than just one product. Yes, you are promised and sometimes get full service, automatic ordering, etc., but then try extracting yourself from it.

Convergence of economies

Not only do companies merge in their quest for survival and profit, but so do regions and even countries. Look at what happened to the world's first manufacturing center. Manufacturing started in the English midlands at the end of the seventeenth century. The baton was then passed to the United States at the end of the nineteenth century. It was then handed off for a time to Japan, then recently to China.

Manufacturing has been seen to evolve from simpler products to more complex ones in waves. In a very simplified version of industrial history, the first industrial wave was in textiles. England began importing cotton from Egypt and the USA. They used this raw material in their textile mills in the midlands. The manufacture of textiles was then followed by the production of increasingly complex items, such as steel, railroads, and cars, now followed by even more sophisticated electronics. The United States took over the textile trade in the mid-1850s, followed successively by Japan, China, Asia, and now South America. Producing textiles began the industrial process that led to increasingly complex products, followed by a wave of services. Just reflect on developments in the USA, Japan, Taiwan, Korea, China, and Vietnam. Consider IT: most computers were once built in the USA. Hardly any are built there now. Instead, more and more sophisticated software applications have replaced the once American-dominated hardware trade.

The latest and very simplified iteration is that China has cornered the market on production while India is dominating the market on software and services. These markets were won based on quantity, price, and hunger for success. It will be interesting to see how this develops. Which countries will dominate which markets next?

This phenomenon was not just limited to one company or area. Often, a whole country or region was galvanized into action for a specific purpose. Think about the glory days of the (now re-named) Rust Belt, Detroit, or Silicon Valley. Wherever a production center locates to a specific place, financing is never far behind. Consider such places as New York's Wall Street, the city of London, or Hong Kong, and the increasing length of their reach.

As local economies grew, so did the opportunity for education. When a certain population becomes more educated, skilled, and wealthy, it develops industries faster and produces increasingly complex products. As the ability to transport products develops, so does the opportunity to produce and sell them all over the world. This global interconnectedness of products, people, and economies even affects how we value economies. In agrarian societies, the amount of land and resources owned was often the gauge of personal wealth and power. As the power of industry grew, this perception shifted to the value of what you produced. Now even this has changed. Wealth is now often measured by what you know and how fast and effectively you then can communicate and apply that knowledge.

Among others, Martin Armstrong of Armstrong Economics points out through his studies of wave cycles that natural resources and land do not alone determine the value of a national economy. Entrepreneurs, workers and a cooperative government also generate products and services and, thus, create value.

Armstrong's poster child is Japan during the 80s and 90s. This island nation, home to hardly any natural resources, produced enough products to generate the world's second largest GDP. How did they do it? Japan became agile. It took the best ideas from around the world and tweaked their industries to make them more efficient. Look no further than the American automobile industry to see the effects of Japan's venture into the 1980s version of agility.

For instance, the premise of the book *Forty Years and 20 Million Ideas*[4] states that Toyota's rise to become one of the world's biggest automobile manufacturers was due to increased internal listening. Toyota embraced the idea of the suggestion box and listened seriously and measurably to each employee, encouraging him/her to contribute even simple and inexpensive ideas in order for the company to be the best. The genius of this concept was further demonstrated by focusing on the quality of the whole production process instead of only on the end result—a quality car. Toyota gratefully rewarded even those suggesting minor improvements in the process of manufacturing cars. This all worked until it didn't. Since then, Toyota's pristine name has been dragged through the mud with more than one scandal to keep the company growing.

In a related example, David Habersham's book *The Reckoning*[5], describes how Nissan (Datsun during 1960s and 70s) executives traveled to Detroit to learn about and improve upon the processes that made Detroit a worldwide name. While their American hosts were openly making fun of them, their Japanese guests were taking copious notes. Then they went back home, implemented those ideas into their production lines, and tweaked them further. It was later revealed that they chose to focus on the quality and effectiveness of the production line itself rather than on the finished product.

One look at what is now left of the market share of automobiles still produced in Detroit[6] compared to those by Japanese auto companies says it all. It is also rather humbling to note that Detroit, which once boasted to have the highest average income in the United States, recently had trouble keeping the public water and electricity systems running. Some of those United Auto Worker hosts must be turning over in their graves as arrivals and departures in Detroit's municipal airport are now routinely announced in Japanese. Can arrogance inhibit agility?

Finally, according to the prestigious Swiss IMP, in the late 1980s, Japan's focus on the manufacturing process measurable threatened Mercedes' lock on the luxury car market. As referenced above, Toyota and Nissan strategically chose to focus on how to create a better-quality production process. Mercedes had instead been focusing on creating higher quality cars. When it came time to ramp up production to satisfy the drastically expanding market for quality luxury cars, the Japanese could do it quickly without sacrificing quality. Mercedes, whose focus had been on each car and not the process, quickly overloaded its capacity. Its customers began experiencing increased quality problems. Eventually, Mercedes resolved this hiccup, but not before a severe impact was felt on the brand in both reputation and profit.

The story does not end here. It is of major importance that thirty years later, Toyota has been suffering from lower margins and quality control scandals just as its Detroit counterparts did a generation ago. It seems that its entrenched leaders continue to focus upon business as usual and their job security, instead of maintaining and improving business agility. In short, they appear to have lost their edge. Through these examples, the hazards of TBTF clearly reveal themselves even in the auto business. TBTF still seems to clear the way for hungrier, lower cost, and more agile producers such as Kia from Korea, Dongfeng and Chery from China, and Tata from India. The process continues as even such quality brands such as Volvo Cars and Saab have now been taken over by Chinese automobile manufacturers. As more than one commercial declares, Volvos are no longer "made in Sweden," they are now "made by Sweden."

Convergence of thought

When two planes crashed into the World Trade Center towers in New York, it was instant news around the world. That is now over twenty years ago! Information travels even faster now. Just ask the Flash Boys, in Michael Lewis' book of the same name. These are traders who make millions of dollars by being a few millionths of a second closer to the stock market computers than the rest of us muppets, thereby making faster, more lucrative, and increasingly questionable financial trades. Fortunes can now be made and lost in just milliseconds.

Just as the one hundredth monkey seems to learn a behavior without direct instructions, so can thoughts spread quickly and manifest in the rest of us. With the help of the World Wide Web, ideas and information are spreading faster than ever. Competing views and different opinions are just as available to anyone if he or she cares to look. Ideas can now incubate into products and services literally overnight, then quickly spread to the four corners of the world. Via social media, opinions and views can also change direction quicker than you can say "damage control." Not convinced? Ask USA President Joe Biden about his son Hunter. Still not convinced? What feelings do the words "Trump" or "Brexit" conjure up in you? Now, did those feelings arise by themselves or were they influenced by what you were bombarded with via mass media, social media, and "friendly" conversations?

With the increasing availability of travel and "relaxed" emigration policies, world cultures are blending into each other at a more rapid pace than ever. Even whole languages are being lost at an increasing pace, as more of us are assimilated into the same (currently English) world mix usually found on the internet. For better or worse, our thoughts, words, and deeds are merging, if not into one, then into two or more increasingly immovable camps. In increasing instances, backlash has also been growing from the refusal of some groups to accept assimilation of others and others from refusing to assimilate into to the local norms. How agile is this and what will the consequences be for your business?

Convergence forces commodification

The faster contact we have with each other, the less location matters. If, for instance, you want to sell an insulated lunchbox at Amazon.com, you can have it produced in China just as well as in the USA, yet usually China sports a much cheaper price. Need a fancy box to package it in? Log on to Fiverr.com and find someone in Indonesia or Sri Lanka to design it for as little as $5. They then send a high-quality pdf file of the carton design to the factory of your choice. There it can be printed and matched to your product. The whole package can then be boxed and shipped by plane to one or more Amazon warehouses in the USA. Get up and running with one of many homepage and e-commerce solutions in a matter of days, then begin selling. The total time from the idea to online sales can be less than two months. The total cost can be less than $1,000. We know people who are making fortunes using this process on a daily basis.

If you recreate this process with a relatively unique product or service, you could also be making thousands of dollars per month quickly. That gravy train will continue until someone more agile than you improves on your previously unique product or marketing process. Suddenly, another innovator begins outselling you and typically at a lower price. Then, the process begins anew.

Congratulations, your unique creation has just become another commodity.

Regardless of whether you sell lumber, oil, milk, electronic components, clothes, legal, health care, or financial services, chances are that your product or service is now, or shortly will become, a commodity. A commodity simply means that price is now the most important decision factor for your customer. Not sure? You can easily check this by timing how quickly the discussion of price comes up during your sales call. The quicker you start haggling, the more evidence you have that all value you thought you provided as an individual or organization has now become a commodity for your customer. Now, the only thing that will ensure your sale is their bottom line.

The lower the price, the more you sell, but the less information you get to know about your customer. More importantly, the quicker they will leave you as soon as a cheaper competitor is discovered. As even more products and services become commodities, it becomes more important to search for and add customer value in every way possible. Otherwise, your customer base will decrease as soon as the new lower-priced, more efficient producer of an improved version goes viral.

There are two clear paths that must be taken to stay in business and to avoid, as long as possible, becoming a commodity. Both of them concern agility. One is to continue to offer more value for the same amount of money, or less. The other is to distinguish yourself and your fellow employees from the competition with more and better personalized service. This means not only a better, more personal level of service, but also an attractive, friendly, and memorable way of doing business. If you forget or ignore these important aspects, expect your customers' loyalty to change when the latest marketing wind blows. Continually doing both well is a powerful step in maintaining and/or increasing your agility and profits. As authors Wouter Aghina, Christopher Handscomb, and Daniel Roma of McKinsesy point out in their March 2020 article, "Enterprise Agility: Buzz or Impact?"[7] agile enterprises that practiced agility experienced increases in customer satisfaction from 10 to 30 percent. Would increasingly satisfied customers more likely to return for more business as well as spread the word even for you?

Convergence means increasing speed and intensity

All of the above trends point toward an incessantly faster pace of development and connectivity. The more these trends converge, the quicker you will need to negotiate them and the more agility will be required. Again, citing the article, 'Enterprise Agility: Buzz or Business Impact?'[8] the authors uncovered gains in operational performance of between 30 percent and 50 percent when the impact of their business agility efforts were measured. Stay tuned for exactly what these efforts can include.

Does convergence equal globalization?

Globalization refers to the growing interconnectedness and interdependence of everyone on the planet. As technology continues to develop, our world continues to get smaller. Going through this process, those of us who are paying attention are becoming more aware of how much our actions and inactions influence others.

For instance, globalization is a wonderful development for the consumer. The consumer can now easily choose from a selection of products, services, and prices from all over the globe. This creates a growing challenge for each producer as there are now competitors from all corners of the world competing for your business. Lobbying to enact stricter laws and tariffs in your country to protect businesses often results in products being outsourced and produced elsewhere and/or just assembled in your country. When your business is affected, in fact before your business is affected, you must remain vigilant, prepared to respond, create and innovate, often in ways you haven't yet imagined.

However, an older belief or force is now being resurrected and refreshed: nationalism. Limits of immigration and open-door policies are now being questioned by grassroots or "populist" groups in an increasing roster of different countries. As middle-class jobs are being threatened by increasing automation and AI, now there is the increasing possibility of a new arrival taking their job raising again the threat to their livelihood. This anti-globalism movement is gaining traction and the uncertainty of how these two ideologies resolve their differences will only increase uncertainty in the markets.

As we become more aware of just how connected we are, it will become dangerously apparent that we can no longer afford the luxury of excluding others. Yet, does this mean that borders and boundaries will cease to matter? What if there is a limit? Just as your liver cannot become a lung overnight, there exists limits regarding what one specialized group can do versus another. Being agile also implies that you can sense where this border is and adjust your organization a little more globally here and a bit more locally there.

With instant access to what happens everywhere at any time, secrets and personal behavior traits will be discovered even more quickly, exposed and dealt with, often by people from places you may have never heard of. In short, it is becoming critical to our common survival that we include everyone in our plans while learning to treat each other with respect. Otherwise, we could easily end up in a *Mad Max* type of future. Unfortunately, shades of this trend are occurring as this is written. Many, otherwise quiet people have become so upset with current circumstances that they are taking to the streets, increasingly rioting and—in the process—destroying more local businesses. These are the same businesses that are already suffering from pandemic lockdowns. More and more wealthy, more mobile residents are choosing to move away from these hotspots, thus putting more pressure on those left to pay for and maintain public services.

CHAPTER 2

Abundance Versus Scarcity

Throughout history, man's struggle for success has been based upon the collective belief in scarcity. All the way up to and through the Industrial Age, scarcity has been a root cause of man's behavior. We will argue later that scarcity is the basis of the entire evolution of business management. Yet recently, something unique has occurred, especially during the last few generations. A feeling of—coupled with some hard evidence of—abundance has made its presence known.

Up until World War I, civilized society had always been somewhat governed by the belief that money had to be anchored in something of value. Different anchors had been used over the years. Between the Napoleonic wars and the first World War, international trade had been based on a gold standard. Most of the 1800s are still referred to as "The Golden Age of Commerce." Look at most historical inflation charts. Notice that if you bought a house right after Waterloo in 1815, its price would have stayed relatively stable until the outbreak of violence in 1914. Interestingly, something unique happened while millions died in the trenches of Belgium and France during World War I.

As the costs of waging war quickly mounted, one belligerent country after another left the gold standard and began to borrow and print so called fiat-money to finance their part of the war. Fiat-money is pretty much just paper that is declared valuable by *fiat* (meaning the law or decree). Economists insist that had England, Germany, France, and others held themselves to the prewar gold-standard, they would have been bankrupt long before the first year of fighting was over! Instead, they threw fiscal responsibility to the wind and borrowed and printed their way through the rest of the war, multiplying new, untold hardship and suffering. To make a long and complex story short, once the so called "Great War" ended and due to the excess amount of money now in the system, these countries could no longer return to the pre-war gold standard, even if they had wanted to. The idea that gold should back a nations' printed money had also become a casualty of the trenches.

In fact, the United Kingdom tried to go back on the gold standard, but was forced to "revalue" (i.e. weaken) the pound in the beginning of the 1930s. Due to the debt forced upon them by losing the war, Germany couldn't comply either. It suffered hyperinflation during 1923–4 in its vain (and understandably half-hearted) attempt to repay the gigantic amount of debt imposed on them by the victors. The last holdout was the United States of America, where President Roosevelt unconstitutionally banned private ownership of gold in 1933. This was publicly justified as part of the way to revalue (there's that word again) the dollar and end the Great Depression. Interestingly, something else also happened on the way to all of these revaluations.

During this brutal, but sweet-sounding process of revaluing currencies, those in charge of their nation's money supply learned something important. They discovered that the average citizen, much too busy with their own daily troubles, did not react or even notice whether those in charge printed and/or borrowed more. They quickly exceeded all sane boundaries of fiscal prudence, yet the average person could not or did not care to connect the dots. An excuse and/or a scapegoat were always found to pin the blame of unemployment and price instability on anything but the people actually in charge.

The Bretton-Woods Agreement of 1944 then made the US dollar, which was still backed internationally by gold bullion, the world's reserve currency. This agreement permitted a few decades of relative monetary stability, but what began happening behind the scenes? In many cases, war debts were paid down, but borrowing and government expansion continued. In the 1960s, with the American war on poverty simultaneously being waged with the war in Vietnam, American borrowing began to increase drastically and negatively affect the value of the dollar, weakening its gold backing. By 1971 this "guns and butter" approach had become economically untenable and American gold reserves were reportedly down by almost two-thirds. In response, President Nixon closed the so-called "gold window" in August of that year and severed the connection between the US dollar and its good-as-gold backing. This was, in reality, a national default and its consequences lead to an even more rapid increase in the money supply, thus reducing purchasing power. By the end of the 1970s, with many more printed dollars flowing into the global economic system, inflation became a household word all over the Western World. Debts also began to rise first geometrically, then exponentially.

With every economic slowdown from the late 1960s forward, it became standard practice for central banks to first borrow, then print more money and inject it into the national economy. Like magic, every economic dip was followed by even better times, especially for the financiers closest to the source of this new money. More money also meant more development and better technology. By the end of the twentieth century though, the world began to develop more capacity than it could use. Just like a junkie needing a bigger hit as his/her body gets used to a drug, world economies began to require more monetary stimulus to regain that same high of prosperity. At the dawn of the twenty-first century, this extra money was now driving manufacturing capacity rapidly into overcapacity, all over the world.

We are now rapidly coming to grips with this enormous and still increasing amount of overcapacity. Standard economic theory tells us that when supply increases more than demand, prices drop. The deeper we get into this twilight zone of easy money, the less this fundamental rule seems to work. This is becoming more evident, especially when it comes to asset values compared to prices. A typical suburban American house, built in the 1960s, which may have originally cost $20,000 can no longer be purchased for less than $300,000 to $400,000. So far, that has been no problem as income has also risen, loans, and even free money now seem to be given away to anyone who can still fog a mirror. Sometimes, it seems the words "fiscal" and "responsibility" haven't been used correctly in the same sentence since before World War I.

Source: US Census Bureau, 2010

Figure 4. The median price of US homes

In attractive areas such as the east and west coasts of the USA and in and around most West European capitals, prices are a few times more than even these extravagant figures. This begs the important question: has the value of your home increased so much or has the value of your money decreased? Could these inflated prices be due to the increase in your nation's money supply?

Recently, housing prices in overheated markets such as London, Vancouver, Hong Kong, San Francisco, and New York have begun to peak and the luxury segment of these markets began to plummet. Not only have these high-end segments been overbuilt, buyers—many who were paying cash—and even those needing mortgages are getting wary and lenders are beginning to require prohibitive down payments. With the advent of COVID-19 demand is drying up and uncertainty is increasing.

This trend in uncertainty seems to be gaining speed as it is now estimated that the world money supply of dollars, euros, yen, yuan, rubles, etc. has increased by the equivalent of upwards of 14 trillion US dollars since what is now being called the 2008–9 Great Recession. With interest rates at unprecedented lows for now more than a decade, large sums of money have been incredibly easy to acquire, especially if you have the right connections. At the same time, the price of money, energy, and technology has drastically decreased. Still, every time there is a crisis, more money is literally thrown at it and in the process our trust in our financial system continues to erode. Has this situation caused you to feel more or less uncertain?

To add insult to injury, the mainstream media, possibly for the first time ever, has been promoting story after story of the "coming recession." Whether it was to strongly urge voters to choose yet another new president in the USA as some media commentators and economists (with questionable ties) have suggested, or that sanity and gravity are finally making a comeback, the resulting recession or even depression, when it inevitably comes, will undoubtedly be dangerously hard to navigate. In fact, we may already be in to it now! In short, what goes up, especially that which goes up more than twice as long and exponentially higher than ever before, will surely come down harder and quicker than the historical norm.

The point here is not to provide a detailed economic history of the last 200 years, but rather to highlight that there is an unprecedented amount of money sloshing around, desperately seeking a low risk with high return home. Safe destinations are now quickly drying up. This is causing financial uncertainty on steroids! Economic fundamentals no longer work as they have since the dismal science of economics was born. When debt is seen as an asset, black has indeed become white. The result is an increasingly volatile and fragile economic climate. The biggest historical difference now is that this is a global phenomenon!

This economic climate is one where the so-called "hot money" can accumulate in a sector or industry quickly and then suddenly dissipate to other places, sometimes on the other side of the planet, literally overnight. With most of this money now being in digital form and transmitted over fiber optic cable, this process has literally progressed to the speed of light. The creative/destructive clash between current abundance and historical scarcity has major and uncertain implications going forward, especially when it comes to your ability to be agile enough to anticipate what will happen next.

Five times more scientific developments

My grandfather was born in 1883. This was when horsepower from real horses and wind power from sails were still two of the most popular ways to move goods and people from place to place. Before he died, he witnessed the birth of the airplane and ultimately watched humans land on the moon. As Neil Armstrong remarked when he set foot on the moon, this truly was, "one small step for man. One giant leap for mankind." Less than fifty years later, even that rapid pace of development is looking increasingly like an even smaller step. Estimates now point to five times more scientific developments over the next one hundred years than have taken place so far in human history!

Our interconnectedness and ability to share ideas over the internet mean the previously high costs of research and development can now be farmed out to skilled workers in much lower-cost countries, immediately. Just this development alone may end up making this estimate of five times more inventions and innovations a shameful underestimate.

Another telltale hint of the acceleration of development came from a conversation with a good friend from Linux developer, Red Hat. For agile players in the IT/Telecoms business, the luxury of separating research and development from operations is now ancient history. This traditional separate but equal(?) configuration has given way to what is now known as DevOps. Thus, two former rivals for shares of the same budget are now forced to work together as one team, drastically cutting down on development-to-market. Their task is to increase the speed and effectiveness of beginning to sell and implement new products while simultaneously developing and innovating them. This forces new projects to be:

- More reality based
- Reduce the number of decision makers involved
- Have more realistic time and budget plans
- Contribute something measurable and marketable quicker

The time to market from good ideas to saleable products must now be reduced to a fraction of the time it used to take. The more development seamlessly merges into operations, the faster this process will inevitably become. For those of you allergic to stress, get ready.

With each new development, and the disruptive technology it causes, comes both the threat and opportunity of even more and greater creative destruction. Need proof? Just look again at what Uber did to the taxi profession or the competition Airbnb is posing to the hotel business.

How about Spotify or Apple's iTunes and the carnage they caused in the traditional music industry? Look at what AI is now doing to the service industry and call centers. Look at what data driven social media is doing to our attention spans, the core family, the community, politics, and life as we know it. Watch how the security and transparency of the blockchain distributed ledger is increasingly threatening traditional third-party actors such as: banks, lawyers, and soon politicians.

Up the down R&D escalator

The best metaphor your authors have found for the disruption caused by this increasingly rapid rate of development is trying to walk up a down escalator. Picture today's rate of research and development as the current speed of the down escalator you now try to climb. To reach the top of this down escalator, your rate of climb must be faster than the speed of the escalator itself. If you just keep up with the escalator's current speed, you will make no upward progress. Even worse, the moment you slow down or stop climbing, the downward momentum of the escalator will immediately carry you back down to where you started and out of the race. Now, what happens when:

- The escalator increases its speed?
- Even more people/competitors get on the escalator and you have to navigate around or avoid them too?

If you are beginning to sense a bit of frustration, welcome to today's R&D and business environment challenges.

More competitors than ever, from all over the world, have more money and more resources to bring even more ideas to the marketplace quicker. Is it any wonder why your job of navigating this sea of increasing change is getting tougher?

How long can you afford to rest before the next wave of technology hits your market niche broadside? Without a healthy and continuous dose of world-class DevOps agility and an increasingly powerful, competent and motivated team, count on losing your competitive edge.

Cheap energy still, for the moment

For approximately the past 150 years, the energy market has followed its own interpretation of Moore's law, which is usually applied to processing power. The number of BTUs of useable energy available has risen while the corresponding costs have fallen, sometimes drastically. Wood, coal, whale oil, kerosene, gasoline, and nuclear energy prices decreased while the energy potential produced in BTUs per unit increased drastically. Interestingly, this noticeable increase in cheap energy has been mirrored by an equivalent explosion in population. How long can/will this exponential climb toward the sky continue? This is an important question.

Until this trend does change, increased energy efficiency keeps exploding our boundaries of development. Abundant, cheap, and powerful energy gives us cheap electricity, cheap fertilizer, cheap food, and cheap building materials to fulfill our wildest dreams. Cheap energy has provided abundant power to produce abundant inventions and innovations. Yet nature has a habit of shaking things up when we least expect it. Considering how much of our current Western standard of living depends upon cheap energy, any disruption to this supply could quickly cascade through our economy and society, causing massive dislocations and hardships. Although Hubbert's "Peak Oil" scenario has so far been successfully avoided, remember the "peak" refers to the relationship of availability and power to price. Right now, the cheaper the cost per barrel gets, the more rigs are taken offline and the more oil companies struggle to make a profit. Putting wells back online takes an enormous reinvestment and is sometimes economically impossible.

Also, according to many reports, America's Shale Oil Industry has only been successful because of abnormally low borrowing costs. The price per barrel of Shale Oil produced is quite a bit above the current market price and most Shale Oil companies are struggling to secure new rounds of financing.

A new phenomenon is now also hinting toward a major shift in our relationship to energy, oil, and our environment. Mention the name of Greta Thunberg to virtually anyone with a TV or internet and you will hear how she is shaking up the younger generation and causing environmental behavior change. This change, sometimes referred to as the "Green New Deal" is directly aimed toward our law makers and politicians. With

Greta's and COVID-19's help, it has now become almost shameful to fly. Many young people are choosing not to learn to drive and those that do are choosing alternative energy sources to power their cars. Trends indicate that especially those under thirty years old are creating a completely new paradigm when it comes to energy, sustainability, and the environment. This is shaping up to have a large effect on customer behavior and societal purchasing patterns worldwide! This is before we even talk about what is now being called the Great Reset.

Competitive global expansion in all industries

Look at Alibaba following ever closer on the heels of Amazon. Look at the growth of the automobile industry in China. Chinese investors even bought Volvo Cars and SAAB cars. Until recently, both companies were icons of Swedish quality and engineering! As this trend of interconnectedness and cheap financing continues to develop, companies can quickly start and/or relocate to lower cost locations. Hungrier workforces, who are willing and now able to do a quality job at a fraction of the cost, are increasingly getting the call. In the process, they are evening out former great gaps in wages between their countries and the previously rich ones.

As of this writing, the cost of finance, resources, and transportation are all still sinking, but evidence suggests the rate of decline is beginning to slow down and freight charges have just now begun rising astronomically. With the cost of borrowing at historic lows, this has made it easy to produce and market products all over the world, profiting from wherever the best conditions for your particular business happen to be located. Shifting production, sales, and service from one place to the next can be done relatively efficiently, putting more pressure on price and on those looking for a job in the wrong place, or with the wrong competence and/or training.

This is creating a whole new class of workers with uncertain futures. These workers are now being referred to as the Precariat. As professor Guy Standing points out in his book *The Precariat, The Dangerous New Class* (Standing, 2011), "job insecurity is a defining feature" of this new class.

The above trends show no sign of abating and, like so many other issues discussed in these pages, they all seem to be speeding up and intensifying. As of this writing, the recent trend toward inflation has begun to accelerate due to increased transportation costs and wages plus a decrease in availability due to the effects of the pandemic. Although there still seems to be an abundance of products and services in most industries, with more choices coming online every day, we could rapidly see a monumental shift back to prohibitive pricing and scarcity.

There is an old proverb in the sales profession that states, "you are only as good as your last month." With the trends that are now accelerating, we may want to update that to "you are only as good as your next week." Why? Except for checking if a competitor is gaining on you, looking backward now only distracts you from preparing for your next challenge or opportunity. Looking backwards, you are less likely to spot the next opportunity or threat ahead. Still not convinced? Keep reading and don't look back.

Explosive growth of mergers and acquisitions

As of this writing, Mergers and Acquisitions or M&A (as this industry is referred to) is having yet another banner year. There is still an unprecedented push toward merging smaller companies into larger, worldwide operations.

Why?

In an era of colossal change and shorter cycles, more companies will try to accelerate the time to market of their products and services through increasingly aggressive M&A and marketing practices. This focus on marketing synergies, rather than operational synergies, is turning this historically slow process of finding the right operational fit into a frantic search for the quickest and cheapest way to find, rebrand, and distribute a new product or service. For example, what if Samsung made a deal with Nokia to repackage and sell their products with a Nokia logo? Could a partnership like that have helped one of Telecom's former leaders to at least maintain their now drastically shrinking share of today's telephone market? One they were instrumental in creating?

What this all means is that the M&A process is undergoing its own transformation. Maybe it too should be rebranded from finding synergies in R&D and production to one of finding them in marketing and distribution. The crush of time to market has now become so unforgiving that to develop a new product often takes more time, therefore shrinking its window of opportunity, than can be afforded. For instance, if your newest telephone has a sales life of one year, but it takes more than one year to develop and produce it, you have significantly cut your chances of making a decent return on your investment. It will be much more effective and profitable to instead merge, acquire, or ally with a company that can develop it faster or has a killer app ready to go. Then you can focus your precious resources on convincing the market that it looks and feels like your other products.

Therefore, as this trend accelerates, your M&A and marketing focus will become more important and probably require more resources, whereas your R&D and production focus will diminish, unless that is where your focus lies. Faster time to market dictates the shortening of this make/buy decision. Strategic partnerships, such as one between former rivals Ericsson and Cisco, will become more commonplace and divestitures will increase when an internal department or unit's usefulness wanes. Yet what if the tendency also increases to choose speed over prudence, causing many well-intentioned M&As to crash and burn, due to quick, ignorant, and/or sloppy due-diligence methods?

Disintermediation

"Disintermediation" simply means eliminating the middleman. Although this is by no means a new trend, it is now also beginning to accelerate. What is the cause for this rapid acceleration? Economics and technology.

With the focus on producing even more stuff at an even lower cost, many have intensified their search for ways to eliminate all middlemen. Most everyone feels a sense of pride when they have a chance to go directly to the source. Direct access usually saves both time and money. Fewer moving parts and connections means less to go wrong. The agile among us love inventing new business models to serve us in our search. In the IT business, disintermediation is commonly referred to as peer-to-peer transactions. Yes, it's another sailing metaphor that describes going straight to our destination without any stops along the way. This is efficiency. And in a world where efficiency is becoming a primary measuring stick, disintermediation is a quick and natural response to producing the best product or service at the lowest cost.

With the increasing investment in blockchain technology, this pace is destined to increase further. One of the most touted results of blockchain technology and their "smart-contracts" is the elimination of third-party intervention. Yet now it is not only limited to industry: threats to banking, politics, and even the legal profession arise as you no longer need to trust someone else, only mathematics and electricity.

Like life itself, disintermediation has its advantages and disadvantages. Here is an incomplete list with the aim of getting you thinking more in these terms:

Advantages:

- **Lower cost and faster delivery**
  As less participants are involved
- **Greater access and more control**
  Easier to see and access the whole delivery chain
- **More choices**
  Lower costs mean easier entry for competition
- **More security**
  Decreased chance of points of entry/failure due to fewer links in the chain

Disadvantages:

- **Increased responsibility and greater burden**
  You need to be able to respond more quickly and comprehensively. There are fewer involved who you can either praise or blame regarding the consequences of your choices and actions.
- **Time-consuming**
  You are now in charge, which also means you need more time to do your homework and find what you are looking for. Not only that, but you need to find it from a trustworthy source and constantly check that source is still trustworthy, as well as still the best deal.
- **Greater chance for bigger mistakes**
  Less links in the chain often means bigger consequences when things do fail.

This trend is showing up in other places too, such as our access to information. It is now possible to get a live video-feed direct online from an important event or disaster. Yet "fake news," very partisan views, and social-media algorithms designed to feed you only with news that you choose or prefer, can skew the truth drastically and increase the need to closely check what really happened. It is becoming unavoidably obvious that there are many partisan players with political or economic axes to grind. Also, it seems that journalists are either becoming increasingly sloppy with their fact checking, intentionally bending or leaving out the truth, or both. Thus, the need (and trust) we have for our traditional information handlers, now collectively known as the Main Stream Media (or MSM), is eroding at a rapid pace. For instance, in the USA upwards of 90 percent of the traditional media outlets are now owned by six large conglomerates, and our trust in them has reached historical lows. Is there an opportunity here to "spin" the information they produce toward a particular goal or ideology? What do you think? And more importantly, has your own trust in the news increased or decreased during the past few years?

The rapid rise of the so-called alternative media and independent journalism has now been attributed to this decrease in trust for traditional media sources. More and more people are beginning to question the information they are constantly bombarded with and are seeking other sources to verify or refute what they hear on the news. What do these alternative media channels represent? Peer to peer communication that short-circuits the preferred and carefully crafted "narrative" that has traditionally kept the masses in check. Hundreds and thousands of independent researchers, many (but not all) with close or previous ties to the information source, generate unfiltered information directly to social media and their own internet-news sites, thereby disintermediating the big main-stream players. They often report on stories too wild or too sensitive for the MSM to touch. In an ironic twist, the more the mainstream news tries to cancel/silence or undermine the validity of this pesky—yet growing—source of alternative news which, more often than not, challenges the accepted narrative, a number of things happen.

- Authentic, real-alternative news sources have to become even more transparent and must be meticulously careful to document and verify their sources are telling the truth. One false story and they lose whatever trust, viewership, and revenue they have built up to survive this long. In more and more cases, some are intentionally silenced or "shadow banned" for telling documented truths deemed too radical and oppose the "accepted narrative." This is often accomplished by shaming the character of the reporter, regardless of whether their reporting is accurate or not. Look no further than Julian Assange to see that "killing (or in this case silencing) the messenger" is still trendy.

- So-called internet "trolls," paid or not, human or not, lurk in the background to provide disinformation and confuse viewers, as well as sway opinion for or against a hot issue. This confusion causes viewers to become even more wary of trusting even formally trusted sources.

- The more the Main Stream Media actually adds fuel to the fire and encourages more people to seek alternative news. Look no further that the #walkaway or #nevertrump movements in the USA to observe the effect of this increasing barrage of alternative information.

E-commerce

Online business

After a slow and cautious start, doing business online has become widely accepted. The figures are growing exponentially. As far back as the Christmas Rush of 2014, it was estimated that for the first time, the value of presents bought online either equaled or exceeded over the counter sales in brick-and-mortar stores. Since then, this trend has exploded to the point that entire shopping malls are now closing due to a diminishing stream of steady customers. With the advent of COVID-19, if you are in retail and you are still in business, congratulations! Yet for those of you who are still alive, what does this rapidly increasing trend portend for you and how you market and sell your product or service?

First, it was the disappearance of the main or high street family-run shops. Due to the growth of suburban shopping malls, then later due to the big box stores, the small family-run shops and boutiques could no longer compete. Now we are experiencing the next step in this process as entire shopping malls and strip centers close. The reason for this latest change is e-commerce. Why pay more at a store when you can buy something through your smart phone anytime, from virtually anywhere and get it delivered to your door quickly at the same or often a lower price?

Most of those few customers, who bravely risk getting infected by still visiting their mall or an old-fashioned store, go only to gather the necessary information to make a competent purchase decision. They then order by phone or computer, increasingly while still in the store! This is obviously not profitable buying behavior for your local store owner's long-term survival, regardless of their size. How often do we now end up saving a few bucks and then become shocked to learn that our favorite store was closed due to a lack of customers? Looking now at all the empty store fronts in such shopping meccas as 5th Avenue in New York or Rodeo Drive in Los Angeles and it can seem surreal!

The latest retail innovation before COVID-19 was showrooms popping up in malls where you look at the product, ask a question, but then instead of taking your purchase home directly, you are instructed to order via the internet. Tesla is a prime example. It remains to be seen if even this innovation will survive the current virus scourge.

Now, factor in the realization that e-commerce can be initiated virtually and literally from anywhere in the world. Products can now be purchased, shipped, and consumed anywhere. Thus, your ability to respond to changing market conditions needs to be sharper and quicker than ever before. Sales figures for online purchases have skyrocketed again since March, 2020.

Customer capture to permission marketing

Voting with your wallet has turned passive customers into passionate, active ones who expect increasingly sustainable, environmentally friendly solutions and great service. We have come to expect to be able to choose what we buy. Unfortunately, some chains don't understand that this trend is creating a new and upsetting level of commerce whereby consumers are being forced, rather than invited, to transact business. To retain customers some chains have forgone creating customer loyalty and morphed directly into what is called "customer capture." All kinds of traps, clauses, and purchasing labyrinths have been devised to keep you chained to their business model. Some have now even begun requiring an exit interview before they will set you free from their grip. Didn't you read the fine print?

Some of this consumer frustration is surely caused by too much rapid growth for company back-office systems. Increasingly complex customer service systems and the administration they require prohibit the often poorly-trained staff to effectively keep up while serving each individual customer. Anecdotal evidence also points to either bad or possibly sinister decisions made regarding customer support. Regardless, word travels fast! If consumers get wind of a company or product that forces a purchase or (intentionally or not) captures your business, it will become increasingly tough to generate new or retain loyal customers.

Although figures are improving, it is still estimated that in the online world of shopping, up to 50 percent of filled shopping carts are left at the website checkout because of some small shipping charge or handling fee that suddenly appears at the last minute. Take that often small yet absolutely irritating sum away or bury it in the expected price and the conversion rate increases drastically.

The current internet marketing model called "funneling" often starts with offering a free teaser product, usually to capture the name and email address of the curious viewer. This is followed by a gradual increase in value of what you receive and a corresponding increase in price for that value. Get this balance wrong and expect at a minimum to never see that buyer again. Place an email address on a mailing list without the owner's permission and expect your mail to be, at least, irrevocably marked as "spam." In Europe, the new GDPR data base law makes retaining customer information a dangerously costly proposition, should you not inform or document it correctly. All of this means you must listen more often and more closely to your market trends and each potential customer's needs, wants, and wishes. Also remember that even if you do get the right balance, most people will still only mention you and your product when something goes wrong.

People are finally getting tired of being manipulated while increasing their sophistication. With the overabundance of products, services, and places to buy them, customers are increasingly flocking to outlets they feel they can trust and where they feel they are given the most respect.

It is also worthy to point out that customer service is increasingly farmed out to independent call centers. This is one of the few remaining and growing industries for those just starting a career. Having said that, the pay is lousy, most bosses are young and inexperienced, which together create a very stressful atmosphere. Many of these call centers experience employee turnover rates of over 80 percent every six months! One of my daughters tried this and after six months, she was one of two remaining from her initial class of twenty-seven.

Finally, as a small but increasing aside, what do you think of the trend of being hunted by mail, text, or phone for feedback on every single customer contact experience you have? Could this (increasingly annoying) trend backfire as well?

From volume discounts to free

Digitalization has also ushered in an entirely new cost of production relationship. The industrial age was based on economies of scale, which means the greater the production volume, the greater the savings. Save security costs and copyright concerns, the new information age model brings the cost of duplicating a digital product down roughly to zero. Once you design and produce the product, and then set up the necessary delivery and security systems for each new unit you sell and deliver, the cost for each new sale drops to nearly zero. Here are just a few examples:

- An extra subscription on a telephone network costs little or nothing to implement once the network is up and running.
- The cost of an extra e-book is virtually zero once the book has been written, formatted and the secure file produced.
- The cost of an extra song or film file also is close to zero once it has been produced.
- Adding one or one hundred more students to a virtual course costs nothing extra.
- The financial risks of adding another borrower to your portfolio, once you have your risk parameters in place, costs virtually nothing.

In each of these examples, the marginal cost for each new unit, once the investment costs to produce it are recaptured, is virtually nothing while the price remains at market level. Thus, if you create or find a winner, it can be a mega winner! Yet, if you produce a product via traditional means and a digital competitor enters your market, you could also be put out of business in virtually no time. The margin for error in this process continues to decrease as competition from the entire world continues to increase.

Major shift in corporate power

From McKinsey again, "If you think the world's largest companies will remain in the West, think again. Research points to those emerging economies' share of Fortune 500 companies will be more than 45 percent by 2025. This is compared to just a 5 percent share in 2000."[1] What if the main reason for this dynamic shift is the agility of emerging economies?

With a younger, hungrier workforce, fewer laws, regulations, bureaucracy, health, pension, and legacy costs, these start-ups are quickly running circles around established competitors in the developed world. Going forward would you rather remain "developed" or train to become even more agile? Ask yourself if development is more a path or a goal?

CHAPTER 3

Disruptive Technologies

Given current and future technology trends, Gary Smith, the co-founder of UK MSP Prism warns:

"Technology is moving so quickly, and in so many directions, that it (becomes) challenging to even pay attention before we become victims of the 'next new thing' fatigue.[1]" For instance, are you also suffering from "Zoom gloom"?

Technological advancement continues unforgivingly, driving economic growth and, in many cases, unleashing disruptive change. Economically disruptive technologies—like the semiconductor, microchip, the internet, or good old steam power in the Industrial Revolution—radically transformed the way we live and work, enabled new business models, and provided openings for new players to upset the established order. Are you and your team prepared for the next one? The McKinsey whitepaper (James Manyika, 2015) explains:

"Business leaders and policy makers need to identify these potentially disruptive technologies (and services) and carefully consider their potential, before these technologies begin to exert their disruptive powers in the economy and society."

New technologies are continually destroying business as usual and creating new opportunities simultaneously. Just look at what:

- **Uber** has done to the taxi industry.
- **Bitcoin, Ethereum, Cardano, and other blockchain projects** are doing not only to banking, finance and commerce but also to long held ideas of money itself.
- **Spotify, iTunes, and Pandora** have done to the music industry.
- **Airbnb** has done to the Hotel Industry. Now you can put an extra room or your house up for rentals quickly, effectively, and relatively safely.

- **Fiverr** is doing to task work. You can get SEO optimization, a referral, a logo for your company, a jingle for your sales campaign or a short video to promote your product for five dollars.
- **Kahn Academy, Praxis, and EDX** are doing to the justification and sanity of paying taxes for schools and rocketing tuition costs and a sinking interest in attending college.

All of these opportunities and many more like them are forcing us to rethink what business looks like. This entire trend of unrecognizable change is now accelerating faster.

Again, from friends at McKinsey, "Whether it's an old or established systems perspective or an institutionalized technological habit of getting business done, the ever increasing and now almost hyper-speed of technological change may indeed be perceived as a disruptive force, at first. But it needn't be. Change is always, and only disruptive as long as there is resistance. Resistance in the form of thought-patterns, practices, systems, and ultimately institutions, that are different or opposed to what is emerging. Once you open up to the possibility of the receiving and perceiving the underlying potency inherent in all change, you may find yourself gazing upon hugely broadened horizons.[2]"

How willing are you personally to open your mind, discover your points of resistance, and relax your body from those learned or conditioned defenses? Your answer to this often-uncomfortable question will be crucial to address if and when you are ready, willing, and able to become more agile. By becoming open and willing to entertain and incorporate disruptive technologies into your organization and your life, you increase your chances for success. For the duration of this exciting journey, you are invited and encouraged to test and develop your curiosity and openness. Now is the time to discover and learn what is necessary to master the rolling seas of uncertainty while increasing your ability to change course with ease and grace. Yet we must remain aware of serving others in a way that pleases.

The following occurred in a showroom in Stockholm, Sweden. A gentleman was ready to sign for a brand-new Mercedes for almost US$100,000. Everything was complete. The sale was down to the last line in the agreement. Literally, on the last line the buyer noticed an unexpected title transfer fee of approximately US$80. The customer, surprised and annoyed by this last-minute development, politely stood up and walked out of the showroom.

Big Data

According to the 2013 BBC Horizon documentary program, *The Age of Big Data*, this age was launched on the day we first got a search button on our browsers. The prospect of accessing information anywhere, anytime became a reality. Since then, there has been a rapid dumping of all information, from dusty and all but inaccessible books to the latest kombucha recipe, into instantly and easily accessible bits and bytes stored on the internet. Yet according to Big Data experts, this is only the opening salvo of an incredible informational and societal shift.

Figure 5. Big Data word cloud

More and more information is coming online daily. This data deluge is incredible! Now with the use of algorithms, we are able to discover and chart hidden data patterns as well as reveal personal and societal behavior in completely new ways. These algorithms have the ability to transform raw data into useable information instantly. As more and more sensors and RFID chips are planted in more and more products and even in and on people, even more data becomes available to analyze. This so-called Internet of Things or IOT opens up a whole new way of looking at our environment and ourselves. This too is only just beginning.

For instance, a poignant anecdote was offered in this Big Data program. Target, a well-known American retail chain, began a project to collect data on the shopping behavior of expectant mothers. The goal was to identify those mothers-to-be based upon what they had been buying, in order to better market the specific products they would need as their pregnancy progressed. One irate father called his local Target store to complain that his eighteen-year-old daughter was being bombarded with such advertisements. Unaware of this internal marketing project, the Target manager, who took the father's angry call, apologized profusely for the "mistake" and promised to get to the bottom of it. A few days later, he called the father back to inform him of the internal marketing project and to apologize again for the mistake. But now, it was now the father who apologized. He had since learned that his daughter was indeed pregnant. Of course, Dad was the last to know.

This type of surgical marketing is both very controversial and growing exponentially. With this marketing power and potential available, it's no wonder why:

- Your grocery store often sends you ads for your favorite cereal
- Your favorite internet sites offer ads you have recently Googled
- Facebook posts ads on your timeline regarding something you mentioned in a conversation
- You receive invitations to book a place for your next big round-numbered birthday before you even realize you will be having one
- You walk through a neighborhood and suddenly sales and specials in the stores you pass pop up on your screen
- There is now a number of projects such as the one between Telia, the Swedish telephone company, and Folksam, a large Swedish insurer, to connect your automobile's "black box" to your insurance policy. Your driving behavior will be monitored and compared to the speed limit and stop signs you pass. Then your rates will adjust according to how close or not you adhere to those traffic regulations.
- Facial recognition software is becoming very sophisticated and is being implemented in all the cameras you walk past "for your safety."

- China's recent implementation of connecting your "social score" to your ability and access to travel (this concept is now being tested in the USA by a company called Sidewalk Labs as a for profit enterprise. According to The Globe and Mail, Google is using Sidewalk Lab's "yellow book" as a guidebook to set up so-called smart cities where your information would be accessible for city services, the tax authorities, and police, among others. Detroit, Denver, and Toronto were mentioned as test sites.)
- Much has been written and proposed regarding vaccine passports: pricing at different shows and venues is already being adjusted based upon whether you have or have not been vaccinated. From Broadway theatre to rock concerts, proving you have gotten the jab can save you money!

Some estimates say that Amazon has up to 100 various data mining projects going on at any one time. As a plus, these methods are much more effective at reaching particular prospects, saving the uninterested from unwanted and intrusive ads. As a minus, any sense of privacy you may have entertained is now part of a comfortable, isolated, and distant past. It is going surprisingly fast for people to get used to software that tells complete strangers so much about their behavior, but like it or not, that is our current and future reality. What may be most interesting to note is the most common response to the question, "Aren't you concerned about your information being available to all over the internet?" The reply? "Well, I am not doing anything wrong." With an estimated 40,000 new laws enacted every year in the USA alone, how can you be so sure? Even more startling may be the title of author Harvey Silvergate's book, *Three Felonies a Day: How the Feds Target the Innocent*. If you think this trend is only happening in the United States, think again.

Another important point is the real cost of "free" Facebook, Instagram, Twitter and other social network accounts: free service always implies some kind of trade-off. For those of you who still think you are getting a free, no-strings-attached social platform that permits you to keep up with what your friends ate for dessert, enjoy your ignorant bliss. Facebook is constantly improving their data mining capabilities to monitor your behavior and then packaging this information to sell. This "market analysis" of your personal behavior traits goes to companies with products directly aimed at you and your wallet. Again, it has been estimated that these algorithms have become so sophisticated that by just liking eight posts they can create an accurate profile of you and predict much of your "buying" behavior. We mention Facebook as only one visible example, but this opportunistic behavior can readily be extrapolated to not only all other social media sites but to many other sites as well. As such, "data mining" continues to get more sophisticated and intrusive.

This is why you are getting fewer ads in which you have little or no interest. On the other hand, get ready to become the target for even more ads specifically tailored for you and your situation, and with even more convincing arguments (which address your specific behavior, feelings, and predictable defensive responses) to buy "what you need now." You have now become the product!

Not only that, a growing amount of people now rely on their favorite social media platform for their news, even though it is algorithmically tailored to what they prefer and often filters out or blocks all opposing views. As the film *Social Dilemma* painfully points out, the richest corporations in the history of mankind are now the internet and social media giants. Their business models all rely upon keeping you addicted to your smart-thing and their specific app. With the help of AI, that app learns all it can about your behavior and then feeds you with those "choices" that your behavior to which it is most likely to respond. In short, to be profitable, each of these companies design programs to manipulate your behavior so that your choices can further enrich their balance statement.

Yes, you benefit also, but what if that is just a very small part/cost of their business model equation. Bits and bytes do not have feelings! The algorithms are logically designed to maximize your participation by catering to your feelings and then keep you "hooked" to that app, site, and product. The longer you remain connected, the more ads they can pump into your mind. Your continued attention is gold for their business.

Big Data will also open up countless opportunities in just about every other conceivable niche of society. For instance, soon you will be able to access real time information about all sorts of currently frustrating rapid transit situations. Think of Uber and your ability to know where and when the next driver will reach you. Then multiply this at a minimum by every train, bus, and plane. Happily, the days of not knowing if your ride is on time are just about over.

Also, the amount of medical information being gathered on you and others is immense. Count on the state of your health and well-being becoming known by, and probably marketed to, many other people, organizations, and companies. Based upon your history, current behavior, and whether you care enough to act or not, your probability of coming down with anything from a common cold to heart disease, stroke, or cancer will be available to not only to you, but insurance companies, employers, and others. Issues of defending your medical privacy are already being challenged from all sides. Issues relating to the ongoing pandemic have only increased this trend. Currently there are a number of blockchain projects such as Medibloc that intend to collect all your medical information into an encrypted file or wallet to which only you have access. You would then take this portfolio (digital wallet) with you whenever you have a checkup or a medical problem. The days of being charged again for a perfectly good x-ray you just had taken at a competing hospital will soon be over. As a bonus, you could now also charge researchers for interesting medical information relating to specific health conditions you may have to offer. In the name of progress and profit, count on most of these challenges to maintain your privacy to escalate, including a monumental battle as to who has ultimate ownership of most of the details of your life and health.

Don't forget about the famous scandal regarding the hacking and exposing of *Ashley Madison's* database of 37 million married people who were looking for love in all the wrong places! Talk about a divorce lawyer's wet dream. Let this be a warning! For better or worse you now leave your digital signature on every site, transaction, and on all forms of digital communication in which you consciously or unconsciously participate. Those so-called internet "cookies" can be much more than just harmless, tasty digital snacks.

Add to this another mention of the very real trend of interconnection. Data is being increasingly shared, often whether it is legal or not. Most government databases are now being hooked up into one seamless sea of instantly accessible information. Although this can be a boon to, for instance, honest peace officers actively trying to track down a known criminal, it can quickly become a very powerful tool for oppression when put in the hands of less-than-honorable "public servants." What if, as a wise Hollywood monk once said in the movie *7 Years in Tibet,* "there is no honor in politics" is becoming increasingly correct?

Look no further than the US National Security Agency and its giant database facility that is now online in Utah. Every phone call, bankcard transaction, text message, and email you make is now being catalogued "for your protection." This is happening worldwide.

The above examples are currently stretching the boundaries of the word "legal." Then you have all the illegal hackers, many private "entre-preneurs," yet many others organized by various intelligence and security services in different countries. There is a lot of money to be made from hacking databases, so a lot of big money is being invested to increase the sophistication of their tools. A listen to just one of the late John McAfee's rants about cybersecurity on YouTube is enough to make a sane person pull the plug on their computer. Yet, according to him, even that may no longer be enough.

Whether you like it or not, Big Data is here to stay and it will now be up to us to figure out how to deal with it. As with any tool, Big Data can be used to enhance society, expand our individual freedoms, and quality of life, or alternatively intrude on society, your personal freedom, and limit your quality of life. The line between sharing information and intrusive surveillance gets grayer every day. Sooner or later, we may even solve this problem. The blockchain and the transparent security it offers is a noble start. Until it is solved, increased individual awareness, vigilance, and agility should be developed and prized.

Artificial intelligence, or AI

Artificial Intelligence (or AI as it is known) is just as exciting as it is confusing. Even defining what it is varies on what source you use. Examining only six definitions, contributor Bernard Marr states in his Forbes Article, "The Key Definitions of Artificial Intelligence (AI) That Explain its Importance"[3], ". . . while the foundation is generally the same, the focus of artificial intelligence shifts depending upon the entity that provides the definition." According to him, in the original 1956 Dartmouth College summer workshop hosted by John McCarthy he proposed, "The study is to proceed on the basis of conjecture that every aspect of learning or any other feature of intelligence can in principle be so completely described that a machine can be made to simulate it."

More than sixty years later, this still seems a distant dream although we have come exponentially closer. To paraphrase Marr, AI has become a subfield of computer science and how machines can imitate human intelligence (being human-like rather than becoming human). He continues by explaining that the focus and most of today's AI development is to use human reasoning as a model to make better products and services. This still falls a bit short from a computer that can think on its own. Yet even with AI still in its infancy, look what has been accomplished:

- **Alexa:** Amazon's home help can listen and decipher conversations in our home, look things up on the internet, play music, and be the smart homes central contact point.
- **Siri:** Apple's digital personal assistant can book meetings, send messages, give directions as well as learn from our requests to better predict and interpret what we want to do. Apple admitted that its i-products have the ability to listen to when we are having sex, "but only for the first few seconds."
- **Cogito:** this is a mixture of machine learning and behavioral science designed to help telephone professionals interact better with customers.
- **Spam filters:** AI is an important part of keeping your email box under control. They scan for metadata and other hints which reveal certain emails as annoying to some, welcomed by others. These filters use machine learning to try to keep up with new and creative ways for online marketers and other less honest mailers develop to reach your mailbox.
- **The IOT or Internet of Things:** This whole new branch of Big Data that connects all of your electronics, from toasters, to TVs, to cars, to buildings, etc. means that all we say and do is subject to being scooped up, analyzed, packaged, and resold to the highest bidder, thanks to a little chip in each product.

Other more bizarre applications include self-driving cars (such as Tesla's), Chef Watson's recipes designed with what you have in the kitchen here and now, Infervision's deep learning and image recognition, which can help diagnose cancer. Then there is the voice and facial recognition software that is being deployed very often in our phones and on our city streets.

The important point regarding AI when it comes to business agility is that it can definitely be called a disruptive technology. When all the bugs are worked out of self-driving cars, who will need a taxi chauffeur or a truck driver? Telephone trees are getting more sophisticated and eliminating human operators. Pandora and Spotify have pretty much made record and even CD stores obsolete. And again, this seems to be just the beginning.

AI's limitations

Yet there is something that AI cannot and probably will not be able to do for a very long time to come, and that is to feel.

Although this may not sound like a big deal, especially when you think of all the business conducted online today, feeling is still the missing link when it comes to building loyal relationships. Machines and software can solve problems, mimic behavior, and even improve on it (within programmed parameters), but what it cannot do is convert knowledge into understanding and creativity.

As motivational speaker Kjell Enhagen says, "Understanding is knowledge mixed with an emotional cocktail." Knowing something involves memory while understanding it so that it sticks with us and can alter our behavior requires both memory and feeling.

Translated, this means that work will be found long into our futures and our value as employees and leaders will increase the more we can create, maintain, and enhance human relationships. Here are some professions that, regardless of AI, still have a promising future:

- **Healthcare:** Technology will continue to improve our ability to provide healthcare, but having an understanding doctor or nurse who is there to comfort, listen and explain what you have and what needs to be done about it, is a soothing and integral part of making an often traumatic experience palatable.
- **Sales:** Yes, you can buy more and more complex products from machines and the internet, but certain products and services will

continue to require a human that not only knows the details about what you are considering buying but can confidently calm all your doubts and ensure you that you are making the correct decision. Salesmanship is still based upon the trust we have in those who stand behind a product or service.

- **Customer service:** There is absolutely nothing more aggravating than not being able to voice your concerns and complaints to an actual human being! Especially when your expectations have been crushed by something that went wrong with your brand-new toy.
- **Teaching:** Yes, Khan Academy, Intrepid Learning Systems, Minerva Group and others are changing the face of digital learning, but the value in having a real, live teacher available to listen, understand, explain, and support you when you get stuck will become more important as complexities increase.
- **Leadership:** Management and decision-making software is constantly improving, but how would you follow it even if you wanted to? Leadership is to people what management is to things, to paraphrase Admiral Grace Hopper. Being able to listen, understand, feel, and communicate in a way that encourages and empowers listeners into action will only become more valuable in our turbulent future. There is nothing more stressful or frustrating than the feeling of being managed by a human controlled, in turn, by some spreadsheet or algorithm.
- **Transhumanism:** Adding computer-based chips and even redesigned cells to the human body is now beginning to emerge. Enhancing human performance via man-made innovations has the potential of recreating what we think of as human. How will this exciting and scary trend affect us and our business? Who will ultimately decide what gets put into your body, by whom, and what for?

The blockchain

A trend that has now established itself, and is definitely worth monitoring, is the rise of blockchain technology. You may not have paid much attention to it yet, but it is the technology that started with Bitcoin and other so-called cryptocurrencies. Since its inception just over ten years ago, it has grown into an industry that is poised to potentially overtake business as we know it. Remember, the PC and internet started life almost as a joke, quickly growing to engulf society as we knew it. The blockchain trend might even surpass those "jokes" with its impact. The reason this technology is so groundbreaking is that it is literally disrupting business, finance, commerce, and even money itself with the following attributes:

1. It is encrypted and therefore offers a drastically increased level of security.

2. It works peer to peer and is therefore trustless, meaning that the middlemen such as banks, lawyers, and even doctors can be eliminated as you no longer have to trust the other person, just mathematics and programming.

3. It is borderless, so if you have access to the internet, you can participate regardless where you find yourself in the world.

4. Quantity is limited by a mathematical formula making it impossible to print more or inflate. For example, only 21 million Bitcoin and 84 million Litecoin can ever be minted.

5. It is distributed, and with so-called distributed architecture there is no single bottle-neck, person, or entity that can control it. Transactions are distributed on identical ledgers all over the network so changing one ledger without changing all, simultaneously, requires prohibitive amounts of energy and resources.

6. It is transparent, as each transaction is visible on that blockchain. The identities of the parties involved is protected, but the transaction itself is visible and distributed over the entire network to all who care to look up that particular blockchain explorer.

7. It is outside the current monetary and financial system and therefore does not have the same risks of control and failure the current system has. It indeed has its own risks, but should the current and increasingly antiquated system fail, as many predict, this may become a plus.

Money versus currency

What if the difference between currency and money is that one is a freely agreed upon, borderless vehicle of exchange between free market players, while the other is dictated by legal "fiat" and then forced upon a market as "legal tender"? A problem arises when people lose confidence in the value of their money to purchase products. Whether it's tobacco leaves or dollar bills, this can happen to fiat or state-run money. Confidence in currency has disappeared in such places as Germany in the 1920s, Zimbabwe in 2010 (and again recently), and too often in Argentina. It even happened way back in Roman times as silver was "clipped" and cheaper metals substituted as Rome ran out of money—slowly at first, then quickly.

Gresham's Law states that, "bad money drives out good money," and when our money's purchasing power weakens, we tend to hoard the older alternatives by taking them out of circulation. The belief is that the older one will maintain its value better. In Rome, when the money began to be "clipped" and cheaper metals replaced silver, wise people began to bury the old, unclipped silver coins in their backyards. Many of these hoards are still being discovered today, providing evidence that things got so bad for so long that the owners either died, moved away, or forgot where they had buried their treasure. Variations of this behavior have happened multiple times in history: in France in the 1700s, the smart French money moved out of France during the time of John Law's bubble, and during World War II, many refugees sewed their gold coins, jewelry, and even gold threads into their clothes when escaping their tormentors. This may be happening again with central banks recently buying more gold than they have during the last few generations. Also, more and more people are now piling into Bitcoin and other cryptos to further diversify their holdings.

The famous gold investor Jim Sinclair coined the term GOTS meaning "Get Out of The System." This has been his advice since the Great Recession of 2008–2009 as he and others see trust and confidence in the current system eroding at an increasing pace.

Human behavior continues until another, newer agreement is reached freely or is forced upon us by using the threat of violence or incarceration. Look no further than John Law and his printing of livres and how it collapsed the French economy at the end of the eighteenth century[4].

In a closed or fiat market, you are usually stuck with monetary decisions designed by the rich and powerful to keep them rich and powerful. You are forced to stand by, helpless to control it. If the powers that control your money decide to print more of it without your consent, your purchasing power decreases, since there is now more of it to chase after the goods you desire. Sometimes they do the opposite by declaring old bills to be replaced by new ones. For anyone still holding Italian lire, German deutsche marks, or French franks, good luck buying something with them! You can even risk jail should you choose to use something other than your country's "legal tender." In other words, you're stuck!

Keep in mind, since the Great Recession crisis of 2008–2009, it is estimated that central banks, worldwide, have printed a total exceeding the equivalent of more than US$14 trillion in leading world currencies, to shore up this increasingly uncertain system. This has sometimes been lovingly referred to as Quantitative Easing. However, if you or I did this, it would be called counterfeiting. This begs the question, whose money do you have in your pocket or on your bank card/chip, really?

Increasingly, governments are trying to reign in this situation as this new technology represents a major threat to bankers' and lawmakers' control over "your" money. At the same time, blockchain technology may also represents a major opportunity for you to take back control over your money and your personal sovereignty. This is part of the genius behind blockchain technology and why so much is now being written on money laundering, etc. blockchain technology limits and possibly even neutralizes the control the banking system and local lawmakers have over your money. This represents the biggest threat ever to business as usual. With the recent addition of Decentralized Finance (DeFi), blockchain technology is taking direct aim at the financial sector by enabling peer-to-peer transactions, loans and contracts that are independent of the banking sector. Again, as long as you trust mathematics you no longer have to trust the person on the other end of your transaction.

Some very sharp people are now waking up to this challenge. Bitcoin, Ethereum, Litecoin, Monero, Ripple, Cardano, and many other crypto projects have now been developed based on technology that puts an exacting limit on the number of units that particular currency can create. These currencies currently work seamlessly over national borders making them a threat to the current national system. So far, they have not been fully controlled by any certain government.

In short, cryptocurrencies have been created as a decentralized and supranational agreement. They offer the opportunity to take back private ownership of your buying power and ownership of your personal data. This new form of disintermediation could signal the beginning of an epic battle on what form our future money will take.

Facebook first proposed its LibraCoin, but this was met with much skepticism and resistance due to their less than stellar reputation of handling personal account information. This was in addition to their increasing ties to overzealous governmental scrutiny. As money still "makes the world go 'round'," this struggle showcases the latest issue of what you can freely choose or are legally forced to use for money. Stay tuned for the CBDC or Central Bank Digital Currency. Recent projects in China, Europe, and even the USA point to that our current money will go digital first slowly, then quickly, while bans of non-governmental cryptos can become tougher. How this trend develops could easily affect how we view and use money going forward. How it will affect the way we do business will require an agile mind to figure out.

After the last big run up on crypto prices in late 2017 (when Bitcoin hit almost $20,000) prices have crashed back in some cases by over 90 percent. Most of those who bought on the way up have either sold at a loss or have chosen to hold on for dear life (or HOFDL) until, hopefully, the next wave of investors pours in. An update to this suggests that a new surge began in late 2020 and is continuing as of this writing. Bitcoin recently hit $65,000, for instance. Congrats, so far, to those who bought and HOFDL at the lows.

More importantly, what has happened behind the scenes is that many companies and projects that had good ideas, strong backing, and good financial managers, have now developed and launched their block-chain projects. Platforms such as ICON, EOS, and Cardano have been launched or drastically improved their offerings. Distributed Applications or DAPPS (as they are known in the crypto space) such as SIA storage, Enjin gaming, BAT (the token driving the popular Brave Browser), and others are up and running. Many others are coming on line almost daily. Whole new branches such as DeFi and Non-Fungible Tokens (NFT) are also on the upswing. Although those who speculated to get rich over night from cryptocurrency have taken a decisive beating. Yet the excitement and innovation from those remaining HOFDL-ers has increased drastically and is slowly beginning to spread. So-called "on-ramps" for blockchain neophytes have also been drastically simplified making access to this technology, especially for non-technical people, much easier. Cryptos go in and out of the spotlight, but to dare call them dead may be much more than premature. The blockchain seems destined to further confuse the ongoing struggle between centralized control versus personal freedom and, therefore, will contribute greatly toward economic, governmental, and societal uncertainty.

For instance:

- What will happen to foreign exchange rates and the entire FOREX industry when you can just "atomic swap" one currency (crypto or not) to another via a DAPP (Distributed Application (on the blockchain)) through your smartphone?
- How fast and cheaply will you be able to move money, twenty-four seven , when these individual blockchains are fully connected to each other? What will this do to the current SWIFT payment systems monopolistic control over the international movement and pricing of monetary transactions?
- How will taxes be levied or collected when it isn't completely clear who owns that particular crypto account today?
- What effect will it have on public service and runaway government spending should they be limited to taxing diminishing fiat money transactions while new and even better encrypted transactions increase in volume and speed?
- As both the current system and the blockchain rely on electricity to function, is the blockchain really scarier or safer than the current, electricity-based fractional reserve system we have in place today?
- How are cryptocurrencies already affecting the way you do business?

This same new technology is said to allow for secure, direct voting. This could also eliminate the need for representative government and those increasingly expensive full-time career politicians, many of whom now openly masquerade as our "public servants," while acting and getting paid more like royalty.

Blockchain conferences and specific crypto conferences are being held annually all over the world. Among others, the Netherlands, Lithuania, England, and Switzerland seem to be morphing into new "Silicon Valleys" for cryptocurrency development. Large banks such as Goldman Sax, JP Morgan, and even SEB in Sweden have poured big money into blockchain technology R&D. They understand that the security, portability, and anonymity that cryptocurrencies offer are beginning to threaten their fundamental reason for existing.

Banks are realizing that service which has value and financial agility are now first priority when it comes to actively retaining their customer base. Large tech firms have now also begun pouring money into crypto R&D and they see the possibilities of smart contracts and payment systems with increased speed security and privacy. The fundamental question of what your money—and even business—will look like in the future is far from resolved.

Fractional reserve banking, DeFi, and cryptos

Again, Fractional Reserve Banking means that only a fraction of the physical money we have in our bank accounts actually exists on reserve. The rest of your hard-earned cash is just a digital accounting entry in some centrally run electronic ledger, guaranteed by the statistical probability that you and everyone else will not withdraw your money all at the same time (causing what is known as a traditional bank run). Yet the bank run may also be a thing of the past, since the latest push to eliminate paper money.

Yet electronic or paper, our current, or any monetary system works only as long as there is public trust in our bankers and their financial system. What happens if, or increasingly when, that trust erodes?

This situation has been amplified since the Great Recession in 2008 as most western countries' banking laws have now been changed (and most of us have not even noticed).

Since the chaos of 2008–2009 and deep behind the scenes, laws were enacted transforming the money you have on deposit into an asset of your bank. Translated, any money you have on deposit is no longer your money! Thus, during the next inevitable downturn, the so called "haircut" that occurred in Cyprus in 2013 will, courtesy of your local banking lobby and their favorite politicians, can and will occur again, now in many countries—maybe even yours. What happened in Cyprus was that any bank accounts with more than €100,000 in them suddenly had €100,000 remaining. The rest went to "save" the banks. On top of that, limits were set on how much cash you could withdraw on a daily basis. According to BusinessInsider.com:

"After the two-week closure, a €300 a day cap on cash withdrawals was initiated for individuals; business transactions over €5,000 per day needed central bank approval; credit card spending abroad was capped at €5,000 a month, and travelers could not export more than €1,000 at a time."

Comments ranged from "blackmail" to "robbery" when this solution was introduced.

Interestingly, during this time, the price of Bitcoin rose from approximately $20 in January 2013 to $95 by the end of March, while daily trading almost doubled from ca. 65,000 to 110,000 Bitcoins per day during the same period, according to Cnet.com. This little bump was the first of many in the price and transaction volume of Bitcoins (and subsequent cryptocurrencies). In December 2017, the price of Bitcoin reached almost $20,000 before crashing to ca. $3,200 in January 2019. Another upswing started in 2020. Most importantly, volume in this recent cycle went from a low of ca. $100 billion to a high of $2.5 trillion (according to Coinmarketcap.com). Although still small compared to the estimated $8 trillion gold market, the rapid increase of the amount invested and the number of investors, both individual as well as corporate, should give cause for surprise. Agile fortunes have been made and lost in this space quicker than ever before!

Blockchain supporters suggest that this important trust problem will be eliminated using cryptocurrency, as there is a limited supply and each individual transaction (not the individual participant) is posted on that coin's distributed ledger (documented on all miners, all over the world, simultaneously). They further suggest your currency will be available for peer-to-peer transactions as long as you have access to electricity and internet. Thus, according to cryptocurrency advocates, this new system can function completely separate from the traditional banking system, as long as there is electricity. Regardless of whether you are a Bitcoin fan or not, does this information regarding the new banking regulations and cryptocurrencies make you feel more or less certain about your own and your organization's business model and financial future?

By the way, how much safer will your current holding of traditional (electronic) fiat assets be if electricity suddenly disappears? It's not only the worry of a brownout or blackout of electricity on your cash; there is also the consideration that many people and companies own millions, some even billions, of electronically traded stocks. Nations also have their bonds in electronic format. How can you really be certain that, in a crisis, the correct number of electrons representing your holdings remain in a place you can access? Most brokers handle stocks using what is known as "street name" meaning they are in a pool with your broker's name on them, not directly in yours. You are only allocated those shares that you have purchased on an as-needed basis—for example, when you buy or sell them. Otherwise, your shares are normally held by your broker in their name. There have already been scandals in both the stock market and in the crypto space that when there was a run on a certain share or token, the broker or exchange in question was either forced to buy more shares from the open market, to cover the transactions made by their clients— or they went bust trying. Can anyone say fractional reserve shares? This mega trend of electronic transactions definitely increases the availability and flexibility of investing and making money. Yet with each new innovation, there are also more ways to lose your hard-earned cash even quicker, making yours and everyone else's financial future just a bit more uncertain than most are aware.

Space

From the resurgence of NASA in the USA and Elon Musk's SpaceX to the new American Spaceforce and the enormous and growing space junk problem orbiting our planet, space is beginning to again capture the minds of forward-thinking people who are restless to travel. After an almost fifty-year hiatus, US NASA seemed almost forced to gear up again as interest in space has spread all over the world.

Russia is still active, China has now aggressively joined the party, and the Europeans are continuing to progress, among others. Yet what may become the biggest game-changer is the entrance of private entrepreneurs into the fray. With notables such as Elon Musk and Sir Richard Branson as visible icons, private business are now trying to develop ways to profit from expanding into space. NASA has now even contracted privately owned SpaceX to fly missions with reusable rockets to the government owned International Space Station or ISS. It has now been declared that landing humans on Mars is the next great goal, at least for the USA.

On another front, threats of space domination have created the need for expanded military interest in space. Former President Donald Trump's creation of Space Force is probably the most showcased example, but that is (according to him) in response to what is happening in other powerful countries. It seems that there are different types of threats that are being built—or are already circling the globe—that can cause damage via laser and other forms of focused radiation. More and more observation and spy satellites are monitoring us from above and are tapping into the already enormous collection of communication satellites currently in orbit.

In fact, there are so many satellites, both alive and dead, plus debris from older missions, orbiting the earth that the risk for this junk causing an orbital collision has increased drastically. The environmental movement now officially has a new dimension. This also means that the risk increases daily that some of this stuff can literally fall out of the sky and land on us. This must sound and feel like a business opportunity for some enterprising person. The question is, who do they contact to collect what? Compound this problem with the fact that much of this "junk" was, or probably still is, classified as top secret, and this means that if entrepreneurs are not careful, they may get shot out of the sky for tampering with trash best left alone. It may soon be time to produce and sell lightweight yet heavy-duty space debris umbrellas that also protect you from the mid-day sun. "Space, the final frontier." Is it creating problems, opportunities, or both?

World-class information and education everywhere

Before COVID-19, education was in the middle of a big shift. Since COVID, that shift has been accelerated at blinding speed. With the help of Big Data, social media, and multimedia, the latest generation of students was already experiencing a profound educational shift. The internet has thoroughly destroyed the traditional relationship between money, privilege, and higher learning. The internet was already breaking down barriers between education and class. Now because of the lockdowns, education has been forced online. Not only are our institutions having to reinvent their business models in order to survive, but now everyone can really learn from the best!

Ever since formal learning became important, access to higher quality education has been both a privilege of the rich and powerful, as well as an obstacle for everyone else attempting to upgrade their class or status in society. The relationship between money, power, and status to education has long helped to keep the ruling class ruling. This barrier is now being fundamentally altered.

Inexpensive computing and the World Wide Web allow people from all over the world direct and instant access to the world's store of knowledge.

With the introduction of Massive Open Online Courses or MOOCs, this trend of education anywhere, anytime, is now accelerating rapidly.

Prestigious citadels of learning such as Harvard, MIT, and UC Berkley now offer their courses online (and often for free) at places like edx.org![5] What were once guarded secrets, accessible only to the offspring of the privileged elite, are now equally available to the determined son of a fisherman on some beach in Sri Lanka. All that one needs is a laptop and/or smartphone with an internet connection to get world-class learning here and now.

Inventiveness and curiosity have been proven not to be God's gift to the rich and privileged alone. Keep in mind that this trend is also only a few years old. We have not yet begun to see or feel the enormous potential and implications of what MOOCs can do. You are welcome and encouraged to ponder what this exciting development means for our collective future! What if estimating how determined and hungry for knowledge this exemplified Sri Lankan fisherman's son is may be a sign of how agile and competitive each one of us ultimately chooses to be?

Figure 6. Gutenberg Press, France

For those willing to look deeper, it is now common knowledge that it wasn't just Martin Luther who was responsible for the Reformation. He had the winds of change at his back, primarily due to Gutenberg's invention of the printing press. In retrospect, his press is now considered to be the "internet" of its time.

Just as the Lotus 1-2-3 spreadsheet (Ringstrom, 2015) ensured the success of the personal computer, the printing and distribution of the Bible in the local vernacular, such as Luther's and Gutenberg's own German, suddenly lifted the veil off the well-guarded secrets of the Catholic Church and thus exposed what the Bible really said. All of a sudden, by translating the Bible into the local language of the people, the Catholic Church lost its monopoly on how God's word could and should be interpreted.

Consequently, much of the power and synthetic superstition that came with the Church's interpretation (that had kept the Vatican in power) was severely diminished. It became apparent, to those willing to read, how limiting access to the Bible had been the secret behind the power, wealth, and domination of the medieval Catholic Church. Church officials had amassed large sums of wealth, literally in "the name of God," by anointing themselves as the only way to heaven, and by charging the faithful indulgences[6] to gain personal access to paradise. As William Manchester wrote in his *A World Lit by Fire,* at the end of the 1400s, it was estimated that the Catholic Church owned 85 percent of all that could be owned in France. Since then, both the Church's monopoly on information and its wealth have lessened (but by how much, no one is really sure). Five hundred years later on, what if the history of increased information access and its effect on power is now repeating itself, only on a much broader and grander scale? What would happen if most of the current fears of political unrest, threat of war, societal divisions, environmental collapse, etc. were discovered to be contrived by those who currently wish to perpetuate their rule?

Now, many long-kept secrets of how our world actually works (and who is really in charge of what) are being discovered and revealed to anyone with the patience and gumption to search for the deep, factual information. Could this sudden and massive transition of well-guarded secrets to public knowledge, via (among others) the new and growing alternative media, cause increased uncertainty? Is the Pope still Catholic?

Additionally, everyone who wishes to contribute his/her own personal knowledge and findings to the rest of us can now do so instantly. Through various alternative media and social media sites, Wiki-pages, personal blogs, informal networks, and institutional and professional organizations, the accessibility to facts and documented evidence is expanding rapidly. These sites, coupled with more effective search engines, make it easier than ever to quickly find and share information with like-minded people online from all over the world.

We will shortly see faster developments and new innovations coming from even the most remote places on earth! Instant access also means that informational-critical mass can now be reached overnight, such as on the implications of a significant scientific breakthrough, a burning political or financial issue, a previously easy-to-manage scandal, or a closely-guarded secret. Just ask Prince Andrew. If you haven't yet been exposed to some sort of information leak that affects your trust in a leader or organization that you currently hold in high esteem, it is probably just a question of time.

Professional networks such as LinkedIn and others like Innovation Global Network are also contributing to and building upon each other's work. Sift beyond all the recipes, cat videos, and selfie photos on Facebook, Twitter, Instagram, etc. and you will also find a wealth of knowledge (and what is taken for knowledge) spreading here too. This trend to share your knowledge is catching on and spreading like wildfire. Again, it is crucial to understand that we have hardly begun to feel the tremendous power and acceleration of this global megatrend of information dissemination. How fast will today's information blossom into tomorrow's inventions? Who knows? Still, two things are fairly certain: The rate of change will accelerate further. The more agile you and your organization become, the quicker you will be able to shift your energy and resources to invent or at least innovate something of value. Think, you may suddenly be ready to launch the next big thing!

Enablers of world-class information

Have you:

- Started your own blog or podcast yet?
- Tweeted today?
- Called someone on Skype, Viber, WhatsApp, Signal, etc.?
- Posted an article on LinkedIn, or a video on YouTube or Vimeo?
- "Liked" a post on Facebook or Instagram?
- Updated your website?

Some genius has estimated that the amount of documented information, from the beginning of time until now, has doubled during just the last two years. This may or may not be true, but perform any Google search you can think of. Notice how many hits you get. Each one references anything from a mention, to an article, to a full manuscript. More people than ever are expressing themselves online. Be it via blogs, Vivo/YouTube clips, Instagram, Tweets, TikTok, or whatever, more people than ever are finding their e-voice and using it. What's causing this avalanche of information? It is the explosion of information enablers that are increasingly facilitating online communication.

Inventions, innovations, and totally new businesses now appear overnight. Globalization, as we have come to understand it, seems to be getting another shot of adrenaline. What will the next thirty years bring when we begin to see the effects of MOOCs? From the MOOCs providing education for free, to AI, to Big Data analytics and data mining services, information has increasingly become cheaper, and we are now only scratching the surface of what this means for our development as individuals and as a society.

Is formal education the only answer?

A textbook case of the challenge to the institution of education and knowledge is what Khan Academy[7] is doing to traditional education. Without formal educational credentials and with very little money, Salman Khan started his online education crusade in 2006. His mission according to his khanacademy.org website it is "to provide a free world class education to anyone, anywhere." Since then, his company has grown way past 71 million registered and unique course participants. What is most interesting is teachers in their traditional educational settings are now beginning to use Khan Academy's course material, often piping it directly into their classrooms. How will this affect educational traditions? Tradition holds that a teacher in the classroom is the only proven method to deliver quality education. How can that still be true when traditional teachers are now using Khan Academy material?

What does it do to a school's business model? Now multiply this by COVID-19!

What does it do to the teachers' value to the students? Do they repackage themselves as coaches?

As blogger Gary North pointed out, "[Khan] has turned the entire teaching establishment into the equivalent of teacher's aides."[8] To paraphrase Mr. North further, if one person with no formal teaching background can teach 71 million registered learners (2018), why should any person with common sense spend time and money to get an official certificate that permits him/her to teach a class of thirty? How will this realization affect the established and expensive path of formal teacher training as well as the costly educational apparatus and the exploding public pension burden that has been built to accommodate it?

Look what is happening in the wake of the coronavirus lockdowns. Public education budgets and university teaching programs are finally being forced under the economic microscope. Many universities are in deep financial trouble. If you love education and have taken a stand to make the world a better place by teaching as many people as possible in an effective manner, which path would you choose: the limited old or expansive new?

A recent poll showed that over 60 percent of college graduates in the USA have had to take a job in another area than their chosen field of study. Could they still be the lucky ones? There are now also more people, up to thirty-five years old, still living at home with their parents than ever before. Many of these people have student debt and little or no way to pay it back. In many cases it costs more to get a job and begin paying this debt back than remaining unemployed on daddy's couch. Yet the number of outstanding student loans continues to break records, despite increasing defaults, combined with the diminished possibility (in the USA) of bankrupting their way out of the burden.

Alternative education, both online and offline, is gaining a foothold as the cost of traditional education channels, such as college, become too expensive and the quality deteriorates. With the advent of COVID, we are seeing an accelerated trend of college closings due to exorbitant costs and decreasing chances for graduates to land a job in their chosen field. With the job market for your average young person under extreme stress, the focus is beginning to shift toward educational tools students can monetize directly.

Startup companies, such as Isaac Morehouse's learning startup Praxis[9], offer one-year training programs which allow you to study in the evening while working during the day with a prospective employer. The company gets your services by paying your modest tuition to Praxis and you get practical, on-the-job training, plus an education, all by volunteering your time and energy. You also directly enhance your future employment opportunities in real time, as just about everyone gets hired by their employer directly after graduation. What will Praxis and other less expensive online and blended learning startups do to what blogger North calls traditional and boring "conveyor belt learning"?

There is now so much information available that it easily overwhelms even the most determined researcher. More researchers are becoming necessary in order to sift through all this information, and find out what is relevant, true, and from a reliable source. Making matters more challenging is that much of the information available is free. The problem is, even when the information is literally sitting at your fingertips, you must first find it, be able to understand it, and then verify it before you can responsibly use it. The old saying that "there are no free lunches" still holds. We are noticing a trend that can best be summed up by saying that, "information is free, understanding costs." A prime example of this is that Wikipedia, even quoted in these pages, is no longer recognized as a viable source of reference material. Keep that in mind as you read, and always first and foremost trust your own verified sources.

More importantly, how will the skills of these hungry, ambitious, and freer-thinking individuals affect the job market for those who choose to follow more traditional routes? How will these new young managers who will eventually become CEOs lead and manage? Well, we believe they will be more determined to accept agility as an important trait of both their people and organizations. As these people are used to instant gratification, they will probably be allergic to any change inhibitors they encounter and thus become more restless, bored, or angry with any delays experienced. It is also worth considering how they will be more agile and within what parameters.

Other disruptive technologies

Emerging technologies such as 3D printing are slowly turning areas as diverse as traditional manufacturing to medical practices upside down. Already today, you can print anything from body parts to guns and now even houses on a 3D printer.

The medical profession is also being expanded with the use of digital and biotechnologies. Growing body parts in laboratories, laser surgery, and long distance surgery will help people to live better and much longer lives. The spread of information also allows laymen to not only understand health issues better, but also shop worldwide for the best medical deal. This seems to scare the medical profession for at least two reasons: One, they are losing their long-held monopoly in medical information. Two, after googling one or two pages of information, an increasing number of patients—sometimes arrogantly—believe that they have the same knowledge as their doctor.

Crowdfunding platforms such as KickStarter and others are not the only challenges to traditional bank loans. Transaction platforms from PayPal to Bitcoin and now the upstart industry known as DeFi are challenging our beliefs as well as our behaviors about banks, financial transactions, and investment opportunities.

All this and did we mention that we're just getting started?

Moore's law and shorter life cycles on all products and services

You hardly have time to purchase a new smartphone before another smarter, better, and not always cheaper one is released. The research and development cycle is shortening constantly. How will this continuously accelerating development trend impact your organization's agility and propensity for change?

When we started our careers before we authored this book, the internet was unknown. Not until the personal computer revolution, starting in earnest with IBM's PC entry in 1982, did personal computing become a reality. It took another ten years to make these devices into what we would now recognize as somewhat user-friendly. Then it took about another ten years before true mobility and connectivity became possible. We who were in the computer business back in the 1980s used to joke even then that a common calculator had more computing power than the first Sperry Univac. Moore's law was already demonstrating its power.

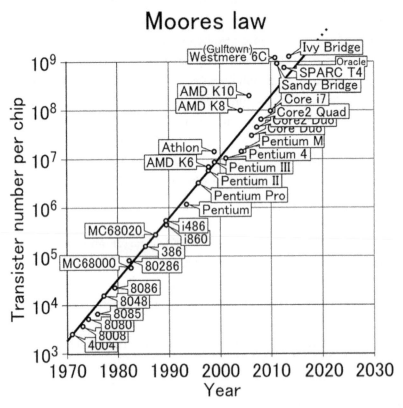

Figure 7. Moore's law timeline

As a reminder, Moore's law[10] states, "The complexity for minimum component costs has increased at a rate of roughly a factor of two per year. Certainly, over the short-term this rate can be expected to continue, if not to increase. Over the longer term, the rate of increase is a bit more uncertain, although there is no reason to believe it will not remain nearly constant for at least another ten years."—G. Moore, 1965

The year of this quote is not a misprint! If the pace of development seemed fast then, fifty years later it is downright blinding. To this day, most people in the IT business agree that our current growth rate is still increasing in-line with or even faster than the rate that Dr. Moore predicted.

IOT: The "Internet of Things"

Look at the following graph of what is being called the "Internet of Things." This depicts the connecting of all the stuff we use to computer-based systems. Even now, you can hook your room lights, your coffee machine, your security system, and your thermostat to your cell phone. This graph points to the continuing explosion of this IT trend while also pointing to a drastic increase in our interconnectedness not only with each other, but even with all of our stuff.

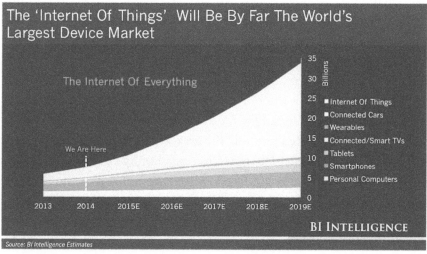

Figure 8. The Internet of Things, Time Magazine, January 2015

This now ancient chart from *Time Magazine* clearly demonstrated that, even then, we were just getting started. Already we have speakers and TVs like Alexis and Samsung that listen and interact with us, and apps, such as Siri and Alexa, that are programmed to listen and respond to us. Soon, we will have refrigerators that order our food as well as cars that tattle on our driving habits to our insurers. Do you think the powerful combination of IOT and AI will increase or decrease most of the other megatrends we have mentioned?

Increased misinformation and propaganda

"Whatever you think it is, it's not."
—Ancient Chinese proverb

With the advent of e-mails and search engines, the likelihood of receiving massive amounts of incorrect, massaged, or downright deceptive information has also increased dramatically! The use of fake news and internet trolls is increasing. Trolls are people who are often paid sizeable sums to misinform on an issue, or at least cause serious doubt and uncertainty. This growing trend makes your job of finding the truth that much harder. We will discuss the subject of climate change again in the "Perfect Storm" section of this book. For now, it is enough to quickly mention the controversy over climate change and question whether the most touted evidence is real or doctored. The same goes for the enormous amount of both information and opinion regarding the COVID-19 crisis.

The only thing that most of us can absolutely agree on is that the climate continues to change all the time and diseases have come and gone as long as people have been around. The area where Sweden sits, for example, has had about twenty ice ages so far, each lasting up to 100,000 years. Some of these cold spells produced an ice sheet on top of the countryside estimated to be about two miles (or three kilometers) thick. This is enough weight to compress the ground so that even today, it is still rising a few millimeters each year. Thus, water levels and climate continue to be influenced by changes and trends that started thousands of years ago. The Spanish Flu outbreak of 1918 was estimated to have killed around 50 million people. The Black Plague of the 1300s has been estimated to have killed between 25 percent and 50 percent of the European population. Evidence is now surfacing regarding a plague in 536 AD that was even worse. Yet, only one pandemic so far has resulted in a lockdown of the healthy.

> "The North Wind made the Vikings."
> **—Ancient proverb**

Did you know that in this same Scandinavian area there have been an equal number of warm periods with sub-tropical temperatures of about 40,000 years each? Many scientists now agree that Scandinavia is again nearing the end of such a warm period; but not all of them. Statistically, Scandinavia can "soon" (meaning within the next 500–2,000 years) expect a 100,000-year frigid era probably rendering the area uninhabitable, again! So much for the current global warming threat if you live in the land of the Vikings. Yet there are committed people with supportive data and deep pockets on both sides of the argument. Uncertainty is still king, but time will ultimately provide us with the correct answer.

Timing is everything

If you are a decision maker, making the right decision within the appropriate time frame is at least as daunting as admitting that a decision you already made was based upon false or misleading information. This includes some or all of the technology you have at your fingertips. In either case, you may have to reverse course and probably take a noticeable hit on both the original time frame and budget estimate.

> "I fear the day when technology will surpass our human interaction. The world will have a generation of idiots."
> **—Albert Einstein**

These chilling words, coming from one of the greatest minds that ever lived, should be taken very seriously by any decision maker. With the overwhelming amount of information coupled with your ability to tailor your searches through it using your background, education, and beliefs, does this make you vulnerable to missing the correct answer by a mile? The "cancel culture" that is currently all the rage literally cancels out voices that deviate from the politically correct norm. If you are wondering why the word truth is missing from that sentence it is because there is little or no place for it if you fear that what you say may be interpreted as a threat or insult, even if it is true!

What if the more you train to base your decisions on a blend of pertinent factors using your knowledge, experience, gut feeling, and ability to communicate, the better decisions you make? Do you still dare to display a strong sense of curiosity, in the current (and toxic) politically correct cancel culture we now find ourselves in? Could you still become quicker and more effective at actually solving problems, once and for all, if you addressed them at their source?

"Creative destruction"

The economist Joseph Schumpeter coined this phrase to describe the continuing procession of new game changing inventions that replace or destroy established industries and business models. It is the dismantling of long held business practices, known as business as usual, that will make way for innovation. For instance, buggy whips (and the skilled people who made them) were no longer needed when the automobile took over. National postal systems are now suffering and also reinventing themselves to counter the advent of email and pdf documents. 3D printing, nano-technology, and biotechnology are just some of the many game-changing trends coming over the horizon. Many decision makers miss or laugh off these game changers and end up paying the ultimate price of irrelevancy, which leads to bankruptcy. Then there are the agile leaders who can sense change. Bill Gates once reportedly said something like, "How come there are no railroad companies that now own an airline?" This was his reply to justify why Microsoft would take the huge step in their bid to transform their successful software company into a dominant internet player. That fateful, agile decision not only kept Microsoft in the game, it allowed them to expand further, continue to be relevant, to dominate, and to prosper further.

If you are not agile enough to handle game changers and megatrends, then you become vulnerable to the next creative/destructive trend. Regardless of your past success, if you are caught, for instance, expanding into another downturn, recession, or depression, it's usually game over. Being agile means also remaining vigilant.

CHAPTER 4

Societal Shifts

Let's take a quick look at just some of the megatrends that will be influencing society going forward.

Population explosion

By definition, overpopulation occurs when the number of people exceeds the carrying capacity of the region occupied by them. Overpopulation can result from an increase in births, a decline in mortality rates, an increase in immigration, or a decrease in the resources necessary to sustain the people in the area. The idea of too many people in one area is nothing new. In fact, the first real mention of it occurred in 1798 by Thomas Malthus in his famous work, "An Essay on the Principle of Population."[1]

The human population has been growing since we began as a species. According to Wikipedia and many others, the most significant increase has occurred within the last fifty years. This is mainly due to energy, agricultural, medical, and sanitation advancements. As of 2019, the world's population is estimated to be 7.7 billion by Worldometers. info. This exponential population increase is again raising concern, since it seems that we are again getting close to the newest and most improved limits of "peak population." Challenges associated with overpopulation include the increased demand for fresh water and food and consumption of natural resources, which can create deterioration in our living conditions.

So far, every time we have reached our perceived limits, some new invention or technology has saved the day. Malthusian fears of mass starvation due to the lack of food have been postponed since 1798 by the development of better energy sources, industrialization, and fertilization. The crop yield from one acre of arable land has increased drastically over the past one hundred years. Many believe that technology will continue to save us from a tragic reckoning. This remains to be seen.

Recently, due to concerns about the environment, finance, energy needs, and the breakdown of traditional family roles, the birthrate in the West has gone under the 2.1 children per family needed to maintain the current population. With the advent of the coronavirus crisis and what is now known as social distancing, the birthrate may begin to decline again. At this stage it is uncertain, since the opposite could be true as people were forced to spend more time together due to the lockdowns. We should know in nine months. The negative effect has not yet been noted in, for instance Africa, where the population continues to explode.

One thing is for sure: the rate of population increases. Changes in demographics, migration, and thus the effect on your market will remain uncertain. Yet as long as this trend continues, it will create more mouths to feed, along with even more creative ideas being launched daily. These trends and conditions will continue to put pressure on your need for greater agility.

Health, longevity, and adaptability

Research now points with some certainty toward the idea that every other child being born today in Sweden (and other countries) will live to reach his or her one hundredth birthday. Some have prophesized that the first person to live to be two hundred years old years old has already been born. If someone reached one hundred just two generations ago, it was front page news. It is also becoming more obvious that these new generations will remain relatively healthy and active longer. What are the ramifications of increased longevity for our society? How will it influence markets and business?

Focusing on just the OECD countries, the healthcare and leisure industries that cater to older people are already racing to keep up with the exploding demand. Given the recent economic boom, many retirees are really enjoying their golden years, due to fat pensions and retirement accounts. Some of this wealth has already begun trickling down to their lucky children. As each economic earthquake gets bigger and more frequent, regal retiree and inherited money lifestyles could rapidly change and with history as pretext probably will. Until then, many pensioners and offspring will continue having a ball, often at the expense of younger colleagues who are forced to work to support them. This situation will increase societal friction, as those forced to work watch their own retirement prospects get dimmer. The prospects for these two powerful trends to eventually collide with each other are increasing every year.

Retirement, more work, or both?

Yes, a global retirement crisis is brewing and will play out for decades to come. Experts predict its consequences will be far reaching. Many workers will be forced to work well beyond the traditional retirement age of sixty-five. Laws are already being enacted to gradually raise the retirement age to help straining pension budgets. Expect living standards will fall while the chance of poverty rises for the elderly, especially as they continue to stretch the already overstretched actuarial tables. This will be especially true in wealthy countries that built comprehensive and expensive safety nets while simultaneously raising retirement expectations. Unfortunately, demographics have changed drastically since these wonderful plans were formed and promised. How long will you be willing to support the lavish lifestyle of a pensioner while your own income continues to shrink and your retirement plan disintegrates due to increased taxes, service charges, social costs, and budget tightening competition? The younger you are, the more pertinent this question becomes.

By no means does every retiree experience this "golden age." Many workers are now realizing too late that they did not save enough or that circumstances have limited or destroyed their retirement plans. Others see a chance to add to their retirement income and also do something productive in their spare time. This realization is causing shifts in the labor market as older (often perceived as more reliable) workers are postponing their retirements, often for financial reasons, and taking jobs traditionally held by young entrants into the labor market.

The baby boomers' certainty of a long retirement era that some still refer to as "golden years" is now predicted to come to a surprising and abrupt halt all over the Western world. This is due to the mathematical certainty that boomers are retiring faster than their pension funds can afford. Pension payments, contributed to by boomers for most of their working lives, have not kept pace with the underlying funds needed for future redemption. Many funds are moving slowly or quickly toward bankruptcy, especially those covering governmental and municipal workers. California and Illinois are already coming to grips with massive retirement budget deficits. Cities like Chicago and Detroit have pretty much given up. Many companies like Northwest Airlines declared bankruptcy and, as part of the settlement, they liquidated or severely limited their pension plans. In Northwest's case, this still wasn't enough to save them. So, if you have all your money and your trust tied up in this increasingly fragile system, you may soon discover that your hard-earned retirement funds have been misused, legislated away, speculated with, or outright stolen from you. Mastering agility, even as a retiree, may be wise.

These problems are now growing exponentially in the USA as the baby boom generation moves into retirement. Not only that, but many of their children are beginning to realize that the luxurious level of their parents' retirement is quickly fading for them. As we have seen, many are now forced to live in their parents' basement to save money. For a lucky few, inheritances will be their saving grace, but not for all, as many boomers are enjoying a lavish retirement, some earned, some borrowed. Yes, there are many retirees who have chosen to loan money on their houses to finance a more lavish retirement lifestyle, betting they will die before they have to pay it back. Most people aged sixty-five and older are struggling to live on their retirement checks. Emily Brandon wrote this in an article for *US News and World Report*[2]:

> The oldest baby boomers have already turned sixty-five, and those in the oldest population brackets of the USA are beginning to swell. The sixty-five-and-older population grew 18 percent between 2000 and 2011 to 41.4 million senior citizens, according to a recent Administration on Aging report. America's first wave of baby boomers is now retiring at a rate of 10,000 per day. And these numbers are expected to further balloon over the coming decade.

As baby boomers continue to reach retirement age, the traditional retirement age of sixty-five years old is being called into question. It is often stretched beyond the original retirement promise.

Ken Dychtwald, president of the consulting firm Age Wave and author of *A New Purpose: Redefining Money, Family, Work, Retirement, and Success*[3] states, "The boomers will be the first generation to overwhelmingly not receive some sort of guaranteed benefits from employers." He also says, "We now live in a 401(k) world where people are responsible for their own savings, and baby boomers have not done a very good job. It's a generation that is going to struggle in old age in the absence of reliable anchors and support systems."

Baby boomers have also begun retiring in Europe. This marks a demographic shift that will reshape European labor markets over the next twenty years. It will also widen the skills gap many companies are trying to fill. Europe's aging populations are now forcing countries to rethink traditional retirement plans. The recent financial crisis has highlighted the fact that many aging Europeans, raised on the front side of socialism's bell curve, will be forced to work into their later years mainly (surprise again) for economic reasons. Japan, compared to these examples, is a basket case. They have more retirees than any other industrialized country.

In developing countries, the tradition of children caring for aging parents is still very common. Yet rising expectations may be dashed if their governments cannot afford to finance a retirement system to replace this tradition (and many children are already moving away).

For companies in all countries, this precarious lengthening of the job market age presents both opportunities and challenges. On the plus side, mature workers tend to have valuable and practical experience. Therefore, they can be wiser and more efficient than their younger counterparts. In entitlement heavy countries such as those in Western Europe, employers are learning that they can also avoid major disruptions caused by long maternity/paternity leaves by using older workers. This also lowers extravagant consulting and mentorship expenses and older workers are less likely to change jobs. This saves employers lots of extra recruiting and training costs.

On the other hand, workplace friction can increase. Often, older (and usually slower) workers with behavior patterns formed in another age are more often forced to report to younger managers. They also are more apt to want to do things "their way." Older workers have historically demanded—and gotten—higher salaries and health care benefits, but even that is changing. They also may have minor disabilities and need special rules or treatments. These issues can require a large, forced dose of understanding from younger colleagues, who already feel irritated. With people getting older and either willing or forced to work, how will this situation impact your market, products, and employee relations?

This shift sometimes occurs with heart-wrenching results. In a Dunkin' Donuts store in Northern Maine, one of your authors witnessed a sweet little old lady, who looked to be at least seventy, taking our order from behind the counter. We saw her get yelled at by her twenty-something boss for being too slow. The tension and frustration of the situation was evident from both of them. It was plain to see that they both wished this sweet but inefficient lady was somewhere else. From the look of the situation, "somewhere else" was not an option. The way she sheepishly took her manager's abuse could easily have been due to the unexpected destruction of, or the lack of, a viable retirement plan. This precarious situation will only increase friction between the older generation of perceived haves and the younger have-nots. Plan on your ability and your agility to respond powerfully to these issues to be tested.

Now add the coronavirus lockdown situation to this, and the uncertain future of retirement gets even more murky. Due to an often complete lack of cashflow from either a shuttered small business or a salary drop from an affected small business, optimistic retirement funds and the plans made with them have quickly gone up in smoke. Many have been laid off or are working much less than the pre-COVID era. This has affected a wide swath of people and businesses all over the world. Many middle-class and IT related jobs can easily be done via internet from home, but those on the lower end of the wage scale usually have to go to work at a restaurant, beauty salon, building site, or some other fixed place of business. These are often the places that were closed first and, in many cases, have remained closed. Retirement for them usually takes a back seat to both a roof over their heads and food on the table. If these people make up a significant part of your turnover, then your agility to replace or cater more convincingly to them is a priority.

Staying put

Again, from Emily Brandon's *US News and World Report* article from May 13, 2013[4]:

> While many people fantasize about moving someplace sunnier or more interesting, most people retire where they spent the final years of their career. Between 2011 and 2012, only 3 percent of people age sixty-five and older moved, compared to 14 percent of people under sixty-five. And older movers stayed in the same state (83 percent) and the same county (61 percent). Only 16 percent of people who traded spaces after age sixty-five relocated out of state or abroad.

Health and disabilities overcome, for now

Health coverage is less of a problem for the current batch of retirees. This may soon change. It is absolutely going to change for future generations. Currently, Medicare, Medicaid, and the remnants of "Obamacare," plus supplemental retirement packages, mean that many can still afford the increasing cost of medical care. "Sixty is the new thirty" as even now most people who reach the age of sixty-five can look forward to a relatively long and active period before older age, and the common ailments it brings, catches up with them. Living longer and healthier lives also permits them to remain active in the workforce, so far.

Currently, "about 13 percent of Europeans have some sort of disability," according to Luk Zelderloo, secretary general for the European Association of Service Providers for Persons with Disabilities. He has also said that, "another 25 million Europeans will be added to those ranks by 2025. This increase will mostly be due to age related problems."

Still, according to these experts there remains an optimism that technology will develop and permit many of these people to actively contribute to society in their own way. How will that look?

Only time will tell, but recently one of your authors saw a twenty-three-year-old war refugee working his smartphone, with what remained of his left wrist, faster than your author could feverishly work with all ten of his functioning fingers.

Global family consciousness

The younger generation is dropping (or not being taught) many of the traditions that older generations were forced to learn and respect. No longer bound by social, hierarchical, class, religious, and sexual limitations, they are free to form new, cross-border social platforms that often encourage expanded humanitarian and environmental ideas.

With the help of the internet and social media, it is no longer a problem to connect with likeminded people anywhere on the planet. The subsequent exchange of ideas and friendships can greatly contribute to a more homogenized, and hopefully a more forgiving, worldview for anyone with a computer and internet access.

Even on a biological-cellular level, it is increasingly evident that we are all connected. Studies from the University of Michigan have shown, for example, that even when a group of observers hidden behind a one-way mirror focuses on a subject's right thumb or left shoulder, sensors on the subject detect a temperature rise in the particular tissue or body part in focus. Somehow, even through a one-way mirror, we humans can still sense the presence of others twenty feet away, behind glass, and connect. Count on even these soft skills to be developed and improved to advantage in our brave, new, and uncertain world.

At the other end of the spectrum, studies by Armstrong Economics and others show convincingly that world financial and market flows are ultimately connected and will continue to influence each other even more profoundly, going forward.

The cancel culture

An interesting side effect of all this freedom that our younger generation perceives has been their ability to turn off arguments that are contrary to their views. Our many years of abundance (or spoiling?) have given many the perceived option to "cancel" those who beg to differ. Regarding the environment, migration, and politics, to name a few, the traditional voice of reason has, in many cases, been curtailed and speakers with an opposing view to that being presented have had their talks "cancelled" to avoid hurting certain listeners' feelings. The media has often helped feed the flames of this fire of separation and tension by either suppressing views that are no longer politically correct, or enhancing the PC argument to a size bigger than its believers. Media manipulation has caused a rise in violence and open opposition from both sides. Movements like the French Yellow Vests, Black Lives Matter, the Antifa movement, the Green movement, and others amplify an us-versus-them social divide. This trend to divide left from right, haves from have-nots, older versus younger, male from female, is increasing in both size and vigor, causing political, environmental, and market uncertainty (to name a few).

Cancel culture is now in full swing. If your view is not appreciated you can be "cancelled" as in being erased from your favorite platform for violating their often confusing and constantly changing "terms of use." Worse yet, you can be doxed, and all of your personal information can be leaked out on the internet so that your enemies can find and often abuse you even more easily. The result is that many are now being bullied into keeping their opinions to themselves. Even while writing this book, it became increasingly important for us to think about and navigate the quickly changing norms of what is and is not acceptable to actually write.

X-Box generation is not bound by time/space-mindset

Gen X and Gen Y are beginning to make their mark. Today's younger people have grown up in a time of abundance, entitlements, and often raised by so-called "curling"[5] parents who doted over their every need. (This term comes from the winter sport of the same name, played on ice, in which you make the path of the curling stone completely free of any hindrances or debris by frantically brushing it all out of the way.) Many have never experienced want, much less accountability. In fact, many have been conditioned to expect everything to be solved and delivered, by someone else, instantly. If you doubt this, ask an average twenty-something to change a light bulb or mow the lawn. From blockbuster movies, to food, to finance, it can seem like nothing exists, especially for those born in the 90s and later, unless it is immediately available. Like interest rates, attention spans for these privileged youngsters have decreased to zero and sometimes negative rates. Many friends of ours, trying to relate the lessons of history to their children, often experience that their advice is met with either boredom or complete disinterest. What if this pretty much ensures philosopher George Santayana's famous quote "those who do not learn history are doomed to repeat it"?

Regarding entitlement, way beyond voting with your wallet are the "snowflakes." This is the name given to oversensitive people who will not or cannot tolerate hearing or experiencing people or topics outside of their self-determined safe zone. The term snowflake seems to be a reference to how delicate their sensitivities are and how quickly they can emotionally melt if a hot/controversial (politically incorrect) topic is discussed. This snowflake movement seems to have started on college campuses and was closely linked to politically correct views and word usage. This seems to be a mostly liberal phenomenon as many conservative speakers were literally banned from speaking on various campuses because of the violent backlash that appearance was expected to create. This can have very serious effects on the right to freedom of speech versus cancel culture going forward, and evidence is already piling up.

For instance, Charles Taylor posted an article on Forbes.com on January 15, 2019, called, "Why Gillette's New Ad Campaign is Toxic."[6] In an apparently very poorly researched attempt at corporate social responsibility, Gillette launched its "We Believe in the Best in Men" campaign. Gillette presumed it was time for their main customer group to "stop making excuses and renounce" the old adage "boys will be boys." Sales figures would suggest that their main market disagreed as many demographically-average men stopped buying their razor products overnight. Their new ad suggested that "toxic masculinity" as perceived by middle America was just plain wrong. According to Charles Taylor, it seems even this particular group did not like being told what to do.

The "great awakening" versus the "woke" and questioning authority 2.0

Many of us are trying to avoid feeling the true extent of the complexities and stress in our lives by canceling out uncomfortable input. Many others are questioning beliefs and even institutions that probably should have been questioned long ago. The internet now provides us access and information to many more facts as well as different viewpoints and opinions. Not all of them comfortably support the status quo. Here's a small taste:

- How can you solve today's public or private debt problems with even more debt?
- Why do many spend money they don't have on items they don't need?
- Is it healthy or wise to eat genetically modified foods or use seeds that, among other very unnatural traits, can no longer reproduce?
- How long can we continue to use up resources faster than we can replace them?
- Is it right to kill others in the name of peace or democracy because your current leader says so?
- What gives our public servants the right to expect to be treated like infallible and unapproachable royalty? Please explain why our "public servants" need bulletproof cars and heavily armed security paid for with taxpayer money?
- Why should questionable job performance in corporations be rewarded with large incomes and perks?
- Won't using antibacterial products sooner or later increase our susceptibility to diseases that our bodies don't recognize or are no longer prepared to handle?
- What is the wisdom or health ramifications in vaccinating yourself this year against last year's virus strain?
- Is there really no harm to the water table (and our health) when the chemicals commonly used in fracking have caused kitchen tap water to burn?
- Why does the Federal Reserve "Open Market Committee" meet behind closed doors?

With instant access to information, many of us are waking up and beginning to "follow the money." Some are realizing that not everything told to us by opinion makers on what is now known as the Main Stream Media may be in our best interest. One of the USA's Founding Fathers, Thomas Jefferson, wrote "The price of freedom is vigilance."

This may be more appropriate today than when he said it. What if falling asleep in front of your smart phone eventually ensures the loss of that freedom?

At the same time, there is a diminishing need for young people to seek or gain the approval of others, especially their elders. An interesting side effect of being "curled" during your childhood by doting parents seems to be an inflated sense of self. One of the most interesting traits of many young people is their fearlessness to being published or to instigate an instant public response about an issue via social media. Look no further that sixteen-year-old, environmental activist Greta Thunberg. She was recently compared to Jesus Christ by the Swedish Church for her outspoken efforts. For better and for worse, this type of indomitable doggedness found in this latest generation of activists will make it much harder for those wishing to "control the narrative" to succeed.

This will undoubtedly encourage even more social division and market turbulence. A real split seems to be festering between our ambitious, articulate, and increasingly media savvy youth and the masses of so-called "sheeple"[7] who have actively or passively chosen to sacrifice their freedom and their self-expression for a (false?) perception of security. The older "don't rock the boat" seems to be giving way to the younger "no guts, no glory!"

From your authors' anecdotal experience of reading between the lines, most people we know who "hit the wall," burned out, or suffered a nervous breakdown did so due to being unwilling or incapable of sacrificing their integrity any more for that perceived sense of security. Although our interpretation is far from how they describe their situation, reading between the lines and examining the evidence, there seems always to be a great deal of unease between how things for them became and how they should have been. Most could no longer pretend to support a task in which they had lost their belief. This realization drained them of their energy, integrity, and ultimately their health.

What is even more fascinating is that many who hit the proverbial wall and successfully come out the other side often develop a powerful sense of their rediscovered—and now reinforced—personal limits. If for no other reason than survival, when they begin to say "no" more often, they often develop a complementary ability to see through many falsehoods that they used to politely overlook. As saying "no" now often means maintaining their regained health, this decision takes on a much more powerful and grounded context. They develop a stronger voice and begin daring to call a spade a spade. Also, it seems that many children react to a parent's burnout by resolving to never wind up in the same situation. They begin early to question their parents' beliefs and assumptions, then actively refuse to sacrifice their own integrity for a paycheck. Questioning authority, by this so-called "woke" generation, seems to be making a comeback. How will this trend contribute to and change our world going forward?

CHAPTER 5

Environmental Consciousness on the Rise

Talk to any student today about the environment and you will probably hear the name "Greta." Although Greta Thunberg is Swedish, she in now known all over the globe. Something resonated in her commitment to strike from school for the environment and has caught fire worldwide. Greta and her defiant call to arms is a far cry from the collective apathy and ignorant denial that plagued those first brave Earth Day protesters in April, 1970. It is highly unlikely that anyone reading this book would question our need and responsibility to clean up our environment and shrink our environmental footprint. Yet how we do this and what laws we pass to strengthen our resolve and the results may have drastic effects upon our ability to conduct business.

Sustainability and the green movement

What started out as a fringe movement has now become a major trend, blindly supported by those we elect and more often by those technocrats we don't. More of us seem to finally be waking up to the fact that we can no longer ignore the consequences of treating our earth as a garbage dump. Although some large, multinational corporations will probably be the last to admit that this trend has to be taken seriously, this grassroots movement to get greener, buy local, and save the planet is impacting profits now. This "voting with your (green) wallet" movement has started to catch fire, especially when it comes to our environment.

More municipalities than ever are legislating the sorting of your trash to encourage recycling. Think also about all those email signatures that urge you to "think before you print" and save trees by minimizing paper usage. Buying produce at the local farmers' markets is becoming both a marketing trend as well as a social event where neighbors finally meet, even in pandemic times. This trend is being fueled by the increasing distrust of the prepackaged, newly-termed "manufactured food" being sold in large chain stores. It is evident now that nearly everything sold in a box, can, or bag has questionable additives that include salt, sweeteners, all kinds of preservatives, and additives ranging from unhealthy to downright sinister. "Better living through chemistry," once the proud motto of a large chemical conglomerate, has now morphed into a sarcastic poke at chemical additives that range from a slight untruth to a negligent, fraudulent, and often dangerous lie.

Most city air is now cleaner than it has been for generations. Even Beijing recently experienced blue skies for the first time in decades. The efforts of Greenpeace, the Sierra Club, and organizations such as the Swedish eco-labeling company Swan now have the wind at their backs. Helped in large part by the availability of instant information from the internet, consumers are actively voting with their wallets to purchase more ecologically friendly products and services. Even legislation is being enacted that protects the environment. All these steps contribute to making the world a little better for us all. Staying abreast of this trend requires more flexibility to respond quickly to these wallet voters.

Greta Thunberg, the Green New Deal, and other green proposals

Back to Greta. What started out as a little girl with pigtails' crusade to strike for the environment has now caught the attention of a large portion of the world. Greta Thunberg, still a minor at this writing, has spoken in front of the United Nations and taken to task those leaders for "stealing her of her childhood." She has literally become the poster child of the environmental movement and children (remember those kids who have lost their fear of authority?) have become motivated, sometimes to the point of violence to promote their own version of this green movement. Even though some point to her being used as a tool to promote a new level global taxation without representation via carbon credits, one thing is for sure: she is motivating generations of people to be more environmentally responsible.

Never missing a chance to ride a powerful social wave, many politicians have capitalized on Greta's breakthroughs and proposed all kinds of environmental legislation. One of the most controversial plans is from a newly elected representative to the US House of Representatives, Alexandra Ocasio Cortez. Her masterpiece is called the Green New Deal. The details need not be discussed in this context other than that the price tag for this proposed bill being put into law would be astronomical; some estimate $90 trillion. Should it be enacted, where would the money come to pay for even a fraction of this bill? What would the consequences be for your business if it became law? This is just one proposal from only one country. There are many others with the most ambitious and perhaps scariest one being a worldwide carbon tax or base corporate being imposed on an international basis. This, of course, would require a whole new international layer of governmental oversight largesse to enact and enforce it. So far there is little to no mention of voters getting to vote on either the proposal or the people destined to run it. Can you say, "taxation without representation"?

Greta is an important part of this larger green movement looking to eradicate the use of fossil fuels and implement the so-called 2030 Sustainable Development Agenda. This whole environmental movement is both exciting from the perspective of really cleaning up the earth, yet challenging when we really look at how it will affect personal freedom, the way we will do business, and our pocketbooks going forward. To affect a livable balance between these factors and the committed people on both sides will be an incredible challenge. Get it right and it works for all. Get it wrong and we may all revert back to medieval serfs.

It is now even being touted that the COVID-19 pandemic is being used to implement something called the Great Reset. This is the name given to a complete revamping of our economic system to make it environmentally friendly. In the process though it will curtail our individual freedoms regarding travel, money, and even health. Nothing is yet clear as of this writing other than that this entire movement will create more uncertainty before everyone agrees upon the correct course of action. As powerful players have now committed to supporting this green agenda and this reset, we also have to prepare to navigate the effect of such statements as, "In five years, you will own nothing and be happy," spoken by the influential chairman of the WEF at their annual meeting in January, 2021.

As the most ardent supporters of these newer, more radical environmental makeover are still in school, this trend is really just beginning. How it develops and effects how you and your company do business will be decided in the years and decades ahead. What is clear though is that should you be caught napping or have your eyes focused backward on historical KPIs or Key Performance Indicators, you could quickly be legislated or socially shamed out of existence. Or, you could catch this wave and surf it into a completely new dimension of environmentally friendly products. Becoming more vigilant and agile will definitely help.

Success accelerates asymmetrically!

To "get rich quick" has never been easier!

Matt Callen and his group at Amazing Selling Machine[1] has produced incredible results for people who want to start a business selling products online, such as on Amazon.com. They have helped hundreds of people to make $10,000 and much more per month by following their ASM system. Recently, they held a webinar to announce the newest round of their successful eight-week course. Five thousand people signed up, for almost $5,000 per person, during this online webinar. This hour-long extravaganza ended up generating $25 million to ASM from excited participants all over the world!

This type of efficient and effective sales and marketing is increasingly common on the web. Success like this still takes lots of preparation, but when it finally arrives, riches can go asymmetric and viral immediately. This new model offers you globally compounded results, instantly. This is, of course, providing you have prepared a system robust enough to handle the rush of traffic. Many other great ideas have failed miserably because of an overloaded spike of interested participants onto an unprepared website or too many buyers who end up causing confusion, delays, and frustration. This leads to the killer: too many bad reviews.

CHAPTER 6

Negotiating Megatrends Demands Agility

Hopefully, these few megatrends listed here offer a taste of what we see on the horizon. We encourage you to think further about the opportunities and consequences they can provide. Again, our purpose is not to document in detail, or argue for or against each trend, but to provide an in-your-face experience of what is happening and encourage you to wonder how you will be affected. More importantly, we urge you to consider and plan for how you choose to meet these trends and tackle the uncertainty they will provide you and your organization going forward.

If not already, soon one and probably more of the following will powerfully affect you and your organization:

- Information overload
- Exponential development
- Increased globalization
- Changes in travel and communication behavior
- Increased competition
- Uncertain and ever-changing laws and regulations

The increasing pace of faster, better, and cheaper solutions is, for now, unstoppable. This means a continuing acceleration of shorter and more intense cycles. Trying to suppress, avoid, or ignore these shortening cycles will, at best, only buy you a bit of time. Learning to navigate them nimbly is a much wiser and more sustainable strategy. When facing major changes, shocks, and surprises, the more agility and resilience you can muster and master, the better you can handle what comes your way. In Part Three, we will be using the metaphor of sailing a yacht to help us all better understand how to navigate safely through the threats and boldly toward the opportunities that lie ahead. Whether you are the captain or a distinguished member of the crew, knowing what to do and being agile enough to do it, even in the roughest waters, gives you and your entire crew a better chance of success. This is not only true in sailing, but in business and life as well.

Agility also means knowing when not to act.

Understanding and distinguishing this important difference increases your level of responsibility. When you increase your ability to respond when navigating a big sailing yacht or company becomes simpler, easier, and safer. As Peter Senge mentions in his excellent business book *The Fifth Discipline*, "There is a major difference between reacting and responding. Reacting is automatic. It comes from Latin and literally means to 'act again.' Responding is a more conscious act. This word comes from old French and literally means to 'answer back,' after consciously reflecting over your different options," (Senge, 1990).

As life and business get more complex and turbulent, simplicity, ease, and certainty become both more important and more elusive. The more you learn to consciously answer back to circumstances (and practice with the tools, methods, and processes we present in this book), the better you will get at responding instead of reacting. The result will then be a more controlled and conscientious path to success.

PART II

The Perfect Storm

Figure 9. The perfect storm[1]

Ever since the year 2000 movie with the same name, the perfect storm has come to mean a giant storm combining several sizeable storms together, where each one could be very deadly in its own right. This weather analogy is very much in line with the situation we seem to be currently facing in the world today. A number of seemingly unrelated factors, each of which could be an economy killer in its own right, look to be coming to a boil at roughly the same time. Should they combine, we would face an even greater perfect storm, like none we've seen before. Some, but not all of these factors are:

- Economic uncertainty rising
- Environmental damage mounting
- Political and geopolitical tensions increasing

- Health risks increasing
- Societal strains and personal stress reaching their limits

Like the Four Horsemen of the Apocalypse (plus one), these five broad issues are beginning to integrate with each other while gaining further momentum, leverage, and speed. Underlying this entire storm is the diminishing trust and, in some cases, growing distrust and (in some places such as Hong Kong, UK, Germany, France and Chile) outright contempt that more and more people seem to be feeling for those supposedly in charge.

As with the first part of this book, the points we present here and others are much more comprehensively documented in other places than here. The point we are striving to make is that any one of these individual forces could upset the global economy and your business all by itself. When taken together, hypersonic agility may be required to navigate through them and provide you with any hope for survival, much less success. Being able to consciously and deliberately handle them in the manner of a nimble samurai or agile sea captain will take both training and special equipment to be effective. That's the point of this book.

CHAPTER 7

Economic Uncertainty Rising

Turbulence and market uncertainty have historically been cyclical and their cycles appear to go hand in hand with each round of society's progress. With each new round of development, a feeling of excitement ensues; things then grow until reaching a boil and finally collapse to start fresh again.

Economic deterioration

How can your job possibly be sustainable if it costs your company more to maintain your workload than the value you measurably contribute?

With the possible exception of a governmental post, the days of hiding in the corner of a big organization without contributing much are long gone. Even though the idea of contributing something measurable to the growth and success of your organization over what you cost has become distorted, it is still mathematically intact and easier than ever to measure. The consuming nature of taking more than you give has worked for a while (even generations), but in the long run this process must consume its host. Look no further than what is left of Detroit, Michigan to see the effects of entrenched labor, unrealistic wages, and retirement benefits in the context of a globally competitive manufacturing environment. The results can be devastating not only for an industry but also to an entire city! For instance, during the 1940s, Detroit boasted the highest per capita income in the entire United States and probably the world. Today, they are having trouble funding the maintenance of the city's water system.

Economics: A seasonal comparison

Economic historians and occasionally distinguished economists have long understood that economic cycles can be likened to the four seasons. Some economists have predicted these cycles with such certainty that they have been persecuted, locked up or killed for their prescience. Kondratieff of the former Soviet Union was so clear about his work on cyclical patterns and what it said about the Soviet Union that Stalin chose to send him to his death in the *gulag* rather than listen. Note how that finally turned out. Recently, Martin Armstrong was sent to prison on trumped up charges that were later dropped, potentially due to his programming skills, which in part enabled him to program a computer to accurately predict upcoming economic events. Armstrong asserts that it was this program (called Socrates) based upon cycles that his accusers sought. The charges were ultimately dropped and he was released. He chose to continue his research into the history of economic cycles and is again a consultant to central banks and large institutions while building a growing and loyal group of small investor followers. What do these types of men have in common? They discovered and documented similar and predictable patterns or waves that keep historically repeating in economic as well as just about all other cycles.

Kondratieff likened his four cycles to the four seasons of the calendar year. Simply described, the growing season works like this: After a winter of collapse and retrenchment, dormant seeds begin sprouting again in the spring sun with warmer, moister, and more favorable growing conditions. During the summer, crops reach their peak growth, helped by peak sun, much rain, and sometimes fertilizer and pesticides. The cooler breezes, increasing clouds, and shorter days of the autumn follow and wise farmers harvest their crops in preparation for the colder months ahead. Winter inevitably follows with its harsh environment, freezing and damaging anything or anyone unprepared. Then the whole cycle starts afresh, once again.

In the economic sphere, a cold winter of overwhelming debt and diminishing demand paves the way for fresh and optimistic entrepreneurs to begin springing into action. Their ideas sprout so-called green shoots and capital is raised to help them cultivate these startups. More and more monetary fertilizer is happily poured on them to make full use of summertime prosperity. Sooner or later, the market starts to wane as the economic days become shorter and colder during the autumn. Wise entrepreneurs harvest their gains then by selling out or saving to prepare for the cold and unforgiving winter season just ahead. Yet human nature seems programmed to resist these natural cycles; others yearn to and do whatever they can to keep the economic growing season going.

Especially in the autumn, they continue to borrow more and expand right into the colder and darker months of winter. As the harsh reality of winter takes over, many of these optimists become overextended. Their dreams collapse along with their company stock prices, credit ratings, and often their fortunes. Their mistakes cause a chain reaction of hardship for others, such as: suppliers, bankers, shareholders, and their customers, and all disappear into a *winter of discontent*. Everyone is forced to hunker down in this harsh economic environment while savings, non-performing debt, and other claims are washed clean from the cycle. The whole process then starts afresh with the warming and fresh, new optimism of a new spring. This full cycle of business can be easily tracked a number of times since the early 1800s and even long before that. Each cycle is often connected to leaps in communication or transportation technology, for instance:

- **The Canal Boom of the 1830s**

  Transportation time and cost decreased drastically with the use of canal barges. This lasted until overinvestment created an overabundance of canals and shipping prices collapsed.

- **The Railroad Boom of the 1870s**

  Once the collapse of the Canal Boom was complete and the debt from it was washed clean, a new boom in technology, called railroads, took hold. Tracks were laid all over the Western world until overcapacity and cheap finance once again crushed the transportation pricing mechanism.

- **The Automobile Boom of the 1900s**

  At the turn of the last century, it is estimated that there were anywhere from 300 to 800 automobile manufacturers in the city of Detroit alone. By the end of the Great Depression, only a handful remained.

- **The Mass Communication Boom of the 1930s**

  The stock of Radio Corporation of America, better known as RCA, reached a height of about $400 per share right on the cusp of the 1929 stock market crash. It reached a low of approximately four bucks a few years later. The products kept improving, yet overcapacity, deflation, and a collapse of demand directly affected its value.

- **The Air Travel Boom of the 1960s**
  What a great time to fly and to invest in the rapidly expanding airline industry. High service and high margins made this one of the darling industries until hijackings and increased fuel costs of the 1970s dampened all the fun.

- **The PC and Internet Boom of the 1980s and 90s**
  At the beginning of the 1980s, there was no limit to what could be accomplished with the developing computer, software, and internet technology. Ask anyone who was fully invested in the peak year 2000 how this cycle ended.

- **The Real Estate/Mortgage Boom of the 2000s**
  Many people made money by "flipping" houses. It worked until it didn't. We are still feeling the effects of this cycle.

- **The Global Debt (bond) Market**
  The Global Debt (bond) Market is next, according to the experts who profess to know. These debt markets are estimated to be at least ten times bigger than the world's stock markets. The unfolding monster known as the derivative situation will not help.

- **The Transformation Boom**
  And now . . . the Transformation Boom, where agility and even newer technology will be the key to sustainable and enjoyable success.

In each of the above examples, the momentum of what "Sir" Alan Greenspan famously called, "irrational exuberance," got the better of even the most conservative business people. Investment turned into speculation and manageable credit transformed into overwhelming debt. Keep in mind that in each cycle, even prudent business people were finally forced to participate. They were often well aware of what they recognized to be a very uncertain play, but they ultimately had to participate just to remain competitive and keep their clients happy. Why? Among other things, it has now been proven that the *high* created by riches influences the same parts of the brain, as do stimulants like cocaine. The comparison stretches further as those who become addicted to the market upside believe (just like a junkie) that they will know when to quit. You could say that we are "programmed" to get so involved in our excitement that we become addicted and then happily and willingly throw prudence to the wind.

Charlatans and con artists, who smell the potential of making a quick buck, also love to help encourage this process to ultimately exceed all rational or prudent behavior. In all of the above examples, technological change is fueled by the increasing ease and availability of finance and favorable legislation until such time that there becomes an overabundance of both. The whole process inevitably collapses upon itself and then begins anew.

Although we are fully capable of being conscious of this process and agile enough to leap from an old trend to a new one, most have yet to master this delicate dance. Below are some symptoms that suggest, for the agile among us, new opportunities to practice and master their own capability for increased agility are arriving as we write.

Abundance equals overcapacity and commodification

With such easy access to financing and billions of new workers from the still developing east entering the market, it has recently become very easy to set up a plant to produce just about anything almost anywhere. As the current business cycle inevitably nears its next economic winter, it is becoming clear that there is overcapacity emerging in just about every industry. Latecomers such as Indonesia, Vietnam, and Cambodia are now challenging even China and its ability to produce cheap products in excess. Yet the question so eloquently posed by writer and publisher Bill Bonner[1] remains: "How long will Americans (and other westerners) continue to buy stuff they do not need with money they do not have?"

Production versus consumption society

Buying stuff has become the new religion. "He who dies with the most toys wins" has now been transformed from a cute bumper sticker into a tempting lifestyle. As the shopping mall became our new place of worship, our society shifted focus from production to consumption. The capacity to produce faster and cheaper also moved from the West to the East and Asia now produces most of the stuff that we buy. It is estimated by the

Federal Reserve Bank, among others, that over 70 percent of the US economy is currently based upon consumption. Borrowing has increasingly been filling the gap between working to produce enough money to afford a trendy lifestyle and our ability to pay for it. Want proof? Look at all the ads for borrowing even more money and consolidating loans, so you can borrow more.

Could it be that this process is also consuming our ability to produce? If this is true, then we have also been consuming a large portion of our skills and resources with which we formerly used to produce. If you have children, you may have noticed that their drive to create, produce, and earn a living is drastically different than yours probably was. The biggest point here is not what has happened to our ability to produce, but our entire mindset. Increased stress, taxes, and homelessness, for instance, would suggest we have also consumed our understanding of why losing our ability to produce matters. This becomes especially important if the US, the UK, or Germany, for instance, want to remain global competitors.

Many now look down on those forced to work in factories. Somehow, it has even become more glamorous and sometimes more profitable to be unemployed than it is to get your hands dirty on a factory floor. What if we have consumed our work ethic? Martin Armstrong of Princeton Economics and Bill Bonner of Bonner and Partners have both done very good jobs of explaining that a country's ability to produce what the market wants is how you measure its value. According to their writings mixed with a good dose of common sense, fifteenth century Spain and 1980s Japan exemplify, from opposite directions, the point that the wealth of a nation is not indicated by the amounts of money, oil, or gold it holds in reserve. Instead, it is determined by how much value-added product it can produce and sell.

According to Bonner, Spain became extremely rich by relieving the Americas of their gold during the time of the conquistadors. Unfortunately, instead of focusing this newfound wealth on producing things, they spent it fighting wars and buying fineries from all over the globe. After they had spent their gold on a lavish lifestyle and had borrowed even more to finance their continuing wars, the Spanish economy collapsed. Other than the current riches enjoyed as a result of Spain's recent travel and condominium boom, the stature it reached as a world economic power around the time of Cortez has never been regained. Now with the COVID situation and its draconian lockdown policies, Spain is reeling from the effects.

By contrast, according to Armstrong, Japan has hardly any natural resources of its own. The country began importing raw materials and producing finished goods to sell to the rest of the world, from before the Second World War until after the bubble burst in 1989. Companies like Toyota, Sony, and Mitsubishi have become household names all over the world. For a time, real estate prices in Tokyo became some of the highest in the world as well. Even though it has now been mired in a recession for over thirty years, Japan is still one of the top three nations when it comes to GDP. This is with a population that is shrinking and aging at a record-breaking pace. The factor that continues to make them economically viable is their ability to produce things domestically that others, all over the world, wish to buy.

How long will the US and Europe be able to maintain their world dominance while their economies are being consumed from within by buying more stuff than they can afford? It has now gotten so strange that since the Great Recession of 2008, central banks have gone from lending money at unprecedented low rates of interest, to printing it (Quantitative Easing again) out of thin air to "stimulate" their economies and to keep the consumption party going. If there is one thing that has historically sabotaged every country's ability to remain agile, it is being weighted down with debt that can never be repaid and printing the purchasing power of that nation's money into oblivion. Just ask Argentina or Zimbabwe.

Increasing everything

Along with this abundance trend there is a growing realization that we are finally reaching boundaries that had so far remained theoretical. You have no doubt heard of peak oil, but what does peak actually mean and what can it teach us about the big picture?

Peak oil does not mean we will run out of oil anytime soon. On the contrary, with its recent drop in price there is more available than can currently be used! The peak refers to the economical peak where the finding, harvesting, and refining of oil uses more energy and resources and actually costs more than the revenues generated by energy produced from it. Producing oil over peak production is uneconomical and the more that is produced, the more money is lost. The active ongoing debate as to whether we have already reached this point seems to have been postponed for the moment, but not really. For example, it is currently estimated that it conservatively costs $70 per barrel to produce shale oil from the Bakken fields in midwestern USA. The current price has been near or under this for most of the past ten years. Some analysts still expect oil's price to go down to the twenties and it is now trendier than ever to trash the Oil Industry and vote green. Thus, money is being lost on almost every barrel produced. The difference has so far been made up by an unprecedented run of low interest rate loans. What will be the long-term consequences of that, especially when the rate of interest inevitably rises from the ashes? What will happen to all the investors, creditors and banks that loaned billions on business models based upon oil at $70 per barrel? Could this same phenomenon be playing out sooner or later in virtually every other commodity and industry?

Overcapacity in production

Since China became the world's go-to place for manufacturing, the price of producing goods has decreased virtually every year. With the rest of Southeast Asia and South America now coming online, more and more producers are entering the market. With financing so cheap and making factories easy to build, this further distorts the manufacturing market and its your pricing.

Add to this the current escalating trade wars and all the COVID-19 lockdowns, for the first time in at least one generation, growth is contracting. The full extent of this damage may not be known for years to come. In the meantime, many workers are going from temporarily to permanently unemployed.

Another game changer that will add to this problem of overcapacity is the decreasing price and increasing sophistication of robotics and 3D printing. Count on this making a large portion of the remaining industrial complex obsolete. Why order a small part even from China if you can produce it efficiently in your own home? The time of mass-individual home production is not far off.

And . . . has the balance of power clearly shifted from suppliers to buyers?

Shorter cycles, greater competition, and deflationary prices naturally tip the scales in favor of the buyer. This translates to an extreme weakness in pricing power for anything even smelling of being a commodity. High margins and customer loyalty are becoming memories of a distant past.

Increasing litigation

The legal profession has expanded all over the world, yet nowhere has it expanded as dramatically as in the United States of America, where ethical standards are also declining significantly. Although there are still champions that use their legal skills to do good for individuals and our society, many more have been compelled to or consciously chosen to stoop to ambulance chasing and worse. On a recent drive through a lower middle-class neighborhood in the state of New Jersey, many billboards were observed. A surprising number were pasted with advertisements promoting divorce lawyers boasting that, "Now only one consenting partner's signature is needed!"

When it comes to corporate law and legal proceedings, the horror stories keep piling up. Whether to defend sinister products, services, and questionable research or to challenge negligent or criminal products, services, and research, bad law has gummed up the courts and cost untold fortunes. An unknown lawyer who commented, "You only get to eat what you kill," seems to have sarcastically summed up the current legal situation.

When money is involved, people often become ruthless in pursuit of winning their case. In big tobacco, food, finance, and oil cases, to name but a few, their pockets are so deep that they can literally exhaust a smaller challenger's resources by continually throwing money and lawyers at the problem. This is regardless of who is ultimately in the right. Evidence suggests that the spirit of the law is clearly now of inferior value to the letter of the law. Here again, the power of accessible information and forces such as Wikileaks and Truthout are slowly, but surely exposing more and more blatant abuses of power. As trends forecaster[2] Gerald Celente has often said, "Justice is now spelled *Just us*" and honest business people are starting to wake up to and more often fear this message. Recently, some small business owners were fined for not cleaning up the human waste and dirty needles littering the sidewalk in front of their stores. There are many examples of police stopping a law-abiding citizen and confiscating any cash the owner had. The excuse? The owner could not prove where it came from.

There also seems to be many tactics at hand to hide, suppress, and distort the truth. Many of these less than forthright agendas are slowly, but surely, being revealed. This is resulting in an increased distrust for the darker practices of large, corporate business as usual and its cozy use of questionable litigation. Just google "special interests and corruption" and you currently get tens of millions of hits. To anticipate and deal with a growing legal minefield will require any serious decision maker to be extremely prepared and agile, especially when it comes to issues of the rule of law versus the rule of men.

It is a big problem for society when litigiousness becomes a way of life and that problem is now expanding rapidly to the rest of the world. Below are excerpts from a white paper written by Hans Amell on the US Legal System. Please ponder the following excerpts:

1. Is it true that every OECD country apart from the USA has the rule that "the loser pays"?

    In all other western countries, if I sue you and lose, I risk having to pay for your defense. Here in the USA, who ends up paying for what has to be negotiated. Consequently, this makes initiating a case a viable business decision or option. For instance, this means that in the USA you can use litigation as a delaying tactic, even if you know you are in the wrong. Examples are big tobacco and big pharma.

2. Is it true that every OECD country except the USA has an established relationship between injury/damage and the penalty? This is to say, the greater the neglect or injury, the higher the financial penalty. This is the norm in all OECD countries, with one exception. In the USA, the norm is: "How much punishment/greater sanction will it take to ensure that the culprit does not repeat the action?" If I lose my little finger in a door stop on IBM's premises

due to a faulty installation, I can sue for millions of dollars to maybe get a couple hundred thousand. Yet if I lose my finger in my neighbor's door, I may only get $500, if anything. The same situation, but different pockets.

3. Is it true that every civilized country has some type of jury system, but only the USA strictly stipulates the need to have a "jury of your peers"?

    It is these "peers" who eventually decide whether you are guilty or not. The problem is nowadays that many top-dollar lawsuits are extremely complex and need the explanation and understanding of true experts. If it is a complicated biological, psychological, medical, or financial issue, most normal "peers" neither have the training nor the experience to comprehend the level of detail necessary to reach a responsible decision. Only in the USA are experts called upon only as witnesses and even this has to be negotiated! Tragically, a jury, often without the necessary understanding of the pertinent hard facts, is charged with assigning guilt in complex cases. Often, their judgment ends up being based upon their emotions. Hire a good lawyer, one who has mastered playing upon people's feelings, and you directly increase your chances of winning, regardless of who is telling the truth.

4. Is it true that all OECD countries except the USA prohibit lawyers from taking commissions? Their reasoning? It undermines the necessary level of trust. Therefore, ambulance chasers are a uniquely American phenomenon. What if this makes trying to teach personal responsibility to our children a real challenge? For instance, how hot should coffee legally be? The result is the USA is the most litigious society on the planet. Bizarre cases of assigning guilt happen regularly to others instead of the person who probably should have been more careful or responsible in the first place. Ethics often end up taking a back seat to greed.

5. Is it true that the USA has about twenty times more lawyers per capita than the average OECD country? Why is it that the USA needs about one lawyer per engineer whereas all other OECD countries have fifteen to thirty engineers per lawyer?

6. Is it true that the USA also has about twenty times more lawsuits per capita than the average OECD country? If number five is true, then this would make perfect sense.

7. Is it true that the US healthcare and insurance systems are between two to seven times more expensive than an average OECD country? How much of this difference has to do with insurance costs due to more exposure to legal risk? It is interesting to see how even the current healthcare reform costs so much while avoiding the two areas most in need of reform: malpractice and cross-state competition for insurance plans. After all, insurance costs are based upon statistics. Wouldn't it be better to discover and address the root cause, which is the legal system, instead of the victims who are the people and livelihood through exorbitant healthcare, insurance, and other costs? Maybe the reason is in the next point.

8. Is it true that over 70 percent of all congressional delegates are lawyers?

    This still means there are on average four to five times as many lawyers in government as in other OECD parliaments. We also enact something like forty thousand more laws each year from local to federal levels. This would give credence to the old saying, "If you are a hammer, the whole world looks like a nail." How will all of these questions affect your need to be agile?

    This is without yet mentioning all these elected lawyers legislating over business, environmental, defense, and financial issues (to name but a few) that they have no training or understanding for; all the while spending most of their time soliciting contributions for their upcoming campaign or paying off the debts from their last one.

Although the above points are focused on the US, we clearly face a challenging dilemma as this "lawyering up" trend is expanding globally. For instance, the UK is well on its way in the same direction. In the US, it is an obvious and uphill struggle to have "lawyers" take any decisions whatsoever against those in their own profession, especially in view of the last point. Yet how much money could we save if we reformed the legal system before we tackled, for instance, healthcare?

After the presidential election of 2016, most of the time spent in congress and covered in the media went toward resisting and impeaching the president. Who actually took the time to lead the country? Regardless of your position on this increasingly sensitive issue, do you think the Founding Fathers meant for this to happen when they wrote in the Constitution about checks and balances between the three branches of government?

"You either have a legal system based upon laws or upon people."
—Unknown

Being subject to the whims of those currently in charge of the legal system only creates more uncertainty. Agility is most effective when the risks are visible and known. Agility is much less useful when employed against the whims of opinion, deception, and manipulation of those in power. Maybe if more people took these concerns to heart, something more positive might come as a result of these observations and—in the process—lower the current level of uncertainty. What could we collectively accomplish then?

Overcapacity of decisions?

With all the information we are bombarded with, is it any wonder that our ability to make decisive choices has been eroded? Only two generations ago, most families had one phone bill, one bank, one or two favorite stores, and one school system to deal with. When you went into a store you would have fewer choices when it came to what you would buy, but you could normally and quickly respond with a rational purchase decision.

The word "decide" comes from the same Latin family of words as homicide, suicide, and genocide. The suffix -*cide* means to end or kill and in the case of *de-ciding*, it means to end or kill the other choices. Now, just like in *The Terminator,* the choices keep coming relentlessly. How and when can you be sure you are making the right one? How do all these choices make you feel when you land in a decision-making position?

Go into a store and choose a loaf of bread and you will easily be faced with over thirty different and attractive choices. Multiply this just by the type and brand of soap, the cat food, and the shampoo you need and the choices you need to make expand exponentially. The same is true for all the different retirement plans, telephone/internet providers, banks, healthcare, and school choices that now confront you. A few can be avoided, some others delegated or postponed, but most need to be addressed, as time is always "running out." There are so many choices now that some business models actually take this into account and prey on your information overload by making it economically prohibitive to cancel your subscription and switch to a competitor.

Customer capture: The new business model

Whether the intention was genuinely helpful or not, many companies are going to a subscription type of service. Later, after you have signed all the paperwork or accepted all the terms, you often find that it is extremely hard to extricate yourself from the service. This form of customer capture is becoming more prevalent as we drown in a rising tide of excess data and decisions while being drained of the time and energy to address them. The cost per month may only be a few dollars, but how does this feel not being in control?

How many subscriptions do you now have? Have you also noticed an increase in products and services you used to be able to buy one-off to which you now must subscribe?

From cell phone subscriptions, to Microsoft Office 365, to eyeglasses and others, you can now choose or are now being forced to pay a monthly or annual fee to maintain access to your services and products. Yes, exciting updates are included, but your ability to switch providers becomes more and more complicated and often you continue to get billed or auto-renewed without your conscious consent. This information is usually buried on page 37 of the customer agreement small print you have no doubt read and memorized.

The result is customer frustration, an increased feeling of helplessness, and more time, energy, and resources devoted to game changing ways to combat these intrusive and constraining ways of doing business. This is the textbook opposite of creating and maintaining customer loyalty.

And this still does not include all the fake sites, scam operations, and the hucksters behind them, all actively looking for someone to fleece.

Renting versus buying

> "In ten years, you'll own nothing and be happy about it."
> **—Klaus Schwab, Chairman, World Economic Forum, Jan 2021.**

The business model that started with big ticket items like buying a house and later a car has now trickled down to much cheaper and more mundane items. As prices continue to increase, everything from perfume, to vitamins, to eyeglasses, to carwashes can now be leased, rented, or subscribed. Many consumers have little or no choice as otherwise the price tag and often their credit rating would prohibit them from acquiring them. Others, including potentially those who are reading this, choose this model for its convenience. Regardless, will this trend increase or decrease and what will the ramifications be for your particular product, service, and business model? As the quote above suggests, not owning anything might be the endgame many authorities today are aiming for. If so, how will this major trend change affect your business, if you still are permitted to own it?

Easy credit and the temptation to buy forward

The issue of when credit becomes debt has been and will further be discussed throughout this book. We bring it up here only to mention forward purchases. Every time you use credit to make a purchase, you buy something that you are betting that you will have the money to pay for in the future. More importantly, you increase the time delay before your next purchase of that item and help push future market demand forward.

No better example exists right now than the effect of six, seven, and eight-year car leases on the softening of demand in the new and used car market. Due to increased regulation of safety and environmental costs, as well as increasing health and pension costs for auto workers, new automobile prices have exploded. Cars have become so expensive that most customers are now forced to borrow money or lease. In fact, just ten years ago, the author tried to get his usual discount for buying a car in cash, only to learn the salesman actually now made more money through financing the car than selling it. To qualify for the monthly payment, many have to apply for the longest-term lease available. As autos are lasting much longer and many that can afford to buy one already have, those who can least afford a new car are again just squeezing in to what may end up being the tail end of this incredible era of frenzied auto buying.

Now, add to this:

- The increase in city auto pools
- The increasing gridlock in urban and suburban areas
- The trend to rent instead of buy
- The affordability and dependability of Uber and others
- The trend of urban dwelling young people not to get a driver's license.

With these trends as background, Ford Motor company projected this could reduce future auto-purchasing demand by up to four-fifths of the current volume. How optimistic would you be in this critical global industry?

The question then becomes: "Which industry or industries are next?"

Colossal government and personal consequences

In the interest of maintaining the important image of control, those who govern us have been very active in passing laws. More and more of these laws seem to have less and less to do with serving the public and more and more to do with serving special interests, getting reelected, and maintaining or grabbing even more money and control. Just a quick look at recent headlines will reveal that the term "public service" has lost whatever shine it still had.

- What does the monitoring and cataloging of every electronic communication and transaction have to do with freedom of speech? How about the increasing cancellation of social media accounts that question or challenge the chosen narrative *du jour*?
- How does the militarization of the police contribute to their image as "peace officers"?

- How does de-funding the police help them to "protect and serve"?
- Why do public servants need expensive bulletproof cars, extensive bodyguard details, and then use your taxes to pay for them?
- Why do they demand more gun control while being guarded by heavily armed and expensive security details?
- How do lockdowns contribute to personal freedom and the right to, for instance, "life, liberty and the pursuit of happiness"?

What if we have too many laws as it is? Ask yourself when was the last time you heard about a spring cleaning of obsolete, irrelevant, or ridiculous laws? Laws that increasingly slow down your ability to do business. Just like cleaning out a large closet and getting rid of two pairs of shoes for every new pair you buy, wouldn't it be healthy and popular for legislators to install a self-rinsing mechanism along the lines of "for every new rule, you have to retire at least two old ones"?

Right now, certain watchdog groups estimate that average law-abiding citizens in many countries break an average of three laws per day, most of which they are unaware. Off-duty police have been sheepishly heard to admit that they often remain silent about their profession in social gatherings. According to them, guests often avoid talking with them once their profession is revealed, for fear of, consciously or not, saying something incriminating.

In summary, we are now seeing a breakdown of civility in large cities, open protests against draconian laws that were never taken to a vote, plus the flight of wealthy and more mobile taxpayers out of the rapidly eroding services still provided by once gleaming cities. This is causing a major shift in demographics which has and will continue to cause uncertainty and destruction to a company's balance sheet, should management be caught napping.

Keeping the economic party going

Most of us would love an endless summer; hardly anyone likes a good party to end. As we have previously mentioned, the business cycle seems to consist of waves. Much like wanting to continue to enjoy a great, late August beach party, most of us long for just a little more warm and sunny weather. Also, it is well known that we humans are physiologically wired to seek pleasure and avoid pain. Metaphorically for the past thirty-five years, most of the developed and developing world have enjoyed a long, endless summer party, especially when it comes to economics and societal development. For anyone interested, evidence now points to that the continuation of the good times now increasingly relies upon financial shenanigans such as: cooking the books, larger debt burdens, and currency printing rather than upon solid, organic business growth, less rules, and lower taxes. These disturbing trends increasingly beg the question, "What if you don't need government negotiated trade deals as much as more freedom to do honest business with whom you freely choose?"

Since the first real taste of an economic winter since the Great Depression of the 1930s, estimates are that the world's central banks have printed US$14 trillion extra worth of their currencies (rubles, dollars, euros, yen, yuan, etc.) during the Great Recession of 2008–2009. One unofficial, but provocative reason given for this behavior is to shore up growing uncertainty in debt markets. Record levels of both governmental and corporate debt have again been reached and exceeded. Small business owners (the recognized backbone of a solid economy) all over the world are being forced to close while cheap and increasingly creative financing allows big multi-national firms to continue to grow.

The difference is mainly due to the access that big business enjoys to this easy money, plus new, favorable legislation allowing higher volume with lower costs. High quality jobs are being replaced with low quality ones and low-quality jobs are being replaced by robotics. Most troubling is that much of the money made by these multinationals no longer stays in the local community, but is sucked out of it and transferred back to an offshore HQ. Profits are larger, but who really benefits? Questions are becoming increasingly unavoidable as to how much longer this unstable model can continue or how much longer already debt burdened consumers will be able to afford to buy even more?

Measuring inflation and deflation is much like taking a temperature. As it grows colder, it takes more energy and fuel to keep warm. Since the 1930s, when an economy cools or deflates, Keynesian economics has preached fueling the fire by borrowing and spending more money to revive it. The idea of borrowing our way to prosperity has worked since John Maynard Keynes first suggested it during the Great Depression of the 1930s. Could something now have happened to suggest a sea change in the perceived sanity of borrowing even more?

People, corporations, and even governments seem to be reaching the limits of their borrowing capacity. Attempts at austerity, of actually cutting back on expenses, have been tried, but generations used to efficient and cheap public services are becoming increasingly unhappy with their decline. Just look at the civil unrest in Greece, France, Venezuela, the UK, the USA, and Chile to see the result. Since our current monetary system is now fully based upon increasing debt, talk of more austerity puts the whole financial system into jeopardy.

Due to the financial system's current structure of charging interest on every dollar, euro, yen, yuan, ruble, etc. printed, there will never be enough money in the system to pay all the accumulated debt—plus the interest—back. The act of paying off interest on this newly issued money requires the issuance of even more new notes and the vicious cycle deepens. Since each of those new notes will also be subject to even more interest payments, it doesn't take a "quant"[3] to realize our system has a large black hole right in the middle of all this money printing. Just like a black hole, sooner or later, our whole current monetary and financial system must inevitably collapse into itself. Many now point to the Great Recession of 2008–2009 as the start of this volatile and dangerous process.

Financial repression

Another storm warning that is also a direct threat to any plans you may have to save for a better future is called financial repression. It is a financial tool used by governments and central banks to keep their borrowing costs manageable. It is a legislative slight-of-hand that has dire consequences for business and investing. It is the practice of forcing interest rates below the rate of inflation. This increases the government's ability to borrow even more money without significantly raising the total amount of the payments. Although it can (and should) be used to help pay down existing debt at a quicker pace, it is now used to borrow more. Unfortunately, the flip side of this is that anyone trying to maintain their savings, or possibly get ahead, is faced with serious financial and legal headwinds. As long as the interest rate on savings is below the inflation rate, any money being saved for a rainy day loses future purchasing power. At your expense, this allows your elected (and increasingly unelected) officials to borrow even more, creating an even bigger hazard.

Ten years after the introduction of below market interest rates, the result is that even prudent investors have now been forced to chase greater risk just to break even! Want proof? Look at recent action in the crypto market. Most large loans as well as bond offerings, for the past decade, have been taken at below market levels, an increasing number at negative interest rates. This has screwed up the market's ability to correctly price financial instruments thus measurably contributing to even more volatility. This, of course, increases the amount of "hot money" sloshing around in the system. This is money that quickly hops from one investment to another in order to increase return. Can you guess what happens to your ability to judge, let alone price risk, in this situation? The longer the financial repression continues, the bigger the waves of uncertainty have to become. We are now in the longest wave yet of interest rates below inflation rates ever and that is before considering the believability of the reported figures. How and when will this end?

Governmental debt equals increased economic tension

If most western governments were to use the same accounting rules they apply by law to commerce, all, save possibly Russia, would have had to declare bankruptcy long ago. Since governments increasingly make their own rules, they have so far been able to increase their debt loads way over what would be acceptable to a responsible company or an individual law-abiding citizen. Unfortunately, the gap between governmental fantasy and fiscal reality may be beginning to narrow more quickly. Importantly, more constituents are beginning to notice.

Although Greece garnered most of the headlines a few years ago, when it comes to the effects of austerity and borrowing more to take care of a debt problem, other countries are quickly catching up. World leaders like France, the UK, Japan, and even the USA have had their national debt downgraded over the past few years. This is due to an increasing level of doubt in their long-term ability to repay it. Even the financial rating agencies that rate creditworthiness have been accused of playing favorites, thereby eroding economic confidence even further.

Countries have either tried, or been forced into, austerity programs to lower costs. This has resulted in budget cuts on the very social services that more people have been forced to rely upon. While health, sanitation and infrastructure costs are postponed or minimized, military budgets are maintained and, in some cases, increased further, adding more weapons to use during an eventual threat. Case in point, one of the biggest expenses still on the financially challenged nation of Greece's balance sheet is defense.

Debt and the bond market

> "Gentlemen prefer bonds."
> **—J. P. Morgan**

The debt market is what currently makes our world go around. This global market is estimated to be at least ten times bigger than all the world's stock markets combined. Bonds have traditionally been the safest place to park big money for a low but safe return. Yet with the advent of Zero Interest Rate Policy (ZIRP) and now Negative Interest Rate Policy (NIRP) this is no longer true. Now many fund managers are either forced to chase yield in riskier markets, forced to receive no interest or increasingly even pay for the privilege of saving. Even in the case of traditionally rock-solid Swiss bonds, you now have to pay for the privilege of owning them. Retirees and others who were planning on living off interest income are now forced to seek greater returns and more risk in so called "junk bonds" or the stock market. Or increasingly, they just spend it.

The effect of this downward manipulation is fourfold.

1. Risk can no longer be effectively valued or priced, measurably increasing the risk of a major financial dislocation, which is just another fancy term for financial ruin.
2. The pool of savings where businesses and corporations traditionally went for money to grow their companies has now been hollowed out.
3. As long as the inflation rate remains higher than what you can earn in interest, you are penalized for saving and encouraged to spend.

4. Funds for investing in future expansion and development (especially for small and medium size businesses) are unavailable.

These historically low rates have contributed to, and some even say created, the necessity to print more money in the form of what is now called Quantitative Easing. This freshly created money has been used to support (buy) this ever-increasing worldwide debt load.

An average interest rate cycle in the sovereign bond market has historically been about thirty-five years from one interest rate low until the next. Our current interest rate cycle has now been steadily going down for more than thirty-five years alone. Interest rates are not only continuing to go lower, but have now going negative, meaning the lender pays! A negative interest rate literally means it is actually more profitable to put your cash under your mattress or buy something riskier that produces a return (and a commission for your banker/broker). Could this be the real reason behind both the inexplicable rise in stock prices and the latest trend in legislation toward a digital/cashless financial system? What do you think will happen when this extremely tightly coiled spring of artificially repressed interest rates finally ends? Can you say, "no bid"?

Continued safety in government paper?

With the exception of Argentina and others, buying government issued bonds from most western countries has traditionally been considered a safe and reliable play for most of the last few generations. For most of the last thirty years it has been a very profitable investment also. Since interest rates reached dizzying heights in the early 1980s, the price of bonds rose with each interest rate cut, for anyone who, consciously or not, kept their bonds. From the early 1980s, long-term bonds have had an excellent run. Since then, different bond markets have had different fates, but with the growth of transnational investing, many interesting situations have arisen in the world of national and corporate finance.

It started with the Yen Carry Trade and has extended to and developed in other countries since. This is where financial institutions saw much less risk in borrowing money in one currency, at a low rate of interest, then invest that loaned money in another country/currency for a greater return. For instance, the Japanese yen was used for many years, due to its extremely low borrowing costs. Yen were borrowed in order to invest it in another government or corporation's debt, which return a presumably safer but still higher yield, which does make sense. Why would you risk lending money to a private company in a turbulent market when you know governments hardly ever dare risk a default? Although this is true superficially, there are lots of things that can happen behind the scenes, such as:

- The borrowing of more and more money. Look at Japan's debt/ GDP level now!
- Rating agencies, for one reason or another, rate a country's ability to service debt higher than it really is.
- Printing of more money to repay maturing debt (Quantitative Easing).
- Even more wacky legislation to pay for even more unaffordable and questionable programs.
- Shifting of expensive long-term debt into cheaper short-term debt (inverted yield curve).
- Increasing long-term certainty of ultimate debt market collapse— but when?

The more these types of shenanigans take place, the more volatile world markets become. More and more of all of these shady practices are being exposed (sometimes bragged about) in markets all over the world. The result, rarely talked about openly, is the increasing uncertainty and risk. It doesn't take much to turn that uncertainty into a default situation like Argentina again or even Russia experienced in the 1990s, except the next time it could be on a worldwide basis.

In addition, every time the interest paid on bonds is pushed down further, it naturally requires purchasing more of them to achieve the same amount of return. For anyone that counted upon retiring and living off the interest on their savings or bond portfolios, their dreams of a safe (and fair?) return have now been crushed. Anyone wishing to safely live off the fruits of their labor is now forced to chase bigger and more risky returns in the private market. Even as the return on government bonds continues to decrease (to levels not seen, for instance, since records began being kept at the Bank of England in 1696), many investors still prefer or are forced into the perceived safety of this guaranteed rate of return. Yet for how long?

Inflation, deflation, or both?

If you have recently bought groceries, paid a medical bill, or been smart or crazy enough to invest in an internet or drug stock, you will have probably noticed a price increase. But, if you have recently renegotiated your mortgage, bought a new cell phone, or new clothes, you may have enjoyed a drastic price reduction. What gives?

The short version is that with all this excess liquidity (printed and borrowed money) sloshing around the globe, it is causing more booms and busts in different industries at an unprecedented and ever increasing pace. For instance, the junk bond financing of the Bakken shale oil field exploration and development in the USA, while demand softens due to environmental and pandemic concerns. OPEC simultaneously seems to be losing its ability to influence prices. This has caused a glut of gas and fuel, until recently when pipelines were shut down for various reasons. The energy shortages and consequential sky-high prices that slammed us ten years ago were replaced by low fuel prices not seen in an even longer while. That trend has recently reversed again with growing inflation fears. This has caused massive volatility in transportation costs on many products? Many brush these increasing gyrations off as simply a matter of market timing. How consistently good is your ability to time these increasingly volatile markets?

Thus, easy money is metaphorically very much like wetting yourself in a pair of snow pants. At first it is warm and wonderful, but it rapidly becomes wet, cold, and uncomfortable. This so-called financial dislocation phenomenon is taking place in more markets, as easy money reduces the borrowing risk to get into an already crowded game. Trusted names with high legacy costs cannot compete with new, more agile, or cheaply funded startups without a "wink wink" bailout. Look no further than home electronics and the cutthroat pricing wars between big box chains and global producers. Even trusted household names such as Sony have been challenged by low-cost producers popping up virtually everywhere on the planet. We now also face the risk of more "zombie corporations" who have been given below-market loans or government grants to remain in business. Theses zombies continue to compete with fiscally responsible companies, causing even more market dislocation. For some, borrowing risk drops (temporarily?), but what about all the other risks?

This entire process causes increased turbulence and creates greater uncertainty when it comes to planning; for example, how much will tomorrow's energy costs be? How can you make long-term forecasts, much less order more raw materials, for instance lumber, when you are not sure of how much the product will cost to produce and transport and how much future exchange rate and carrying terms will be? These pricing dangers multiply every time you nostalgically look back at your historical records instead of peering forward toward the financial horizon.

When credit becomes an asset

This creative destruction process even calls into question what money and debt have now become. Now that money can be printed with the push of a button, allowing governments to quickly monetize their debt, it begs the question of what functioning definitions of money and debt really are? With government and huge corporate interest rates that slid all the way to "negative," this literally means that you could get paid for borrowing money. Does this mean that credit became an asset? With interest rates showing signs of rising and inflation heating up, how long will this remain true.

A little-known fact is that although the dollar became the dominant world currency after World War II, it was finally cut loose from its gold backing by President Nixon in 1971. More importantly, there was another major decision taken at the same time. This other decision was that US Treasuries could now be used as collateral or credit for borrowing money. Sovereign credit and/or debt could now be used to finance even more debt. Not surprisingly, the use of US dollars as the world's reserve currency began increasing drastically all over the world. People, companies, and even governments could now invest in US Treasury bonds (government debt) then use them to loan money against. Individuals and businesses began putting their "savings" to work. The debt market increased exponentially and US dollars and US treasuries were bought and used all over the world, and why not? Wasn't the US dollar and the treasury market "backed by the full faith and credit of the United States government"? Was it still as good as gold? Now, fifty years (and counting) later, we may still soon see.

In other words, as of 1971, this strangely named debt instrument (still referred to as a treasury or savings bond) was magically transformed into an asset, which you could borrow even more money against. Black indeed became white. Some governments tried to object to this, but the genie would not go back into the bottle, especially by the government that caused it. As Nixon's Secretary of the Treasury, John Connally (credited with creating this financial innovation), arrogantly quipped to a visiting and upset dignitary, "It's our dollar, but it's your problem." This may ultimately cease to remain true and that time may be approaching. There are currently a number of movements by China, Russia, the BRIC countries, AESEAN, etc. to unseat the dollar as the world's reserve currency. What happens when the CBDCs or Central Bank Digital Currencies shortly begin deploying?

Repackaging different forms of debt, especially government and Mortgage-Backed Securities (MBS) as assets also worked brilliantly for quite a while. It helped fuel our massive and unprecedented worldwide economic boom. It worked very well at least up until 2007.

Yet something different seems to have happened that fateful year. The world economy contracted. First, came the collapse of American MBS market due to too many questionable house loans, followed by the collapse in value of pretty much everything else. This collapse in asset value was further exacerbated by the loss of confidence investors began to feel. Investors sold and prices collapsed from October 2008 until March 2009. Our world economic system was only saved by a massive worldwide effort (evidently, sponsored by the same people who caused the crisis) to borrow and print more money. Massive amounts of freshly printed and borrowed money flowed into the system while interest rates were simultaneously forced to unprecedented lows. Even so, the demand for more debt slowly began to weaken. Looking behind the headlines, a fair question to ask became "who is actually still buying all the new governmental debt?" Who in their right mind would pay for the right to own a debt instrument, expecting little or a negative return? Can you guess the answer? Also, how did this colossal and historic infusion of new money affect the market's (your) ability to accurately price things? How is not knowing the fair price of an asset, consciously or not, still, more than ten years on, affecting your market confidence?

It just may turn out to be the 2007 collapse of United States' housing bubble and all the borrowed money supporting was opening signal to the end of this current and unprecedented phase of global growth. Now in the wake of this Great Recession, even the safety of the US Treasury market and the policies of the US Federal Reserve Bank are increasingly being called into question by the rest of the world. Will debt continue to be treated as an asset or will it go back to its more traditional role, meaning reverting to being a claim upon something else? Could the timing and impact of this "reversion to the mean" cause you even greater volatility?

Since the above words were first written in 2015, the answer has been even more growth using more extravagant, often theoretical tools and methods! A number of increasingly desperate measures such as Quantitative Easing (basically money printing), unprecedented ones such as negative interest rates, point to attempts to postpone another financial catastrophe. The continual and deliberate adjusting of the metrics used to measure employment and GDP doesn't help. Are these exciting attempts to keep the party going the same as solving the problem? We may soon see.

What if printing money, debasing the money supply, and tempting people to borrow even more, with negative interest rates, only further hollows out the value and trust in our currencies? Regardless of how this is packaged, mathematically it must ultimately fail. Finally, how long can these increasingly creative emergency measures continue to function? Especially as the trust people have in the current system and those running it further erodes?

When credit becomes debt

As long as a company, government, you, or I have the means to repay a loan and clearly see the possibility to make a profit on the money we borrow, then the money borrowed can be considered credit. When the money borrowed exceeds our ability to repay it, and/or the possibility to make more money by borrowing more ceases, this amount of optimistic credit suddenly converts to a pessimistic burden of debt. This may be over-simplified, but just try saying these two words: credit and debt. Then allow yourself to get a sense of which feels better to say.

Most economists, be they Keynesian, Austrian, Chicago School "Supply Siders," Austrians, or whatever, now finally agree that most current governmental debt can never and will never be paid back. Increasing amounts of corporate and private debt even further are also now openly being questioned. In fact, many "solvent" banks are only still solvent due to taxpayer bailouts and very favorable/questionable legislative changes that govern how their solvency is currently defined. In short, a strong case can be built that we are now collectively broke. It increasingly seems that it is just a matter of time before ordinary people wake up to this nightmarish situation of a breakdown in trust. Until that mass revelation, you still have time to prepare and get agile!

Loan sharking made legal

Not even this is the whole story. It has now once again become profitable to lend to more questionable debtors. Stories abound about the so-called NINJA loans made at the height of the housing bubble to people with no income, no job, or no assets. Recently, variations of these irresponsible forms of finance have begun appearing again. The victims always seem to be the least educated, lowest paid, and unsurprisingly, the least agile among us. The trend has now caught on for NINJA auto loans. Loans to people with questionable credit histories can now be found with terms from six to even eight years! Although the monthly payment is temptingly low, by the time you are finished making payments on such a loan, you have paid for your car a few times over. These loans also have a nasty habit of defaulting more easily, long before that lofty goal is ever reached. This tendency to default naturally increases whenever the economy begins to sour. In this topsy-turvy market, even this type of business is somehow still profitable, but again for how long, and what will any long-term consequences be?

Micro-loans are also controversial, as they allow entrepreneurs, even in third world areas, to borrow money to start company and contribute to the local economy. Take a closer look at Muhammad Yunus, a Bangladeshi social entrepreneur. Many question the Nobel Peace Prize committee's decision when it comes to giving a prize to this banker. Yes, he did introduce micro-loans to help local poor people, yet it was later revealed his generous largesse came with very high interest rates. Loaning money to people with good ideas, but few options, at high interest rates, made him enormous amounts money. Were his gigantic profits made unfairly off the backs of the same poor people he was honored for trying to help? One thing is now certain: in the process he became Bangladesh's first billionaire.

American student loan debt has exploded to over $1.5 trillion. With a change in the law a few years ago most of this new debt can no longer be written off, even in the event of personal bankruptcy. As job prospects become more challenging, this situation becomes more precarious. What suffers in this situation most is our trust in current business-as-usual practices. Uncertainty and risk for the perfect storm increase again.

Bigger balloons

As world economy fundamentals continue to deteriorate and our leaders strain to prop them up further, by borrowing and printing more money, it becomes probable that new financial balloons begin inflating and popping all over. This "whack-a-mole" trend has become obvious to anyone interested enough to look for bubbles since the 1985 Plaza Accord was instituted to devalue the US dollar. The rapid devaluation of the dollar that followed this agreement is now thought to have been the culprit behind the rapidly rising stock prices leading up to the October 1987 crash.

The Black Monday crash of 1987, too, forced investors into the perceived safety of Japanese stocks and caused its markets to rise into a second great bubble, which occurred in the Nikkei index in late 1989. When this bubble burst, it was the emerging world market's turn. From the Four Asian Tigers to Mexico and Ireland, investment money began to chase yield in many former third world, now rebranded developing economies. This was until 1996 when these bubbles too began to pop. This is when savvy global investors moved their hot-money again to the emerging high-tech market in the USA. Silicon Valley became the place to start your internet business and young entrepreneurs were financed with billions on the flimsy basis of clicks per view. This bubble finally went pop in 2000. With the help of easy money from Sir Alan's now irrationally exuberant Federal Reserve, the next bubbles started to quickly inflate in the American real estate market, in the raw materials market, and in anything Chinese. The "real estate bubble" burst in 2007 and with crashing house prices, the mortgage market, which had made those insane housing prices possible, crashed too. This subsequent bust became so bad that the US government was eventually called to the rescue when the overheated mortgage market collapsed in 2008. This "big short" brought world stock markets down with it. This seems to have caused what is now known as the Great Recession. The hot money shifted again into raw materials and precious metals until that bubble also popped in 2011. Since then, more money has been printed and loaned making these previous highs look modest. An increasing number of central banks (USA, Japan, and European for instance) have resorted to REPOs or repurchasing of their own bonds with newly minted or digitalized money.

Since 2009, trillions of freshly printed and digital dollars, yuan, euros, yen, etc. have been thrown at the problem of reviving the world economy, but views on the resulting successes are at best mixed. Predictably, those financial firms closest to central bank printing presses have benefitted the most. The next and possibly final big bubble to fear in this amazing and prolonged cycle is in the various bond markets and this alarm seems so far to be very under estimated. Since the various debt markets are at much larger than the corresponding stock markets, a loss of confidence or a rapid rise in interest rates could cause another cataclysmic financial dislocation. This could shut world commerce down on a scale larger than the recent pandemic or even the Great Depression. With all these bubbles, it is a fair question to ask what the current fair value of your company is? Is it two (five? ten? twenty? thirty?) times earnings? And what will it be tomorrow?

During the big internet and dotcom extravaganza, many IT/Telecom companies where trading at a hundred times earnings and multiple times revenue. Only recently Pfizer, the pharmaceutical giant, offered two times revenue for its takeover of AstraZeneca. Sometimes high valuations are a mystery, but historically they seem to balance out at around ten to fifteen times projected earnings. For large corporations, larger multiples must be supported by special underlying reasons. Either these reasons are extremely unique and often only temporary, or they are fabricated and subject to collapse, usually when you least expect it.

Often, aggressive growth objectives create their own problems. In Pfizer's case, their enormous size alone, forces them to continue to conduct aggressive mergers and acquisitions in order to keep on growing at a pace that continues to excite their shareholders. The excitement can become addictive, mesmerizing, and ultimately untenable. Even with unprecedented pharma profits from the pandemic, market uncertainty increases.

Zombie companies

These and other behemoths became zombie companies because they caused disruption in their markets while responsible companies that do play by the rules are now forced to compete unevenly with companies that are literally handed free money to survive. Both government with our tax money and banks with our savings have chosen to continue supporting these untenable businesses. It seems they fear the consequences of them going bankrupt more than throwing more good money after bad. What this practice of what is now referred to as crony capitalism does to the future of our free-enterprise system remains to be seen, but it may not be pretty.

A most interesting issue arises here with regard to the discussion of agility. This is that these monster companies ended up needing these special favors due to their being everything but agile! Now, ten years later, the number of zombie companies have increased, grown even bigger and, by definition, become even less agile! Moreover, they seem to have become even better at throwing their increasing financial and legal weight around to protect their very profitable, but increasingly non-agile, way of continuing business as usual . . . and why not? This contrasts directly with those recent studies by McKinsey[4] pointing to companies committed to agility programs producing 30 percent gains over their previous business-as-usual practices. It may be worthwhile wondering what will become of them and us when the next inevitable downturn starts in earnest?

Too Big To Fail (or TBTF) is both a symptom of and a threat to the current business-as-usual system that, like a cancerous growth, slowly and inevitably kills its host. The bigger these giants become and the more they strive to protect their way of doing business, against a freer and more agile market, the bigger the repercussions will be when TBTF is ultimately revealed as untenable.

Already there are signs that the leaders of these behemoths cannot and do not know, in manageable detail, what is happening inside their companies. Look no further than all the documented cases of price fixing and market rigging that have been exposed, to which no CFO or CEO has yet been charged or held responsible. Can this mean anything more important than either the CEO is totally incompetent for not being aware of crimes being committed on his/her watch, or that he/she is blatantly disregarding the law? Recently, a few cases of price fixing have been tried in the commodities area, but whether this is a trend or a fluke remains to be seen. When the law is bent or disregarded, uncertainty increases.

How can you effectively adjust to accommodate and anticipate the capricious market changes that may or may not take place when you and your business are forced to play in rigged markets? Like it or not, as long as this untenable situation keeps morphing into new and uncharted waters, these highly uncertain variables will need to be dealt with. Using an increasingly outdated and inadequate set of traditional tools on untraditional and often radical challenges is quickly a becoming recipe for business suicide. Finally, the grey areas of accepted business ethics are also increasing as interpretation of traditionally held norms become, dare we say, more capricious? This increasingly uncertain situation will eventually require a superhuman level of agility, navigation, and a lot of luck.

Buybacks

Another game being played in the boardroom of large companies that contributes to this zombification process is taking advantage of these low interest rates to issue debt in order to repurchase their own stock. Since most executives enjoy compensation packages that often include options to buy stock, it is definitely in their interest to inflate the stock price. As they ensure their future security with an increase in the stock price, the temptation to increase that price is too great to be done just through normal increases in sales, research, development and production. Decreasing the number of shares on the market helps considerably. By also issuing debt to fuel their ability to fund this process and further cutting R&D, they literally consume the company's future by jousting for bragging rights to their market's biggest year-end bonus. They get richer by weakening their company's ability to fund new research and development, or to expand, renew, and improve the company's production capacity. This short-term strategy of capital consumption invites long-term failure in agility, competitiveness, and sustainability.

The predatory business model

Compounding this problem, more companies and government services are beginning to nickel and dime their customers with small fees on everything. In the beginning it was just another annoyance; now, it is morphing into big business. From congestion taxes to drive your car into cities like London and Stockholm to roads that you previously paid to build with your tax money that you now have to pay a private company to use. From a charge for every paper invoice you receive, to a hefty sum plus a labyrinth of paperwork to switch telephone carriers. From little or no interest on your money deposited in your bank to a service charge to move it anywhere or even take it out of an ATM, these small charges add up quickly to large burdens that can cripple a family budget. Each one is an irritation by itself, but together, it is becoming a sort of stressful stealth tax where everything is costing more in ways other than just traditional price rises. This practice also ensures that any reported inflation statistics will be underestimated and less reliable.

This practice is now spiraling out of control as more and more companies figure out ingenious and nefarious ways to add charges here and there. Those charges seem to be rising at an increasing rate. Look no further than the cost of ecological food. It now actually costs a measurable amount more to not have poisonous chemicals sprayed on produce! Think of the stress for someone on a fixed income or on a salary that is not keeping pace with these costs, who only wants to do the right thing. The room they have for economical maneuvering is diminishing daily. An increasing number of people are beginning to have to choose between two products that they used to buy without question.

If your product happens to be one of them, you may suddenly realize a drastic reduction in sales almost overnight when your customers are forced to drop yours. This situation is not helped should your product or service be the one they resent the most, due to all the small, extra charges they have had to suffer. This is regardless of whether or not you were forced to add them just to stay afloat yourself.

The United States Bureau of Labor Statistics even calculates this trend into its Consumer Price Index statistics in the form of what has been called chained CPI[5]. This means that reported inflation statistics are lower because families that, for instance, used to purchase lots of hamburger shift and purchase fewer steaks when the increase of price is higher for the hamburger. Too bad that creativity and agility are not the same thing.

Complexity

As the markets become more and more interconnected, they also grow in complexity. Just a quick review of what we have already talked about, multiplied by their interconnectedness itself screams complexity. The markets are tied together more than ever and an event in Hong Kong in the morning can often influence the markets in Europe mid-day and the USA in the evening of that same day. Just one look at the size of Deutsche Bank's derivative book and how the growing uncertainty of it affects its stock price.

Derivatives

According to Investopedia[6] on June 6, 2018, the total value of the World Derivatives Market in June of 2018 was approximately US$1.2 quadrillion. Some analysts estimate this now three-year-old figure could be ten times higher than total world GDP! What are derivatives? They are bets, they are also bets on bets and they are even bets on bets on bets on underlying assets such as stocks, bonds, real estate, Forex, and other derivatives. What happens if something upsets this market and causes a chain reaction?

The Great Reset

Add all these storm threats up and you have what is now being referred to as the Great Reset. The Great Reset is a larger but what has become a relatively normal shift in what we define as a monetary system. A shift seems to happen, on average, about every forty to fifty years. For instance, the last shift occurred in August 1971 when President Nixon closed the gold window. This was where other countries could cash in their US dollars for gold. French president Charles De Gaulle is credited for prompting this shift after he rightly understood the USA could not continue financing the "war on poverty" while simultaneously fighting a war in Vietnam without debasing its good-as-gold dollar.

Something had to give and it was the increased printing of the US dollar. Therefore, De Gaulle began converting as many depreciating dollars into gold as possible which caused Nixon to react. Although Nixon said this closure was "temporary," it is still in effect today and no dollars have been exchanged for gold to rebalance trade since. What has occurred since is the unbridled printing of paper and digital dollars, yen, rubles, euros, etc. Conservative estimates are that there may now be twenty times more dollars in circulation than 1971. It is very questionable whether all the Ctrl-Alt-Prnt digital currency is included in that figure. And this does not include any and all other national currencies, which have been forced to follow the same path called "our dollar, your problem."

This house of cards of printed money has now been expanded to the point where a sudden event could cause a cataclysmic shift in markets around the world. Then those holding a suddenly and drastically deflated currency would be crushed. Those owning hard assets such as profitable companies, commodities, and raw materials would experience a great reset in price, but would they still own those assets?

Further distinguishing the proletariat

Over 150 years ago, Karl Marx began exploring the future of what he named "the proletariat." Very simply, he defined it as the working class who created value with their hands. He further distinguished these workers by also defining "bourgeoisie" as the ruling or owner class. Over the next hundred or so years, the working class both expanded and became more entrenched. What started out as a necessary cause to reign in the habits of the "Robber Barons," eventually morphed into something much bigger and much bolder. It then began to stratify with ever more "rights and benefits."

According to professor Guy Standing[7], these benefits expanded to include:

- Health insurance
- Unemployment
- Minimum wage
- Retirement and social security
- Job security
- The right to organize and unionize
- Stock ownership

Each one of these benefits naturally started out as a good idea, but over time, the "do-gooders" who established these benefits and especially their followers expanded these good ideas way past their ability for management to responsibly fund and support them. This then led to an increasing cooperation between unions and aspiring politicians and their banker friends. Each well-meaning program gradually became a non-negotiable entitlement or "right." This was not seen as a problem until recently, when management began to wake up and suffer from the increasing costs of it all, in total.

These so-called "social costs" of employing someone else to replace a new retiree only gradually begin to mount until retirement growth snowballed. The damage to your bottom line begins to reveal itself when you start multiplying them by the increasing number of entitlements, their individual growth, and the growing number of employees you have. Each one incurs an additional and growing cost to your bottom line. The further we get into this cycle of working-class entitlement growth, the more each new employment opportunity will cost. To keep in touch with reality, these costs must always be weighed against potential income and profit that each new employee can generate. This is before we include the mounting costs of all the promised "boomer" pensions now maturing.

Many employers are now realizing they can no longer justify these new-hire costs and have actively begun seeking alternative ways to get the needed tasks done. The evidence? Just look at the explosion in part-time employment that slips under the rule of mandated employee health insurance. The result has been accelerating erosion of secure and high paying jobs. This trend of insecure or precarious jobs seems to keep increasing, for the moment, due to among other things:

- Off-shoring
- Temporary employment
- Contractors and sub-contractors
- Automation and AI

This growing trend has caused an increase in fear and uncertainty for those who still have a traditional and (for the moment) secure type of employment. It also causes growing frustration, anger, and resentment in those who don't. The increased implementation of robotics will only increase frustration, tension, and unemployment for the unskilled.

It is now hard to believe that the idea of wage deduction for income tax started during World War II. It was sold (again) as a "temporary" solution to finance the war effort. Yes, the withholding tax was passed as another temporary solution, yet quickly became the primary (and permanent) income source for ever-expanding governmental services. Now, even this temporary source of tax revenue no longer covers continuing governmental expansion. Other more creative ways to capture public money were needed and now have been devised. The result is now that the whole "progressive"[8] system of ever-increasing laws and taxes is beginning to choke further business expansion, especially for SMEs. Increasing corporate taxes and charges are now putting more and more traditional jobs in jeopardy due to their costs.

Entrepreneurs recognize that it has become much more profitable and much less of a liability to have work performed outside of the company. It then becomes a business expense, instead of it resulting from internal, salaried, healthcare covered, retirement-conscious worker output. This worldwide trend will continue until people get so fed up with paying more money for less services that. Now, take a closer look at Greece, France, and Chile, so far.

Is collective bargaining an anachronism?

Action and reaction

The labor movement began as a reaction to dangerous and inhumane working conditions and destructively low wages the average factory worker received at the dawn of the industrial age. In fact, you could easily trace these recurring symptoms back to different peasant revolts which took place during the Middle Ages. In short, management got too greedy and the farmers/workers couldn't take it anymore. Some little spark erupted the masses and the revolt was on.

These revolts are first met with total disinterest from management and the owner class. Then, the activists and leaders' reputations are slated for sabotage to undercut their believability and keep everyone else in line. Next, the revolts are met with violent resistance often with help from the local ruler or government. Look no further than the combative rise of the United Autoworkers in Detroit and United Mine Workers in the mining districts of the USA.

Finally, when all resistance by management is exhausted, concessions are made and some sort of new balance is achieved between management and the workers. Yet, as life itself and human nature constantly swings from one extreme to the other, the story eventually repeats.

One of the most powerful forces in labor for the last one hundred years has been the power of collective bargaining. Trade unions existed to force management to reassess the relationship between them and their workers. Great headway was made to improve the worker's situation and environment during this time.

Like almost every other cycle we have talked about in this book, the reliance on the collective bargaining cycle may now actually be hastening its own demise. In many countries, the power of the unions has decreased precariously over the past generations. The USA is a prime example of where unions once reached a powerful enough bargaining position to force companies to accept unsustainable wages. As a result, whole industries that were influenced by collective bargaining have now moved to areas with cheaper production costs and where unions were either weak or non-existent. Two prime examples of this are Detroit with regard to automobiles and New York City with shipping.

Right up until the late 1960s, New York Harbor bustled with shipping. The docks that lined Manhattan and Brooklyn bristled with activity. Getting a job as a long-shoreman was almost like hitting the lottery. Yet a very disruptive technology made its presence known on the docks in the late 1960s and early 70s in the form of the shipping container.

Up until this time, each ship had to be loaded and unloaded piece by piece. Due to hard-nosed collective bargaining, the only people who were allowed to do this backbreaking work were card-carrying members of the Long-Shoremen Unions. With a lock on dockyard labor, they charged a price way over what the market would soon reveal was actually competitive. When containers began appearing more frequently, the unions went on strike and, for a while, maintained their grasp on the shipping business in NYC. In retrospect, the bargain was ridiculous. All ships were now forced to have the Long-Shoremen unload the containers on the boat, carry the contents off piece by piece, and then repack the container on shore. The reverse was necessary for filling up outward-bound ships. What would you have done if you were a cargo ship owner or a freight manager with limited resources?

It didn't take too long for shippers to reroute their cargo to competing ports where containers were welcome to be used as they were designed. Now, fifty years later, there is hardly any trace left in the Big Apple of this once robust industry or the jobs it produced.

Collective bargaining can temporarily give its union members a false sense of security. Evidence in New York City and Detroit would also suggest so. It may even last a few decades, but change will eventually prevail. Skim through David Halberstam's 1986 book *The Reckoning* and observe the difference between how Ford Motor Company and Nissan chose to handle the emergence of a worldwide car industry. In retrospect, it is obvious what the outcome had to be, but it is still amazing to read about the devastating effect that Detroit's insulated arrogance had, leading to the slow erosion of an entire industrial mecca. It is the difference between adapting to change and the old adage of "Give him enough rope and he'll hang himself" comes to mind.

A quick search on the internet for pictures of Detroit's iconic landmark buildings, then and now, provides a tragic glimpse of what can happen when the ego overtakes the ability to sense and react to a changing reality.

The strangling of the salariat

Ten years on, professor Guy Standing's book *The Precariat* is well worth a read, as it provides much needed insight into the precarious future of employment. He takes Marx's use of the Roman proletariat and subdivides it further into what he calls the "salariat" and "precariat." The salariat he defines as those privileged workers who still have a "real" job where there is insurance, job security, sick leave, and other benefits. Benefits that most of older, now retiring, employees used to take for granted. For the sake of this discussion, the precariat contains pretty much everyone else who now works primarily for money and has few or no rights, benefits, or job security. People in this category can include everyone from migrant workers, cleaning crews, and contract workers, to an expanding list of professionals.

As our business environment grows more uncertain, the precariat continues to grow in size, while the salariat continues to decrease. As this phenomenon grows, it has begun infecting the precarious nature of more and more company business models. For instance, in many "developed" countries, it is becoming economically suicidal to hire salaried employees to populate a precarious type of business. Sooner or later, the expanding square peg of salaried worker laws, regulations, and taxes will no longer fit your round and shrinking salariat way of doing business. Those still left in salaried positions, unions, and in publicly funded (tax financed) organizations, which have relied upon this cozy employer/employee way of working, are finally beginning to take this threat to their entitlement-bound lifestyle seriously.

You as captain of an older, salaried crew will inevitably face a situation where everyone around you has been trained and conditioned to feel they are entitled to a certain way of working or a certain outcome, regardless of the current economic weather. One look at the darkening sky and having read just some of the ideas suggested in this book, you suggest something else. Something more in tune with today's business environment. Something more agile.

How receptive do you think your crew will be?

If fact, how can you expect your listeners to even hear your enlightened message, much less decide to adapt to it quickly? Chances are, entrenched corporate culture will probably inhibit or filter out your message of change, as it is completely alien to what they have been trained and conditioned to understand. In other words, the bigger the entitlement legacy, the less listening you can expect, the more resistance you will encounter, and the more certain eventual disaster will become. Think France!

The growing precariat

All of the above have contributed to a growing sense of disenfranchisement for an increasing part of the global population. According to Guy Standing again, if there is a positive side to this growing, restless, and resentful group of employable people, it is that so far, their movement has yet to find any type of unified voice. "Finding one," he says, "is the danger going forward." So, don't bank on this diffusion to remain. All the above shifts to business and society referenced in this book will continue to nurture the growth and promote the unification of this group of precariat's into a powerful, creative force with less and less to lose. The precariat is also overrepresented by younger people with even less to lose. We can count on their anger, resentment, and creativity to continue to grow. Do you think certain groups that have suddenly sprung up around the world to riot, take over parts of cities, and cancel opposing opinions may be the uncomfortable evidence of this growing movement?

Also, witness the growing number of young people forced to live with their parents long after they have graduated from school. The price of housing and rents have now increased way beyond the affordability of most working for an entry level wage. Worse still, with every table they wait, burger they flip, or sale-priced blouse they sell, their costly university skills decrease while their anger grows. This is not what they envisioned four years of college would lead to. Now, with former retirees also competing for those remaining jobs, automation and the online sales increasing drastically, even those few remaining jobs are now threatened.

McDonald's, Walmart, and other low-paying companies have to deal with constant increases in the minimum wage laws. Their response is twofold: reducing the number of employees and automating the increasing number of jobs that become available to automate. The automation process is often slightly incremental, meaning one tiny task at a time, but eventually these incremental effects snowball. As we have discussed earlier, with the twin rise of technology and globalization, those jobs that can be replaced either by machine or computer/software are growing. This increases pricing and downward wage pressure on remaining jobs, which aren't yet at risk of being automated. But they do risk being exported to lower cost countries, the most blatant examples being China for manufacturing and India for services. Now, how would this make you feel if you had just spent four years going into massive debt to get a degree that is losing its power and status to help you land that well-paying job?

Some have even gone so far as to suggest that higher education should come with a money-back guarantee in the event you do not get the type of job that you trained or paid for. This may seem a bit outlandish, especially given that a good amount of the work in landing a job has to do with the individual's persistence, not to mention their choice of a concentration or major. Yet, the mere fact that it is now on the table and being discussed further supports this precarious trend.

Polarization of the workforce

It is becoming increasingly evident that the polarization occurring in the political, environmental, health, and even family spheres is influencing the work culture. Divisions within the workforce regarding, race, politics, health, and gender issues among others, is pitting former team members against each other.

In any organization that is profit driven or not, there must be a common goal to galvanize everyone into efficient action. If the goal is obscured by societal issues, accomplishing it becomes difficult to impossible. Although corporate politics has always lurked in the background, it has recently jumped to the foreground with issues including, but definitely not limited to:

- Are you vaccinated or not?
- Do you wear a mask or not?
- What is your view on climate change?
- Who did you vote for?
- How you dress for work or a meeting?

With the help of a less than balanced media and too much time spent alone in front of some sort of screen, whether it's television or a mobile device, issues that used to cause interesting conversations at the water cooler have now become flashpoints that can limit or even cancel the cooperation necessary to work as a team.

Possibly the biggest problem facing organizational efficiency is an individual decrease in tolerance for other's views and opinions. Regardless of where you stand on any of the spectrums listed above or any other, observe how easy it has become to just shut down a discussion.

Whether you de-friend someone, label them a conspiracy theorist, block their email address or telephone number, or just walk away when that sensitive subject is breached, conversation and the possibility of finding common ground for a constructive dialogue abruptly halts. What can be accomplished together without vibrant and creative conversation?

Employment dislocation

We are already witnessing a direct consequence of the increase in the precarious nature of working. As more and more private companies reduce staff, the biggest organizations still routinely hiring seem to be governmental. Even with a recent uptick in employment, the number of those who have given up looking for a job still stands at all-time highs. This is also notwithstanding the fact that these numbers are not even calculated the same way they used to be. It may be worth visiting www.shadowstats.com to get a feel of how the measuring of economic and employment statistics has become much more "accommodative" over the years.

Recently, a number of studies from Oxford University[9] and CBRE Genesis[10] have pointed to the possibility that up to 50 percent of current jobs will disappear over the next five years. The CBRE report further states there will be new job opportunities popping up: "Organizations with twenty to forty people can be just as impactful as large corporations, and by leveraging technology while being 'unhindered by legacy processes and mindsets,' they will easily disrupt existing corporate models."[11]

In fact, they go on to state the following: "Corporations will not only need to be lean and agile, they must also be authentic to attract talent, authentic in their values, and in making a real contribution to the social good." Will you and your company be agile enough to handle this increasingly turbulent, efficient, and authentic employment market?

Labor shortage with increasing unemployment

There is another problem that is becoming a ticking time bomb especially in Europe. Some young people are not even getting the chance to work. In Greece and Spain for instance, the number of unemployed people under the age of twenty-five surpassed 50 percent during the recent turndown. The longer these young and energetic people are denied a chance to develop their skills and their self-confidence, the less of a chance and drive they will have to seek employment in the future. As the *Trends Journal*[12] forecaster Gerald Celente says, "People who lose everything and have nothing left to lose, lose it." What happens then? This trend of youth unemployment does not look like it will be disappearing any time soon.

Result: The working dead

You meet them on the train, when you are going about town, in the car beside you, behind a mask, and in just about every line or queue in which you are forced to stand. Their eyes will be either extremely focused to the point that they look hard. This may be a glare of indignation, or the opposite: a kind of vacant gaze that gives you a strong feeling of hopelessness, resignation, or complete surrender. If any notice of your existence is taken, it is only as an obstacle or threat placed in their way.

Whatever kind of visual contact takes place, it will be distinguished by a gnawing sense that they are not present here and now with you, but with some distant thought. They are often preoccupied with their smart gadgets or seem to be staring straight ahead at nothing. They can easily and unconsciously disappear either into a loop of debate, defense, or into resignation and despair. Despite this, they often bravely keep doing what they are paid to keep doing, as they often have no choice.

The ultimate result of this detached behavior is the creation of a legion of working dead. The entitlement to a paycheck as long as you do your job, combined with a more omnipotent and permeating computer grid that monitors all aspects of life, seems to create a growing sense of what Pink Floyd member Roger Waters once defined as being "comfortably numb." This is a state of mind that encourages other people and sophisticated systems to take care of what to think for you. As most of us are inherently on the lazy side and like being taken care of, has this system now grown into a comfortable and addictive form of societal cancer? A cancer that threatens to kill its societal host and with it all our individual pleasure and creativity?

You may get a better sense this feeling of resignation by noting or sensing that:

- Something is just not right
- There are too many things to do
- Whatever choice you make, it ultimately won't matter
- You no longer have time to care
- Instead of relaxing, you collapse on your couch after work
- You feel guilty when you are doing nothing
- Someone else should do it, but who?
- Authentically expressing yourself puts you in danger of being politically incorrect
- There must be more to life than TV and social media

These and many other thoughts may trigger this sense of resignation, but the end result is that it causes you to detach from being fully conscious to what is going on around you. You may see it happening, you may sense that you should do something, but you ultimately remain in a passive, functional coma. Look again at those victims who were caught in the big tsunami. Many well-educated tourists probably sensed something was not right, but how many reacted to the threat to turn and run for the hills in time? Agility? Not!

Now, what makes you fundamentally different?

Entrenchment from the top down

Inhibiting change not only happens from the factory floor up, it is just as devastating from the ivory towers of management downward. H. Ross Perot, former presidential candidate and founder of Electronic Data Systems, was given a seat on the board of General Motors when GM purchased his EDS.

A few years later, he doubled his money when he was "politely" asked to leave the board and was forced to sell his shares back to GM. His agile style and his harsh Texas honesty clearly did not fit in with the "traditional" business culture at GM. In order to silence his criticism and attempts at (badly needed) reform, could he have been offered a large enough bribe just to walk away? Whether the following anecdote is true or just an urban myth, the following is none-the-less offered. The drop for this decision reportedly came when he addressed GM's board with something that was riddled with his stinging Texas sarcasm. Mr. Perot was supposed to have said, "I cannot understand why it takes six years, from concept to show-room, to build one of our cars and it only took four years to win World War II!"

Did he possibly have a point? Since then, the automotive history of Detroit seems to support him. There was a time when it was said that, "When General Motors sneezes, the US economy catches a cold." Increasing international competition has now eroded that time and the destructive arrogance that accompanied it. It may be worth a moment of reflection on what could have happened if GM's board had opened up and listened to Perot's comments and chosen agility.

Entrepreneurship

Entrepreneurship is often mistaken for the ability to be agile. The fact is that many, even famous, entrepreneurs can be extremely hardheaded and stubborn and not agile or flexible at all. They just happen to be in an envi-ronment without inhibiting legacies or just in the right place at the right time. They end up riding a new wave of creative destruction or new busi-ness that is independent and or better than the current established way of working. Anecdotes abound about Apple's Steve Jobs' stubborn hard-headedness and genius. Many new and successful companies also have or are creating entrepreneurial legacies, but most of them won't be proven until things once again get tough.

> "Luck is opportunity meeting preparedness."
> **—Deepak Chopra**

Preparedness is great, but what if you can further increase your chances of success by listening closely to what your market is saying and then being agile and entrepreneurial enough to act upon what you see developing?

No guts, no glory! To be successful you need to act!

Acting requires good information, agility and a resolve to trust yourself, right or wrong. Is there any better way to sum up the successful traits of an agile entrepreneur? The level of your success will probably hinge upon these traits along with the quality of information you have to work with. Basing an overwhelming portion of your time to focus on the forward horizon will also make you more successful than by just showcasing your past performance.

Hard, transactional business versus soft, relational business

Over the past thirty years, focus on the application of technology in business has contributed amazingly toward getting more produced and sold in shorter periods. This process was boosted sharply with the improved technology available to track and analyze each transaction and do business with a much tighter margin. Great, right?

Absolutely, especially if you happen to be a big box retailer, one who also has access to virtually unlimited credit at record low rates. You probably also have the shiniest new business system to back it up too. Yet if you are one of those small shop owners on your town's main or high streets, congratulations to you if you are still in business! In fact, how in the world have you managed to survive the increasing level of global competition, drone delivery, and money-back forever guarantees? Good on you!

If you are still in business, the reason will probably have something to do with the phrase customer relationship. That is that wonderful and respectful way of doing business where people will usually pay you a little bit more to feel like they have actually dealt with a compassionate human being. It is a form of business that encourages you to respectfully see, hear, and understand each customer's needs, wants, and wishes.

We now have over thirty years of proof that you do not need a human being present to transact business. An entire transaction can now be accomplished by machine and most likely at unbeatable prices. But what happens when something goes wrong or if you wish to change suppliers?

Transactional business only requires sense when it comes to measuring stuff. If you can measure it, you can manage it, whether it's the amount of money, the color of the item chosen, the delivery dates, and/or logistics to name just a few measurable parameters. All of these metrics can be sensed using cheaper and cheaper computers, sensors, and/or chips.

Sensing, in terms of feeling what the customer needs, wants, or wishes, and how satisfied or dissatisfied they are before, during, and after the transaction, is tragically being forgotten or discounted because presumably that kind of labor-intensive attention costs too much.

As the complexity of the transaction increases, so do the chances of something going wrong during the process. Resolving the situation satisfactorily still ultimately falls back on an individual in your ever more overworked and frustrated service staff. Navigating your way through endless telephone trees, to find someone who actually cares, only increases customer frustration. It also heightens the chance that when you finally do find a sympathetic customer service person, you will be too upset to sense their concern. How agile is this for anyone? More importantly, how important is individual customer satisfaction becoming when it comes to measuring your ability to be agile? How can you ever hope to distinguish your product, service, and company from your competition? What if agility now must include increased soft skills?

The trend toward transactional business seems to be nearing its peak. With yet another reminder to recent studies from McKinsey pointing to measurable gains in profitability and effectivity from more agile customer service practices, the challenge of getting what you want, when you want it, and at the cheapest price, is beginning to become noticeable.

It is also worth noting again that recent figure that 47 percent of online customer carts that reach the website checkout are never completed. The reason is an unexpected or additional service or handling charge that was added at the last minute. The computer may not feel a thing as it automatically adds this surprise charge, but tracking metrics clearly demonstrate that your customer certainly does. Pay attention! Almost 50 percent of a web shop's business is left in the shopping cart unsold, if even only a few pennies are unexpectedly added to the expected purchase price! If that sounds high, ask yourself if you would be more or less motivated to buy if an additional and unexpected cost was added to your purchase at the last minute? How easy do you think it will be to regain that lost customer's trust and future business?

Being agile enough to relate to each of your customers, on their terms, can be enhanced with the use of technology such as Client Relationship Management or CRM systems. You are still fooling yourself and your future chances of success if you think even this sophisticated AI technology can replace the personal touch of a real human being. It is that conscious, human interactive element that will allow you to heighten customer trust and your sales margins. Otherwise, you, your product, and your company become a commodity where the only distinction is ever lowering prices.

What if, in our haste for efficiency, we may have thrown the customer loyalty baby out with the relational bath water, in favor of transaction efficiency and quarterly profit. Short-term, this will goose earnings and possibly even your profits. In the long-term, without constant heavy sales and marketing expenditures, this strategy usually fails, completely. Now it's happening even faster as your typical customer is quickly harnessing the power and reach of social media to get reviews and comments before they shop.

On the other side of this transactional/relational coin, your ability to increase margins in an oversupplied world drastically diminish, if all you have left to distinguish your offer is a lower price. Research now proves what should be common sense. The road to higher margins is paved with personal and sustainable relationships. It is further enhanced by mastering the agility to quickly and consciously adapt to volatile market situations and changing customer tastes. These important soft-factors often defy even the best AI tools. This newer and more sensitive customer service requirement demands newer, increasingly sensitive and more agile marketing tools!

Creative destruction case studies

To really rub these points in, here are just a few examples of trends and game changers that have turned conventional business-as-usual practices into mush. The internet is shattering one traditional business model after another. If you look at how the path to success in just the following industries has changed over the past few years, you will hopefully sense an accelerating trend. That trend is the need to become more focused on what will happen rather than what has happened.

- **The recording industry** suffers from profits that have been declining for years, due to both piracy and increased competition from internet providers. Both now allow you to listen to only the songs you want to hear, when you want to hear them. Long gone is what some called the reverse piracy (referring to the excessive record company profits) gained by being forced to buy an entire album just because you like one particular tune.

- **The movie industry** is suffering from the same online pressure as the recording industry. The distribution of the latest films can no longer be tightly controlled, due to the rise of torrent technology and the ability to stream a film online, often without paying for it.

- **The retail business** is transitioning from the traditional chain store to internet sites that are open twenty-four seven. The need for retail space is plummeting. Amazon.com is just the biggest example. They are opening forty new distribution centers in the USA alone. Drone delivery is now being tested. In some parts of the country, entire shopping malls are closing down and turning into forgotten ghost towns, looted for the materials that can easily be pried off the walls and sold.

- **The banking industry** has been too profitable for too long not to notice. This is causing both increasing jealousy and resentment. After the banking crisis of 2008–2009, people have slowly begun to wake up to what Fractional Reserve Banking really means and its consequences on a personal level. Also, from interest rates, to Forex, to commodities, it seems one price fixing scandal is being revealed after another. Trust in your local bank has drastically eroded to the point that many in the bank and finance industry are sarcastically referred to as "banksters." With the advent of the internet, blockchain, and now DeFi technology, more innovative products are being introduced and adopted at a quickening pace. Names such as Pay-Pal, Polka Dot, Ripple, UniSwap, and Pancake are offering innovative alternatives to banking as usual. Their development is no doubt fueled by almost daily revelations of more shady dealings and corruption.

- **The fast-food industry** according to Zerohedge.com there was a recent strike by fast food workers. Their demand was higher pay.

In hindsight, the strikers could not have picked a better time to provide a textbook example how to hasten the demise of their own profession. A San Francisco based start-up called none other than Momentum Machines[13] introduced a burger-grilling robot that can produce almost 400 hamburgers per hour (with no wage complaints). Possibly sensing the fantastic opportunity that lies before them, yet understanding the dislocation their technology will cause, Momentum issued the following statement:

"The issue of machines and job displacement has been around for centuries and economists generally accept that technology like ours actually causes an increase in employment.
The three factors that contribute to this are
- The company that makes the robots must hire new employees,
- The restaurant that uses our robots can expand their frontiers of production which requires hiring more people, and
- The general public saves money on the reduced cost of our burgers. This saved money can then be spent on the rest of the economy."[14]

Whether this is true or just a vain public relations attempt, one thing is for sure. Just as the eighteenth century English Luddites[15] found when they destroyed textile machines in the English Midlands (to retain their jobs), progress waits for no one.

Black swans

Nassim Taleb's best seller, *The Black Swan* (Taleb, 2010), possibly sums up the challenge we face better than our following description of a perfect storm, especially with regards to uncertainty. As Taleb has now stated in different ways, the idea of predicting a black swan is preposterous! "The very nature of a black swan is that it cannot be predicted." Even so, they happen.

This is why the whole idea of agility is becoming more important. He makes clear in his book that the probability of one or more economic black swans is increasing. Although they are impossible to predict, just by their nature, to stay in the game we need to increase our vigilance and be agile enough to handle them.

The dark side of AI

Dr. Ben Goertzel, Founder and CEO of SingularityNet and chief science advisor for Hanson Robotics and an expert on AGI (Artificial General Intelligence), makes an interesting point in one of his London Real YouTube interviews. Currently, the focus of AI is mostly toward four areas: "selling, spying, killing, and gambling." This may not be the best start when the point of artificial intelligence is to create systems that learn from their mistakes.

His rather upbeat message is that AI and AGI can be a boon to humanity, but it needs to also learn compassion so what we create doesn't end up like Skynet in the Terminator movies. This, of course, has to happen before the singularity occurs. Otherwise, at that point computing will learn on its own faster than we can keep up with it. He agrees with Ray Kurzwell that a rough guess of when the singularity will occur is approximately the year 2045. Into this deadline, everything having to do with AI and AGI will continue to accelerate at an increasingly faster pace. His point is that AI will be a boon to humanity, but there will definitely be some growing pains along the way.

Core family values dissolving

Although there is much debate regarding its cause, the idea of one husband, one wife, and a few children living happily under the same roof is becoming rare. All kinds of new family constellations are popping up and a growing portion of the population lives alone. Various studies state that, statistically, these lucky children from families still consistently get better grades and adjust better to adulthood when raised in such antiquated environments. Unfortunately, today's trend seems to be for parents to choose a lifestyle that suits them first, then let their children adjust while everyone hopes for the best. For instance, there are many parents that after years of encouraging their children to get entertained by the computer or TV screen (so that they can work just a little bit more) become shocked when they can no longer pry them away from it. A number of children's daycare centers have been forced to impose steep fines on parents for each minute after closing their children were not collected. Most parents hit with a fine obviously felt more drawn to answering one last text, email, or telephone call rather than spending time with their offspring.

Not surprisingly, respect for authority, even in the home, is plummeting. This trend is tragically evidenced by stories such as the following. One of your authors has heard from two principals/rectors from two different schools that they have been scolded by parents because "it is the school's job," not theirs, to raise their children! We will leave for another time the issue of what, if anything, parental responsibility means.

One look at how people currently dress, talk to each other, and take care of themselves confirms that the result is pointing toward a more chaotic society rather than a more organized one. Indeed, comparing a picture of a crowd today to one fifty years ago and it would appear that the more antisocial you look, the cooler your status should be perceived. Just look at any fashion magazine. It seems that the message is something like, the more you look like you "just don't friggin' care," the more attractive and successful you will become. Yet is this mixed message actually true? But wait! Before you answer that, isn't it high time for a selfie?

Recent trends of homelessness and opioid abuse are skyrocketing. In San Francisco and Los Angeles there are increasing complaints of people using the street as their toilet. With these problems and others too interesting to mention, California is suffering an exodus of wealthy, educated, and mobile residents. This trend will only amplify the problem as more and more people, dependent upon handouts from a rapidly shrinking tax base, demand more and more services. Good luck with that!

Restlessness or boredom, seldom in the middle

Instant gratification, as in the rock band Queen's "We want it all and we want it now" seems to be the rallying cry for the current era. Although meditation and spiritual practices are slowly catching on, many still crave that "rush" of dangerous excitement, just to feel alive. Whether it is jumping out of a perfectly good airplane, free running, or any other type of daredevil experiences, the underlying motivation is, more often than not, to feel less like a "human doing" and to get even a brief sense of becoming a "human being" again.

Today's food and drink are now so loaded with sugar and other stimulants that the natural alternative usually tastes dreadfully boring. We have also become so addicted to outside input that we often do not know what to do when we suddenly find ourselves offline. Regardless, we are still faced with the GIGO principle of garbage in, garbage out. When was the last time you took a conscious look at what you typically feed your mind and body?

Dr. Joe Dispenza is adamant about the influence of smartphones and screen time on our youth. In his interviews with Brian Rose on London Real, he warns that children are so used to being stimulated by all the action happening on their smart gadgets that they do not know what to do with themselves when that stimulus is taken away. For any parent, this is probably no surprise, but what does this do to their creativity, their ability to think freely, and our future as a society? Where will all the progress come from when most everyone of working age is absorbed in some sort of activity on their screen of choice?

What if we have unconsciously allowed ourselves to become more easily "programmable"? We allow ourselves to be constantly bombarded with information, usually without even noticing it. How much time do you spend reflecting over the underlying message, its source, or the quality of the information you are currently digesting? We have known at least since Freud's nephew, Edward Bernays, wrote *Propaganda* way back in 1928, that, given the correct tools and motivation, it is very easy to manipulate public opinion:

"Universal literacy was supposed to educate the common man to control his environment. Once he could read and write he would have a mind fit to rule. So ran the democratic doctrine. But instead of a mind, universal literacy has given him rubber stamps, rubber stamps linked with advertising slogans, with editorials, with published scientific data, with the trivialities of the tabloids, and the platitudes of history, but quite innocent of original thought. Each man's rubber stamps are the duplicates of millions of others, so that when those millions are exposed to the same stimuli, all receive identical imprints[16]." Edward Bernays, *Propaganda*, 1928.

There is a difference between education and indoctrination. Royalty and savvy politicians have known this for centuries. With this in mind, is it any wonder why it is so easy to become bored, restless, or just collapse in a heap when things go silent? What if we are trained to crave a constant stream of comfortable and repetitive information? In this information rich, content poor environment, how easy is it to get your message across in a way that moves others to act? Creating agreement and action in a typical conversation becomes much more challenging when you compare it to the shock, awe, and excitement found instantly on TV and the internet.

Result? Increasing high risk of deep market crisis

The Baltic Dry Index[17] is one of the most followed indicators of world commerce. It measures the cost per day of renting a cape size freighter. A cape size freighter is a ship so big that it is unable to pass through the Panama or Suez Canals and therefore must sail around the Continental Capes. The higher the price, the more robust the need for raw materials and thus, the better the world economy is perceived to be doing. The Index has recent memory made lows never seen before and now, due to the pandemic, is suddenly skyrocketing!

Government activity is increasingly taking a larger and larger slice of the economic pie while small and medium enterprise business is contracting even further. Also, according to the US Federal Reserve's FRED educational website, the current velocity of money[18] (the approximate time it takes one dollar to circulate through the economy) is at one of the lowest frequencies in decades. This is historically interpreted to mean that people are hoarding their cash in fear, rather than spending it. This is a global problem, but due to the differences in national currency laws, governments are taking different paths to combat it. Built into some CBDCs is an expiration date where the money will expire unless spent by a certain date. Most are quickly trying to cancel printed money and go all digital. The USA may have the most problem combatting this as its dollar is still the world's reserve currency and as such, most resides outside of its borders.

Meanwhile, record debt is being recorded in the public and private sector, and why not? Interest rates would suggest that it is safer and cheaper to borrow money than it has been since tracking statistics were invented. Banking and financial institutions are still recording record profits. What's not to like?

Unemployment looks relatively low, but take another peek under the hood again at John Williams' site Shadow Stats[19]. A quick look at his figures, based upon their original metrics and then compared to the recent changes, demonstrates that United States unemployment and inflation numbers are much different. So, how do you make it easy for your team to win? Just keep moving the goalposts to a more favorable position.

These indicators and others portend that while official world trade figures look good on paper, the reality may actually be increasingly different. Does this contradiction fill you with confidence? How do you plan for this future and what figures will you use? Uncertainty seems to be the key word here too. This does not bode well for business as usual, but where there is risk there is also reward—for the agile businessperson!

CHAPTER 8

A Holistic Look at Agile Impacts

Geopolitical tensions increasing

It is becoming clear to anyone with common sense (and who dares to look behind the headlines) that many of today's geopolitical tensions could be solved if rational dialogue was used instead of saber rattling. It seems that even this kindergarten-level solution to a grown-up disaster will take more time and destruction to resolve. Until we get sick enough of killing each other to understand that real courage comes from resolving conflict without violence, we need to prepare for more, physically, mentally, and financially.

Trust

When it comes to both finance and politics, trust is the glue that holds the current system together. As long as you and I believe in our political and business leaders' promises, things have been in the habit of continuing because business as usual does come with some comfortable qualities. As long as trust is there, we often leave the business of governing up to those who strive after the levers of power. The same goes for businesses. Yet, when things go too well for too long, symptoms of greed inevitably appear. Add to this mix entire industries that continue to be created just to provide you with even more entertaining distractions. It is easy to get so involved with your latest smart gadget or app that you forget to look up and see who is running the show, and why. It becomes just too tempting for some. Many of the following issues originate from this annoying and reoccurring human flaw called a lack of trust.

Major geopolitical upheaval

It is no longer a well-kept secret of how to remain the bully on the block. Just make sure your competitors stay mad with each other and you have succeeded in "destabilizing" that relationship. Their infighting allows you to remain in charge. Do it with finesse, and you may even look like a savior, even when it was you who caused the instability in the first place. Does this sound familiar, especially on a geopolitical level? Study any reliable foreign policy report from the biggest power on the block since at least Roman times, and you will probably come across a reference to this type of policy. From Caesar to Napoleon and beyond, all you have to do is successfully divide and conquer to remain in power. The key is to get the factions to fight among themselves. You get extra points and income by supplying both sides with weapons. Although this type of strategy is getting easier to see, it is still occurring and thus must be reckoned with and prepared for.

There are also increasing signs that power and wealth are shifting again from the West back to the East. The powers of the Orient are flexing their increased economic might. They are setting up their own investment banks and payment systems and buying anything gold that isn't nailed down. Many of the problems outlined above are exacerbating this shift of power. As China, India, and other eastern powers amass great fortunes in production and trade, the powers of the West are going deeper into debt to keep their good times rolling.

Evidence suggest that the age of the petrodollar seems to be giving way to a more international payment system. Slowly but surely, countries like Russia, China, and even India are looking to pay or buy oil in currencies other than the US dollar. At the same time China's yuan has been accepted into the Special Drawing Rights or SDRs basket of currencies maintained by the International Monetary Fund, IMF. China is also setting up direct payment accounts with most of their trading partners, thus bypassing the need for converting into US dollars. Along with Russia, they have set up and are now testing an international settlement system to compete with the American SWIFT system. Although this is a relatively recent occurrence, expect its importance to increase over the coming years. This is before breaching the topic of the oncoming wave CDBCs. What happens when all those dollars circulating around the world are no longer needed to transact business between two non-American nations?

What was once seen as attractive American humility, up to and including the Second World War, has since morphed into what an increasing number of non-Americans are calling arrogance. The rest of the world has now gone from tolerating this to creating systems to actively bypass American hegemony. This trend of globalization looks set to continue, relegating the US to a more appropriate and diminished role in a more balanced mix of geopolitics. But, don't think for a minute that this process will go smoothly. Just like a wounded animal feeling threatened, someone used to getting their way often becomes much more aggressive if the position and status they are used to controlling is challenged or taken away. Since the United States has, by far, the largest military and military industrial complex to support it, they may begin relying on it even more to maintain their self-called *exceptionalism*. Whether the source is American or not, how will you adjust your business sails for these kinds of potentially volatile geopolitical winds?

Government agility?

Perot's focus was always said to be on the customer, and this focus kept him, those who worked with him, and his business endeavors agile for the times. It is interesting to note that a strong reason why many believe that he was not taken as a serious candidate for president in 1996 was that his agile style of leadership would have upset the way politics as usual was conducted. This was deemed to be too uncomfortable for those who ran the show. Has this trend toward comfortable entitlement changed?

Now, a generation later we have more outsiders competing with our political royalty. It has been interesting to follow Donald Trump's adventures and how he responded to the American market of eligible and disenchanted voters. The divisive issues he showcased during his presidency may still be gaining in potential to tear the fabric of this over 200-year-old experiment in personal freedom, known as the United States of America, apart.

Get agile or change the law?

With the rise of the lobbying industry, an alternative to training to be agile has become to stack the legislative deck in your favor. According to CNBC1, nearly 12,000 lobbyists populated 300 firms in the Washington, DC area in 2019. On the other side of the Atlantic, the British newspaper *The Economist* estimates that there were over 25,000 lobbyists working the corridors of the European Union in Brussels in 2020.

Paying former lawmakers lots of money to talk to their friends, who are still in the legislative branch and can write a law in favor of you and your product or industry, now seems to be considered sound business practice. These laws often include increased barriers for potential competitors, with fresher, more agile ideas, to enter your market. This comfortable strategy has worked brilliantly for the past few generations. Among other things that have been enacted into law are:

- Legal stipulation regarding the size and curvature for bananas marketed in Europe. This law strangles African and Asian competition by championing the interests of a few well-known multi-nationals with expert lobbying skills.
- The use of genetically modified foods in the United States and the increasing use of patents on certain types of food and grain.
- Energy-saving light bulbs to replace older fully functioning and much less poisonous incandescent light bulbs. Both in the EU and the US, the traditional and cheaper alternative to light up your room was outlawed for these more expensive energy-saving ones. Yes, they do save energy in the long run, but now you have no choice especially if you are on a limited budget. If you look at the profits General Electric and Philips have generated since "assisting" with this legislation, it might be worth pondering how much of it was generated from a few advantageous changes in the law.

The only problem is that, as this way of doing business has expanded and the laws become progressively more outrageous, the legislature further loses touch with the realities experienced by customers/voters. Morals, environmental concerns, fair trade policies, and ultimately profits all suffer. More and more people are beginning to wake up to the fact that they have become victims of a system that is becoming harder and harder to enter or keep up with. There is a growing feeling of alienation and it is beginning to dishearten and anger both voters and consumers greatly.

You can't fool all the people all of the time. With increasing awareness of the option for us to vote with our wallets, entire companies are rising to success and falling back to failure at a frantic pace, due to public perception. This is without the noted impact of those high frequency traders, which author Michael Lewis refers to as the "Flash Boys (Lewis)" who can now make and break a stock price of companies in nanoseconds. Whether this practice becomes illegal or just remains controversial, it can still rain havoc on the capitalization of your business in the blink of an eye.

America's standing in the world?

Especially with recent events in the mid-east, President Wilson's so-called "Arsenal of Democracy" is beginning to be seen by many in the rest of the world as a spoiled, self-absorbed, exceptional bully. Foreign policies directed by a motivation to destabilize, and the chaos and death they cause, are slowly being revealed as raw power plays. Which western child, raised during the cold war, could have ever dreamt that Russia would grant amnesty to an American whistle-blower, whose allegedly "treasonous" crime was revealing the level of governmental spying taking place on its own people?

Rules and regulations regarding international transactions are growing. In their wake, more incentives are being created for other nations to work around American-based systems. An Asian competitor is now challenging the American-controlled SWIFT international payment system, and even the Washington, DC-based International Monetary Fund or IMF will soon have the Asian Infrastructure Investment Bank or AIIB to contend with. American-led international payment restrictions and banking requirements are slowing the velocity of money (the rate of the amount of business being done) considerably, all over the world. These incidents and many others like them, coupled with the increasing uncertainty that the governmental debt will ever be paid back, is causing a slow but measurable erosion of the image and prestige of the United States and its role on the world stage. Ask any American expat who has recently tried to open a bank account in another country.

Free enterprise versus?

> "Fascism should more appropriately be called Corporatism
> because it is a merger of state and corporate power."
> **—Benito Mussolini**

If you care to notice the power and influence that business and banks now exert over our politicians, you will see that Mussolini's definition of fascism is alive and well. Nowadays, it may have more to do with finely tailored suits than with jackboots but with the rise of certain groups promoting the use of violence against opposing ones, who knows? Although lobbyists may be making too much money to even think of themselves as the corporate tools of fascism, this may be exactly what they have become. Here are a few examples:

- The government bailout of private American banks in the autumn of 2008
- The running of many American jails is now a very profitable and private enterprise
- The influence of Big Pharma over health care policy increases drastically
- The increasing amount of money donated by Political Action Committees or PACs to US election campaigns
- The selling of public corporations to private (chosen?) ones at very undervalued prices, such as postal and telephone services, in many countries
- The rise of "natural news" which is another term for news written specifically to promote a product or service (often without the audience knowing it)

These and many other examples should provide a taste that your individual vote may increasingly countless, especially when compared to the influence of moneyed business interests. All of these actions further the chances of business as usual going forward, having more to do with your savvy political correctness than something you planned. The need for business agility increases.

Increased risk of military intervention

As domestic concerns increase, focus upon external military expeditions seem to increase in parallel. Local conflicts are morphing into regional ones and regional ones are attracting larger and larger players. For instance, with the United States squaring off against a rejuvenated Russia in both Ukraine and the Middle East, the stakes are increasing as quickly as is the risk of large-scale warfare. Look in any economic history book, and it is obvious that the risk of open warfare quickly puts business and society on a defensive footing. This causes already weakening international trade to tighten further. If you happen to be expanding into such an atmosphere, you could quickly find yourself overstretched in a market that no longer exists.

Environmental damage mounting

People have been preaching to "save the world" since long before the first Earth Day in 1970. Yet only recently have we begun to really suffer from the impact of those warnings in a way that seems to finally be moving us into action. For instance, we still have unknown quantities of radiation leaking from Fukushima, Japan into the Pacific Ocean years after the initial catastrophe. There is also a floating and growing island of plastic waste somewhere in the Pacific Ocean, estimated to be larger than the state of Texas. The threat and intensity of volcanoes, earthquakes, tsunamis, and hurricanes continues to escalate. Entire species are dying off at an increasing rate and Greenpeace now estimates that "over fifty percent of marine wildlife has disappeared over the past forty years." According to statistician Dr. Hans Rosling, our population will continue to increase until the end of our current century. How will these challenges impact our way of doing business?

Environmental health versus mental health

As the world population continues to grow and become more affluent, more strain is being put on the ability of our societies to maintain and increase our standards of living. Issues now being discussed include some of the following:

- The sudden decrease of steadily rising crop yields

- Erosion and soil depletion, resulting in less nutritious food
- Big business charging for and limiting access to fresh, potable water
- The health benefits and risks of genetically modified foods
- Ecosystems strained to their limits
- The increase of big business solutions over trust in the human immune system
- The migration of large groups due to environmental challenges and disasters
- Increased risks for big weather

All of these trends and threats are being hurled at us on a daily basis which is creating an increase in general fear. Whether by chance or through shrewd planning, these trends are absolutely influencing consumer and business behavior. More anti-depressant drugs are being consumed that ever before, suicides are on the increase, and an increasing backlash of people who disagree with or actively campaign against this narrative is occurring. This makes your navigation through this sea of hazards even more important to chart correctly.

The violent turbulence around climate change

"There are three types of lies: lies, damned lies, and statistics."
—Mark Twain

The only thing that has drastically changed in the one hundred years since Samuel Clemens wrote this is that there is much more data available from which to create statistics. Now, more than ever, facts and figures can be manipulated back and forth to support, promote, or defend just about anything.

The debate about whether or not climate change is real is still not over, but most everyone interested in this topic is in agreement that something is happening to our climate and weather patterns. The jury is still out on how our climate is changing. Will it be global warming, cooling, or something else? Does it matter?

Many scientists who study climate change agree that human activity is partly responsible for changing the climate. But is this the whole story? Studies on geologic, volcanic, tree, and ice samples also point to large and volatile climate patterns that span decades, centuries, millennia, and date back long before man even existed.

There are many differing opinions, but there seem to be two main camps when it comes to climate change:

1. We are the biggest cause
2. Nature is the biggest cause

The discussion always gets interesting when money is involved. On both sides of this conflict, a lot of money is being spent to sway public opinion. Once you have the data you want, there are always experts who are ready and willing to advocate your point of view, especially if there is some money to be made from doing so and even more so if they believe it too. The more money involved, the bigger push you can make. Package your research convincingly and you can create doubt in even the staunchest supporter of a cause. You may even win an Oscar. This debate is bound to cause uncertainty, indecision, gridlock, panic, and increased market volatility.

One of the biggest actors on the stage on the side of human activity as the cause is the United Nations Intergovernmental Panel on Climate Change (IPCC). According to McKinsey, the IPCC is one of the largest bodies of international scientists ever assembled to study a scientific issue, involving more than 2,500 scientists from more than 130 countries. The IPCC has concluded that most of the warming observed during the past fifty years is attributable to human activities. Its findings have been publicly endorsed by the national academies of science of all G-8 nations, as well as those of China, India, and Brazil.

With these statistics in mind, Google the words "climate change manipulation" and you get more than 11 million hits. Interestingly, the word "fraud" comes up quite often. For every point brought up by those painting doom and gloom, when it comes to what we humans are doing to the planet, there are valid counter arguments as to why this is not true. The most pervasive of these arguments include that some of the biggest names regarding global warming, such as Al Gore, responsible for his Oscar winning film called *An Inconvenient Truth*, still live in homes that consume over ten times the energy of an average size one. Furthermore, instead of cycling or walking to work, many are driven in large limos. If they themselves really practiced what they were preaching, wouldn't it make more sense to lead by example, ride a bike, and demonstrate what a small energy footprint looks like? It is also interesting to note that many of the biggest advocates of the carbon credit system have large financial interests in the market on which they would trade. Isn't that also an "inconvenient truth"?

For instance, an article by Larry Lohmann from *Ecotopia* reveals the following along with names:

"The World Rainforest Movement (WRM) says that many of the authors and editors of the IPCC's 'Special Report on Land Use, Land Use Change and Forestry' (LULUCF), unveiled in June before international climate negotiators, were business people in a position to profit financially from the tree-planting schemes likely to follow in the report's wake."

It would seem that here again, certain business people will put personal gain before the interests of society and thereby further undermine the public's trust in their leadership. Whether or not these arguments are eventually prove true or not, this type of behavior is guaranteed to feed a growing appetite of fear and uncertainty.

Steadily rising crop yields revisited

With growing urban and suburban sprawl, the amount of arable farmland is continuing to diminish. Therefore, farmers need to continually increase crop yield per acre from the already inflated amounts we currently have. Although yields increased drastically from the 1960s up until recently, the era of sensible "better living through chemistry" seems to be coming to a rapid close as the effects of new solutions become more questionable.

More and more consumers are recognizing that there is a tradeoff between quicker growing crops and the quality and quantity of their nutritional value. For instance, adding nitrogen to farmland provided a drastic increase in the size and speed to crop maturity, but it is also estimated that most oranges and apples produced using nitrogen and other additives have lost 50 percent and more of the nutrients that natural, slower-growing crops contain. So even though there may yet be a further decrease in time to harvest and in per acre crop yields, evidence points toward those crops getting blander in taste and weaker in nutrients than current ones. This does not even include the growing issue of what genetic modification does to a crop and eventually to the people eating it.

Erosion, soil depletion, and less potent food

Yearly plowing of the same land makes it easier for rich topsoil to dry up, blow away or get washed downstream during a big rainstorm. The result is less fertile soil remaining to grow crops in and much larger deltas at the eventual mouths of the rivers that flow past these lands.

Take the Amazon, Mississippi, and Nile river deltas' rapid growth over the last few decades as just a few giant examples. Not only have they expanded tremendously; they have also created giant dead zones way out into the ocean, gulf, and sea into which they connect. These dead zones are caused by heightened algae growth, now traced back in large part to all the fertilizers and chemicals mixed with this farmland runoff. It may be worth a moment to ponder the following: if these chemicals are causing so much damage to the water into which they flow, what are they doing to the digestive system and health of each person eating the crops grown with them? Do you really know what your food contains?

Food and water are now big business

The age of the family farm is facing stiff and relentless competition from deep-pocketed corporate competitors. Corporate farming has become the dominant force in the US and is rapidly spreading across the globe. Stories such as:

- Large tracts of Ukraine's bread basket are being bought up by at least one company in Sweden.
- Bill Gates's recent buying spree of arable farmland.
- Thousands of Indian farmers are reportedly committing suicide due to financial stress.
- Lawsuits and harassment by corporate neighbors in the US and Canada on family farmers who are caught "using" modified seeds to grow these modified crops on their lands. Although blown there

by wind, many farmers, fully committed to planting naturally occurring crops using normal seeds that generate by themselves, are being sued out of business for *stealing* these "patented seeds."

- Big business buying up reservoirs and water rights in regions and municipalities all over the world then leasing or selling that same water back to the community at a big profit. As usual the poor locals who are affected by this are in no position to complain, resist, or pay. As we continue to use up and pollute our remaining reserves of drinkable water, the shrinking remainder is being systematically bought up and cordoned off by large corporations. They plan to, or are already, exploiting this resource by charging those who can least afford it to regain or have continued access to it. Something we took for granted, such as access to potable water, is rapidly becoming a commodity to monetize, exploit and profit from.

- Whole earth and permaculture farmers who are facing increased scrutiny, harassment, fines, and even destruction of their crops and herds by local authorities, due to trumped-up "health concerns." SWAT teams have even been called in to harass these normally peaceful farm-folk and slaughter their often newly legislated, "illegal" herds.

- Many are already talking about water being the next oil. Potable water is being consumed faster than it can be replaced. Aquifers are being drained faster than they can refill. California is suffering from the longest drought on record.

- There are also more and more reports that the new oil extraction method known as fracking is causing the contamination of underground water tables. There have been many documented and often covered-up cases of fire and water coming out of a kitchen tap!

All of this and more points again toward the increasing trend of short-term profit triumphing over what was previously considered common sense. Wiser, more natural, and sustainable based farming methods are down, but not out. In one way this era of peak industrial farming is literally sowing its own seeds of eventual destruction, as it is continually forced to employ harsher and more heavy-handed methods to maintain business as usual. For instance, by having more and more legislation enacted with the help of lawmakers who are clearly either idiots, on the take, or both the word is slowly but surely spreading to buy local and support your local family farmer.

Farmers' markets have been resurrected from the dustbin of history to once again become a local community fixture. Even some local sheriffs are beginning to support neighborhood farmers suffering harassment from unwanted officials. Members of the Constitutional Sheriffs and Peace Officers Association have assisted farmers in getting law-abiding sustainable farmers out of intrusive government's way. Although these are positive trends, they are still a long way from being the prevalent method of raising crops. As long as consumers choose price over quality, whole earth farming will have an uphill battle against their larger, cheaper, and more "resourceful" corporate counterparts. Staying on top of this important health and environmental issue and its inevitable shift is important, especially if you want to remain healthy, agile, and in business.

The health risks of genetically modified foods

Others more passionate about this subject address this issue in much more detail. The important thing here is that there now seems to be evidence to cast serious doubt on the claims that these *manufactured* foods are as safe as their natural counterparts. With larger marketing budgets and more legislators willing to "cooperate," getting an unbiased view of this picture from the mainstream media is challenging. Whereas, the amount of alternative information sources via the internet is increasing. The point to be made here again is that whenever uncertainty enters into the picture, even concerning the food we eat, increased vigilance and agility are needed.

Ecosystems strained to their limits

Bee populations have been diminishing at an increasing pace in many parts of the world. Reasons for this rapid decrease range from the increased microwave activity and intensity from cell phone networks to new types of pesticides that were brought to market before they were adequately or properly tested. Whatever the cause, bees play an important role in the pollination of just those crops we rely on for food. Fewer bees will lead to less pollination, which can result in a drastic reduction in food.

According to Melissa Breyer of the Mother Nature Network,[2] "There's a definitive lack of apples, avocados, bok choy, broccoli, broccoli rabe, cantaloupe, carrots, cauliflower, celery, cucumbers, eggplant, green onions, honeydew, kale, leeks, lemons, limes, mangos, mustard greens, onions, summer squash, and zucchini—all foods that rely on bees."

With the travel limits imposed by the recent pandemic, migrant workers have now been prohibited from travelling to the farms where they are relied upon to plant and harvest certain crops. This is exacerbating the food shortage problem and can not only affect the availability of certain food products, but it already seems to be having an effect on prices, too.

Figure 10. Catch of the day, but for how long?

Reduced production is now being documented regarding the decline of marine life, which has been taking place over the past forty years. The World Wildlife Fund[3] recently released a report stating that "up to 50 percent of the aquatic life they were tracking has been fished out or disappeared over this time period." A certain contributor to this devastation is again the toxic run-off from farmlands. It kills the coral reefs that have been responsible for protecting and nurturing a large portion of the marine life habitat. This trend is still increasing. Many other examples abound, but the evidence that our current way of living is now having serious consequences on our ability to keep living this way is becoming unavoidable.

As consumers wake up to this reality, increased scrutiny will be placed upon the environmental impact of companies and their products. Even now, receiving bad press often spreads instantly and virally over the internet, whether or not it is warranted. Should you, your product, or your company get caught in this hysteria, agile actions on your part may be your only hope.

Increased risks for big weather

Typhoons, hurricanes, monsoons, La Niña winds, and tornadoes have been increasing in both intensity and frequency during the last few years, causing increased flooding, drought, heat waves, and major snowstorms.

Regardless of whether or not this is naturally cyclical or induced by our lifestyle choices, sudden changes in the weather can shut down factories, interrupt transportation, and cause general mayhem to all your plans to conduct business as usual.

Earthquakes and volcanic eruptions have also begun increasing in intensity. An earthquake in the Indian Ocean in 2006 caused a large tsunami wave that resulted in approximately 250,000 deaths and complete devastation along hundreds of miles of coastline, from Sri Lanka to Indonesia.

Hurricane Katarina pummeled the Gulf Coast region of the United States and practically destroyed the city of New Orleans, Louisiana. Bureaucratic red tape impeded the rescue response time and the FEMA bureaucracy received enormous critique for their slowness to act decisively. For a while the southern United States looked more like a dithering third world landscape than a robust part of the world's most influential country.

The eruption of the Eyjafjallajökull volcano in Iceland disrupted air travel in twenty different countries for a period of six days in April, 2010. This eruption affected over 10 million passengers and their travel plans. To even get home during this period required lots of agility and often lots more money.

The Fukushima disaster of 2011 put in serious question the safety and sanity of nuclear-powered electricity. More than ten years on, we are still not sure of the extent of the damage, further undermining our trust in leadership.

These four "black swan" incidents disrupted lives and businesses on levels rarely seen. These are just four of the most recognized disasters over the past decade. There have been many more. The point is that if you look back in time it is seldom that you find so many powerful and diverse natural events occurring in such a short time.

You cannot prepare for everything but it's increasingly important to be aware of the environment you are sailing into. Right now, environmental events are increasing in both intensity and frequency. The better you understand the possible situations you may face and your own capabilities to handle them, the better you will be able to deal with whatever comes. These situations can range to placement of new factories, to which markets you wish to enter, remain in, or expand.

The urbanization of society

The migration of people from rural areas to urban ones continued, until it didn't. This trend started in earnest at the beginning of the industrial period. It really took off once industry began expanding in and around urban areas. Although this phenomenon started in the Western Hemisphere, the eastern one is now breaking all records when it comes to the movement of people toward cities. Estimates of up to 300 million of China's inhabitants shall be moving from the country to the city into the next ten years.

In 1800, just 3 percent of the world's population lived in cities. By the year 2000, this had increased to 47 percent. In 1950, there were just 83 cities with populations over 1 million. By 2007, the number had risen to over 400. The UN now forecasts today's urban population of 3.2 billion will rise to nearly 5 billion by 2030.

In 2000, there were eighteen megacities such as Mexico City, Mumbai, São Paulo, and New York City with populations in excess of 10 million. Tokyo now has 35 million making it a so-called hyper city. By 2025, according to the now defunct *Far Eastern Economic Review*, Asia will have at least ten hyper-cities, defined as those with more than 19 million inhabitants. Some Chinese experts now forecast that their cities will contain 800 million of their population within another five years.

Cities are the most inhospitable places to live unless there are effective support systems to keep everyone housed, fed, and in good health. As the size and number of cities continue to grow it puts an enormous strain on the infrastructure and resources needed to support them. So far, technology has saved the day when it comes to food, water, and energy. Whether or not this will continue is always in doubt. Uncertainty will remain an important factor in the growth of our cities.

Problems that have always accompanied urbanization are still with us and multiply with its growth. Homelessness, crime, drugs, domestic violence, and the spread of disease all continue to increase in direct proportion to the density of population.

On the other hand, with the growth of the internet and more efficient transportation, selling and delivering products has never been easier. As traditional mass marketing is losing its appeal, micro marketing to larger groups becomes easier as people with the same tastes and interests group together and increasingly share their thoughts online. Although this is an almost embarrassingly simple example of the challenges and opportunities of the urbanization process, it should suffice to underline that doing things as we have always done them is becoming unsustainable. Just the increase in affluence alone has caused the purchase of cars to expand to the point that there is gridlock in most major urban areas on every working day. No longer is there easy access to the resources nor the space to add to a developed city's road system without extravagant costs. Even so, more cars are bought each day.

Whether this trend toward larger concentrations of people continues toward infinity or systems start breaking down, human behavior will either continue to adapt or change outright. Almost right on que, there has now been a major break in this urbanization trend. With the rules and limitations imposed by the pandemic, many people are opting out of their urban lifestyle and moving as far away from the city as they can afford. Prices for farmland and houses in small towns have risen drastically, while the reverse is true in large metropolitan areas. The wealthier and more mobile are moving first, taking with them their disproportionate part of the city tax base and thereby hollowing out what was left of the municipal services, including water, sanitation, police, fire, and rescue, which urban dwellers depend on.

Looking in your rearview mirror to ascertain when these changes occur will not help you quickly enough to do anything in time. Searching for them on the horizon in front of you will be a much more effective way of keeping up, or better yet to stay ahead.

The sixth great extinction

According to several sources such as Stanford University, *The Scientific American*, and *National Geographic*, the interpretation of archeological evidence indicates that there have been five great mass extinctions on planet Earth. According to these sources, we are now in the midst of the sixth. The big difference is that this one, now referred to as the *Holocene Extinction*, has a unique cause—ourselves. This seems to make sense, if only from the points above.

Yet according to experts, this newest extinction actually seems to have started approximately 100,000 years ago, just about the same time humans started moving out of what is now Africa. We started by hunting and killing for food to exist. Now we have become so "clever" that we are destroying whole habitats and, in the process, impacting our own. This latest extinction seems to be happening quicker than all the others and easily contributes more evidence that we are indeed connected to everything. Estimates by the WWF now put the loss of species currently at about 50 percent[4]. Agility in this case will include a lot more than just business.

Government to the rescue, again?

With all the hype surrounding our influence on climate change, it is good to keep in mind a quote used again and again by certain manipulative leaders, "Don't ever let a good crisis go to waste." Regardless of the natural versus man-made impact of climate change, the certainty in the equation will be *more new laws*. Well-meant or not, they will be enacted on our "public servants'" schedule, not yours. If you happen to be caught sleeping, you may miss the chance to avoid or profit from the coming changes. Staying on top of your game and aiming your products and energy toward creating a cleaner environment and monitoring new and unexpected legislation is becoming an unavoidable goal for the businessperson who wants to remain successful.

Societal strains reaching their limits

Many indigenous people express it in different ways, but all point to some sort of mega change for the world and humanity when two things begin to occur with increasing frequency:

1. Natural catastrophes begin increasing in size and frequency
2. We neglect and ignore our children[5]

Pick up any newspaper or watch any news broadcast and you will certainly see evidence of an increasing trend for both. Natural catastrophes are one thing, but once we take our focus off of our children, and how we guide them into adulthood, we are basically committing societal suicide. From increasing cases of depression and teenage obesity to school shootings, it isn't hard to connect the dots. Clearly, our children are feeling more and more disenfranchised. That is a very wimpy way of saying that they feel alone and unheard. If the message they are being taught and conditioned to accept is one saying "we are too busy to care," what do you think they will teach or not to their kids?

Coronavirus time and forced lockdowns

If you still aren't convinced that business agility is now a necessity, just compare January 2020 to now. Since then and for the first time in history, most of the known world has been affected by the now infamous coronavirus, or COVID-19. This pandemic has created the rational and/or excuse to lockdown most of the world's economy. This lockdown has sent a shockwave through most every business both large and small, all over the world!

Yes, many people have been infected, a large number have suffered greatly, and many have died a gruesome death. Yet the world's population is becoming increasingly confused, irritated, and impatient as to whether this tragedy justified locking down the world's economy.

The reason we bring this up here is not to debate whether this was medically justified or that it is some sort of global conspiracy with a deeper and darker goal, but to advocate yet again that events are happening even quicker with more measurable impact than ever before! The result has already been a wave of bankruptcies and unemployment, the likes of which haven't been experienced since at least the 1930s and the Great Depression. And there seem to be more challenges coming. For instance, at the time of this writing, it is estimated that only 8 percent of commuters have returned to their offices in New York City, roughly 10 percent in London and 13 percent in Stockholm. Many workers who can are learning to like working from home. Just one example, what does this trend mean for the commercial real-estate market and all those employed in the building and maintenance trade?

Those businesses that have survived, consciously or not, were either very lucky or had to become very agile, and in some cases, transform their business models and even business cultures overnight! Still others have flourished during what can only be described as a catastrophic situation. How did they do it?

Yes, some had the luck of being in the right industry at the right time. Some surgical mask producers, ventilator producers, and big pharma vaccine and therapeutic producers have hit the jackpot. Online retailers have also taken a large, irreplaceable bite out of the remaining brick and mortar retail market. Food and liquor stores have also benefitted as have streaming services, online gambling, and gaming companies. For the sake of argument let's just call a good portion of these players and others lucky. Lucky for being in the right place or industry at the right time. What is more impressive and worth studying very closely are those agile players who consciously and quickly acted to deliberately transform their business in an industry hit head-on by the lockdown.

For instance, in the restaurant business, many restaurants were quickly forced to fold from rental costs which their empty tables could no longer cover. Others transformed their businesses into takeout emporiums with optional delivery available. Thus, many agile restauranteurs have weathered this perfect storm quite well. One restauranteur on the Outer Banks of North Carolina is in fact celebrating by buying a yacht at a massively discounted COVID price due to his chain's quick transformation from sit-down to take-out model. He does not plan to fully reopen his dining rooms anytime soon, yet business is obviously good enough for him to go sailing. The question remains as to how many others will be agile enough to tackle this enormous challenge to their livelihoods? The answer is still uncertain.

Although this should maybe go into the megatrends section, it is simply too uncertain to leave out of the storm section. One of the trends that could leave a lasting mark on our society is the growing use of surgical and other face masks. Children have a hard enough time navigating childhood these days without adding the next challenge of not being able to learn and understand facial expressions. Having studied body language for decades, it is hard enough to read body language when a face is fully exposed. Try reading someone's expression behind a mask! We are now training a large part of our newest generation to function without understanding basic facial expressions. That masks have as yet even been clinically proven to be effective makes their exploding usage a possible societal and interpersonal communication catastrophe in the making. Finally, it is interesting to note how many used masks are ending up on city streets and anywhere but a medical trash bin.

The rise of fear

With almost every media available saturated with pandemic information, is it any wonder that many peoples' fantasies have given way to dark and foreboding thoughts? Combined with increasing financial, geopolitical, and environmental uncertainty, is it any wonder even well-educated and affluent people are worried about what will happen next? Worry causes stress and when you are stressed your ability to be agile declines.

Integrity

What is integrity?

Integrity means that everything is integrated and completes the whole. Just as a balloon demonstrates its integrity when it is full of air, a person demonstrates his/her integrity when they stand for, radiate, and work from consciously chosen values and principles. Not knowing or selling out what you stand for signals an opposite lack of integrity. You may become rich, but at what price? It is unbelievably hard to remain agile or attract others to follow when your integrity is leaking.

Integrity also implies a willingness to look deep within, plumb the depths of who you are, and consciously choose to improve how you want to be seen and remembered. Those leaders among us with integrity and a personal willingness to master life will demonstrate this by listening to others and adjust their behavior according to what they hear. They will consciously do their best to balance this with the principles for which they stand. If their desire is to be more congruent in thought, word, and deed then they are often grateful for well-meaning feedback.

Those lacking integrity don't listen, are always prepared for a debate, and often sacrifice any remaining integrity by justifying or arguing for why their actions were "necessary." In fact, there is a term that probably comes from the bombing missions of the Second World War. It states that, "the anti-aircraft fire is always the thickest and most deadly closest to the target." Meaning, a liar will justify, explain, defend, and scream the loudest and most intensively as you get closer to that inconvenient truth. One can wonder how some of these less than forthright public figures can sleep soundly, and there is more and more anecdotal evidence that many do not.

Integrity or what price vanity?

Current fashion, music, and movie trends lay bare the tip of the iceberg when tracking societal values. According to many social researchers, we are living in one of the most narcissistic eras ever. The major focus of many, regardless of age, seems to be "look at me." Just as Narcissus spent most of his time staring at his reflection in the mirror, most of us have been conditioned to seek or at least seem to desire recognition from others. The drive to be a celebrity for the sake of celebrity is a popular theme regardless of how vain and empty it inherently is. Want proof? Just watch a so-called reality show.

It seems that as long as you look good on the outside, it doesn't matter if you are morally and financially bankrupt within. Image seems to be what counts.

This self-absorbing behavior also influences our values and goes a long way to explaining the current epidemic of scandals and corruption that has seeped into every level of society. The need today for being known for something, *anything* arguably overtakes common sense.

For those of us interested in running an honest business, this increasingly noisy background makes our quest for loyal customers all the more challenging. As people become increasingly numb to corruption, it becomes harder to maintain a stand of integrity.

Disconnected from body and planet

Even casual observations reveal that skinheads, cultists, and others with anti-social tendencies are attracted to each other out of a basic human longing for meaningful contact. Despite even social distancing, we humans are sociable. We feel better when we have and interact with other people around us. Although it may be worthwhile to examine the context, the principle remains; we feel much better and more valuable when we are in contact with those who hold values and views akin to our own. For most of us this means being able to stand for and be proud of our beliefs. Companionship is good, but without something of mutual value holding it together it will inevitably collapse. Therefore, basic listening skills, some common sense, empathy, and compassion also helps.

With more and more uncertainty on the horizon, many of us are starting to search for something deeper. The rise in popularity of spiritual retreats and the return of fundamental religious beliefs are both trends that seem to be on the increase. Many former criminals turn to religion, spiritualism and meditation to heal old wounds. Spirit literally means "everything is connected," and there remains hope that many of us are beginning to realize just how disconnected we have become. The next step is actually doing something about it. This an important step in being able to start healing all the current and gaping societal wounds and could become a new business model, if done authentically.

Even in present times, many of our parents or grandparents either grew up on a farm or knew someone close to them who did. Most everyone alive then knew that food did not originally come from an attractive box or can in the store. Today, many children may have only seen a farm on TV. Even fewer actually know how to grow, catch, or prepare their own food. The further away our food gets from its source the less nutrition it usually contains. This is due to the processing of it. The shinier and more colorful the package is, the emptier it often is of nutritional content. Even so, we keep stuffing these manufactured "treats" into our bodies and strangely become heavier and sicker with each bite.

Even though we may get an immediate sugar "kick" that makes us feel like Superman, the net result is just like pouring gasoline on a fire. The food often causes more damage than nourishment. Add to this the amount of stress we usually encounter on a daily basis, and this pulls us further away from what our ancestors would probably view as a more healthy and natural flow of life.

Not surprisingly, this trend of empty foods dovetails exactly with today's exploding obesity trend. Many of us seem to have disconnected ourselves from our feelings and self-esteem. Some still don't seem to notice or care about the connection between what we put into our bodies, how we take care of them, and how this ultimately makes us feel. Others do understand, yet suppress doing anything about it, often out of pride or resignation. Many eat more just to deaden their pain and some to create an even bigger boundary between themselves and reality. Although some are waking up to this, many are still "asleep at the wheel" of the vehicle representing their own health and well-being. Look around and, if you dare, into your mirror. Notice if "garbage in, garbage out" applies.

Working with body language, it becomes painfully obvious, very quickly how little we pay attention to the cheapest, most available, and important communication tool each of us has, our bodies. For instance, someone near and dear to me works with obese people looking to lose weight, without surgery.

A key element to this life-changing choice is exercise. For many, losing control of their eating habits also means losing control of their bodies' motor function, often with tragic effect. According to a source in the over-weight treatment business, when asked to simply lift up one of their feet, many patients will hear the command, yet their feet stay put. The reality of separating their foot from the ground only becomes apparent when the therapist physically bends over and lifts the patient's foot off the ground! This has happened too often with too many different individuals to be a coincidence. Could this be shocking evidence that many of us are also asleep at the wheel when it comes to the reality of converting thoughts into actions? Think of the cause of much of the tragic loss of tourist life in the tsunami of 2004. How often and in what circumstances do you forget, avoid, or neglect to act when you know action is called for? This discon-nection from our ability to act is a giant challenge for everyone joining us on our crusade for more agility.

The term "guilt money" is now almost antique, but its consequences will be felt for a long time to come. Parents, many even still living together, who are so busy with everything else, often do not take time to spend with their offspring. Instead, they throw money at them to relieve their own guilt and, *poof*, the problem seems to be solved . . . or is it? Children are fast learners and quickly understand and master this type of behavior. Being kids, they are also fast to exploit it. What if they begin training their parents and even encouraging them to continue this destructive behavior? What lesson is being taught here, whose behavior is being modified, and by whom?

One fourth grader in my daughter's class bragged that if he threw his cell phone against a wall, went home, and told his parents that he dropped it, he would quickly get the latest one. Sure enough, it was true. He proudly showed off his brand-new smartphone the very next day.

If these anecdotes are not enough to encourage you to take this social disaster of disconnection seriously, take a look in any drug store or supermarket at the availability and number of different types of headache remedies, stomachache remedies, and painkillers. The amount of people who are taking both prescription and non-prescription drugs are at record levels. This trend has increased drastically as this lockdown craze has widened and deepened. In short, more and more of us are relying upon synthetic remedies and not just to make us feel better.

We are increasingly relying on drugs to treat or deaden the symptoms. Deadening the symptoms shuts down the search for the underlying causes of your disease, perpetuates the need for continued and increased use or addiction to those drugs. Not surprisingly, profit-based pharmaceutical companies do not readily demonstrate a problem with supporting and encouraging this type of behavior. Recent research points to that you now have a ten times bigger chance of dying from a misused medication than from a gunshot wound. It seems that quarterly profits have become more important than the Hippocratic Oath[6] to "do no harm."

If you have any interest in becoming more agile, yet find yourself resonating with any of the above anecdotes, then it is time to act! Not doing anything trains you to become less agile over time; just as training to act and do something makes you more agile. It always boils down to a choice: to act and practice agility or not! This choice, its resulting behavior, and the results produced are yours to make and enjoy or not.

Reflections on human beings/doings, "sheeple," and zombies

When things are going well, you often feel inspired and engaged. When you are enjoying that feeling, you may feel connected to something bigger than yourself. You may find yourself in what is now often called "the flow."

When that happens you are usually in, or contributing to, a virtuous circle. In sports, this means that you have entered the zone. In music, it used to be called, the groove. You feel empowered. With that feeling of empowerment you consciously become a bit more human even while going about your daily routines.

Unfortunately, we are designed in a way that we can often get so wrapped up in what we are doing that we easily become unconscious to it and start doing it more without thinking or feeling anything for the people involved or the consequences. When things spin further out of control, stress increases, and you turn inward. This makes some try to do more, while some become paralyzed or lethargic. Either way, the result is that we usually feel less. Focus turns even more to the task directly in front and it is easy to become distracted from and eventually disinterested in any and ultimately all consequences. Many become more willing to intrude into other people's integrity and have less and less concern about preying on others, as long as it seems to lighten their own stressful load. For many it is easy to throw someone else under the bus, especially if they are perceived to be of lesser importance than them, or if they are led to believe this person, group, or country may represent a threat.

Those who understand the psychology involved in this process are also well aware that your willingness and energy to question begins to wane with the more stress experienced. When we become stressed and our feelings begin shutting down, we forget our integrity, become more easily convinced, and often accept to do more intrusive and predatory tasks. These are often tasks that, under normal circumstances, you would probably have raised an issue with. Think running concentration camps. For many, these types of resolutions usually have an "If I do this, will you leave me alone?" factor in them. For others, often burdened with unexplored or suppressed psychological baggage, an opportunity to boss others around seems to fulfill some unfulfilled need or heal some sort of emotional scar. Just observe the behavior of various airport security personnel, parking lot attendants, and bouncers. But is it fulfilling, especially if and when you take the time to reflect over your behavior, its effect, and consequences?

Regardless, the more burdened and stressed with issues you become, the more distracted you get and easier you become to manipulate. If you also happen to be worried financially, the promise of a steady income will often be enough to get you to go along with all kinds of intrusive, essentially anti-social, even anti societal behavior. Remember, Upton Sinclair said, "It is difficult to get a man to understand something when his salary depends on him not understanding it."

Figure 11. Light's on, but who is home?

Perpetuating this passive behavior further disconnects you from the flow of good feelings and positive experiences. Your stressed, anti-social behavior can quickly and easily become habit. Since misery still seems to love company, the more you are surrounded with others on automatic pilot, the more you will be constantly reminded and conditioned that this is how things must be for society to work. The result is the more this type of intrusive behavior inevitably becomes the societal norm.

This type of behavior amplifies resignation, and we literally become human doings who easily forget to take the time to be human. No wonder so many of us feel lonely. Somewhere deep down, most of us still have some sort of moral compass. Yet this process easily eats away at what is left of that compass, as well as our dignity and lust for life. Resignation to "do what you're told" can easily become the norm. Not convinced yet? Look at any train platform at rush hour and gauge the level of inspiration from your fellow travelers. What if, when the gap between what we are doing and who we remember and still feel ourselves to be becomes too great, it can cause us to "hit the wall," burn out, suffer a heart attack, or cause some sort of nervous breakdown?

Two terms are now being regularly used to describe this feeling of chronic disconnection and resignation: "sheeple" and "zombies." Just as their names seem to imply, one is more passive and the other more active. The term "sheeple" seems to refer to those of us who just wish to be left alone to get on with their lives and off-load responsibility and challenges to their all-too-willing shepherds. This is not to imply that they are against rocking the boat, it seems more that their stress dampens any thought of doing so. Many of us are so caught up in the details of running our lives that we become too resigned to initiate anything when time is left over. If extra time is found, we would much rather use it to collapse or disappear into other people's excitement on Facebook, Instagram, World of Warcraft, or one of the many cooking, reality, or entertainment shows available on TV. To relax and let others run things is the path of least resistance, as long as you continue to have faith in your shepherds.

Problems arise when those you trust to lead are finally revealed to be more concerned with their own welfare than yours. This is where "zombies" play a role. Basically, they are very much like "sheeple" with the exception that, just like the fictional monster they are named after, consciously or not, they take on a predatory behavior, especially when they are mandated by those in charge to force others around.

We the "sheeple"?

Just like a deer that freezes in your headlights, the more we become dependent on our technology, the more we seem to be losing our ability to be present here and now. The expression, "the light is on but nobody's home" comes to mind when you stop and observe how preoccupied many of us seem to be. The term "sheeple" seems to imply that more and more of us tend to act like sheep and sleepwalk through our day. Just like sheep we often choose to follow the crowd. Take a walk down any crowded street and see how many people you pass who seem present, filled with the excitement of being here and now. Chances are you will notice very few, especially now when many seem to have been muzzled with a facemask. If, on the other hand everyone appears to be more present to you, then you may want to take another look at how present you currently are.

Take some opportunities to observe the body language of people you pass and take notice to how automatic and mechanical much of it seems to appear—especially their eyes. Probably the most obvious and frightening piece of evidence to this trend is the following realization: many you encounter will see you not as a fellow human to acknowledge but more as an obstacle or contagious threat to be avoided. Can you really expect that we are suddenly going to become more agile and pull together in times of great trouble when we currently do all we can to avoid others on the street? This may not be so everywhere, but this tendency does seem to increase in cities and in colder climates. Really. How can we expect to accomplish world peace when we don't dare to even say hello to a stranger?

The more we shuffle along and disappear in our little electronic gadgets, permitting people and companies with undeclared motives to dump information directly into our raw senses, the more we succeed in disconnecting ourselves off from the natural flow of life.

Not very long ago, my daughter's school sent out an alarming notice to all parents. The teachers had observed that the cafeteria had gone silent. The students were still there, sitting in their proper place, but only a few of them were actually talking with each other. Most sat silently, staring vacantly into their smart gadgets. The teachers raised the alarm because these healthy, energetic early teens now sat there like docile sheep(?) totally disconnected from their friends and from life! What is happening to the agility of youth? Is this the future you wish your children to be raised into?

Many of us who used screen time as a passive babysitter in order to handle just one more errand or task in the evening have eventually been surprised to discover how hard it is to start a conversation with our now screen-time-conditioned children. Once they are trained to seek excitement online, how can a dull parent compete with the action available just a few clicks away? Quite a few concerned parents eventually seek professional help but often only for their children when they see how hard it is for them to leave their screen for any reason. Want to compound the problem? Try taking the gadget away!

All of this seems to be contributing toward a society where healthy individuals are being trained to behave more like sheep; hence the term "sheeple." The drive to think for yourself and to create something new is being replaced by a fear of not fitting in to the politically correct flock. Or there is an overreaction to the other side to begin dressing differently to stand out. Notice the increase in what psychologists call "cheap signaling," which means piercing, tattoos, non-natural hair colors, and interesting clothes.

More and more adults and frighteningly many children are now suffering from health problems such as depression. Most of us like to follow the flock and blend in with the majority, but not to the point where we lose our identity. Becoming a sheeple is a trend that seems to both cause and result in good-hearted and well-meaning people who just want a little peace, generating more fear, uncertainty, and worry.

Zombies

The increasing number of "zombified" people among us does not make the plight of the sheeple easier. These are those "human doings" who have, for whatever reason and consciously or not, decided to take on a task or job that intrudes upon someone else's integrity. For instance, whether or not the threat of increased violence is perceived or real, what if the increase

Figure 12. Zombie or tired co-worker?

of those employed in the security and protection sectors are currently outpacing the corresponding threat? Taxes and surcharges have also increased to help pay for all this increased protection providing more jobs for both public and private number crunchers. Big government keeps getting bigger as the encouragement of fear continues to overtake reason, common sense, and empathy.

There are unfortunately many among us who have no problem with—and actually enjoy—having the mandate to tell others what to do. This is the distinguishing behavior factor separating docile sheeple from predatory zombies.

The more we continue to sheepishly react to all the fear around for example, terrorism, the more zombified behavior we are likely to meet and the less freedom we are likely to retain. As Benjamin Franklin once said, "The more you are willing to sacrifice your freedom for security the less you will have of either." If you wish to avoid becoming a sheeple, and the more you understand the challenge you and your conscience ultimately face when you realize what becoming a zombie really means, the more you will recognize the value and utility in improving your agility.

Some questions to reflect over:

- Have you noticed that an increase in your stress level encourages you to shut out the concerns of those around you?
- Do you relax comfortably on a Friday evening or collapse into your couch, exhausted after a full week's work?

- How many choices and tasks can you handle responsibly during the day and for how many days running?
- Does your job give you a mandate that requires you to intrude on another's integrity or personal space? If so, take a moment and reflect—how does it make you feel?
- What if being more agile is also a function of minimizing stress and being and feeling more human?

The culture of cancel, revisited

Censoring used to be the domain of tyrants and dictators, yet something happened on the way to being a PC (a.k.a. politically correct) society. We began turning off the people and channels of communication which we disagree with. Black indeed became white when the University of California, Berkley began cancelling events that disagreed with the prevailing liberal mood on campus. This was, in fact, ground zero for the "Free Speech" movement of the late 1960s. What happened? Dissident voices are now being "cancelled."

Be it in the form of so-called shadow banning or outright cancelling of your account, most of the prevailing social media platforms are no longer hiding these practices and sooner or later we will all suffer from it. Should you say something that goes against the grain of whatever the current accepted narrative is, be prepared to have your voice cancelled. This is regardless of whether your comment was your heart-felt truth, a mistake or even a typo. If your words could be interpreted as offensive to someone, some group, or someone's algorithm, be prepared to have your voice (and in many cases) your livelihood cancelled. This book may put your authors in cancel jeopardy.

Public servants or masters

To appease the PC gods, let's now limit this broad conversation to just our ability to easily transact business. Do any of the above examples of human behavior make it harder or easier to have a happy, healthy life and run an agile, successful business?

What if, in their interest to preserve and enhance business as usual, our current batch of leaders are increasingly impeding our ability to conduct business? As the costs, barriers, and frustrations of doing business expand, will more or fewer people take the plunge to start a new business? Before COVID-19, figures revealed pointed to a drastic contraction of new business startups. Since COVID-19 that trend has exploded. Of course, this makes sense. When the economic environment demands a more vigilant and protective behavior, we seem wired to respond accordingly.

Since small businesses account for the majority of the GDP of nations and their respective tax base, does it seem like a wise choice or an effective use of diminishing public resources to try to monitor and control every aspect of a small business? What about shutting it down?

Yet even this simple question is made more complex with the access to creating as much digital and regular money as needed. All talk of the impending Great Reset also includes the promise of guaranteed basic income. Yet how many of you, dear readers, will be satisfied sitting on your couch collecting your basic income? And how long will it be before those who do have been fleeced out of their guarantee?

It doesn't take a very high IQ to predict the future consequences of such a poorly thought-out plan. In fact, look no further than California, Illinois, and New York State and see the figures and demographics of those moving out versus those moving in. Most of us have to make a living. In the midst of this drastic increase of red tape, exciting possibilities still exist for agile business leaders who understand and can navigate according to how the future is changing.

This process is sometimes called reframing or creating a paradigm shift. You basically define the tenets that have given rise to a specific industry or profession. Once you have them clearly defined, it is just to challenge a specific one until its weakness is revealed. When this is done, the old, accepted business model will eventually give way and everyone who did not see the change coming will be swept away as the traditional way of conducting business as usual comes crashing down. Once again, look to Uber, Apple's iTunes, Cable TV, PayPal and others for current examples of this process.

This is the same process that ended up fracturing the Catholic Church's grip on Europe when reformers such as Calvin and Luther challenged its dogma and found it wanting. Some unknown genius once stated that, "when you assume, you make an ass out of 'u' and 'me'." What are the current beliefs of your business model and indeed your life, which you may assume cannot be challenged?

There is a saying that seems to be grounded in common sense, which states, "Pure service is transparent." What this means is that the more you stand for service, the more you and your ego disappear into the experience you are creating for those whom you are serving. Just as an excellent waiter disappears into the background when they are serving you a great meal, so do all other forms of service disappear when performed correctly. In fact, the only time you should even be aware of service is when it doesn't work. Only then will the lack of it make it an obvious target. When it's functioning properly, pure service should blend with its surroundings. With this in mind, we again ask why more and more public servants now need bulletproof cars and security details?

Unfortunately, politics is now an embedded lifestyle, especially in the United States where many of the founding fathers considered themselves to be farmers, brewers, merchants first, and politicians second. Politics has now become a lifelong profession. This makes lifetime politicians little different than the royalty of old. The reason this is so crucial to you as a businessperson is that if officials we elect are primarily focused upon being re-elected, then what kind of laws and what kind of enforcement of those laws can you expect? Would you agree that the diplomatic answer is increasingly uncertain?

Just us?

Gerald Celente, founder of trendsresearch.com[7], well known for more than thirty years of researching trends, coined the term "just us" for what is currently being called justice. From the fact that many large banks have begun treating fines for illegal conduct as a cost of doing business, to the shenanigans that went on in a few impeachment trials, compared to the still current brushing off of evidence of what the opposition has done with China, Ukraine, etc., to the fact that since the 1925 Judiciary Act, the US Supreme court can choose[8] the cases it will hear, it seems that if you are in the club, you do not have to worry about criminality.

Compare this to the many common people who are locked up, often for a long time, on minor drug charges, and you have a large and still growing gap when it comes to trusting the legal system. A small number of corrupt police who confiscate property, just because they can, up to those cops who have murdered and got off scot-free, provide ample cause for concern and even anger over the current state of the justice system. Over the summer of 2020, many small businesses were looted and destroyed during "peaceful" protests, which took place all over the world. In many large cities, especially in the United States, large retail stores which have been in business for decades are closing up and moving out of downtown because they no longer can count on police protection. Fifth Avenue and Rodeo Drive are two landmark examples. Will decriminalizing shoplifting and removing or defunding police protection increase or decrease uncertainty for you and your organization?

Our culture of entitlement

Entitlement is the belief of an implied right to some sort of benefit. It is basically a form of expected pleasure. Therefore, discontinuing an entitlement can often imply real or imagined pain. Could this be why people are so protective of their entitlements? For instance, all a politician has to do is hint they may look at the growing imbalance between social security underfunding and what you receive in payments. They can then be assured of losing votes at the next election.

How long do you think a system can continue where one employee retires then underfunded pension funds and taxes must then pay for both this new retiree as well as their newly hired replacement? Multiply this by the estimated 10,000 American baby boomers now retiring per day and you may sense how the entitlement system called pensions will sooner or later gum up our already overtaxed system. You may even agree that cancelling or decreasing these pension entitlements, often paid for with your taxes, is a very good idea, as long as your retirement fund is left alone!

What if our continuously expanding entitlement society combined with governmental largesse are together destroying the remaining agility in our society?

"The problem with socialism is that sooner or later
you run out of other peoples' money."
—Margret Thatcher

Facilitating entitlement through IT

Could this trend of avoiding pain through increased entitlement now be supported and encouraged using IT systems and AI? What does placing every aspect of life into a computer matrix, an organizational flowchart or any kind of digital box do to agility and creativity? What does it do to our ability to remain conscious?

Take Sweden as example. A top Swedish business leader recently expressed his concerns about entitlement by saying publicly that the primary goal of the Swedish workforce has become to create an "eternal vacation." After venturing into some Swedish business after spending my whole life abroad, I must sadly concur. Most Swedes now seem to be so indoctrinated and cozy with their "nanny state" of entitlements, that recent polls show that the satisfaction generated from an honest day's work has unfortunately eroded down to a third or fourth place priority. Do you think a Chinese, Vietnamese, or Mexican poll would produce the same results?

Although it may be noble that family priorities in Sweden still come first in this workaholic era, they are closely followed by travel, exploration, self-development, and more "me-time." These all seem to be much more important than producing a product or service of which you can be proud. And why not?

First of all, current labor laws in many western countries make it hard to almost impossible to fire someone. Then, even if your company is successful in getting rid of you, the social safety net will probably protect a large portion of your accustomed lifestyle. In short, you will feel little or no pain. In fact, with more and more low-paying jobs replacing high-paying ones, it actually becomes more economical for a crafty Westerner to look like they are searching for a job and instead collect unemployment as long as possible. This phenomenon of searching for work only to guarantee your next unemployment check has increased drastically during the pandemic.

Many restaurants are now being forced to look toward service automation as reports have appeared where twenty or so people will come to an interview for a waiter position and no one will come back to accept it.

Most social service programs have been developed on the premise that we will need a really "big mama" government to nanny our every move from the cradle to the grave. What if democracy has become autocracy, as many vote for those who tell them the best story? What if most voting has finally evolved into choosing the candidate the voter expects the best entitlement from for the least amount of personal engagement and strain? How agile is this?

This begs the question as to whether twenty-first century democracy has finally degraded into mob rule. The most important and enduring aspect of this whole "nanny state" structure is the question of who will pay? The trend of increasing social costs and rules for new hires is rapidly increasing. Not surprisingly, the number of low-paying jobs with no security or benefits are rapidly increasing, while salaried positions with benefits are in decline. This trend ensures that cracks are beginning to be noticeable and felt in the ability for leaders to deliver on their promised levels of public service. This is making the prospect for some form of basic income more and more tempting for both politicians and the less motivated among us.

Basic income

The latest trend to be announced by progressives around the world is basic income. This is basically free money. You get a small income provided by the state to take care of your basic needs. Depending upon your business, this might be a boon to your customer base as now more people have money to buy, for instance, food, toilet paper, and other necessities and also perceived necessities such as soft drinks, chips, fast food, and lottery tickets. Yet there are at least two major concerns with this plan:

- Where does the money come from for this plan?
- What does this plan do to someone's already compromised work ethic?

That money needs to come from somewhere and that somewhere is usually from someone who still has some money left or, the alternative, of course, is that it is just printed, thereby diluting the value of money made the old-fashioned way.

For anyone who is not motivated to develop themselves, having an income appear every month without doing anything for it is like a dream come true. Yet, will this suddenly inspire them to do more as some straight-faced experts predict, or will it instead provide more incentive to be even more docile and spend even more time in front of their screen of choice? Of course, the more they are conditioned to depend on this handout, the more they will want it to continue or increase. What a field day for our political "public servants" looking to get reelected. Socialism just shifted gears.

Agility and progressivism

Progressives have a nasty habit of structuring most entitlement programs on the notion of the "bell-curve." Each program is formed to serve the "average person." Is it any wonder then that mediocrity always seems to take the upper hand? Would the likes of Edison, Tesla, Einstein, and others ever have had the chance to contribute their epic inventions should they have been forced to go through any current public school system? In fact, many now argue they would all have been forced to take medication to tame their eccentric (or dare we say agile?) behavior. Their genius would most likely have been medicated away rather than allowed to flourish. This of course, begs the question of how many gifted, but eccentric, geniuses are now having their creativity suppressed with medication or incarceration before it can bloom?

Add to our list of megatrends that can quickly morph into a perfect storm, the trend that tries to force the increasingly round peg of a creative individual into the square hole of conformity. Even with a generous sweetening with social entitlement, hopefully it is clear why the future is starting to get harder to control. Is the current system the best we can do to promote creativity, resilience, and greatness?

Most importantly, are you still feeling creative?

Most leaders still seem to subscribe to the notion of Pareto's 80/20 Principle, where 80 percent of the value of any organization is created and driven by 20 percent of the people. Those 20 percent hate the silly rules and restrictions built for accommodating their "average" co-workers and colleagues.

Now, think about all the rules "good," progressive, democratic intentions have created to chasten those who strive for excellence; take speed limits, for example. Think now about how rules to increase the entitlement culture have blossomed during this time. What if this whole mediocre process of protecting the sweet spot of the population bell curve destructively undermines the creativity, agility, and entrepreneurship needed to remain world-class? Would this also sow the seeds for entrepreneurs to move and find more open cultures and friends, or to create ways to quickly topple this unstable paradigm? Would agile behavior be an advantage? What was it that attracted all the immigrants to the United States between 1850 and 1950? What is it that is forcing people to move from San Francisco, New York, and Chicago, not to mention France, today?

When successful, rich, risk-taking entrepreneurs move from an area due to crushing new tax burdens and less social and ethical constraints:

- Who remains to start new businesses?
- Who chooses to remain?
- What is still attracted to move there?
- Who is forced to stay because they have no choice?
- Who will now pay, and with what, for the necessary societal services?

The increasingly precarious nature of the organization

The precarious nature of employment is not happening in a vacuum. The turbulence brought about by globalization, and the competition it causes, has put enormous stress on business margins all over the world. A certain rebalancing between the high wages and benefits of the West and the low wages in the East is causing massive dislocation of work from one end of the globe to the other. In order to survive and thrive, companies have been forced to seek out the most efficient places in the world to get what they need done. The destination keeps changing at an increasing rate. This, of course, adds to the instability of employment and quality ultimately suffers. For those of you old enough to have purchased a "standard pair" of blue jeans forty years ago and compare them to the quality of a standard pair today will notice a distinct difference between both price and quality.

How can you be expected to concentrate on doing a good job when you are preoccupied, worried about what you will be doing when your latest temp job is over? Just as importantly, how can you—as a business leader—concentrate on delivering a quality product when you are forced to focus on saving costs and moving locations all the time?

The death of socialism?

Consider the amount of debt that has been issued since the progressive movement started in the end of the nineteenth century. Recently debt has begun multiplying exponentially as the financial shockwaves from the 2008–2010 Great Recession continue to reverberate through the global economy. Without going into the detail that can easily be found by Googling the phrase "world debt," one question stands out: "How will governments, funded by taxpayers, ever repay all the debt that is now outstanding?"

Getting votes by promising more than you have resources to pay for has become a way of life for career politicians. The only way this system has been held together so long is by the use or implied use of force. Paraphrasing economist Murray Rothbard, "With government's monopoly on violence, the chances are that when 'other people's money' is mentioned it will probably mean yours." What if the cornerstone of socialism is the government's legal ability to take from you the money you have earned and then distribute it to others? How is this accomplished? It is done through the implied threat of violence using a police officer's gun, the threat of incarceration in prison, or both. What if the more voters a savvy politician can turn into beneficiaries of other people's money, the better their chances for re-election? The tighter the grip on power, the more promises need to be made. What if this works until such a time when the amount promised can no longer be taxed, borrowed, or printed? Increasing evidence, such as basic income, suggest that this is the reality we may now finally be waking up to.

Just like the erosion of quality in blue jeans over the past forty years, no matter where you live in Western society you are probably beginning to notice deterioration in the quality of public and private services offered. You don't have to believe anything above. You are still offered an invitation to observe the increase in crises occurring and the corresponding increase in laws and regulations sold to you as "for your own good."

Look no further than your face mask to see something that has not been comprehensively nor clinically tested, yet is being touted as necessary to stop the spread of a viral infection (by public servants often filmed removing them once after delivering their scary message).

> "Just remember, a genuinely deadly pandemic doesn't require 24/7 advertising to remind you it exists. Real pandemics don't need marketing campaigns and endless propaganda . . . but psychological operations do."
> —**Unknown**

This current situation may still suggest that becoming more vigilant and agile is a prudent and perhaps healthier choice.

Volatility, confidence, and trust

Increasing amounts of evidence are now being revealed that point to the theory that economic booms and busts are not financial in origin, but rather a phenomenon based upon levels of public trust and confidence. When people are confident in their futures, then they are more willing to spend and thus the economy grows. As Armstrong Economics points out, "We are more willing to take a loan out, regardless of the interest charged, if we know with confidence that we can make money on it." On the other hand, when confidence in the future begins to wane, the economy begins to contract. People begin saving and hoarding. How does the current economic climate feel to you and your team and how can it affect your business going forward?

A reminder of Rome

There is lots of information available comparing the rise and fall of the Roman Empire with our current state of affairs. The major point here is that what started out as an agile step forward in human progress ultimately collapsed and self-destructed, with the help of the Huns, into the dark ages. Historians and even economists point to many examples of the greed and self-absorption of many of Rome's rulers. Interestingly, it has also been noted that toward the end of the Roman Empire, war, sex, entertainment, and food were the focus while Roman society disintegrated. Sound familiar?

The pursuit of personal pleasure, in the midst of societal decline, became the order of the day. Most Romans apparently didn't seem to notice when their ability to maintain their lifestyle began to disappear. They seemed to be quite content with "bread and circuses," which is a reference to the poet Juvenal's famous *panem et circensus*. Most only noticed after the government had bled Roman society's money, energy, and creativeness dry. Roman homeowners actually began abandoning their homes for the wilderness when taxes became too high. At that point, it became easy for the "Barbarians at the Gates" to open those gates and pick over and destroy what was left. Even today, buried Roman treasure is being found, usually far from a city. These coins seem to have been deliberately taken out of circulation, hoarded and hidden. Evidence seems to suggest it was buried by families to hide it from predatory authorities and in the hope of being able to put it to use in building a better future. This buried evidence would suggest that the future they hoped for did not return in time.

In short, the great Roman society failed when an elite few tried to inhibit the creativity, energy, and agility of the many. Rome stopped looking ahead and instead focused upon consuming what was already available. "The older I get, the better I was" may be a catchy slogan, but it sums up the danger of a person, organization, or society that loses that vital sense of focus on the future and their drive to master the ability to remain young at heart and agile.

A coming collapse in confidence?

Although many have written both positively and negatively about finance as the ultimate confidence game, research by Martin Armstrong of Armstrong Economics has tracked the collapse of societies going back further than the fall of Rome. His well-documented conclusion is that what ultimately causes a country's or region's economy and then its society to collapse is a loss of public confidence in the contemporary system and hence, the ability of those leaders who created the mess, to lead.

Take a closer look at what is happening in Europe, particularly to Greece, Italy, and Spain. Look at Japan and what is referred to as Abenomics and see if you can make common, logical, or business sense of it. Look at how much money is owed by each citizen in the US, especially if you include what is both 'on budget' and 'off budget.' Estimates range from the official $17 trillion to more than $200 trillion if all future governmental commitments to pay are included. Divide that number by the 309 million citizens, or better yet by the estimated 150 million who actually pay taxes and you may begin to get a sense of why anxiety and distrust continues to build.

Despite a rising stock market due to the cheapest money possibly ever, our current global economic situation continues to rot from the inside, while we continuously wake up to newer and stronger laws regarding taxes and money flow. More and more, it seems just a question of time before we are forced to collectively look for more agile, outside-the-box solutions, which may increasingly not have the blessing of our current batch of rulers.

You need look no further than the turmoil against politics-as-usual to see that the public seems to be losing faith in their ruling elite and their "market tested" message. From Brexit to the US presidential elections, voters are starting to turn their backs on the candidates and advice served up to them via traditional mainstream media outlets. This growing rejection of politics as usual seems to be slowly spreading all over the globe, cultivating increasing uncertainty for the future. Could another term for this rising interest in outside-the-box politics be agility?

The dangers of business as usual: The *Titanic* revisited

Figure 13. The *Titanic* on that fateful night

How can we start a serious discussion about being agile and using sailing the ocean as a metaphor without one last, reflective look at a saga-like catastrophe, known to the world as the *Titanic* disaster of April, 1912? Imagine being on the maiden voyage of a ship reckoned to be so safe that the management only installed half the lifeboats needed, ostensibly to make more room to walk on deck! The ship was commanded by a certain Captain E. J. Smith, who was on his final cruise and had been taught to speed up when entering an iceberg field to get through it faster. You were to be saved by a crew that had little or no emergency training. A ship that was so big and had such a small rudder that turning quick enough to avoid icebergs turned out to be a textbook example of "too little, too late." Safety was compromised again and again in favor of headlines and firsts. These hubris-driven mistakes cost two-thirds of the passengers on board their lives. Although the term wasn't invented until much later, the *Titanic* and her crew also had all the characteristics of being Too Big To Fail and yet it failed miserably. It might be more food for thought that this black-swan catastrophe occurred in the middle of a crystal-clear night on a mirror-like sea.

This is before we even consider that there may have been manipulation in the background. For instance, why did most of the firemen, those who shoveled the coal, decide to quit and leave the ship when they reached the first port of Southampton? Why did J.P. Morgan, a major owner of the White Star Line and never one to shun free publicity, decide to cancel his ticket, at the last minute, on the maiden voyage of the biggest, most prestigious ship, which he indirectly owned?

Today's challenges, only some of which are mentioned above, could cause disaster one by one. Yet the danger exponentially increases due to their increasing interconnectedness. A fateful comedy of errors was much in evidence with the loss of *Titanic*. Moving away from our nautical metaphor and back to our current situation, all these forces are increasingly becoming interconnected and are building in intensity at a growing rate. Being able to meet them will require an extra strong dose of agility coupled with a much faster, plus more decisive and practical response time.

Even "crash and burn" may present opportunity!

"Everybody has a plan until they get hit in the face."
—Mike Tyson

With human nature being what it is and with human history documenting our nature again and again, it should be of no surprise that current behavior often becomes habitual, until some great crisis or catastrophe forces us to change. It is Dr. Lipton's growth or protection again. This is the nature of both cycle theory as well as our tendency to seek pleasure and avoid pain. In other words, we are programmed to try to avoid pain and just get on with our lives until the pain becomes often ridiculously and sometimes tragically unavoidable. With all the geopolitical uncertainty, the health threat and subsequent economic lockdown, could this be the situation we are again beginning to face?

This behavior also gives us a physiological explanation as to why agile growth, from a cellular level upward, predictably morphs into a protective type of business as usual. Therefore, considering the incredibly good run we have had for the past thirty-plus years and unless human nature has fundamentally changed, we can expect another cycle of crash and burn to appear on the not-too-distant horizon. Keep in mind that down waves usually happen quicker and with more force than the upward ones. With the laws of physics being also what they are, the longer you postpone a given outcome, the larger and more powerful the consequences usually become.

Yet even during the height of the Great Depression, fortunes were made for those who chose to be creative, look forward, and gingerly respond to the prevailing market conditions. For instance, Charles Ives, a famous composer of that period, made a fortune up to and during the Depression by running his own insurance company. In 1930, he retired from business and eventually won a Pulitzer Prize in music. Another story was that of Irving Weiss, a young investor who sold all his stocks before the Depression and borrowed money from his mother at the market low in 1932 and began buying trusted names, at bargain basement prices!

Perfect storms come and go. Yet just as Mother Nature never gives up, neither do the agile among us. Right now, navigating through all the obstacles currently aligned against you may be your greatest challenge ever, but for those of us who thrive on challenges, this may be the most opportunistic period ever. Agility will help!

PART III

Get Agile Now!

Get agile now!

Congratulations! You have now successfully navigated through some exciting megatrends that we see are now influencing us. You have also been introduced to a collection of our favorite major storm warnings currently appearing on the horizon. Making it to this point in the book you can now justifiably take a breather and ask yourself the best business or life question there is: "So what?"

The answer to this important question and our heartfelt invitation to you is:

Get agile and do it quickly!

If you already understand and agree with us why agility will be the deciding success factor going forward and now just wish to get some practical management tools and advice on how to use them, please feel free to skip directly to section four.

Regardless of whether you continue on a rosy megatrend path to growth and success or "crash and burn" as forces of a perfect storm overwhelm you (or experience a powerful combination of both), one thing seems unavoidable: the rate of change looks likely to increase with every breath you take. Success can, of course, crush you as easily as failure. The most sensible and effective path is the one leading to surviving and thriving in this uncertain world. The name of this path is agility.

Returning to our nautical analogy, success in sailing a large boat depends upon seizing the moment and acting wisely, forcefully, and nimbly. The tactician must see and understand how market and environmental shifts can affect stated objectives, then quickly determine and implement alternative actions. With this information your navigator plots the optimal heading to reach the objective, and your skipper is there to coordinate all actions and, when necessary, override ineffective decisions. We see this same proven combination in the business team of CEO/COO, CFO (Chief Financial Officer), CMO (Chief Marketing Officer), and CHRO (Chief Human Resource Officer). Each of these officers must contribute as a key player in the integration and building of an effective sailing team. Please read on to discover what their toolboxes will need to contain going forward. Learn the steps of how they can listen, collaborate, and better work together toward success.

This book describes how any corporate ship, even those with thousands of logged miles at sea under their keels, can practice and master becoming even more agile. The following deck plan gives you an idea of our suggested cabin configuration. You will notice that the front of the boat consists of those cabins or departments that are and should remain focused upon the horizon. In the middle of any boat and placed somewhere above the middle of marketing, R&D between manufacturing and operations is the bridge. In the back, focused on creating and maintaining a powerful and true wake, is your powerplant and all your ship's supporting systems. These consist of finance, legal, and all administrative functions. We suggest your corporate ship be set up in the same way. This will offer you maximum agility. The key here is to keep your corporate yacht on an even keel even when the sea turns against you. Often it is too easy to run toward the back of the boat and to check and recheck your power plant and gauges, instead of focusing upon the horizon and the storms and rocks dead ahead. Just by staying in the more stable and comfortable part of the back of the boat will in no way calm the seas that you will shortly be sailing into. Vigilance and a clear view will be necessary to maintain agility.

Very often, established companies such as those that have been honing their business models for the longest time, can have much better staying power and resilience than many entrepreneurial start-ups. Their biggest challenge remains to get their systems, organization, culture, and processes in more agile shape and then re-focus forward toward the new and changing horizon. To encourage this process, the following deck plan may be worth framing and putting up on a prominent wall on your corporate bridge.

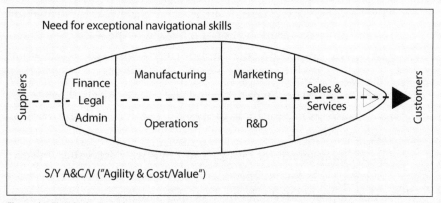

Figure 14. The deck plan of your corporate ship

The final and crucial ingredient is the ability to overcome the most common inhibitors to this process and take conscious and decisive action. The first batch of our powerful tools to help you will be discussed in the fourth section.

The prior two sections, "Megatrends" and "The Perfect Storm," strive to convincingly describe how increasingly volatile our world is becoming. They also indicate that globalization, information, and new technologies will create exponential growth and encourage radically new ways of doing things. This massive wave of innovation and disruption will continue to dramatically shorten all product, service, and business cycles!

This fact will naturally create new challenges for the leaders of both corporations and institutions. As some of the more potent new technologies, such as big data analytics and AI, evolve, targeting, speed, and accuracy of decision-making will improve further, leaving execution of those more accurate decisions as the greatest leadership challenge. What if many current leaders will be found to be weak, irresolute, and lacking integrity? They may well be discovered to have no clear muscle when it comes to achieving short or long-term aims under increased pressure. Many leaders who have consistently received high scores in their rhetorical prowess will find themselves cornered by serious circumstances and will receive zero scores in measurable action. Although there will certainly be some charlatans in this group, many goodhearted leaders will buckle mainly due to inexperience and the grit necessary to handle a real crisis. The consequence of shorter product/service cycles will force the governance of corporations and institutions alike to get serious about practicing:

- **Exceptional navigational ability** and the need to stringently focus forward toward the horizon instead of the wake.
- **Dramatic improvements in both strategic and operational agility,** to better anticipate and execute the next move. They must be nimble enough to act quickly and decisively through the company's entire business process to continually improve their competitiveness.
- **Building a selective, quick, and effective cost/value culture,** where people know what a cost leak or threat and/or an extra value opportunity looks like, as well as what to do. They must practically respond to stop more leakage by selectively adjusting the value, price or cost on popular products and features.

CHAPTER 9

The Age of Agility is Here

Want to know what happens if you choose not to personally get agile?

Take a bus or train or look into most cars on the way into any major city during rush hour and notice the quality of life around you. Chances are that you will witness the "working dead" we have already mentioned. Are you inspired by what you see?

More often than not, you will probably be surrounded by those who are still lucky enough to have jobs, sitting there in some level of resignation. Look closely at their level of enthusiasm:

- The way they shuffle and drag their feet
- How they seem to breathe just enough to survive rather than inspire
- How they stare through the windshield and tightly grip their steering wheel
- The preoccupied "light is on, nobody's home" look in their eyes
- How they treat you as an obstacle in their path

The older they look, the more resigned they often appear. On the way to work, most are trying to distract themselves—with their smart gadget, book, or music—from all the challenges they will soon face at work. On the way home, many will have their eyes shut or their headphones in, blocking out as much outside stimulus as possible, while they seem to sit collapsed into their seats. Granted, there are those bubbly, intrepid people that you meet who seem to thrive on adversity, but how many of your fellow travelers look a bit more subdued?

Especially for those nearing retirement, it is now obvious that most people still working are responsible for the tasks of what two to four people used to do. Not only this, but when you subtract inflation, current average wages have now shrunk back to levels not seen since the 1970s.

Prices have risen drastically since then, especially recently, and most of us now need to work much harder and longer to make ends meet. The prognosis looks to be more of the same or worse. How are you, as a leader, going to get your increasingly urgent message of yet more change to emotionally move your inhibited, system-oriented, business-as-usual people into quick, decisive, often radical action?

As computers and robotics continue to improve in performance and dexterity, many jobs and even careers that were safe a few years ago are now in jeopardy of becoming extinct. We mentioned that McDonald's is responding to employee demands of fifteen dollars per hour wages, not just by caving into these demands, but rather by installing new self-service ordering and grilling machines. There are now capable robots that can take orders and payment; others fry hamburgers perfectly, without the need for coffee breaks, and have zero wage complaints. Can you guess what this means to an unskilled, less-agile service worker? For the rest of those workers in retail, the thought of self-service machines combined with drastically increasing competition from the internet is now driving a perfect storm in the traditional brick and mortar retail model. And these words were written before COVID-19 accelerated the robotic trend exponentially. Even Walmart's continued success and bottom line are now being questioned. Is it any wonder with paychecks shrinking and the threat of unemployment rising that the amount of inspired-looking commuters is reaching all-time lows?

Make no mistake. This same phenomenon described by Joseph Schumpeter as creative destruction works on both a personal and company level. The bigger the company or personal ego, the more it takes to retain or enhance your agility.

Regardless of whether you are unemployed and capable, unskilled and working, middle class and worried, a successful entrepreneur, or a rich and fully invested corporate titan, the quicker you become more consciously agile, the more you will be able to remain being "the captain of your ship."

What if "get agile or die" is more than just our catchy meme?

Too big to fail, and succeed versus agility

One of the biggest impediments to change, as well as another important reason that we will be hard pressed to avoid an inevitable perfect storm, is the advent of Too Big to Fail. It seems to have started in the banking business but has quickly spread, for instance, to TBTF government. In each of these cases, companies and governing bodies have merged and grown into untenable behemoths. If we believe their well-paid-for hype, they are now so big that it would create tragic consequences for society, should they be allowed to fail. Even a rudimentary understanding of history or a memory of that childhood saying, "The bigger they are, the harder they fall," will remind you that this will not end well. Now ask yourself if this behavior makes any business sense at all.

Through mergers, acquisitions, attrition, and easy money-fueled growth, some large organizations have increased in size to the point of being untenable. What became very clear in the Great Recession of 2008–2009 is that some organizations were seen, at least by those in charge and their friends making our laws, to be Too Big to Fail. The story sold to the public was that certain financial and industrial behemoths, such as some large, well-known banks and even General Motors, to name a few, were given a special treatment based on that if they went bust, it would be catastrophic for the American and possibly the world. Therefore, they were bailed out with public tax money and given special super-legal rights to allow them to keep operating beyond the point where most a sane or honest accountant would have declared them bankrupt.

Who besides the benefactors will benefit from something that, by all rational measures of business performance, should have failed, but was forcibly kept alive? Just in the context of this book, propping something up further that is destined to fail while continuing business as usual is about as far from agile as you can get. These organizations are almost always politically connected and routinely lobby for laws to further protect their existence and thwart younger, more agile competition. If this isn't enough, in the last crisis, your tax money was used to bail out and save these private companies. If we pay attention to history, all these band-aids will work until they don't. If you are not agile enough to respond when this house of TBTF cards finally collapses, good luck.

This adds yet another dimension to the words "business agility." What business agility really means is that you not only have to be agile enough to handle the megatrends and the perfect storm brewing on the horizon, but you also have to be agile enough to handle all the "emergency legislation" enacted to protect this privileged, connected, and moneyed few. This is probably the toughest challenge, as they can and usually have changed the playing field over a night or weekend to better suit their needs. This trend of TBTF combined with what is referred to as crony capitalism is no longer hidden in the shadows. For instance, the trans-Atlantic and pacific partnerships were laws, brought forth by your elected "public servants," were so secret that their contents could not be revealed to voters until five years after their passing. This stunning, extremely anti-democratic fact was uncovered and disrupted by a certain president who, surprisingly, was ridiculed by those lawmakers that crafted and voted for these partnerships!

Don't forget that when the famous 2010 Obamacare health bill was up for a vote, the Speaker of the House, an elected representative ostensibly for the people of the State of California and Speaker of the US House of Representatives, was quoted as saying, "We have to pass the bill so that you can find out what is in it, away from the fog of the controversy[1]." Do you sense a disconnect in the "representative Democratic process"? Who now represents whom or what? This method of doing business depends directly upon who is in power at that moment, their personal agenda, and often to whom they owe a favor. This is a public confirmation of "it's not what you know, but who you know," a nation of people rather than a nation of laws. Avoiding being agile enough to sense who is in whose pocket, leaves you one new piece of legislation away from business catastrophe. For the honest and agile businessperson, this adds an extra dimension of stress, as who being of sound mind would dare take a political promise at face value any longer?

To even act at all may turn out to be the wrong decision. Yet not acting may also be equally as destructive. How will you know when the situation can change and then change again overnight? We humans are designed to change behavior to accommodate new situations. Unfortunately, if we do not understand the situation or are blindsided by some totally unexpected occurrence, we will probably end up acting irrationally, further helping to "dislocate the market." As economist John Maynard Keynes once wrote,

"The market can remain irrational longer than you can stay solvent." Yet, the longer imbalances persist, the smaller the catalyst needs to be to create havoc. Think of that one extra snowflake that lands on an imbalanced ledge of snow, high up on the mountain, causing a catastrophic avalanche into the valley below, which shows you that agility is nothing without a sense of timing.

This uncertain environment supports and indeed adds fuel to the precariousness of both the market and your employment situation. It absolutely confounds the ability of even wise and experienced corporate leaders to plan for the future. For now, there doesn't seem to be any complete solution for the precarious nature of today's market and the moneyed players controlling it; yet becoming more agile cannot hurt.

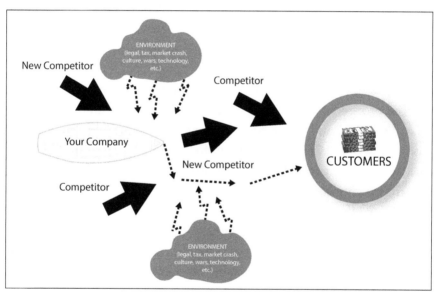

Figure 15. Your need for business agility

The agility imperative

"Lead, follow, or get out of the way."
—As seen on the desk of CNN's founder, Ted Turner

What do the few opportunities and challenges we have outlined in these first two sections of this book point to? They demand an increase in your business agility and leadership ability in order to more effectively lead, follow, or get out of the way, faster. If you want to remain in a profitable and sustainable business, the demands to do so keep rising. There is little to no sympathy for those who miss even one important market signal. By making just one bad decision, becoming cancelled due to one questionable post, or missing one important new piece of legislation, you and your organization may be out for good. And even this blinding pace of change is still accelerating.

Viral agility

Business agility needs to become a lifestyle, one that is taken on at all levels within an organization and by each individual. At this point you may agree that the decision to get agile is a no-brainer, but what if that makes it akin to implementing a budget cut?

Everyone is for saving money!

That is, as long as the cuts occur in someone else's department.

The process of becoming agile is bound to reveal inhibitors, traditions, behaviors, and systems that are not only ineffective, but also well entrenched and desirable to maintain for someone, even you. Resistance that inhibits changes in these "legacy" issues are bound to cause irritation and confrontation. Yet to really become agile they must be addressed, quickly and effectively.

In terms now used on the internet, business agility needs to go viral. It needs to seep into every nook and cranny throughout your organization and into each individual team member's cells in order for it to really make a measurable and decisive difference.

With agility, both privilege and risk increase for those in responsible positions. Getting everyone on board and empowering your whole team, even with understanding all the megatrends and the perfect storm clouds, will be challenging! A new level of agile collaboration, cooperation, and connection will be needed to stretch from your shareholders to your boardroom, embrace your organization, extend out to each individual customer and beyond. Heartfelt internal cooperation, accurately focused upon servicing individual customer needs, wants, and wishes must be constantly strengthened, cultivated, and reviewed.

Every process needs to be looked at with conscious curiosity, increasingly revisited and updated, throughout your entire organization. This means even looking at relationships between, for instance, management and employees, HR and unions, customers and customer service. To be effective going forward also means dealing with the fear of internal competition and the destructive behavior it can encourage. Finally, it is critical to begin appreciating and cultivating a culture of empowerment.

What if knowledge is power, but understanding leads to empowerment?

Parents usually feel they have accomplished the task of correctly raising their offspring when their children enjoy better life, filled with more opportunity than they did. This mindset needs to become the norm for business leaders, too. Management needs to tackle their role and transform themselves into worthy and respected leaders, capable of mastering their role of cultivating people to become better than they are. Empowerment inspires and expands.

To manage or to lead an agile group?

To become agile, fundamental traits and roles will have to be re-examined. Tools, methods, and work roles, developed for the industrial age, no longer provide the same level of impact. They are increasingly becoming a heavy drag on development. For instance, what if something still as accepted as the conventional manager role is also a stubborn holdover from the industrial age? What if the traditional role of manager has now become an industrial age anachronism?

Think about it. The role of management was developed during a time of scarcity; scarcity of resources, time, and capital. Resources in those days included bricks, wood, nails, and water. Resources also included an extra pair of hands and a stronger back. As we have discussed, we now live in an era of abundance. Resources are cheaper and more accessible than at any other time in human history. Unfortunately, the word resources still routinely includes "human resources."

Rear Admiral Grace Hopper once eloquently observed that, "You manage things and you lead people." The more you make people feel like things, the more they will either resent it or resign themselves to it. Regardless, their dignity as human beings will decrease, their energy will dissipate, and their performance will suffer. The ultimate result will be that your customers will no longer remain loyal, and your bottom line will pay the price. To paraphrase Admiral Hopper, your leadership must inspire, empower, and expand your fellow colleagues or it will revert to being a compressive management of things.

Most millennials you will meet have never known want and are irritatingly used to having their own way. They are also the most educated generation ever and although they may often not act like it, they are very responsible, and capable. Most of all, they will accept being inspired to do something, but they absolutely do not like and usually resist being told what to do.

Now, what is a manager's traditional role?

Their job is to apply scarce resources, in the most effective way, to produce or accomplish a result. This involves taking decisions, directing/commanding resources (both human and not) efficiently, and measuring the results. After all, "you have to break a few eggs to make an omelet."

Right here and now we have:

- Decision-making software that can take more objective and more effective decisions much faster than any human
- RFID chips and ID cards that automatically monitor where people are and give a very good picture of what they are doing
- Cameras and surveillance technology that are well above and beyond what is necessary to ensure someone is working effectively
- An educated workforce that can be given a goal and then encouraged to figure out the best way to achieve it

Leadership means focusing on what's left. Creating specific, measurable goals and then inspiring those tasked to achieve them toward success. Good leaders leave the how up to the ones doing the job. This means letting go, creating more space for things to happen and trusting your hiring, teamwork and leadership skills.

What is the point of someone still lodged in an administrative role, commanding others while being paid more than their colleagues, when those doing the work can and should be charged with, responsible for, and accountable to produce the desired result? This type of management role is finally being revealed as the predatory (and costly) role of babysitting it has now devolved into.

These are all reasons why managing people rather than *leading* them is rapidly becoming a recipe for disaster. Sophisticated software programs can now allocate resources and streamline processes quickly, thereby freeing up managers to focus on leading, empowering, and encouraging people rather than just managing them.

As we have noted already, a large part of being agile has to do with being open, receptive, and compassionate, to name just a few qualities. Interestingly, a leader who easily attracts willing followers demonstrates those exact same qualities. So, if you want to become more agile, learn to lead. If you want to lead better, become more agile.

For instance, what about basing future leadership promotions and raises at least partly upon the number of employees or associates who surpass their boss in the organizational structure? Can your organization any longer afford treating your ability to cultivate your colleagues' skills, to the point that they are better than yours, as a personal threat or failure? Instead, your ability to master teaching others to practice the skills needed to make your organization more agile and successful should be acknowledged and celebrated! Your skill in bringing out your colleague's best needs to be trumpeted as part of your success!

Creating agile awareness

Agility becomes more powerful the more you become aware of what it means. As we are creatures of habit, we usually do what we have always done. That is until we get hit over the head with the realization that it no longer works. With all the stuff you have to do during the day, how often do you find time to discover new alternatives when older, trusted, and comfortable methods/behaviors already exist?

Keep this in mind when you are communicating to customers and colleagues alike. Unless you can clearly demonstrate that you have a better, more agile suggestion that can produce measurable results here and now, your listener may politely listen, but chances are they will continue to do what they know and feel comfortable with. We get bombarded with more and more information every day. This makes it even more important that what you say is not only technically correct, but the message also has to emotionally "move" your listener into action too. The more agile your ability to communicate becomes, the more chances you will have to accomplish this.

Practically, this means that you need to inspire and engage your listeners with both facts and feelings. It is no longer enough to leave your listeners with bullet-proof logic; you have to generate actionable understanding of what you want them to buy or do. Remember, "Knowledge leads to debate, understanding leads to action," and measurable action is what keeps things moving.

Think of the metaphor of something you know sitting in a box on some high but inaccessible ledge. Then think of that same bit of information that is anchored from underneath, standing tall and attractive for all to see and connect with. How often do you leave your listeners with more knowledge instead of taking them to the active level of understanding? What is lacking for your listener to experience an actionable "aha" moment?

This is more often than not a question of simplifying (instead of complicating) your message. Simple is much easier and quicker to action upon than unnecessarily complicated, with more alternatives and bigger words.

"The Mind cannot argue with simplicity."
—Patrick Collard

To move into action, the left and right hemispheres of the brain need to synchronize on the thought. The right hemisphere is more concerned with aesthetics, form, and feeling, whereas the left hemisphere is more concerned with results that can be measured. Synchronizing and harmonizing these two hemispheres is no easy task. Often, if you break your message down to the least common denominator and add your heartfelt passion to its essence, this potent blend will help. Break complicated topics down into bite size chunks and add a bit of emotion, and you will begin to feel the agility. This practice brings actionable results to your brand of leadership. Test and see if you become more appreciated and followed as a leader who can explain things in a way people feel moved to act upon. This is the path of agile leadership mastery.

Compression versus expansion

Agility has to do with anchoring and expanding a possibility into a measurable action. Business as usual is about status quo and limiting or inhibiting new possibilities. When we talk of incorporating agility into an organization, it may be wise to compare your corporate body to your physical one. Compressed tissue stops the natural flow of blood, causing tension and pain. It uses more energy and results in increasing stiffness, pain and entropy. Relaxed tissue is expansive and blood flows through it much more efficiently. It feels good and increases your agility and resilience.

What does your ability to sense compression and expansion have to do with communication, relationships, and business?

This question may be better framed as what sensing compression or expansion *does not* have to do with communication, relationships, and business!

I recently witnessed an interaction between a board member and his accountant over an important accounting question. The answer to this question would basically mean a difference between the company breaking even or being stuck with a large debt on the books. The board member was used to and very good at driving his point home with a series of well-structured arguments and justifications. The accountant was used to bullet-proof accounting practices that would stand the most determined tax office scrutiny. The challenge was that the board member needed the accountant's support to implement his well-thought-out solution. Although legal and viable, his solution landed a bit outside the comfort zone of his accountant's standards and his meticulous accounting practices.

What made this interaction so interesting was that the more the board member brilliantly argued for his case, the more compressed and guarded the accountant became. His willingness to help slowly disappeared and each valid and argumentative point drove him deeper into his defensive shell. Both people wanted to solve the situation, but their well-used communication tools and accompanying behaviors were now working against them. The board member was now caught in the common trap of using his favorite tools, the ones that had brought him so much success, in a situation where their use was making matters worse.

Agility on a personal level means exercising your senses more (especially listening) and training more to recognize how you are, in this case, pushing your listener further away from your goal with each additional word you say. What if instead you tried a few curious and inviting questions, then sought some expert advice from your accountant?

In fact, this ended up happening. At a critical moment in their discussion, the frustrated board member asked the accountant to please give him some feedback on what he saw for possibilities. With this little, delicate bit of coaxing, the accountant thought for a moment, then picked up his phone and called his tax expert to explain the situation. The tax expert responded by going methodically through a SWOT analysis before agreeing to look into how the proposed solution could be implemented. A bitter argument that had been festering for months was moved successfully forward; just by employing a curious question, presented as open invitation to dance.

Now, think how often this same compression phenomenon happens in conversations and relationships within your organization. Just think of how many times your company's relationships and business flow are measurably inhibited by such compressions as:

- A salesperson who oversells someone. In the process he gets politely thrown out, or the customer sheepishly buys what is being offered, only to embarrassingly return it the next day and never be seen or heard of again.

- A manager who commands his staff to spend their increasingly scarce and precious time filling in useless reports for headquarters, without explaining the reason. Rumors start circulating about reorganization, yet management refuses to confirm or deny them. This causes everyone to begin spending more time and energy on checking the latest rumors, protecting their livelihoods, and looking for new jobs instead of performing their mission-critical functions.

- A customer service agent, who is so eager to demonstrate his expertise and efficiency that his well-intended and correct attempts to solve the complaint are interpreted as downright rude. The customer, who feels neither heard nor understood, keeps getting interrupted before she can finish expressing her thought and leaves the call totally frustrated, never again to return.

- An employee throwing someone out of a store or restaurant for not wearing a mask or wearing it wrong (the latest addition). The alternative to this is refusing service to someone because of some sort of political statement on their shirt or hat. These situations usually do not happen in a silent vacuum and more and more are being filmed and later posted for all to see.

In each one of these all-too-common situations, the conversation as well as some of the people involved became compressed. The relationships involved and everyone's resulting ability to do business is damaged or destroyed. The listeners go from growth into protection mode, batten down their hatches and thus impede their ability to hear newer and more viable possibilities. Where is the agility or service in the speaker's presentation or behavior? Keep in mind that in each situation described here, and in many others, everyone on both sides most likely had good intentions, but did it matter?

Becoming agile means practicing to sense when a conversation or relationship begins to compress, then using the correct conversational tools to halt and reverse the process. This magical tool usually starts simply by curiously asking some thoughtful and inviting questions. Then you can invite your listener to brainstorm with you on other possibilities. This is just one of the simple tools you can use to expand any conversation.

Being curious, asking thoughtful questions, and listening closely and respectfully to how others answer separates leadership from management! It invites the kind of give and take increasingly necessary to get something agreed upon and done with busy co-workers in today's stressed environment. Again, the simplest and most agile conversational tools for this process are curiosity, questions, and invitations, followed by a good dose of listening, understanding, confirmation, and action.

Much nimbler in steering our ship

Becoming nimbler is a function of being able to be present to, and gracefully handle, what is going on right here and now. Being burdened by thinking too much or having to remember and invoke the policy on your corporate rulebook's page 132 will greatly inhibit your capacity to be agile. You will be constantly filtering what is happening through all the preconditioning you have ever received. The more you commit to developing systems to minimize your own inhibitors, the more you will increase your capacity for curiosity and creativeness with others.

CHAPTER 10

Agile Decisions, Agile Executions

This book is about being agile enough to execute important decisions effectively and appropriately in real time. Therefore, this book is not written just to show how to make more agile decisions. It is written to help you to *act* and master executing those decisions with increased agility.

If we are successful with this book, then you will have better tools in your toolbox and more effective equipment on your corporate yacht with which to act upon important decisions swiftly, even when they are unpopular. Political correctness is not agility. In times of uncertainty, count on someone's feelings getting hurt. Acting decisively and engagingly is an unavoidable result of leadership, being "lonely at the top." Decisive action is imperative to become a respected leader who is worth following, even if it turns out to be wrong. If a child is playing in the street in front of an oncoming bus, the situation requires action first, then explanation—when safely on the sidewalk.

The art and practice of decision-making has been in focus for many years and there is more than enough good literature available on how to best decide. In fact, with improved AI applications, your computer will continue to handle more decision-making processes much more effectively and objectively than you. What is still sorely lacking are simple, understandable, and powerful leadership tools to effectively implement your decisions, plus an effective way to measure, adjust, and learn from each.

The tools you will soon read about in section four will help execute and implement critical changes quickly and are a major part of what makes this book unique. In the final part of our book, you will be introduced to these tools. You will also be instructed as to the fundamental steps to use them. You will be encouraged to change course quickly and to implement procedures and systems that can prevent you from falling back into business as usual. Practicing doing this by motivating your listeners, rather than dictating to them, will further ensure success.

Therefore, the purpose of this book is to demonstrate beyond a doubt for you, dear reader, that to go forward, it is to not just to get agile or die, but to get agile and thrive. Doing or living business as usual is no longer enough to ensure your company's or your family's survival, much less your success. Training to be and consciously act agile, as we suggest, takes an enormous amount of commitment and energy for even the most healthy and smartest among us. Many of our tools go stridently against convention. But what is the alternative?

As the pace of change quickens and both the opportunities and storm clouds increase in frequency and size, you will need to develop your ability to sense what is happening and sense it in many dimensions. Then you must quickly act and do it decisively; motivate your crew for them in turn to execute their duties with power and grace. Missing a key bit of information or misreading an emotional turning point could result in financial and/or personal disaster.

Peril and agility

Navigating in the Swedish archipelago during a storm is a bigger challenge than a similar storm on the high seas. The reason? Rocks! There is literally a mountain range directly under the surface. Disregarding this extra, unseen level of challenge puts you, your boat, and your crew directly in harm's way. You need to monitor your depth gauges even closer as well as develop an intuitive sense of what lies underneath the water's surface.

The Swedish language has a word for this: *lyhördhet*. It means to listen with all your senses. From a practical sense, how can you expect to increase your physical agility without simultaneously increasing your ability to listen with all your senses? To do this may require you, as a leader, to go against current corporate convention. Increasing your ability to listen with all your senses means practicing to conscientiously feel and intuit what is going on around you. Behaving like this in the current international corporate atmosphere can still get colleagues talking behind your back or get you thrown out of the macho, good ole' boy network. In fact, the biggest critique of this book is this third section and its focus on "warm and fuzzy" soft skills. What do manners and suggestions have to do with running a large and prestigious company? What if the times as well as customer and employee expectations are changing fast?

The traditional, cold, calculating, head-in-the-sand type of behavior of not listening with all your senses can quickly become a liability to those who consciously or not believe in business as usual. Consciously or not, we have now raised one, probably two generations who have little or no allegiance and respect for their elders. They are now beginning to flex their business acumen and muscle. They also are expressing their growing distrust and often disdain for habits used by those currently in charge. Therefore, should you need to, you can justify practicing this non-conventional, soft behavior and compare it to the soft, agile behavior of a samurai or Native American warrior. Both were taught to develop and sharpen a keen and intuitive sense for what was happening within themselves as well as all around them, in real time. Compare that type of behavior to the poet Tennyson's soldiers[1] who were taught, "Theirs not to reason why, theirs is but to do and die." Then ask yourself if you would rather be an agile warrior with your senses highly tuned for any and all input, or a dutiful soldier blindly following orders. Who do you think risks the biggest chance of becoming the business equivalent of cannon fodder?

Ask most soldiers who have survived battle to describe the rigors of combat and they will usually say that it was those most perilous moments, within an inch of death, when they felt most alive. In fact, from soldiering and sailing to leading others, the closer you come to real or perceived personal peril, the more heightened your senses become. Now what if this ability to heighten your senses can be practiced and mastered? How much better would you then become when also armed with the best tools and equipment that current technology and experience have to offer? Would this give you a competitive edge?

This time is different

The greatest challenge is that when things have been so good for so long, human nature invites us to let our guard down. We then justify this and convince ourselves that life will always be as good as it is currently. Intuitively, you probably understand that life just doesn't work that way.

Yet we are wired so good times encourage us to think that this time is really different. Regardless, this comfort zone of Pollyanna thinking is most likely the biggest risk you will ever face. It represents being lured into an unfounded, false sense of security. Just think about the fate of many honest, law-abiding German Jews living comfortably within its borders during the 1930s. Many had even fought on the frontline during World War I. Some surely boarded their last train still thinking that this couldn't possibly happen in the beloved fatherland of their birth. Wouldn't you?

Business is just like nature; it goes in cycles. Why? Because human nature tempts us to be lazy when times are good and makes us get going when times become bad. Just as night follows day, count on cycles occurring, often when you least expect them.

Now the good news is that regardless of whether the future is dark or bright, can you see any downside with training to be more consciously agile? If nothing else, there is the possibility that you may develop further, learn something new, and be even more successful than you have already become. Agility is your razor-sharp edge! So regardless of your darkest fears and even if you are looking forward with hope toward a promising future, get ready for some tips to help you to better survive and thrive.

Does the future always belong to entrepreneurs?

Be careful of becoming too entrepreneurial. Entrepreneurs often tend to be very stubborn. This stubbornness, in the right circumstances, is what is necessary to get through those dark times when most new businesses fail. Yet, when changes are increasingly happening even faster, being stubborn can lead to catastrophe. Although he was later invited back, Steve Jobs was thrown out of Apple, the company he founded, at least partly for being too stubborn.

Smooth sailing . . . and batten down the hatches

There are many ways to describe the roots of human behavior. Since this book has a nautical theme, let's stick to it. When sailing, you either have favorable weather conditions or not. The more favorable these are, the more sails you can set and the faster and truer your course will be. In very stormy weather, crew behavior can quickly deteriorate into an "every man for himself" survival level. Then the outcome ends up depending upon how watertight your boat really is and how well you have trained your crew. Practicing your collective ability to listen and know when to change quickly from one to the other will help you better adjust to uncertain business seas and weather. This will also lessen the risk of missing a big change in it. Keep in mind, when things are going well, how often do you feel like changing your course or your behavior? Then, when you have been hunkered down in protection mode and the wind starts to lessen, how long before you dare trust your sense that the weather may actually be improving?

Ironically, when you have the hatches battened down and are struggling to survive, that is often when you are forced to learn and grow more. Yet how agile do you feel at that particular moment? On the other hand, when things are sailing along smoothly, do you also go out of your way to inhibit change? Think about it. You are up on deck with a cool drink in your hand, the sun is shining, and you feel a warm breeze at your back. How much energy and what level of danger will it take to motivate you to get up and change course, even if you start seeing dark clouds way out on the horizon?

There is less resistance, and it is usually more fun, to remain in entertainment mode, saving work and learning for later. We have already seen that we seek ways to prolong the fun and actually impede change. The process of enjoyment actually encourages you to be a bit resistant and hinders any interruption of enjoyment. Given that we are all wired more or less the same, do you really think most of your colleagues, customers, partners or suppliers will behave any differently? How can they if they are hard-wired into the same genetic pain/pleasure system as you? This is the origin of our human habit of inhibiting change.

Although we might start out being wired the same way, the perception of our circumstances or surroundings may manifest in totally different and generate often conflicting behaviors just around the next island. As captain, you will need to listen to and understand your crew's individual and collective perceptions before attempting to change anything.

Defining and distinguishing agility

The word "agility" comes from the Latin *agilis*[2] and simply means "quick movement." Although this doesn't look so sexy at first glance, if you begin to see how inaction, resignation, and indifference are slowing our society down, agility becomes something to be increasingly sought after. Granted, not everyone is slow, and in fact, those who act using increased agility usually make out better than most.

This obvious fact can breed resentment among those who have resigned themselves that there is nothing that can be done to change the situation. Taking action now increasingly represents a threat to those who, consciously or not, would rather remain resigned. In fact, demonstrating business agility can actually stir up a debate, increase hostility and sometimes even sabotage from those who would rather just be left alone in their misery.

Definition

Donald Sull from McKinsey defines agility as, "The capacity to identify and capture opportunities more quickly than rivals do." But what if even this definition is too limiting?

Wikipedia says: "Agility is the ability to be quick and graceful on the basketball court or in the courtroom. The noun agility can be used for both physical and mental skills in speed and grace. Your mental agility might allow you to follow two conversations at once. We define it as the power of moving quickly and easily. Nimbleness in response time is the key."

Think of the metaphor where you are the skipper and see a boat coming directly at you. Even with a successful career of avoiding boats and icebergs to look back upon, Captain Smith of the *Titanic* missed just one, on the final voyage of his career, and the resulting disaster became the icon for all maritime disasters.

Does it rhyme with stability?

According to Wouter Aghina, Aaron De Smet, and Kirsten Weerda of McKinsey, you still can have your cake and eat it too. In their article "Agility: It rhymes with Stability," they point out that, "Companies can become more agile by designing their organizations both to drive speed and create stability[3]." They make the case that even big organizations can extract themselves from inhibiting traps, act entrepreneurial, be more agile while retaining chunks of their bureaucracy. Is this possible or just wishful thinking?

If we understand it correctly, their point is that their preliminary findings point toward that you can take all the "good" from a startup mindset and become more agile as long as you have a solid core or "backbone of stable elements." Well, maybe. Yet ask any back-surgery patient if they feel more agile and flexible after they have fused a few vertebrae together. Yes, the pain may subside, but that fused core makes being flexible much tougher to achieve. Our version of agility is to make the whole package flexible and to continuously figure out new ways to transform inhibiting traps and inflexible bureaucracy into a more agile way of doing business. A flexible organization around a stable but flexible core is absolutely a step in the right direction, but with the pace of change increasing, your whole organizational structure needs increased capacity to flexibly respond or eventually risk seizing up or breaking completely.

We would adjust their premise slightly and change "backbone" to a platform of stable elements (possibly inserting the word "values" for "elements"). Somewhere deep your organization, your crew needs to have some common ground (or mutual platform of values) to stand for and work from. Upon this needs to rest a common goal or set of goals to strive for, in order for everyone to succeed. Yet the stuff between the platform and goals needs to bend easily and readjust often, as circumstances become more uncertain and change even faster. Just as cranial-sacral bodywork focuses upon the skull and the sacrum in order to create more flexibility between them, in the spine, a company with agreed-upon common values coupled with agreed-upon and inspiring goals to strive for will end up being more agile than one that is anchored in tradition, overly structured and/or micromanaged.

The tools below will help you identify where and when major inhibiting factors and overwhelming bureaucracy may be draining life and agility out of your organization. Then you can take suggested, proven steps to loosen up the compression and build more flexibility into it. Tools such as Rolling Budget, Forward Decision Drivers and Carve-Outsourcing can provide a strong, supple, and responsive backbone to your organization, plus keep you vigilant and ready to adjust to changes happening out in front, on your economic horizon.

Some values of conscious agility

If we really want to become more agile in our lives and our businesses, it is important to get a better grasp of exactly what we mean. Being agile is a good start, but right off the bat, wouldn't being consciously agile give you a sharper edge? What other words would help us get a better understanding of a bigger possibility for agility? What are some of the properties and qualities of an organization steeped in conscious business agility?

The following list of words can be used to start a conversation on which should be used in a discussion of your organization's core values when shifting toward business agility. This is by no means a comprehensive list, but it does offer an invitation to reinvestigate what you and your colleagues stand for and from where you wish to work. Here are some suggestions:

Flexible

To move quickly, you definitely have to be flexible. Unfortunately, this word may not go far enough to describe what we are looking for. A piece of hose is flexible, but does it consciously know what to do with its flexibility?

Supple

This takes flexibility to another level. Sense, if you can, the soft fluid-like presence in this word. Maintaining a supple corporate or human body takes work, as does remaining agile, but the payoff is usually less stress and greater, more measurable result.

Soft and receptive

Soft may not mean just "silky" soft. It may mean the *spongy-like* ability to receive, absorb, and respond to information at a quicker rate. For example, ask yourself honestly, "Do I actually like to listen to understand what the speaker is saying, or am I just quietly waiting for my turn to talk?"

Vigilant

Keeping watch for storm clouds is more informative and practical than burying your nose in a book about bad weather. The more you practice tuning your senses to what is happening around you, the better your chances of making it to a safe hill before the next tsunami hits, be it financial, environmental, or otherwise.

Quick and decisive

Hesitating can sometimes mean the difference between life and death or riches and poverty. For instance, the more you can decisively act or not and how, by killing the alternatives[4], the quicker you can subsequently relax and adjust to the new changes.

Wise

> "We are creating a generation of intelligent idiots."
> **—Unknown**

There is a difference between being intelligent and being wise. This difference usually shows up in stressful situations. Your ability to think things through under pressure, applying a little common sense, may take more time than a snap decision. But, if an unfounded decision is taken too quickly, it may result in tragic damage. Never forget, sometimes it is even wiser to do nothing at all.

Vulnerable

This word has little to do with being weak and everything to do with being prepared, present, relaxed, open, and ready for anything. For any serious practitioner of martial arts, being vulnerable means having all your physical, mental, and even spiritual resources at the ready, to immediately meet your next threat or opportunity with full energy, resources, and enthusiasm.

Responsive

To respond means possessing the wherewithal to thoughtfully go beyond an automatic, programmed reaction, reflect upon the situation together with your options, and only then, answer back to the stimulus. Responding moves beyond those sticky behavioral patterns and those pesky emotional triggers. Agility allows you to use your wisdom, blend it with speed, and respond with the appropriate measure and force.

Responsible

Being responsive also requires *responsibility* or the retention of your ability to respond. This means that you are the source of the decision and/or answer, and most importantly, you own it and any resulting consequences.

Patrick Collard used to talk about the "Credit/Blame Game." This is where regardless of whether you are praising or blaming someone else for the result, you effectively discount your own power as well as your ability to respond. This is not leadership, and it is certainly not agility.

Playing the Credit/Blame game may work (up to a point) in politics, but if you are committed to practicing long-term business agility, sooner or later your lack of responsibility and accountability will be revealed. Count on it. Even when there is ample evidence that someone else is to blame, if you are ultimately responsible for that person you will be implicated at least for bad judgment. Will this revelation empower or erode the trust others have in your ability to lead? Will it ease or strengthen uncertainty around you and the decisions you make?

Being a decisive and empowering leader requires you to be responsive and take responsibility and accountability for all that occurs under you on your watch.

Respectful

Treating everyone with a sense of curiosity and wonder will energize you and them both to do what needs to be done together, even in times of stress. Listening with all your senses so your speaker feels seen, heard, and understood is one of the quickest and most effective ways to demonstrate respect. Curiously and actively listening to demonstrate your understanding that you really have no understanding of who they are will also help.

Compassionate

Dealing with others compassionately will make you a more attractive leader to follow. Empathy and compassion will also distinguish you as a leader of people from most other management types. Especially from those who have checked their emotions and feelings in the closet, in order to be more effective and goal oriented. What if a good dose of compassion will help you to sense what is going on much more effectively than just reading tables and charts? Whereas previous generations almost expected apathy and cold, calculated replies, the newer ones will not tolerate it. If you want to be respected and followed, practice compassion.

Present

Dealing with the here and now directly is much more effective than dealing with your idea of it. This may sound obvious, but until you can separate what you think you see, hear, and experience from what is actually happening in real time, your ability to practice agility will remain a compromised and dangerous shadow of its true potential. Perception is good, but dealing directly with reality, here and now, is better.

Courageous

To act or express from your heart is the origin of this Latin-based word. This is where intelligence and smarts mix with feelings-based understanding and active passion. The better you can emotionally express your brilliant thoughts with heartfelt conviction, the more followers you will inspire into action.

Detached

To truly focus on the horizon in front of you, you must be willing to let go of the wake behind you. This sounds easy, but as we are conditioned to believe that our identities are in large part made up of our past achievements and failures, it is tough to practice. Dr. Joe Dispenza's[5] work on epigenetics, neural science, and human behavior has proven that the brain is only a catalogue of past events and every time we dig into a memory, worry, fear, or even a joyous reflection, we have taken our senses off the present horizon unfolding in front, here and now.

Can focusing forward be much more profitable than looking back? Just compare your pre-pandemic figures to your post-pandemic ones. Are they the same? To consciously detach ourselves from history, we must practice creating some breathing room between our current businesses and our obsession with KPIs and focus upon what is happening now and going forward. Remember, "past results do not reflect future guarantees of performance."

Letting go: A fable

The following is an old saga which demonstrates the qualities, properties, and value of letting go.

Once there were two holy men wandering about. An older monk and his younger apprentice. One day they came to a riverbank. On their side of the river was a beautiful young lady who looked troubled. The older monk politely asked what the problem was, and she replied, "I am so afraid to cross this river by myself." The older monk then surprised the younger one by responding, "In that case, I would be happy to carry you across." The three of them then crossed the river with the older monk gently carrying the young lady.

On the other side he let her down and she thanked him gratefully. He smiled, they parted, and the monks continued on their way. After a short time, it was obvious to the older monk that something was troubling his younger partner. When asked, the younger monk exploded, "How could you? You, who has taken a vow of celibacy, carry that young and beautiful woman across the river?!" To which the older monk calmly replied, "My dear friend, I left the young lady at the riverbank. It seems that you are the one still carrying her."

How often do you continue to dwell in an issue long after it is over? Interesting expression, "to dwell in," as if you live in it or at least are surrounded by it. Don't you have more pressing issues and tasks ahead of you with which to attend?

There is no better training than to practice letting go of old, useless, and troubling thoughts. This frees up time, energy, and space to focus instead upon what is occurring to come. Also, you will get bonus points for testing the following: The more you can focus upon those thoughts and issues that please you and bring you joy, while diminishing or eliminating dwelling in those that do not, the more you will raise your internal frequency and begin attracting more joyous and pleasurable situations.

Don't believe this! But you are warmly invited to test your power of attraction and see if it works for you, too.

CHAPTER 11

Overcoming the Big Inhibitors of Change

It is easy to talk about incorporating an agile business model that goes viral and saturates your organization. Still, count on the change necessary to accomplish this being met with resistance. Why?

Because as you grow you will inevitably run up against one or more of the following biggest inhibitors of change:

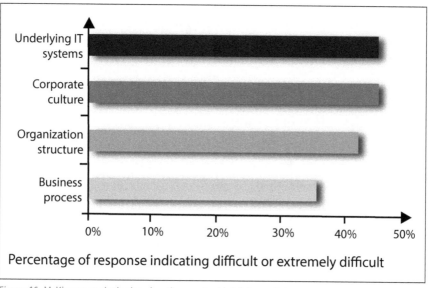

Figure 16. McKinsey analysis showing the greatest inhibitors of change

Systems are surprisingly, inherently systematic; otherwise, they are art. Systemic processes are designed to follow a specific and measurable course to a predetermined result. If you deviate from a proven system or a process, watch its integrity and effectiveness rapidly diminish. Organization and structure bring in human elements, but only slightly. An organizational structure is created so that everyone knows their role and how to systematically react within it. Corporate and personal cultures are probably the toughest nuts to crack as these vary in accordance with the thoughts, feelings, beliefs, and behaviors of each person involved. These factors also change over time. Finally, culture contains many unwritten rules that you must "sense" to practice effectively, even if there are no clear signs to guide you. Discovering these requires openness, curiosity, listening and a presence to everyone and everything around you.

Each one of the following inhibitors should be constantly investigated, reviewed, and improved, especially as the pace of change accelerates. The more you can see and sense that your people are adapting themselves to changing markets and internal conditions, the more flexible and resilient your organization becomes. The more resilient your group becomes, the more you can handle future developments and thus ensure a sustainable level of success. Below we will take a closer look at each of these inhibitors to get a better understanding of how they work and how to address them. Handling them effectively will require a workshop or at least another book.

When IT rules rather than serves

Information Technology starts as machine code. At its roots, IT is made up of either ones or zeros. Each "one" represents an *on circuit* and each "zero" represents an *off circuit*. In many ways, it is very much like Dr. Lipton's cellular *growth* (open) or *protection* (closed) behavior model, only on a digital or electrical level.

In our cells a one would represent an "on" or growth circuit and a zero would be an "off" or protected circuit. This limits behavior to being a direct or some form of derivative of either "on" or "off." This is the source behind the rigid rules and processes necessary in an IT or even AI paradigm. For instance, if your company runs on an Oracle or SAP system, their performance is based upon adhering to the strict one or zero rules of that system in order to produce/(insure?) the anticipated output and corresponding reports. This rigidity is often the root cause for a lot of the strict reaction times and the frustration of figuring out what particular input is causing the malfunction in the output, within a specific deadline. Moreover, by the time management input reaches the factory floor and all the field offices, the ripple effect of a misunderstanding or misinterpretation, especially in a larger organization, can fester and multiply many times over.

The most obvious example of the frustration surrounding IT is security. Although a good case can be made for its need, think about how much time is spent (often wasted) logging in and out, recreating your password if forgotten, and fixing a security issue if it's compromised. If you forget your ID card you most likely need to return home to collect it, otherwise you will be locked out of your office, functions and reason for existence. In very sensitive and secure environments, you cease to exist without proper ID. With the increase in business done on the net and all the temptations it causes, the level and frequency of these annoyances are also increasing. As this is being written we have seen massive cyber-attack on banks, gas pipelines, food stores, and even whole sections of government. Don't forget all of the phishing mails, trojan horse viruses, nasty people and the malicious bots they make to access, steal, and corrupt your systems and data. Data security and board member responsibility has also been a hot topic in the boardroom as of late.

Teleconferencing is also wonderful, when it works; but when your system doesn't function, it can still cause more communication problems and frustration than it solves. With the explosion of different communication channels, the challenge of choosing the most effective one is also becoming critical. As one colleague observed, "It seems the more ways we have to reach people, the harder it is to get in touch with them."

Culprit of IT inhibitor, the data

If you are in a decision-making position, you are certainly familiar with the infamous "budget crunch" that takes place at end of the year. Crunch time becomes an extraordinary inhibitor of change for a number of reasons:

- Being administrative, the process chews up valuable sales and service time.
- It inevitably creates friction between internal groups who already have and those who want more money.
- As your company grows, the budgeting process inevitably becomes more complicated, political, and time consuming.

- Once decided, it is often tough to impossible to adjust something that needs to be changed until the next crunch, even if it is detected the day after the new cycle takes effect.

Why do we even use a yearly budget?

Answer: This yearly process is a legacy left over from the agricultural age. Agriculture is of course, a cyclical growing pattern based upon the four seasons of the year. In order to maximize your harvest, you had to make sure you budgeted your time and resources appropriately for each season's properties and qualities. With the exception of the very few farmers who may be reading this book, how many of you have a business or product which has a cycle that is still critically affected by the four agricultural seasons?

For the most part, our way of living and doing business has moved on. Yes, taxes need to be reconciled every year, but even they can be adjusted to your fiscal year and divided up during the year to cushion the shock.

The Budget Process is also a fine example of what is known as "garbage in, garbage out" or GIGO. The output of your budget process is totally dependent upon the quality of the input. Every number entered hooks into so many other functions and assumptions. If what you input is only based upon your best "guesstimate," then what can you expect to come out on the other side?

A budget is no more than a very sophisticated spreadsheet, which in turn is a fancy relational database. Put something in and out comes the result based upon all the functions to which it is connected. This information then spreads through the whole organization and sometimes beyond, often instantaneously. We will look at the budget process more closely very shortly, but here we want to plant two questions worth contemplating:

1. How the quality and reliability of your input directly influences your output?
2. How rigid and relevant is the yearly timeframe of your standard budget, really?

In other words, if your guesstimates are too optimistic, pessimistic, or just plain wrong, it may take another year before you can change any of the input or the assumptions you base them upon.

Add to this the swamp of many different communication platforms, portals, different or new standards, non-compatible protocols and your whole IT situation can quickly become a pit of quicksand.

For instance, at one point the giant Swedish telecoms company Telia had three different accounting/billing systems in use in different parts of the company at the same time. This caused massive incompatibility issues, wasted lots of time, due to having to re-input figures multiple times. This situation caused extreme frustration for among others, the sales and billing teams. Then there was the internal battle over which system should prevail. The exiting and merger of these systems took a longer ramp-up time than expected. Then the additional time required for training and the need to adjust the system during implementation was enormous. The whole process was a huge source of frustration and for employees, suppliers and customers, not to mention a money pit for investors.

A further example is the Swedish seed company, Nelson Brothers. This multigenerational family business nearly went bankrupt upgrading their IT/business system. What was promised did not function and by the time it was fixed, it had taken the efforts and costs from several companies, installing a few different systems to create a fully functioning solution. This process exhausted their cash reserves and financial resources that had been saved up over generations.

Another poignant example was Y2K. This was the situation at the turn of the last century where billions of dollars and untold hours of manpower were invested because of the need of one extra zero. Great fear was generated out of the worry that all computer driven systems would come to a halt at midnight on New Year's Day 2000. After lots of worry and a lot of reprogramming, hardly anything occurred at the appointed hour, even to those who chose (correctly) to do nothing.

You can absolutely count on your computers delivering accurate information based upon the accuracy and quality of your input. If the input is wrong, is out of date, or just your best guesstimate, the results will iterate further and further from reality. Never forget that all systems are based upon models, not reality. How closely can a model mirror real life and its challenges? No matter how accurate, your budgets will always be based upon models; and those models will be a lot more accurate if they are based upon today's reality instead of yesterday's planting cycle.

Finally, how often do you dare to question a prepared report?

Most decision makers your authors have subjectively surveyed privately admit that they don't usually question a report. Whether it is due to time constraints, comfort, fear, or just plain laziness, most of us take a printed report as the truth, regardless of its flaws. For agile systems demand constant vigilance, more accurate input, and a healthy dose of objective questions.

This challenge of accurate input is challenged on the back end too. Changing input in just one place in your system creates a leveraging effect upon the rest of your organization, often without realizing it. This multiplier effect can skew even small discrepancies or miscalculations into large mistakes, once they travel through your entire IT system!

Even when your accounting system is integrated correctly, it still takes a long time to close the books and get accurate information. To be effective, the agile Skipper needs accurate information immediately. Why can't you close the books every day with just revenue and cost? Because even today, most systems won't allow it! What if implementing a rolling budget system is a more agile and up to date way of mitigating your budget crunch?

Life in a spreadsheet

A little over a generation ago workers were still in charge of their jobs and lives. Computers worked alongside them as a support or aid function. Now, fast-forward more than thirty years from the accepted start of the IT age, i.e., the invention of Lotus 1-2-3 and the cataclysmic shift it provided to modeling, calculating, and predicting results. The power and presence of Information Technology has now become ubiquitous. It is now impossible to remain competitive, let alone agile in today's business environment without IT support.

While this has boosted productivity throughout the organization, it has also handcuffed workers to the rules, regulations, constant monitoring, and evaluation of their performance. All of this comes with being relentlessly under the digital microscope that IT has now morphed into. This intrusive monitoring and measuring now causes an enormous amount of stress and frustration in the organization and within the individual humans who comprise it. In the early 1980s there was much "fat" to be trimmed by reengineering organizations. Profits soared by decreasing unnecessary costs and selling off unproductive departments. As systems became more sophisticated and individual performance was monitored more and more closely, this boon to profitability morphed into a growing threat for those who could not keep up. Now Big Brother monitors and measures performance so well that it is impossible *not* to feel you are being watched. This causes frustration and stress and can contribute to burnout or worse, lying.

Data stress

> "There are two types of computers: the ones that have already crashed and the ones that will."
> **—Computer proverb**

Think about all the extra steps your day consists of just to be able to use your IT system. Are you:

- Constantly logging in or reactivating lost or forgotten login codes?
- Worrying about what has happened to your private information that was probably hijacked in that last headline making hack?
- Often having to stop what you are doing to upgrade software and apps?
- Wondering whether to call for software or hardware support?
- Pondering which hw/sw supplier is actually responsible for the glitch?
- Going crazy trying to figure out what the technical name is for the problem you are having?
- Often rebooting your system when something loads up incorrectly?
- Required to be constantly vigilant for viruses, bugs, phishing, and other threats?

- Explaining your obvious problem to your clueless techie repairperson who seems to speak another language?

No matter how agile you pride yourself on being, working with IT takes time and puts an enormous technical and emotional strain on you and everyone you interact with. Even so it is necessary, since the alternative is shutting down the system and choking off the information and financial flow to your company.

Increasing loyalty by minimizing the need for customer capture

As we have mentioned, customer capture has grown from an annoying irritation to a threat for anyone signing up for a product or service. Although the following observations may not be directly stated in the marketing you read, please note and get a feel of the molasses-like and increasingly frustrating effect you sense with some of the following small but constant and accumulating irritations:

- Paying extra for paper invoices and not being able to easily find or cancel them
- Sometimes being forced to cancel the same payment multiple times
- Having to hunt for contact information, *especially human contact*
- Being forced into a telephone tree only to end up being referred to a chat line or email when you only wish to ask a simple question
- Getting late fees on your late fees
- Not finding your simple question answered in their FAQ (Frequently Asked Questions)
- Not knowing the technical name of your problem or how to express it so you can even begin to seek help
- Getting even more paper invoices after you have spoken with a representative who promised you, "there would be no more"; again
- Standing in a long line to "automatically check-in," getting sent to another line with an equally long wait to finally be sent to a third, attendant-based line, because it is discovered that you have some "priority level" you were not aware of

- Finding out you have unknowingly been paying a premium for this extra level of service for years

In days gone by, you would have had the time to deal with a few of these small irritations quickly, but now when you multiply them by a factor of twenty or thirty similar business models, it eventually slows even the most resilient of us down. These irritations drain energy to the point that you (and millions like you) resign yourselves to the reality that it is easier to continue paying a few extra bucks than have to hassle with fixing it, again and again. Automation and programming make the process of nickel and diming us out of money even easier, as computers do not have consciences. This abstraction of blaming it on programming seems, for now, to allow the programmers to sleep better. Yet, for you (and your remaining loyal customers?), these irritations still manifest and grow.

Interestingly, if you look behind the scenes with these highly automated companies, they often have the highest employee turnover and burnout rates. In some telecom companies, up to 80 percent of some sales staffs can now turn over in a single year! With the quickening spread of information via the internet, even a big company's reputation can now be quickly ruined by too many complaints posted in rapid succession. For the moment at least, TBTF companies can still use their money and muscle to prevent genuine competition and dissent, but is that a trend that can hold? Especially as there seem to be more and more customers who have reached their limit of frustration and may become more active in finding agile alternatives.

New business models encourage new behavior and luckily this is where the agile businessperson can now succeed! What if, just by treating each customer as a valued and respected individual, listening to them and helping them to extract themselves from the prison of your competitor's Customer Management System, you could be seen as different and better and become a success?

Reliance on processes

It was too late to change the direction of the *Titanic* once the iceberg was spotted. When put in motion, most processes can only accomplish the planned result. That planned result is most likely based upon historical data rather than real time or future predictions. With the turbulence we are now experiencing is this a bankable strategy?

Rather than focusing on old and now irrelevant Garbage In, Garbage Out or GIGO, could the solution be to look forward, measure and appreciate the present, then lightly season this information with a little historical perspective? Getting this recipe right can drastically increase your ability to anticipate future conditions and prepare you to navigate through them.

Varied research has shown that corporations are usually looking in the wrong places for information on which to base forward looking decisions. This is especially true when it comes to risk assessment. According to research, "the biggest risk factor is strategic at 86 percent followed by a distant 9 percent of operating risk." Our experience confirms this data presented by the Harvard Business Review, July–August 2015[1]. This further argues that the greatest amount of time spent by auditors is "reviewing operating risks (forty-two percent) followed by strategic risks at thirteen percent." How can you steer your ship correctly into the future, when these actual figures represent looking in the opposite direction of where your focus should be? This fact is further multiplied by both your banker, who finances investments using the exact same, completely misdirected and often backward-looking filters as do most auditors. This will affect your board's decisions and the subsequent marching orders handed down by management, often sending teams off in the wrong direction. This often causes focus on trivial and unnecessary operating issues, while concentration is lost on the more important strategic ones. This backward-looking behavior is a very serious flaw in our current management behavior and its response to risk!

This sort of makes logical sense given almost all popular Key Performance Indicators or KPI systems are based squarely upon the analysis of historical data. Thus, by nature, all KPI and quality processes become inherently constraining. For the reasons mentioned above, even well-meant KPIs, as well as all the analysis built upon them, inhibit agility because they corral and eventually kill off both individual and organizational creativity. What if using KPIs as a spice instead of the main course would help with your recipe to master business agility?

Flawed data doesn't help

For many insecure and/or lazy managers, accurate data represents a clear and present danger to their careers. Think about it, the more accurate the data is, the more the information can be used to objectively judge performance, even theirs. Especially in a large organization, middle management has traditionally had ample time and opportunity to neglect, postpone and fabricate performance numbers in order to look better. This used to be referred to as the Fudge Factor. In the selling profession, this process is sometimes known as sandbagging and is practiced to skew sales figures by more experienced sales people. They simply take their last few sales of the month and delay inputting them until the beginning of the next one. This makes the current month look decent and provides a great start for the next one. Incentives tend to skew the numbers even further, especially when a sales competition starts the next month. This too can be compounded again if sales managers encourage it department wide in order to maximize their own monthly or quarterly bonus. As business cycles are still shortening and costs fluctuate more, how accurate can your ordering, production, and billing KPIs be?

Is context the key?

Therefore, an agile captain needs to always place accurate data in its appropriate context. A simple story that ascribes the dangers of becoming obsessed with the process of measuring everything without understanding the correct context is the Tale of the Two Archers:

Two archers compete by shooting three arrows apiece. The first archer, William Tell, shoots one light grey arrow into the outer border zone of the target. His other two arrows miss the target, but land very closely to his first arrow. Even though all three of his light grey arrows land very close to each other, he only earns ten points. Not only that, but he also only actually hits the target once. The next archer, Robin Hood, lands one dark grey arrow in the bullseye, and the other two miss the target by a wide margin. Yet his shooting earns him one hundred points. The Judges that day are statisticians and technicians and have focused entirely on the rules. They correctly declare Robin Hood the winner. What could be wrong with that?

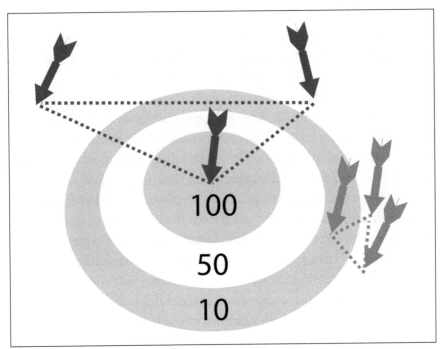

Figure 17. Robin Hood's arrows are dark grey; William Tell's are light grey.

Taking a closer look at how the two archers landed their arrows reveals that although Robin Hood received more points and won, his arrows were spread out over a much wider area. In a broader context, for instance quality, his marksmanship can be seen as less reliable. In terms of quality control, his accuracy was lower than that of William Tell, who landed all three arrows in a much smaller, tighter area.

All William has to do now is to practice shifting his aim closer toward the bullseye and the quality of his shots and the points received will increase dramatically. Yet, this important quality issue is not picked up when dogmatically analyzing the now historical statistics. Without taking notice of the broader context, the difference in quality between the two archer's marksmanship is not fully appreciated. If the context is broadened at the event, in real time with an eye on the future, a different result and winner could be anticipated. Statistics do have a place, but sometimes they (forgive us) miss their mark when improperly analyzed or placed in an improper context.

In this example, just counting the number of points misses the point! This is analogous to today's current dilemma of relying on analysis without honoring its context. All comprehensive measurement practices or systems that just measure hard numbers can easily miss the big picture. This can lead to very damaging assumptions and conclusions. For instance, in the case above Robin Hood's score would most likely make him the best candidate for a promotion. William Tell could easily be chosen for the next layoff. Accurately capturing and analyzing the soft factors and their context are critical when making decisions such as buying, selling, restructuring, etc. If you want to get a real understanding of the whole situation, don't get caught trying to analyze with anal-eyes.

Another potent example is of a top ranked figure skater who wanted to become even better. She enrolled the help of a very well-known but controversial coach. A while into her new training her manager called the coach. She was outraged as the skater was now falling more than ever before! The coach calmed her down by saying, "That's great! She is testing her boundaries." Sure enough, the skater soon began to fall less, while her style, grace, and confidence reached new heights. She began winning more.

Is the glass half-empty or half-full? Train to sense the context.

If you can measure it, you can manage it . . . but at what cost?

This is the challenge with any process-driven data system such as Six Sigma, Lean, or a comprehensive reporting system such as SAP. They are all designed to take the art of measuring, the use of historical data, and stringent procedure to even stricter and more extreme levels. Policy eventually replaces life and people, especially creative ones, and becomes stymied by strict routines like flies in a sticky spider web. They will suffer by being bound to these pre-determined yet often-arbitrary constraints.

For example, creativity is a soft skill and is therefore hard to measure. Bright ideas, more often than not, explode onto the scene in bolts of creativity, just as a lightning bolt strike. Put a creative person into a protected or controlled process and count on their creativeness to eventually wither and die. In the meantime, they will probably focus all their remaining creativity and energy on executing an escape from you, your process, and organization. This is regardless of how effective and well-meaning your system is meant to be.

Remember, every investment disclaimer's fine print uncomfortably reminds you that, "Past performance is no indication of future returns." This warning should also be put on all backward-looking KPIs. They are almost always focused upon measuring processes after they are already complete. At best they take a snapshot of the present, which starts aging as soon as it's taken. This is instead of using indicators created to better help you anticipate and prepare for the future.

Mediocrity rules

Any process-driven company must become mediocre sooner or later. That inevitable outcome is due to its focus on "safely" implementing the most general rules and metrics available. This is done intentionally to make it easier for most members of your staff to follow them easily. A successful process is intentionally designed to harness the biggest statistical slice directly in the sweet spot or the middle of the normally distributed bell curve. Just as in the Goldilocks fable, the process then becomes 'not too much, not too little, but just right.'

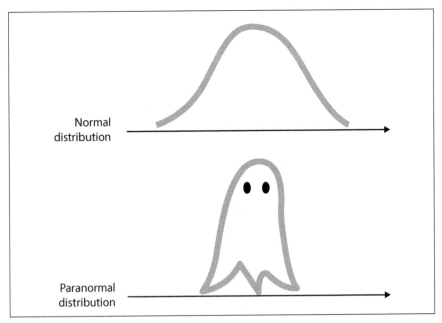

Figure 18. Normal distribution curve and paranormal distribution
(Originally from the National Association of Psychologists)

Could this rush toward mediocrity seem contrary to how life actually works? Think for a moment. Where do you find excitement and creativity, in the cozy middle of a process or on the edge? Think about the middle versus the edges of forests, oceans, and of course, human development. Creativity and inspiration exist on the edges of the bell curve, not in the middle. Just as every rule is made to be broken, it is only by challenging, going beyond, or breaking rules that we get to see what is on the other side. Therefore, by focusing on a process to exploit the sweet spot in the comfortable middle part of your business curve, you will, consciously or not, support and encourage only those bureaucratic individuals in your organization who are most comfortable with the power of the status quo. This is while those bolder few in your organization, who thrive on its creative edges, continue to get their wings clipped, become ostracized, unhappy and, inevitably, begin searching for opportunities elsewhere.

Look no further than the once great company Motorola. This is the company that invented Total Quality Management (TQM). What finally remained of this once innovative giant has now been totally broken up and sold off. More importantly during the process, all the creative genius slowly drained out of it to greener, more creative pastures. Why?

Their exodus was due to the fierce commitment of management to religiously heed to the suffocating constraints of TQM. This very well-thought-out process becomes the "Achilles' heel" to the very creative spirit that built this once great company. Yet could over-thinking also have been responsible for developing TQM? Creativity comes from passion, not logic. Instead of creating and nurturing an environment of freedom and support, management created a prison from which its creative inmates only wanted escape. Compare this telecommunications disaster to what has made Google successful.

At the same time Google has grown into a behemoth, it has somehow managed to both maintain a sense of on-the-edge entrepreneurship, while creating just enough control to ensure that it presents one face to the market. This is a very tough balancing act, especially as the company continues to grow and rapidly add new products, all the while the business environment grows even more uncertain. To maintain this balance, it pays to stay agile. It will be interesting to follow Google's trajectory going forward.

Ironically, Google bought up parts of Motorola's telecommunications business. It will be interesting to see if and how they can revitalize that strict culture, which seemed to have doomed Motorola. With any luck, there are still some agile thinking, former Motorola employees left. Those who can appreciate and promote, to other less agile colleagues, the opportunity that Google's open and agile atmosphere offers them. Experience is golden.

Agility is about steering your organization forward. This doesn't make history irrelevant but emphasizes that input from what lies ahead is more relevant. Working from history makes you more reactive and less proactive. Forward risks are much more important than historical ones and your awareness of this fact must be cultivated. Maybe it's just human nature that makes us focus upon history instead of anticipating the future. History is already finished and is now a memory. This makes it much easier and safer to observe, measure, and analyze it. The risk is lower and, should you care to spend precious time and resources to *anal-eyes* it, you can absolutely support your conclusions with data. This means your risk for your hypothesis to be voted down is low. After all, it worked before, didn't it?! This may make it seem a safer career move, but (especially in the long term) is it really?

Organizational structure

> "There are no rules! We're trying to accomplish something!"
> **—Thomas Edison**

The business leaders who came back from World War II to run businesses often created structures based upon their own recent and often personal experience of the C3 military model of Command, Control and Communication. Leaders being groomed today often have little or no relation to this rigid structure other than it being the traditional and the textbook way to run things. The good news is that tradition is being increasingly questioned and challenged. What is the reason for this?

With shortening cycles everywhere, companies must become increasingly flexible and agile. You must anticipate future requirements while avoiding treating creative individuals as a flock of sheep who require rules and babysitters. Many companies are still falling into the Industrial Age Management Trap of telling employees exactly what to do and precisely how to do it. Do you get inspired when dealing with a resigned middle manager who is so worried about his or her program-generated performance indicators that he/she tells you exactly what to do and when? Feeling helpless in a system crushes both responsibility and creativity while rapidly breeding mediocrity.

Increased competition makes it increasingly difficult for customers to distinguish between your competitors and you. You can have the technical and organizational stuff down pat, but most of your other competitors now have that too. Soft skills are rapidly on their way to becoming the distinguishing factor of choice, yet by their nature they are harder to measure and assess. Soft skills are not easily captured in market research instruments or total quality assessments and that irritating fact limits your company's ability to be agile. As the precariousness of both the company and the worker increases, your HR person will need to become their champion. HR now needs to actively voice employee concerns forcefully, in order to create more stability and encourage creativity. This shift in roles will lessen worry, resentment, and resignation in a time when each individual employee is counted upon to continually do more with less. This shift will also go a long way to healing the artificial rift between workers (unions) and management. In our increasingly competitive and unstable business environment, everyone needs to know and accept their roles in the same metaphoric boat, or one unexpected wave could easily capsize it and drown everyone on board, regardless of rank, political correctness, or affiliation.

The human resource management dilemma

Do you like being told what to do? Productive and creative people categorically do not, especially from people with no practical experience and who are often removed from your organization's core business.

This is the tenuous and sometimes treacherous position in which your HR people now find themselves. They are usually stuck in a corporate backwater, with little or no practical experience from your company's field operations. They are usually seen as an unwelcome and extra cost, especially by those who produce and perform.

This is the dilemma facing most of today's human resources departments. HR's role has evolved into more of an administrative and un-respected function compared to the "Hot Shots" in finance, sales, marketing, R&D, and production. Agile leaders are finally recognizing the obvious; that companies do not do business with companies, people do business with people. Therefore, relationships play a critical role both internally and externally. Put a capable, happy person in an efficient, inspiring environment and marvel at what is accomplished.

The popularity of the HR department can be tracked in direct relation to the health of the economy. When the economy is slowing and the labor market is slack, HR becomes a nuisance. Why? The most vocal critics of HR claim that its focus is too much upon administration and that often correctly HR people tend to lack both experience from the line as well as critical strategic insight. Therefore, HR has often been seen as a hindrance to business development rather than a positive facilitating force. Whether HR is the chicken or the egg in this situation, which came first matters less than how HR will be reinvented, valued, and applied in the future.

Interestingly, human resource management is not handled the same way in all countries. For instance, in Japan HR is often represented in the C-Suite. In India it is an integral part of management. In Europe the HR department seems to be growing in importance. Evidence would suggest that HR becomes more vital in countries and cultures where the people that deal with the biggest societal issues get the most power. For example, environments where work-related legislation is a big deal, such as Sweden, HR is naturally stronger and more influential. In the USA it's marketing and sales that matter. Even so most of the comments on HR, presented here, are focused on the USA market. Of course, you are encouraged to compare, contrast, and profit from our comments with your own experience in your own location and situation.

Just the continued use of the term human resources should give cause for worry. How does it feel to be a resource? Resources, like iron ore, lumber *and* livestock are usually managed, exploited, and traditionally depleted. Many current managers throughout today's organizations still look at new hires as just that—human resources like sheep to be farmed. How does it feel now to be a resource?

This type of management behavior, often unconsciously, encourages issues of resentment and resignation within a company. Think of all the paperwork or screen time you waste filling in reviews, questionnaires and evaluations many of which you never hear about again. In a large telecoms company, your author witnessed one department of highly talented and well-paid engineers dutifully filling out their yearly evaluation forms that asked for their suggestions for improvement. After seven years and seven evaluations, without any feedback or acknowledgement of their suggestions, they were extremely frustrated when this eighth year's evaluation arrived. How much time do you think went toward complaining about this evaluation compared to getting profitable stuff done?

An enormous amount of time and energy was wasted discussing the pros and cons of filling it out again. They felt, and rightly so, that they were not being seen, heard or cared about. Their performance and morale suffered accordingly as did their output.

This lack of love for HR also stretches up into executive offices, too. After all, who do you think requests these evaluations? HR is often excluded on long-term strategy issues. It is very seldom that HR is allowed to take a leadership position. They are often not invited to be members of the C-Suite for two reasons:

1. With so much time being spent on brushfire management today, there are often few to zero long-term strategic discussions to consider.

2. HR is often consciously excluded. This way, management can react faster. They can decide quicker without having to suffer through hearing about employee/union concerns and issues. This creates the effect of making the situation of each employee even more precarious and unstable. Although this would be unheard of in more socialistic cultures, where law often prohibits this, you can bet that there still are conscious and unconscious attempts to minimize HR's participation.

HR's role to assist, advise, and support leaders in workforce planning has been undervalued, at best. How often have you witnessed an HR person transferred to a line position? Most HR people come fresh out of school, trained in administration at least as much as in handling individual employees and their problems. HR has also been considered a backwater, far off the career path to the executive suite. Therefore, sharper and more decisive personalities are seldom attracted to this particular career path. This also creates a stigma where HR becomes a hindrance to career development within the organization it is charged to inspire and develop.

This ultimately causes further alienation, resentment and resignation. HR often gets the blame from above and below. In fact, we have anecdotally experienced that only about one third of the HR departments surveyed were consulted on who should be dismissed during the Great Recession of 2008 and why. Imagine the potential talent that was lost as well as the extra stress and resentment these hasty decisions placed upon those lucky enough to remain.

On the other hand, very few of those outside of the HR department understand how important a structured, well-executed interview process is, in new hire selections. Many people with little or no interview training are too often put in charge of this important hiring function. This short-sighted approach often results in labor disputes, increases the costs of litigation, and drains precious time, energy, and resources for cleaning up the mess caused by poor hires. Adding insult to injury, people in line-management positions often prefer to use external search companies rather than their own internal HR department. After all, HR, in their eyes, is just a group of administrative inhibitors of change. How much extra does this cost in both money and inspirational corporate culture?

Especially with younger workers, arrangements such as working from home were resisted by line-managers up and until COVID-19 forced them to rethink this. There is now growing evidence that this solution may actually be as efficient and sometimes more motivational. Until recently, HR people were often some of the only ones who recognize the growing importance and value of working from home. This whole paradigm has been given a swift kick in the behind with COVID-19. This may actually produce the exact opposite effect where few wish to return to the office. So far figures have been tossed around such as 12 percent of office workers in New York City and 20 percent in Stockholm now regularly commute to the office. This was before round two. This can and is crushing the commercial real estate business.

When it comes to HR management, most of the appraisal systems out there are questionable at best and often are resented in their fabricated design and objectivity. Because of this situation, the best consultant firms such as PWC have abandoned standard performance appraisals. Instead, they are now moving toward a continuous discussion and thus taking this process even further away from the traditional HR power structure. Still at this writing, most firms remain stuck in the business-as-usual morass of traditional appraisals.

The problem then becomes that HR is seen as more of a long-term play, while your business cycles constantly shorten. This paradox creates a mixed and often damaging message, which is that although people are acknowledged as the most important asset in your company, they are still treated as resources, things. Now more than ever, personnel issues must be seriously addressed, even before strategy, and on a human and personal level as much as possible. What if you have the right people in place, they are happy as they feel seen, heard, and understood; don't company strategy and tactics usually take care of themselves?

Rethinking human resources

Therefore, this is an agile time for HR to take the same leap as Finance has already done and become an experienced and bona fide member of the management team. Just as the CFO, CMO, and the Chief Human Resources Officer (CHRO) should become a valued and trusted partner of the CEO.

Expanding your management team to include a CHRO is the best, most agile way to link company financial performance factors to your individual team members and their growing personal concerns. The transition to this new and improved HR department

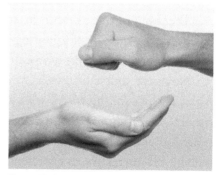

Figure 19. HR hard (administrative) skills versus soft (personal) skills

243

will go a long way toward refocusing on your company's most important resource and it will send a positive and rejuvenating signal to your marketplace.

This will correctly elevate the important task of marrying motivated people blessed or trained with the appropriate skills and their optimal position or task. HR can also elevate the need for more inclusive dialogue between team members with differing/opposing views. Whether they take on a bigger role as moderator or train managers to better handle internal conflicts, based upon external factors, there is no better group to champion this increasingly important role!

Each person's profile should generate a balance between IQ and EQ to get each job done with optimal efficiency. For instance:

- How are you going to reach your results if you have a brilliant technician, who insists upon solving everything himself, yet is in charge of a group of inhibiting creative but frustrated troubleshooters who are itching to apply their talents?
- How will you get your salespeople to sell more effectively when sales managers are more interested in going on sales calls themselves (usually just to show-off their skills) rather than focusing on supporting, teaching, and coaching their teams to sell better?
- How will you rebuild synergy in a team of highly specialized and highly skilled individuals, which has recently discovered they have irreconcilable differences with regard to politics, the environment, or health issues?

The result of these cases is usually the creation of a huge sandbox full of upset egos instead of a homogenized and focused group of focused, professional team players who enjoy supporting and helping each other.

Now, ask yourself how can your HR leader become a true strategic partner when she/he is still seen and treated as a bureaucratic administrator? To accomplish this transition, their knowledge of organizational functions and lines will need to be greatly improved. The best remedy is making HR attractive to experienced line and field people. With its rising importance to the health and performance of individual employees and teams, HR can be the glue that holds company strategy together. HR can literally become the heroes of the C-Suite just by getting people to appreciate the value of dialogue in creating "agreements that stick." Do you think the role of HR as a hero would attract the best and the brightest in your organization? This transition of getting your HR people accepted on the same level as the management team, much less heroes of it will take time. Yet what if time is running out?

Your new HR leader still needs to be able to talk about human capital in business terms; but now, a level of heartfelt respect for each individual in question needs to be factored in. Future HR heroes need to:

- Become adept at analysis to make workforce decisions.
- Be able to make measurable predictions about the types of skills needed going forward.
- Retain a good sense and appreciation of the soft skills each employee brings to the table.
- Develop their senses to feel the pulse of their organization. They need better tools to pinpoint where workflow and team-spirit are present or need to be improved.

That information is not necessarily available to the HR people at all times, nor is it well understood. For the agile company it is imperative to improve the access to and appreciation of this important information of its value and its application. The key? Building better and more respected internal relationships.

The CHRO will be forced to take on a more strategic function in the organization due to a number of factors that include the importance of:

- Placing the right people with the right skills in the right positions and with the right workload. Then re-placing them when the situation or the person changes.
- Understanding the leveraging effect in appreciating what makes each worker happier and more productive, especially in our current environment of decreasing resources, increasing time constraints, and extremely divisive social issues.
- Being able to increase the creativity and efficiency of each employee by understanding what makes each individual 'tick' and providing the right type of environment and training to make it happen. This will require getting to know each individual better.

- Sensing what is happening within the company regarding relationships and morale and then translating and conveying this important information into business and analytical terms for the C-Suite's understanding. Management needs to know how they can make money on each and every personnel issue.

- Making each individual worker feel more welcome and secure. This will happen naturally when HR is placed in a decisive and more appreciated organizational position and given the mandate to speak with authority. This shift will help minimize employee concern about their employment security.

- Empowering and encouraging each worker to be more self-confident, self-sufficient, and self-motivating for three reasons:

    1. Should a worker be let go, they will know exactly what to do and how to quickly handle finding income somewhere else.
    2. Encouraging workers to stay put. If they feel motivated and enjoy the feeling of team-spirit in this type of atmosphere, why would they want to leave?
    3. When they do their job better, the company and they themselves earn more money, insuring a brighter and happier future for both.

- Ensuring that when people are forced to leave, they do so as amicably as possible and ensuring that the door will always be open should other opportunities arise. The arrogance of prohibiting former competent employees a chance to come back is no longer affordable. Everyone makes mistakes.

When all of the above occur, would you feel the need to look for another job?

Another idea is to rewrite the CEO, CFO, CMO, and CHRO roles to cover essential pieces of company strategy. Your HR officer should absolutely be someone who has come from a line function and knows what it is like in the trenches. The more they understand the situation from practical experience rather than from theory or abstract hearsay, the more confident they will be to effectively execute their role in a profitable fashion. HR now needs to be considered part of the management troika.

It will also be a plus if HR gets rid of both routine administration functions and training. Admin functions such as attendance and compensation can and should be done on a much lower level and increasingly by software or a well-designed app. Training should be moved from HR to a department more closely tied with the eyes and ears of your organization. This implies marketing. In fact, we believe that your internal and external communication departments should quickly evolve to become the new natural home for all of your training groups. There, your training staff can experience greater kinship with people who understand and have more appreciation for all their skills and technology. There will also be more appreciation of the valuable information that training routinely gathers and can now interpret. Combining training with marketing and communication will be a considerably more synergistic and relevant placement than the current, typical configuration that places it in a dark and forgotten closet deep in the HR department.

Corporate culture and tradition

Within the greatest inhibitors of change, "culture" sticks out as the most potent. It can easily become a culture for employees to use the other major inhibitors (IT, structure, and processes) as an excuse for poor execution and even total avoidance of change.

In fact, one of our primary inhibitors of change is the inevitable institutionalization of a thought or an idea. As Deepak Chopra has said about the institution of religion, "Before Christianity there was Jesus, before Islam there was Mohammed and before Buddhism there was Buddha." What he seems to mean is these popular world religions, whose followers have sometimes blindly defended to their deaths, were originally based upon the personal beliefs of three single individuals. Evidence would suggest that these beliefs and hundreds of years of revision, reinterpretation, development, and stratification by committees, whose members increasingly have become more vested in a very comfortable lifestyle, have twisted and manipulated these personal beliefs into dogma. This dogma is now defended by extremely well-funded institutions whose role now stretches way beyond their founder's original intentions.

A good little story highlighting this point of missing the forest for the trees, from a slightly naughty, religious tale is this:

A young and curious monk working on updating old scripture once brazenly asked his master, "How do we know these new translations have anything to do with the original texts?"

His master and colleagues were horrified at the newcomer's insolence. They became very defensive, to the point of being angry and screamed in unison: "The texts could *never* have been misinterpreted! Now, to get back to work."

The next day, after a frustrating night's sleep and deep contemplation, his master returned. With a pre-judgmental look, he said to the monk, "Okay! I will go and check." The master disappeared into the depths of the monastery and went missing for three full days. At the end of the third day, the new monk's worried colleagues forced him to go look for their master. The monk finally found him in the deepest, darkest, and oldest part of the monastery archives, relentlessly banging his bloody head against a stone pillar. When asked why, his master responded,

"You were right my son; we should have been more careful to accurately check the original texts. I have now looked at one particular passage which states, 'The men of our calling are to serve, support and safeguard their flock to the best of their ability. Then, on every Sunday forevermore, once the service is complete, they should go celebrate.'

"But," said the master, "it appears that the translation was mistakenly updated to read, 'The men of our calling are to serve, support, and safeguard their flock to the best of their ability. Then on every Sunday forevermore, once the service is complete, they should go celibate.'"

What a difference even a simple spelling error can make, when the original idea or its context is forgotten, overlooked, never challenged or questioned.

Now take the idea of political correctness and intolerant belief; what do you think Jesus would have said about people being burned at the stake because they disagreed with the Church, founded in his name, on whether the earth was the center of our solar system? What do you think Mohammed's comments would be about killing innocents in order to die a martyr and spend the afterlife with seventy-four virgins? Rather than listen to reason and create a flowing dialogue, people have historically defended their points of view and shut out all opposing ones, even to the point of killing others or dying themselves to silence them. Add a bit of money to the mix and watch the intolerance of others' views and rules to support business as usual increase further and faster. How agile is this?

What if the same exact process occurs when a corporate culture takes root? Unwritten rules can often carry more weight than the written ones, causing previously efficient processes to bog down in conscious and unconscious committee wrangling and miscommunication. Unwritten legacy issues often accompany documented legacy costs such as retirement. These weigh down established organizations with outlays that other, younger competitors laugh about, all the way to the bank. Below are some of the biggest.

This issue has recently gotten newer and stronger legs with all the time spent in front of a screen listening more and more to a filtered stream of information, tailored to the observer's personal tastes, preferences in politics, health issues, and environmental concerns. Subjective observations now point to increased debate in routine group meetings in organizations of all sizes. Issues that were previously considered interesting cocktail conversation have now blown up into attacks which can get the speaker fired or banned from social media, just for disagreeing or even worse, asking a curious, pertinent, and objective question. Well-functioning teams have become so divided that some participants refuse to talk to others with different viewpoints or worse, sabotage their efforts to do what they are paid to do. Does this sound like the behavior of a well-functioning, synergistic or dare we say agile, team on their way to success?

Agility also means openness, curiosity, and tolerance. Without these properties your corporate ship can easily spring a dangerous leak. With these properties your team can sail easily past former competitors who avoid or suppress tackling this important issue. All it takes is separating your individual power of observation from your brain's tendency to categorize and judge all input. In short, the more you train to curiously listen with your senses without letting your buttons be pushed, the closer you get to clean, professional dialogue and an agreement that sticks. The best mantra to begin this important process is to keep in mind, no matter what is being said, that "even this is nothing personal."

Policy versus empathy

There is a ferryboat in the city of Stockholm that takes passengers for a beautiful fifteen-minute boat ride from the city's amusement park on the East side of town to its South side. Recently, one of your authors noticed an elderly Norwegian couple trying, in vain, to buy a ticket with their bankcard, but the machine was broken. Although they had Norwegian cash, the ticket taker would not accept it. They finally left the boat totally frustrated as the ticket taker was heard to shout, "What if I accept everybody who cannot pay?" To add insult to injury, the attendant also refused to allow me to pay for their tickets since they had just abandoned their place in line. At that point, I also left. Not content with this, the attendant concluded by screaming, "We have rules, you know!"

> "Policy replaces life."
> **—Patrick Collard**

Out skiing one time, I ended up in the local village hospital with a friend who had fallen down hard. In front of us was an unlucky skier who had obviously broken his right thumb as it was now bent straight up in the air, far from where it should naturally rest. He was in pain! Even so, before the physician would even look at his thumb, he was forced to sign a whole stack of legal and admission papers. The pain was clearly increasing with every signature, even though he wisely chose to sign with an X using his other hand. These two anecdotes are rather tame examples of when the rules and policies we set up take over our capacity to be human. An extreme version is a famous quote from the Vietnam War, "To save the village we had to destroy it."

Going forward, we need to be more agile and forgiving. Just as Captain Barbosa famously said in the movie *Pirates of the Caribbean: The Curse of the Black Pearl*, "They're not so much rules . . . they're more like [long smiling pause] guidelines." As greater portions of our lives come under the rule of technocrats, bureaucrats, bankers, accountants and their computer algorithms, we may also be facing peak compliance too. All too often, these technicians put their measurements and rules in front of the overall picture. Deep throat's famous line from the American Watergate scandal,

"Follow the money," seems more appropriate today than when it was spoken circa fifty years ago. This form of business as usual seems also to be the source of the current rise of popular/third-party or independent politics, which opposes to our old batch of political royalty. After all, who likes to be told what to do when the big picture is either unknown, ignored or intentionally hidden; or when:

- You never personally agreed to the rule or program to which you are now forced to submit
- Both your common sense and integrity tells you to do something different
- You finally notice that you are hearing the same message, often word-for-word, on every form of media you happen to be looking at
- The message either feels disempowering or just wrong
- There are other people, rules and programs that are also telling you what to do, many of which, upon simple reflection, are in conflict with each other
- One of your favorite sources of information all of a sudden disappears

Saying "no" or even, "let's stop and think about this," may not require as much agility as it does plain old common sense and guts. Importantly, it requires the curiosity and backbone to question the appropriate authority, for the common good, as well as your own. Yet how willing are you or anyone else to challenge an authority figure who may hold the keys to your next promotion, your continued employment, or whether your next stop today is home or jail? To make matters worse, for the first time in a number of generations, a rise in intolerance has even been rising in our younger generation, especially on college campuses!

Recent polls show that a growing number of students would rather limit the subjects and speakers they wish to hear than be open to listening to alternative views. This is a worrying trend, since college used to be the most open and receptive time in a person's life. College was originally designed to challenge and test what was currently accepted as knowledge. To paraphrase a speech Ralph Nader gave at my college long ago:

"You students are now at the ideological pinnacle of your lives. You enjoy a cozy, pre-work-life reality and have the luxury of access to all types of information and opinions from all different sources. Don't let this moment of openness and learning go to waste!"

Consciously or not, the opportunity to entertain different points of view, possibly the basis of what makes the pursuit of higher learning so valuable, is now being shut down. More and more pampered students would rather muzzle dissenting opinions than have to listen to and engage a conflicting point of view. Comedians such as Chris Rock and Jerry Seinfeld declared they will no longer perform on college campuses, ostensibly because of the dissent and heckling they now receive from the audience. Does this sound like the breeding ground for open, agile leaders needed to handle increasingly turbulent markets to you?

More and more of us are being forced to either confront situations that are either completely outside of our integrity or to kowtow to an authority figure, only to have to later wrestle with our conscience in private. Talk about stress! Maybe this explains why, for example, there are now more Vietnam veterans who have died of suicide than were killed on the battlefield.

PC no longer means personal computer

One of the biggest inhibitors going forward, with regards to open and free-flowing communication, is being politically correct. Knowing what to say and carefully choosing how to say it so as not to offend someone or some group is reaching plague levels. Your authors absolutely support non-intrusive behavior combined with full self-expression. How agile is it to have to respond quickly, yet have an extra barrier of figuring out how not to offend various listeners' capricious and constantly changing tastes and beliefs? How can, for instance, your HR department do its job if just bringing up the topic of sexual harassment causes offense to certain employees? Agility demands toleration and the ability to hear conflicting points of view in order to make better-informed decisions. The trick is to separate the wheat from the chaff in any conversation. Some call it looking for the 'gold' in what is being said. Getting offended by the message's packaging can cause you to miss the importance of what is being said and to miss recognizing a great opportunity or danger.

Take care to heed the philosophical advice to choose your battles, a phrase commonly attributed to the famous Chinese general Sun Tzu. Some battles are worth fighting and others are not. Could a bit of increased tolerance and empathy to sense the difference increase your agility and play an important role in accomplishing your task? Could your ability to listen, understand, and empathize with your customer or colleague now need to be honored, expanded, and practiced as a business survival technique? Ironically, tolerance and curious listening are often more about unlearning than increased learning.

Sticky thinking

Have you also noticed that the older you get, the more you have to think about and the more you have to do? What if, not only we ourselves work like this, but companies, governments, and societies also? Things pile up and with experience, there is naturally more information to draw upon. This causes more opinions to protect, more to debate and much more to doubt. This deluge of new input ultimately leads to increased or prolonged indecision.

The drastically increasing amount and quality of information that needs to be processed is slowing down the whole communication, decision, and action process. Just think of how many hours you burn weekly just by taking care of the following issues:

- Bank, investment, and retirement accounts
- Telephone bills
- Switching TV channels
- Social media choices and comments
- What to eat this evening and how to prepare it

This short list is offered just to get you thinking seriously about how many distractions there are now that cause you to lose sight of your purpose. Just look in your store next time you wish to buy a box of cereal or a bottle of shampoo. You will be faced with a whole wall of alternatives.

How often do you have or take the time to study the labels of all 200-plus bottles of shampoo or 50 boxes of cereal to choose the best and healthiest choice for you?

Needless to say, the more you have to think about, the slower and more cautious you become when making decisions. This is part of our human nature. Also, the more experiences you have to share and the better you get at articulating it, the more you want your point heard. This takes time. We call this the molasses effect, as the deeper into a discussion you get and the more opinions need to be expressed, the more the conversation takes on a texture resembling swimming through thick and gooey molasses. Discussion easily degrades to a debate and often later to an argument (where it can get very personal). This is the extreme opposite of agility and makes it harder to do what needs to be done to reach your goal in time. How can you streamline conversations and transform debates and heated discussions into dialogues? How about asking more questions? And then listening with all your senses to the complete answer?

The disease of inaction

Inaction can take many different forms such as:

- Not doing anything
- Watching too much TV
- Too much curiosity to the point of indecision
- Eating too much
- Being too worried or scared to act
- Force of habit
- Winning your point rather than compromising and moving forward
- Babbling around a point instead of communicating toward its solution
- Being totally preoccupied with your smart gadget
- Physical or mental challenges that confuse or amplify the situation such as ADD, ADHD, and/or Asperger's syndrome

Inaction can range from annoying to dangerous, as many unfortunate victims of the 2004 tsunami found out. Reference again the many stories about animals running for safety while people stayed put or even went closer to the water's receding edge to get a closer look at the disappearing surf.

Look in every public place these days, from restaurants to buses and trains and you will see the same thing. Most faces staring into a little smart screen of some sort. Everyone is so caught up in their little gadget that many prefer the company of their electronic entertainment than warm and active conversation with a fellow human being. Anecdotal research seems to be confirming that the underlying motivation to turn off the world and bury yourself in your electronic gadget is an increasing level of stress. Psychologists are now screaming for the need for some time offline, alone. Many introverts are quickly learning that just looking like you are pre-occupied with your gadget often blocks others from approaching you. On the other hand, a recent survey showed that 33 percent of the British population had not received a hug in the last six months![2]

There are other social media phenomena that are not simply explained by stress and are increasingly inhibiting commerce. For instance, before COVID, restaurant owners were very confused about packed evenings with fewer profits. They finally uncovered the cause of their financial squeeze. It was due to smart phones. They discovered that their waiter or waitress now needed to come back to each table more often and over a longer period. First, their dining guests now had to "check in" on Facebook, take pictures for their Instagram posts and finish texting their friends, before they could finally settle down to order. In short, tables that used to be occupied by a group for ninety minutes now consumed up to 50 percent more time. Slower turnover and fewer guests per evening mean fewer meals served and less profit, even on packed evenings. The trend of lots of people and lower profits was increasing before the pandemic; now less people and even lower profits are forcing even experienced restauranteurs out of business, many for good.

At the time of this writing, early August 2021, many restaurants have been forced to close either due to lockdowns or just due to customers being too scared to dare dining out. The whole restaurant and hospitality branch is collapsing as no restaurant can stay in business long with a minimum loss of 50 percent of its clientele, basically overnight and continuing. Many restauranteurs are now heavily in debt due to their hoping that this crisis would pass quickly, rather than taking agile steps to meet the new business horizon. A restaurateur and good friend of one of your authors sank his personal fortune, along with many of his relative's money into a new and fresh micro-brewery. After a few costly delays, it finally opened two months before COVID hit. Remarkably, he has managed to stay afloat by making a deal with the landlord and inviting others to invest. He was hospitalized for stress recently and is now back but working at a slower pace. He is still in business on a quarter-by-quarter basis, but unless things change drastically, this quarter may be his last.

Is it any wonder we may be losing the battle of staying conscious long enough to choose?

Entitlements that inhibit

Getting something for absolutely nothing creates behavioral trends. Once you get used to something for free, why would you ever again want to exert yourself to work for it? Agility demands energetic engagement and a heightened ability to think for yourself. Unfortunately, when you are conditioned to rely upon entitlements and other people's opinions (and money), it seems to become human nature to begin expecting freebies as some sort of right. Take them away and you risk social unrest. Evidence would suggest that we are reaching Margaret Thatcher's economic inflection point where we are "running out of other people's money." What happens next? What happens to people who have mastered the art of receiving entitlements as a right instead of training to be agile? COVID has only accelerated the search for this answer.

Reputation

No one likes to look bad; making mistakes looks bad, even if that is when we learn the most. Therefore, those people who quickly and humbly admit to their own mistakes (and those even fewer who choose to learn from them) are few and far between. This becomes especially true when there are prestigious business or governmental/political egos on the line. Remember, it is not the original mistake that makes the situation untenable, it usually blows up when the cover-up is finally revealed. Many a company has gone belly up due to someone concealing what later turns out to be a bad decision or investment. The press loves revealing a good cover-up. For instance, a number of investment houses have been crippled by so-called rogue traders or "fat fingers" who hid massive losses, who often "doubled down" on them rather than revealing their mistakes and seeking help. Interestingly, the sums involved with, for example, Barings and JP Morgan's famous *Whale* make their management's "surprise" a little hard to swallow. This is also a clear demonstration with hard and tragic evidence of a critical need for more agility. Is it any wonder why blockchain technology is making so many inroads to banking and finance? How much more face do you save and how much more agile do you look by not being aware when you are in charge, compared to knowing and being wrong? TBTF anyone?

HPPO (highest paid person's opinion)

Another form of inhibition is being forced to politely concede to the highest paid person's opinion. The further we go into the twenty-first century, the clearer it becomes that the relationship between the Hippo or highest paid person's opinion on how to decide and the most appropriate or effective one are not always one-to-one. Money still talks, and all too often the highest paid person also has the seniority. This assumption is almost habitually based upon past glories rather than reflecting over the current situation. What if it really is easier to suppress your urge to verbally challenge a HPPO and, as a good friend Patrick Collard once quipped, remain polite? He used to say that, "polite also means pissed-off-lightly!"

This phenomenon was taken to the extreme when, according to Malcom Gladwell in his acclaimed book, *Outliers,* that Korean airline crash could have been caused by the extreme hierarchy in Korean culture. According to Gladwell, the 1997 crash of KAL Flight 801 into a mountain on its approach to Guam was due to the co-pilot not daring to question the poor judgment of the pilot. True or not, ask yourself how often you have kept quiet on a decision by your superior that you understood and felt was wrong only to find out how right you were?

Confidence versus nonchalance

If you are sending people off to a course to improve their skills, it is important to do this with a clear motive as well as demonstrating your commitment to what they will learn. It is not necessary that you attend every training course your staff attends, especially when it has to do with their specializations, i.e. a technical or tactical part of their jobs. Yet it is dreadfully important to make a conscious and confident demonstration of the course's importance or better yet, attend the training or event. Especially if it has to do with team building or some sort of kick-off event. Being too busy to attend can be interpreted as nonchalant or even danger-ous. Who, nowadays, isn't too busy? Behave in this way and expect your status as a trusted leader to quickly become tarnished.

Dumping versus delegating

Overworked managers have too much to do. They often take oppor-tunities to off-load uncomfortable tasks on those who cannot say no easily. The resentment of not being allowed to participate in such a choice can build quickly. Leadership is all about confidence and inspiring rather than obligating others to act. Asking the opinion of those affected, creating understanding for the situation through dia-logue—ending in agreement—will go a long way toward gaining their heartfelt cooperation and producing measurable, inspiring, and prof-itable results.

Good and bad habits

We venture to say that most of the processes, cultures, organizations, and systems currently operating in a corporation are designed with the inten-tion to make it easier for employees and staff to act without thinking! An expression often heard in the corporate corridors is, "we have to dumb it down so that people know what to do." This is an extremely condescend-ing, disempowering, and increasingly dangerous attitude, especially when creative, entrepreneurial, and dare we say independent behaviors are now needed more than ever. Unfortunately, most managers still prefer their crew to act like "mini-me's" jumping at their demand.

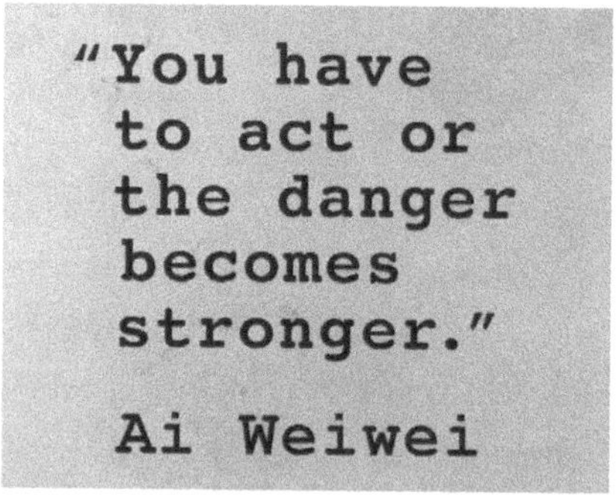

This is very hard when ingrained "habits" are involved. "This is how we have always done this," is a common expression by those who will potentially be affected and are fearful of or are just habitually opposed to change.

The consequence?

An immediate and increasingly critical delay of action and

> "You have to act or the danger becomes stronger."
>
> Ai Weiwei

Figure 20. Ai Weiwei, Chinese artist & activist

one more point for the business-as-usual crowd. It also increases the risk that this new danger will fester and grow. We can also make the argument that this hypothesis is a major culprit in stimulating exploration. Tests have been made that show neurons in the part of our brain called the striatum are much more activated during exploration than after a habit has become imprinted. By then, we act without thinking; why? Because it worked before! In too many teams and typical grouping of individuals from corporations to the military, such safe traits are encouraged and promoted.

"Do not think, just do as I say," needs to be used sparingly, if at all and in a narrow and correct context. Otherwise, the consequences can be anything from discontent to mutiny.

This might be okay if El Capitan is ultimately proven correct, but what if the decision is wrong? Regardless, can we at least agree that it is true that we still are mostly creatures of habit? If so, then conscious change and transformation will naturally be hindered by unconscious, automatic behavior. Add AI to this mix and this creates a challenge to creativity that will demand drastically more attention going forward in this new brave world of constant change. All habits that enforce those systems, culture, organization, and processes that were designed to make work easier and thought-free should be questioned, often. Do not despair yet, some practical things can be done to enhance business agility, and we are coming to that rapidly.

Inhibitors and zombification

All of the above cultural and systematic inhibitors drastically contribute to turning good-hearted, well-meaning and ambitious people, like yourself, into sheeple and zombies. All of these human and system-based friction points wear you down and drain dry your creative energy. Slowly but surely, count on your integrity to begin to erode as maintaining your stand in front of continuous peer pressure and multiple complex systems begin to take their toll. After a while it becomes easier and much safer just to agree and resign yourself to shuffle along with the flock. Can you say *"baa"*? Should you find yourself one day being promoted and in charge of enforcing rules and regulations that would have made you cringe in the past, consider yourself zombified. By then, most thoughts of increasing your agility will have disappeared, possibly never to return.

Factors that make the molasses of inhibition even thicker

Below is a partial/random list of just some of the factors and situations that can inhibit your crew's agility.

- **Rules, systems, processes, and regulations** both written and unwritten
- **Culture and hierarchy**, organizational, societal, economical, and individual
- **Politics** within your group, your company and your society
- **Moods, feelings, and behaviors** of the people involved: simply having a good or bad day can influence how you interact, decide, and your willingness to cooperate
- **Experiences** or history and your interpretation of it: we use experiential filters every time we are reminded of *that past* situation/decision and result
- **Points of view**, opinions, combative attitudes, and assumptions: everyone has these, yet are they relevant right here and now? Are the most important opinions being expressed in a way that can be heard, understood, and acted upon?
- **Listening** to one another: How many people do you meet who are actually interested in your message and listen to it actively,

compared to those who are just waiting to speak their truth? What about you?

This is far from an exhaustive list, and it is constantly changing. However, it should contain enough examples to make our point that agility gets more challenging to maintain or enhance as time passes and these and other behaviors become institutionalized. This molasses effect naturally slows down the whole decision-to-action process until a less encumbered, more agile person, organization, or society enters the picture, then runs circles around you. Whether they arrive with a game-changing technology, a new business model, or new way of thinking, the result is usually another round of creative destruction where only the agile survive and only the most agile thrive.

Your author had the opportunity to work for Digital Equipment Corporation (DEC) in its final days. Even though DEC had been one of the most agile and successful competitors in the mini-computer marketplace, that product and its whole market died a quick and almost unnoticeable death with the advent of the personal computer. The PC quickly took over what used to be the mini-computer market share and DEC lost its whole *raison d'etre*. Suddenly, there was no need for minis any longer. This great company with 120,000 competent, well-meaning, smart, and dedicated employees could not change the course of their proud corporate ship quickly enough to save the company or their jobs. Even though bold, then increasingly desperate decisions were made, those tasked with changing company behavior would not or could not do it. Add to this that most employees had made careers out of DEC's own brand of business as usual. How open do you think they were for someone preaching that their way of life was now doomed, and radical change was needed, fast?

As a result, DEC is now ancient history. Many more exciting crash and burns have occurred since. Yet the molasses of a business culture, internal systems and the (fill in the blank) way of doing business still inhibits the ability to change to such a degree that it continues to destroy even successful companies. Just like a major storm, the market is unforgiving. It just is! Now those storms are coming harder and faster than any DEC or Motorola employee could have dreamed of. The question you and your crew will increasingly face is what can and will be done when faced with a rapid, unforgiving, and market-changing shift in your business as usual? With COVID as witness, these changes are coming faster and more furiously with each passing day.

The consciousness of agile collaboration

An interesting discussion between we two authors occurred while writing this book. Hans comes from the corporate transformation, structural, strategic, marketing, and tactical side of the agility question. He has trained in and made a good living using tools to help companies become more agile. He wanted to focus upon the tools and leave the issue of consciousness as a footnote to the process. Kurt's contribution came from a more "artistic" background in sales, effective communication, sensational soft skills training, teamwork, and body language. Kurt also happened to end up writing a good deal of the verbiage based upon Hans' structure and ideas. The results became this unique and powerful blend of hard and soft skills, which now seems a perfect and agile match for these exciting, dangerous, and increasingly emotional times. What we feel makes this collaboration powerful is our commitment to a conscious roll-out of a soup-to-nuts approach to business agility. Please keep in mind that business agility, without its conscious and flexible application, instantly becomes policy.

Two important definitions

One of the main points of this book is that technology and systems are beginning to take over our way of living, impeding our efforts to become agile. The more we become subjected to policies and regulation, the more people begin to become frustrated and act *anomie* (according to Emilie Durkheim this means a feeling of passivity born of despair)[3]. In other words, we are losing our individuality, creativity, and drive as we become more a part of an uncaring system or we "lose it" and begin flailing at it out of our desperation. Either way, our reactions to these stimuli cause us to become human doings even more quickly, further suppressing our feelings and abilities rather than responding with our full creative and cooperative potential, together.

The second important word here is *amathia,* which is Greek in origin and roughly means "intelligent stupidity." According to a thread on Reddit, it doesn't imply, "an ability to understand, but a refusal to understand." Could this be more evidence of the burgeoning cancel culture and the basis of many disputes? There seems to be an outbreak of very smart people saying, believing, or even worse, accepting the most absurd things. For instance:

- Closing down churches but keeping liquor stores open to reduce infection
- Certain groups using violence to stop what they believe to be fascism
- Wearing a surgical mask while driving alone in a car

We will leave other observations and examples to you, dear reader. Our point here is that you may be surprised to learn that something you have believed or taken for granted for your entire life as common sense is 180 degrees opposite the understanding of those you have responsibility for. Yet it is your responsibility as a leader to talk about it, identify it, and agree upon how everyone defines it, then tackle it, before it causes something to go wrong.

An appropriate anecdote to drive this point home is of a wife making a roast for dinner. After many years of observing the wife cut the corners off the roast before sticking it in the oven, the husband finally asked, "Why do you do that? The wife quickly replied, "because that is what my mom used to do." Whereupon his next obvious question was, "Why did she do that?" After thinking for a minute, she reached for her phone and called her mother. When asked, the mother thought for a moment, then laughed as she replied, "When you were growing up, we did not own a large enough roasting pan. I was forced to cut the corners off to make it fit."

What causes anomie and amathia?

Is it lack of consciousness, curiosity, common sense, or all three?

We humans are creatures of habit. Could our reliance upon conditioned unconscious behavior patterns now be coming back to haunt us? For some reason, we feel more comfortable doing again what we have already done, even when we have evidence that it is no longer useful or efficient. It is the evolutionary equivalent of still using your favorite software's version 1.0 when the latest version will save you time and help you accomplish exponentially more. The more you can learn to dance with the here and now, the more you will enhance your business agility.

Conscious action

There is nothing new in stating that understanding customer tastes and marketing conditions are the new holy grail of business success. This has been an open secret for a long time. The difference is now that with increasing competition and customer sophistication, your ability to create and maintain relationships really needs to shift gears.

Look no further than your own process of selecting someone to do business with. How have your selection criteria changed over the last few years? Not long ago your selection of possible suppliers was more limited and in many cases the quality of both the product and the post-sale service were much broader. With each passing year and with the increasing intensity of the hunt for efficiency and lower margins, businesses were forced to cut more and more corners in order to survive. The fat was trimmed long ago, and now most surviving businesses are cutting into their corporate skeletons to remain competitive. As more and more people are applying for the same good positions, even the cost and quality of employees is eroding. Those employees who still have some sort of work ethic left are being forced to work longer and harder for less pay, increasing stress, and the inevitability of making a mistake, or worse, burning out. With this and the help of more regulation, competing products and services can easily homogenize into a grey, acceptable but uninspiring mass. Just look at how similar different car manufacturers have now made each class of cars.

Creating a more agile organization that your customers can easily distinguish from the rest demands more automation as well as a drastic personal increase in sensitivity to customer needs, wants, and wishes by each and every one of your employees.

Personal agility

Although this book is focused upon organizational agility, it is impossible to do this justice without talking about the personal level of agility. As we wish to make crystal clear, all organizations are based upon and driven by individuals. Remaining conscious of this fact is critical to any attempt at improving individual and/or collective business agility. This increased consciousness and agility should extend to each individual's:

- **Personal health**
  Keeping yourself fit and healthy is paramount to all else. How inspired are you when you are not feeling good physically or mentally? Your agility increases the more you take care of yourself.

- **Personal finances**
  Having responsibility and control over how much you earn, save, invest and how much you spend is critical for your state of mind. Being in debt is not only a drag on your financial agility, it also drains you emotionally and physically. The more money you have at your disposal, the more options you will have and freedom you will feel.

- **Ability to adapt and relocate**
  Just like an agile dog sprinting around an obstacle course, the more quickly you can move from one situation to another, the more options will be open to you and whatever you are focused upon.

- **Ability to listen, communicate, and relate to others**
  It's all about people! Systems are great, but relationships are better. The more adept you are at cultivating relationships by listening with all your senses and dancing your way to agreement, the more you increase your chances for success.

Below are some ways to help improve your personal agility.

Some conscious soft skills

Here we include a number of proven ideas, issues, and examples that can help you consciously enhance your agility into a new dimension of sensational performance. Breaking out of your mechanical and automatic business-as-usual coma is more important than ever, should you still want to think for yourself, remain successful, or improve your success by attracting and retaining more loyal customers. Still, when you are being bombarded with increasing amounts of information and are kept off balance by decisions you are forced to make on someone else's schedule, the challenge to remain conscious and curious increases drastically.

To effectively use the skills presented in this book it will help enormously to practice being here now and bringing a conscious touch to whatever you do.

Here are some simple tools to help you in this pursuit.

Is the fax on?

Before the age of broadband, when telephone cables were the primary way to transfer voice and data to someone else, for a short time we relied deeply upon tele-modems and telefaxes. What these communication tools essentially did was to translate your message into a package of electrons that could be transmitted over the wires and then retranslated back in the receiving machine. To accomplish this, these two dumb machines needed to shake hands first, in order to agree upon how the data would be translated back and forth. This sound-activated process could be interpreted in English to sound something like this:

Machine One	Machine Two
Hello	What?
Hello	What language?
Hello	Oh, English!
Hello	Hello!
Hello	How can I help?
I have a message.	I'm now ready to receive it.

At this point these two dumb machines had established the so-called "handshake protocol" and now could begin communicating in an understandable way.

Take a moment now and ponder just how often you send your message before making sure your listener's fax is on and ready to receive?

Even these two dumb machines are smart enough to connect to each other and make sure they understand the same language. Yet, how often do we begin talking before we even look to see if anyone is ready, willing, or able to receive our message? Or have you ever thrown a ball to someone who wasn't looking at you?

Collaborative urgency

If you feel pressed for time and you are forced to make up your mind on someone else's timeline, then chances are you are being used. After all, if an expert convinces you that time is being wasted, it must be the truth, right? Have you possibly begun to notice that the more someone is telling you that you must act within a certain time period, the more it is probably wise not to?

In a real collaboration, the collaborator will still bring up important deadlines, but the difference will be that they will do this in a dialogue and will try their best to serve everyone and strive to make the deadline mutually beneficial. You may still need to sign and commit before the end of the month, but you are more apt to be aware that your collaborator will now get to go on that bonus cruise and may be willing to shave a bit more off the price to get it. Win/Win! An authentic collaboration will be transparent and cooperative in nature. You should be invited to discover all the profit and/or consequences of acting together within a certain timeframe, but the choice will still remain open and free for you to make.

Relate and challenge

In every era there is a prevailing formula for success. In our post-industrial information age, transactional business was the way to go, as it allowed organizations to expand quickly, emotions be damned. Now, as we approach important limits in virtually every business dimension, the importance of creating loyal relationships is becoming a critical factor in customer retention and development. The price for finding brand-new customers continues to increase and each customer is becoming more sophisticated. This can often mean they are pickier and/or spoiled. In fact, it is not unusual now to see someone talking with a salesperson at a store while simultaneously Googling the competition. This forces the salesperson to use a broader set of sales "arguments" which has to include soft skills that focus on a better service experience. What if the only real value left to add is becoming increasingly personal? Making each customer feel special and even integrating them and their competencies into your sale will create the basis for a sustainable, collaborative, and profitable relationship.

Yet there is one even more important skill that is worth taking with from the golden age of transacting. That is to relate to your customer while challenging them to do even better.

Research undertaken during the Great Recession of 2009–2011 showed that when times get rough, two types of sales-behavior maintained or increased their sales numbers. These two types of personalities were:

- Those that were pros at creating and maintaining relationships and
- Those who challenged their customers to be even better

Not surprisingly, the ones who created and maintained relationships maintained their numbers, whereas those who challenged their customers from a solid relationship increased their sales figures.

Developing trust

In both winning sales models, trust is key, yet here, too, there might be an important distinction.

- In the transactional model trust is focused on the tools, methods, and systems.
- In the collaborative model, trust is focused upon the people involved and their relationship. Part of that trust depends, of course, on their ability to effectively use those tools, methods, and systems prescribed, but trust becomes a powerful leverage point when people and emotions are welcomed and encouraged.

Consciously including the human factor in collaboration is metaphorically a bit like transforming a two-dimensional black and white picture into a three-D color one. But don't stop there, what if feelings and your ability to sense and express emotion is what distinguishes your humanity? It remains of course your choice to live a life of quality or to just exist and transact?

Figure 21. Do you want to live life fully or just transact it? Is working equal to living?

Leveraging agility via confident leadership

The need to get agile is grounded in the emerging crisis of confidence. You can have the best change management and business tools available from the most well-known business consultants in the world. Yet if you as the leader do not feel and radiate confidence, you and your crew still risk foundering on the growing seas of uncertainty. It is also human nature that during times of greater volatility and uncertainty your average crew member will instinctively look to you for positive signals and reassurance from his/her confident leader. Your, conscious or not, chosen role requires you to be confident and ready!

The causes of uncertainty

> "No one ever got fired for buying IBM."
> **—Business proverb**

IBM and other IT companies have sold billions of dollars of hardware and software by playing upon management uncertainty. By heightening feelings of FUD—Fear, Uncertainty, and Doubt—they understand that management will shell out large sums in order to lower risk and *feel* safer. If their sales people fail to demonstrate authentic confidence in their story, the chances of selling themselves and their products rapidly diminish. Fearing the unknown causes uncertainty. The more you feel you are prepared to handle what will happen, the more confidence you will project. One of the keys to increasing confidence is your ability to break large unknowns down into smaller manageable components. This allows you to put a measurable handle on uncertainty. Looking forward, instead of backward, will also help.

The physiological mechanics of confidence

There is one more area needing to be addressed and that is the area of conscious leadership projection. It is important to sense its effect on your level of confidence, your ability to decide and to effectively lead others. What if simply by adjusting your posture and breathing slower and deeper you can leverage your ability to decisively inspire and engage others? What if increasing your confidence is a function of the congruency you create between your thoughts, words, and deeds?

Thoughts versus feelings

It is now almost universally accepted that what you think influences what you feel, experience, and express. Thinking positive is a good start; but combining this with *feeling* positive will drastically boost your confidence.

According to Dr. Joe Dispenza, thoughts are what we silently broadcast out to the world. Feelings are the field in which we receive and experience input back from the world. Could this phenomenon be why even if you are doing your best to think positive, but still feeling worried or scared, you will still attract scary and worrisome experiences? Making yourself wrong—for not feeling as positive as you think you should—only amplifies this incongruency. The trick seems to be aligning your thoughts with your feelings, by first disengaging them from each other and then practicing feeling good for absolutely no reason. This is of course easier said than done, but just may be worth practicing. There are numerous YouTube channels and self-help gurus available on the internet that can assist you in this interesting adventure into distinguishing and mastering your thoughts and feelings. Again, don't believe this, but test it anyway.

Being open to new, even very untraditional paths of learning can only increase your agility.

A simple way to test your ability to increase your chances of feeling positive is to smile. Did you know that regardless of whether you adjust a few muscles on your face or the source is a warm and fuzzy feeling from deep within your heart, smiling will release endorphins into your bloodstream that promote well-being and healing? Take a moment, breathe deeply, and smile. See if you do not start feeling better. When you feel better you also project that out to those in your surroundings. You become a more attractive leader and project more confidence during the process.

Words

Words and conversations can be either compressive or expansive. The words you choose to think and express influence your cells to either focus upon growth or protection. Positive conversations cause your cells, and consequently you, to open up, expand, and actively participate in more of what is happening around you. Negative conversations will encourage your individual cells to close down and compress for increased protection. You become stiff, silent, and usually look like someone to avoid. That defensive message is then broadcast out to your surroundings either vocally, as in angry remarks, or as stone-cold silence. That old childhood rhyme of, "sticks and stones will break my bones, but names will never hurt me," may not be as true or comforting as we were led to believe. Start noticing when your words and conversation are expanding the listening of those around you or compressing and shutting it down. If it's the latter, change course!

Deeds

Want to inspire those you are talking with? Let's start with where the word "inspire" comes from. It is Latin in origin and literally means to "breathe in spirit." Take a long, deep, and inspiring breath. How does that affect the way you are feeling? Chances are no matter how good (or bad) you felt before, you are now feeling just a bit better.

We are essentially wind instruments; the more air we allow to pass through our lungs and larynx, the deeper sounding our voice becomes as more of our body's cells resonate with our words. Increased resonance and a deeper tone invite increased trust. Why do you think most successful radio and TV announcers have deep, dark, rich voices? Because such a voice inspires trust and encourages us to believe in and buy whatever it is they are selling. Just by breathing deeper your voice and you simply become more attractive!

These are just a few of hundreds of tips to consciously increase the impact of your power to positively express and to overcome FUD and a lack of confidence. The more you can align your thoughts, your words, and actions into one congruent package, the easier and more effective you will be in delivering it and the more your listeners will be moved into action.

In our current world of uncertainty there is a distinct lack of confident leaders. Distinguishing them from those confidence artists and sociopaths who have learned to use their body language to deceive us is an important bonus of becoming more conscious of your own body and its language. If you really want to lead others into a brighter future, get more agile. Get more conscious of the messages you are receiving as well as the one you are projecting with your entire, congruent self. Strive to make your message—and yourself—more authentic. Make it something that excites, inspires, and engages everyone!

Getting past behavior

The more understanding you create, the more agile you will become. Those of us who have a few years under our belts come from a past where there was more time to reflect before acting. Today's shorter cycles and increased volatility are now forcing leaders to do away with that luxury. Their crews must learn to adjust their course much quicker than in the past. This implies being agile enough to run the gauntlet of your listener's behavioral triggers. These include all those psychological buttons that you can easily push, sending them into a familiar "do-loop" of reaction that shuts down their listening and sets them into their automatic pilot programming.

Reacting automatically from having your buttons pushed can take the form of:

- Causing a debate
- Projecting your own faults on those you are talking to
- Taking offense

- Anger or rage
- Checking out and daydreaming
- Nodding approval with a blank stare
- Confusion and increased uncertainty
- Checking their phone
- Polite, but clearly detached listening

These are some of any number of other pre-recorded, unconscious, inhibiting, and programmed behaviors.

Collaboration: We're all connected

Each system is somehow connected to many others. For example, next time you board an airplane take a moment to reflect on how many people and systems are connected to your flying safely from one place to another. Think about all of the following people and systems that are in turn supported by others not mentioned or are hiding in the background:

- Travel agents and their booking systems
- Programmers that developed the code and the factories that built all the computers and networking systems
- Miners that dug up and processed all the raw materials and resources that were used to build everything
- Architects, engineers and construction workers who built the airports, roads, and rail systems that got you to your plane
- People and processes that built your airplane
- Airport staff and the crew of your airliner and all the people and systems that clean, support, and train them
- The payment system that allowed you to pay for it

This by no means is a complete list. In fact, this list could include just about everyone on the planet, depending upon how broadly we define connection. Even then we are only considering the practical, tangible plane. The point is that we are all connected and the sooner and more inclusively we recognize this, the quicker we can start appreciating and using this tremendous leverage to our collective advantage. Then we will be able to accomplish exponentially more, together.

Successful vibes

In the movie *The Secret Behind the Secret*, Jerry Hicks explains how he found and examined the original draft of Napoleon Hill's *Think and Grow Rich*. Somewhere, he had heard that essential information was edited out of the first edition. What he found was that every reference of the word vibration was removed. It must have given the publisher some bad vibes.

It would be an interesting discussion of whether this omission of the word vibration was a disservice to the millions of readers who have read this amazing book or if the book would have ever been published had Mr. Hill insisted on keeping this controversial concept in the book. Regardless, this discovery adds more power to this powerful concept of attraction. What if there really are good vibes that you can create and send out to attract even better vibrations back? An entire industry of attraction training has grown up over the past twenty years as more and more evidence is revealed pointing to the power of attraction. Even more than a century ago, the likes of Carnegie and Morgan were talking openly about soft skills. Don't believe us? It may be worth considering that Napoleon Hill's book was based upon interviews with Andrew Carnegie, J.P. Morgan, and other titans. Could the "secret" of the Law of Attraction have been at least part of what these industrial titans believed was behind their successes? Are you agile enough to consider this as at least a possibility?

Service develops conscious agility

What if pure service is transparent? Serving others keeps you present to the needs of those around you as well as keeping you from becoming the center of attention. Test and see if the more you disappear into service, the more you enter an eternal flow that correctly guides you to the next step. Is it really true that you only become noticed when you stand out? This may be important when managing others but can cause problems when serving them.

When serving others correctly, the focus of those you are serving will be on their own satisfaction and accomplishment. You become background, the space for them to experience how well your service satisfies their needs, wants, and wishes. What if this allows them to focus more on their agenda? What if now more gets done and the positive experience enjoyed by your customer increases their loyalty and your future business?

Expertise versus mastery

The difference in these words may appear as just semantics, but there are some deeply important points distinguishing these two states from each other. As we are continually talking about mastering agility in this book, it is important to understand the depth and power experienced on this longer, more challenging path of mastery. The following distinctions do not currently exist in the "real world." They are offered as suggestions to make it perfectly and painfully clear how you choose to use your hard-won knowledge. With this in mind, pretend you now have two very well-versed professionals in front of you; both are highly capable of, for instance, leading others.

Imagine further that they are twins. They have grown up together, attended the same schools, and followed the same career path. Still, there is one major difference that distinguishes these two pros. One considers himself an expert and tends to constantly showcase, justify and defend his managerial decisions. The other chooses to master the art of leadership by asking followers curious questions, listening closely to the answers, then guiding listeners toward the agreed-upon goal and even further, mutual development. Surely, many who probably consider themselves experts today would better fit the following suggested profile of a master. What about you?

Expert (a humbly suggested distinction)

Experts are very good at what they do, having studied a certain field for most of their adult lives for at least 10,000 hours on average, according to other experts. They have built a reputation for having all the answers. They know a lot and take pride in justifying and showcasing that knowledge to you at every opportunity. Yet they have, consciously or unconsciously, chosen to cross a fine line with this amazing amount of knowledge.

Instead of using it primarily to enrich the lives and careers of those listening, they choose instead to exploit this knowledge as a means of bringing more attention, fame, and fortune to themselves. Not only that, if challenged, experts will often do what is necessary to prove and defend their point, increasingly often shutting down, discounting, and even humiliating a curious or inquisitive listener in the process.

Experts love to debate and are prone to use their knowledge as a weapon to defend their reputation, the institution, or the idea they represent. Their point becomes their identity, and pride and ego take over.

Finally, expertise is more goal than path. Once reached, it becomes a badge to show off and defend. Even the expert's body language, stiff and defensive. Notice how often an expert's stiff and ramrod-straight appearance resembles an exclamation point?

Master (another humbly suggested distinction)

Masters are also experts at what they do. They, too, studied their specific area for most of their lives. They have also become the vortex of increasing knowledge in their chosen field. Masters know as much as experts, but somewhere around here is where the similarities end. Unlike experts, masters are usually thrilled and honored to share their knowledge with others in a way that it can be used and developed further. Masters love and seek chances to serve their listeners and to increase everyone's understanding. This is done through open and thought-provoking dialogue, where thoughtful and reflective questions encourage the expression of everyone's point of view. A reflective and thought-provoking question, instead of a bullet-proof statement, is one of a master's most valuable tools. They fully understand that by consciously sharing their knowledge and being open to learn more. They will also continuously expand their own expertise as well as their ability to deliver and teach it. The entire conversation moves forward as everyone wins with a true master. A master is a true leader, as people naturally want to follow them.

Although fame and fortune can and often does follow, personal recognition is not the master's primary goal. In fact, when challenged, a true master will humbly and respectfully ask the challenger to explain in more detail his or her point. There is a curiosity present to see if the challenger has discovered something new, for all to appreciate and incorporate. Debate is seen, by the master, as entertainment at best or a waste of time at worst. The true master will continually seek to create an open, curious, and collaborative dialogue in which differences can be vented and discussed and where even more possibilities can be discovered and integrated. The master's calling card is a mutual "aha" experience.

Mastering anything requires openness, curiosity, and an inherent appreciation of the value and attractiveness of serving others. They constantly practice and test their ability to teach, plus actively demonstrate their own will and willingness to constantly learn and improve. Interestingly, most of us will automatically answer we have these properties, wouldn't you?

Yet how many of us will continue to apply them in our lives, especially when we uncover a contradictory behavior pattern? This is, of course, where exercising these properties and qualities can drastically and truly make a difference in your behavior and your future. That's what makes a discovery like this so challenging. Keep in mind that this discovery can mean that you have been totally wrong, so far.

A master's body language is usually soft, attractive and often resembles a supple, yet grounded question mark. Through selfless and transparent service, everyone benefits from a master. Mastery is more path than goal. This is truly where the master differs from the expert. The master openly admits his or her shortcomings, learns something, adjusts defective behavior and continues forward on the path. The expert often defends his hard-won goal. Which behavior would you choose to follow or better yet practice?[4] Which behavior, expert or master, do you think is more agile?

The practice of mastery

If this suggested distinction between expert and master inspires you to begin walking your own path of mastery, the following points are offered to help you walk that path more effectively. These points can be used in all parts of your life and will absolutely contribute to your personal agility.

- **Remain curious**

    While you're at it, remain young! Take every opportunity to ask questions and find out more about what interests you. Be curious while demonstrating curiosity and wonder to everyone with whom you come into contact.

- **Learn from everything**

    Does that scrap of newspaper blowing down the street actually contain an eureka moment for you? How will you ever find out if you have shut down your curiosity and permitted your own pro-grammed expertise of what you already know dictate the wind and the paper truth? For that matter, you may find it interesting to observe how often you find yourself dictating other people's truths, too. Remember, the best "aha" moment usually starts as an "Oh crap!" moment.

- **Learn, do, and then teach**
  Taught in the best medical schools, this is a powerful three-step process encouraging you to become proficient enough so that by the third time you do something you should be proficient enough to teach it. If this is so, then to what will you need to pay more attention to and learn from during your first two rounds to accomplish this?

"There is no education from the second kick of a mule."
—James Dale Davidson's father

The world keeps changing and the more you can set your corporate ship and its crew on a path of mastery, the easier it will be to stay agile.

Mastering soft skills, the journey

There are many other tools and tips to help you and your process. These should be enough to give you some concrete skills to begin using directly. The most important and most useable point you are welcome to learn from this discussion is that it is your conscious choice as to if and when you choose to expand beyond being an expert and begin walking your own path of mastery.

CHAPTER 12

Incorporating Agility

Not only are your customers getting more sophisticated by the day, so are you. So, when you read about each of the tools described so far and those to come, you are invited and encouraged to be skeptical. From our experience, they have proven to contribute measurably and dramatically to those companies that commit to them. Your commitment to them will be up to you. We therefore encourage you to test them as well as others. As long as you give them a fair trial and they measurably contribute to a more agile stance for you and your crew, they are worth pursuing. As we have written, agility is a lifestyle and will develop over time, just as each of these tools will. We also encourage you to join us on the path of mastering agility. We look forward to your reflections and contributions to this important conversation. On our blog, www.masteringagilityblog.com, we will continue to update these and other tools and you are welcomed and encouraged to read and contribute. The more we share ideas about the best way to master and incorporate agility into each other and our organizations, the healthier, richer, and more agile we will all collectively become!

We again deliberately choose to use the word *incorporate* here. What if just implementing something is no longer enough? Implementing can still leave room for miscommunication through intellectually based misunderstandings, abstractions, and interpretations. These mistakes may be in direct conflict with what you actually wish to accomplish. Incorporating goes a step further. By focusing on the practical implications of executing, managing and embodying what you want to do and then blending this with the spirit or feeling of accomplishing your goal, you add another dimension to the individuals and organizations involved. Just as there is a tangible difference between the letter and spirit of the law, there is also a difference between the intellectual and an incorporated application of agility.

The word incorporate not only refers to building a corporation, but it also means to personally embody something. The more you personally incorporate something, the more it's absorbed into your system right down to your cells. The more this process is taken on consciously, by each person involved, the more effective, profitable, and sustainable your results will be. It manifests, resonates, and becomes part of you. This is the level of the commitment we have seen as necessary to successfully implement these tools in a way that can cause permanent change in your individual and organizational behavior.

Incorporate is such a versatile word when it comes to agility. It conveys the importance of integrating agility into your business structure, as well as into the minds and bodies of each individual in your organization. Incorporate literally means to put into a body; and that includes every type and definition of what a body is, from your own body to the incorporated body or organization in which you work or which you run.

Therefore, to really incorporate agility will require you to:
- Question everything
- Listen with all your senses
- Constantly increase personal and business capabilities
- Lead rather than manage
- Make better use of soft skills
- Practice looking forward instead of behind
- Employ new and effective agile business tools

Question everything!

With everything changing at an ever-increasing pace, holding onto outdated information, beliefs, and dogma becomes a tangible risk. Gone are the days when you could milk the same process for decades and enjoy the same result. To be agile requires you to be open, curious, and question everything from new ideas to behavioral patterns, many that have become so ingrained that they have become invisible.

Agility demands a new level of curiosity, discovery, and wonder. The more you can view yourself and your organization from your customers', suppliers', and employees' perspective, the better access you will have to invisible behavioral patterns that bring you closer to or take you further from your goal of loyal customers and increased business. The more you question, listen, and observe what is happening, the more you will be able to see and even feel the positive and negative ripples that certain behaviors cause. Increasingly, you must accept and celebrate that your customer comes first, last, and always. In the end, it is always each individual customer whose trust and commerce pays for your success.

Constantly increase personal and business capabilities

Increased customer sophistication—and the extra demands this causes—screams for a constant review and increase of personal and business capabilities. To do this and remain competitive will invite a new and innovative look at on-the-job training. This demand for state-of-the-art knowledge is already encouraging all kinds of new applications of online and blended learning. Preparing now for a time when learning and working become so intermeshed that you will not know where one ends and the other starts. Training is an integral part of what business agility is all about and as such we are also heavily involved in pushing its boundaries[1].

Lead rather than manage here, now!

As we have already mentioned, your ability to attract willing and engaged followers will be critical in your bid to become agile. Distinguishing management from leadership will be critical for successful organizations and their key people from here on. This means YOU! The simple explanation is that ancient warrior-based-coercion and the use of force are becoming less-motivating factors and are increasingly being met with disdain and resistance, especially from younger people. Metaphorically speaking, the stick is losing its effectiveness and an authentic and attractive carrot is becoming more useful.

Even in the midst of this latest pandemic, young and capable people do not fear losing their jobs like previous generations did. Even though the traditional job market is shrinking, new, more precarious and exciting ways of earning a living are on the increase. This is occurring while more and more people are testing the waters self-employment. Many are doing this alongside of working full time with the specific goal of being able to support themselves, regardless of the job market. They have realized that the luxury of relying on only one income stream is no longer prudent and many are acting on this realization. This defines agility and this is exactly the type of person you must attract, retain, learn how to motivate, and lead, going forward. In fact, as colleague and leadership coach Jörgen Khilström says, "Our parent's generation could reasonably expect to stay at the same organization for their entire career. Our generation has probably had an average of six employers. The next generation is beginning to understand that it will need to have multiple income streams to insure a steady lifestyle." Do you really think these agile youngsters will take kindly to being managed?

Make better use of soft skills

This topic will be the subject of another book as its ramifications are now just being entering the mainstream thought of how to do business. As our world of transactional business gets more structured; as we get more involved with our electronic toys and gadgets; as we become more and more stressed with the increased amount of work and chores that need to be handled, our ability to communicate—in a way that gets things done—will become more dependent upon our ability and agility to use soft skills. Why?

As we sink deeper and deeper into the complex world of "time-saving" technology, we seem to become burdened with even more stuff to do. People who listen, respect and understand us will become more important as we will be more desperately searching for humans we can trust. Right now, many of us seem to be further alienating ourselves from one another, suspicious of anyone who even hints at wanting to gain our confidence. Isn't it just common sense that anyone authentically trying to buck this trend will begin to stand out more and become more attractive? In our rapidly unfolding future, knowing how to communicate authentically, in a way that makes your listener feel seen and heard, plus using your body language to help get your message across—in a way that moves your listeners to action—will help to distinguish you as someone to trust and do business with. For instance, did you know that by just introducing yourself and saying your name to someone who may want to cause you harm, you will decrease the risk of being attacked by fifty percent? Studies in New York

City showed that it is much easier to rob a "mark," that is someone you don't know. As soon as your name is heard and understood you transform yourself from a mark to an authentic human being. For other than a completely insensitive psychopath, this offers your assailant that most human of moments, to pause, feel, and reflect. It seems there is now science to back up that fact that we become just a bit more human when we strive to connect and get to know each other better.

People need people. People are also now going out of their way and will often pay more to be treated with respect. Wouldn't you?

Practice and incorporate your soft skills then see if you notice more people being attracted to you. Also notice whether you begin to earn more money too.

Some important soft buying factors that can help you win the race are:

- Listening in a way that makes the person speaking feel special and chosen
- Contagious and mutual trust, that ripples out of your people and company
- Personal service, that secure feeling you generate when demonstrating that you and your team will run that extra mile
- Leading edge design and your use of front-running and innovative suppliers
- Better-perceived quality, of your supplier's products and services
- Creating the attractive status and prestige of being a buyer who chooses to buy from you and your team
- Customers who feel loyal enough to warmly and spontaneously recommend a person, a product, and a company

Practice looking forward instead of behind

> "The older I get, the better I was."
> **—(Spotted on an "Old Guys Rule" T-Shirt)**

Spending your time looking at past performance indicators will keep you focused upon the past and prevent you from seeing the sunshine or icebergs directly in front of you. Looking forward is the quality of being vigilant. Lose your vigilance and your risk of being surprised, by something you should have seen coming, increases drastically.

We are trained to and feel comfortable with looking back at what has already happened. This can and often does block or filter our perception of the future, tremendously. Make no mistake; being vigilant is not the same as being naive. "Vigilant" comes from Latin and means watchful. It refers to you staying awake, alert, and aware of your surroundings, while being prepared to act quickly. With all the distractions of twenty-first century life, you no longer have to be physically asleep to lose your watchfulness. Learn to constantly check your six (checking your six is an espionage term referring to checking all four directions around you, plus above and below you for threats and opportunities).

Add to this today's cult of measuring the past. Most measurements that are applied to our success are based on past, short-term performance as well as monthly, quarterly, and yearly historical results. The greatest challenger to your bid for agility undoubtedly is your budgeting process. This process can and often is used as defense for decisions that might or might not have been taken. Budgeting has resulted in truly catastrophic long-term results even if well-meaning management really did not see the "iceberg" coming until after the budget was done. Ask any leader who blindly stuck to 2019's results to predict 2020's COVID-influenced performance. We will deal with this issue more in the next section.

Employ new and effective business tools

Some of our favorites will be the focus in the final section of this book. We have developed and employed a number of tools that now have proven track records of drastically increasing an organization's agility and success. They cover sales, marketing, HR, R&D, and management, to name a few. These are areas of vital importance, when it comes to creating a brighter future, regardless of the weather. The following portfolio of tools is still growing. Even today though, you can create an absolute advantage for yourself and your crew by employing them to get agile now.

While you cannot immediately change or impact large trends, such as the tax code, the legal system, wars, or your own competitive environment, you can improve your ability to navigate these challenges while having even more fun making more money. That is what business agility and these agile tools can mean to you and your organization.

More tips when incorporating business agility into your organization

Build your vessel (organization) to last. Make it sustainable. That means start by plugging known leaks. You cannot realistically think about winning a race or sailing smoothly into the sunset if you are taking on water! Therefore, focus on first things first. If your company is losing money, the first, necessary step is damage control. Focus on finding each financial leak and plug them all.

> "When the tide goes out you will see who is wearing their swimsuit."
> **—Warren Buffet**

Remember, a rising tide lifts all boats. Don't confuse intelligence or business savvy with being lucky enough to be surfing the right trend at the right time. Strive to consciously figure out the mechanics of how and why you are winning. A gift is a gift and is highly dangerous to confuse with a tool. When you figure out the how and why of your gift and where its use is most effective, only then will it become your tool.

One of the most obvious examples of this is the conscious use of body language in selling and leadership. Ask most successful salespeople or leaders, "What is it in your body language that makes your message attractive and engaging?" It is your author's experience that most will have trouble even understanding your question. It is only after cracking the code that they are able to begin consciously using their body language effectively. Until then it is a gift, pure luck.

Always strive to improve your position. This sage advice for driving is also applicable for sailing, business, and living. Continued success requires constant vigilance, a strong will, and an eye for sustainable improvement. Always remember, what may have worked before may not be the best choice going forward.

Agility and what you can do

We keep coming back to the metaphor of a sailing ship and how its crew members, using effective navigation tools, can help the captain to navigate uncertainty. The skipper is the CEO, the crew are all the departments, and the technologies are there to enable the CEO to plan and execute a successful strategy. All these resources, brainpower, energy, and teamwork must be focused upon satisfying individual customer needs, wants, and wishes. These are expressed through your team's clear and curious understanding of their demands.

Focusing on your customers and what each one says eliminates much of the subjective opinions and isolated internal debates that can cause inaction. Many factors are never under the control of the captain, but eliminating friction caused by other, more abstract points of view and uniting around those of your customers will unleash more focus and energy to better satisfy them.

Your captain must always remain very alert and clearly be able to anticipate, understand, and respond to the following factors:

- His own ship's (company's) capabilities
- Specific customer's situation and demands
- Customer alternatives
- The company's ability to exceed customer demands vis-à-vis these alternatives

Your first step, preparing for your Dynamic Navigational System

It is our experience that even large successful companies can still solve their big structural problems, even those endemic to their industries. In order to survive, let alone thrive, breaking through these bottlenecks is now a necessity. To initiate this on your ship we recommend that you employ the following actions simultaneously:

- **Understand** effectively and passionately that your customers' experience is key.
- **Find and discontinue** unnecessary expense categories. Do away with those feel-good categories of expenses that no one understands.

- **Eliminate or neutralize** the financial risk of your customers as well as your own. Make that you sell a secure, comfortable, and inviting proposition.
- **Utilize** more contract personnel to add process flexibility and work more closely with them.
- **Mitigate** problems, inhibitors, and bottlenecks by creating forward-looking information and action using the Dynamic Navigational System (DNS). More about this in Chapter 13.

Training's new role

Is the important role of training still dumped into your HR department?

Take a step back and think about this.

- Isn't training in important skills such as sales, marketing, IT, media, and advertising more naturally aligned with internal/external communication?
- Will research and development do a better job of improving your products if they have the latest data and information from your market?
- What about production? Can you produce a better product by communicating more efficiently what you have learned from your customers?

A free flow of communication, from each customer to the boardroom and back, is critical to maintain and improve what you do, if your company is serious about remaining competitive. Yet budget concerns still usually take first priority, and training is almost always one of the first groups to be streamlined or cancelled when times get tough.

What if this type of old-school thinking now actually borders on crazy?

Correcting these priorities to learn more about the market waters you will be sailing into is now critical to your survival and success going forward! Should your market shrink and/or your competition increase, your customers are going to pick and choose more carefully what they buy and from whom they buy it. If your company's people and offerings are not the most updated, effective, and service-minded in your market, prepare to lose market share. How can you maintain and improve your level of service without the constant, relevant, and timely improvements interactive training can now provide?

Customer, sales, and service training decisions should be held at a divisional level. It is important to remember the value of being able to spread critical knowledge throughout the organization as efficiently as possible. To survive and thrive, training must now be considered as an important and integrated corporate appendage rather than a costly corporate irritation. Therefore, training departments need to be strategically managed from the corporate level. Strategic yet sensitive programs—based upon efficient learning management systems—need to be implemented.

Operational training, such as distribution and product training, should be executed by the respective product or market segments and/ or regional organizations, especially in large corporations. In the end, a decision must be taken in the main office about the role of the corporate parent regarding HQ involvement. Are they running the company in a "hands-on" fashion from the parent or taking a laissez-faire "hands-off" approach? The responsibility of the parent compared to the subsidiaries must be defined!

From now on, a successful corporate training effort needs to become more of a two-way street. Even now, effective trainers constantly have their ears to the ground, looking for changes in the market. They often hear first about shifting product trends, from all of their customers, both internally and externally. Effective trainers stay constantly vigilant for new and better ways of doing what your company does best. Professional training departments increasingly need to employ the very latest techniques and tools as well as the most effective pedagogical platforms and vehicles available. This allows them to mesh with changing participant behavior even quicker.

"Pure-play" training and success

Therefore, small- and medium-sized corporate training departments can, and increasingly should be, open for and subject to takeovers by more specialized, "pure-play" outsourced training companies. These pedigreed training organizations can then offer their acquired employees greater experiences and more challenging careers. Becoming a respected, "pure-play" training company, your training specialists can now serve you plus several other companies with their skills and experience. Their skills will be sharpened, and egos boosted further by having to answer to and serve many different clients and situations. This will increase their understanding of their chosen profession and add a new level of responsibility, competence, and finesse to their job. They will now be responsible to create customer loyalty (and more business) by listening even more closely and being agile enough in their response to satisfy all their clients' various needs, wants, wishes, behaviors, and moods.

Thus, this new "pure-play" model will be a real win-win-win for the company agreeing to the outsourcing of their training department, for their former training department employees, as well as their new outsourcing employer. The result, increased customer loyalty, profit, and:

1. The company gets an upgraded training resource that is now a respected, empowered, and competent open market competitor.

2. The company gets increased market intelligence and information flow from those most qualified and competent to listen.

3. The former company employee trainer now plays a more important and expanded role by having to serve more than one client. This can also lead to more advancement possibilities and deeper specializations within their chosen field of expertise.

4. Each former company employee suddenly gets the chance to be rocketed into the center of the action within his former company, but now as the hired specialist and soon-to-be hero. This is instead of trudging along as some nameless grunt buried in the bowels of a traditional and increasingly dusty corporate hierarchy. A hierarchy which has very little and often nothing to do with his/her chosen craft.

5. The outsourcer gets to expand and develop further while enjoying increased economies of scale. They are able to make more efficient use of specialists and sophisticated (therefore, more expensive) technology and programming. Their reputation and success also benefit as word spreads of their dynamic, professional and profitable "pure-play" offering.

Of course, tips for improvements come not only from trainers. Tips are also gleaned from listening more closely to each course participant as well as from the competition and from our Forward Decision Drivers tool, which we will discuss later as business agility Tool Number 2.

CHAPTER 13

Dynamic Navigational System Tools and Modules

What we have named our Dynamic Navigational System (DNS) could be interpreted as a more forward-looking managerial dashboard-on-steroids. It is a series of easy-to-understand graphs and charts that are routinely updated to provide a clear picture of your current business horizon. The details will be explained below, but the idea is simplified, easy to picture and understand, and an in-your-management-team's-face look at what is developing here, now and looking forward. This is the most sure-fire way to cut down decision time and get more quickly into action to generate results. It should be clear in the descriptions below which tools are suitable for using in your DNS. If you have any questions, you are welcome to contact us.

This book is meant as your invitation to begin building your own physical Dynamic Navigational Center (DNC) to house your DNS by incorporating some or all of the following simple, proven tools and methods. Their use will drastically improve your ability to respond to an increasingly uncertain and turbulent environment. Your ability to consciously steer your organization faster, more nimbly, and effectively will strengthen your chances of success and minimize your tendencies for failure. Below are some of the important and effective tools you will need to accomplish this increasingly vital task. They will help you to identify old-fashioned, slow, and ultimately destructive management practices and then disregard them or re-think and adjust them. Some of them have their roots in either the agricultural or early industrial society and have long outlived their usefulness. Each of the tools below can be implemented via workshops, blended learning, train the trainers, coaching, or as a pure contracted service or a combination thereof. See the end of the book for more details.

Requirements

To create and drive your own *DNS* you will need:

- All current knowledge of your product, your customer, and your competition
- A simple and extremely powerful fact and perception-based system for analytics and effective marketing
- Sales, marketing, and management teams specifically trained in and who enjoy gathering appropriate information to feed and constantly update your new system
- An agile vigilance coupled to an active willingness and ability for decision makers to respond quickly to changes in their competitive landscape
- An open mind and a willingness to commit to testing and measuring, in order to keep learning and improving (upon what we suggest below)

If this sounds highly sophisticated as well as expensive to implement, it's not! In fact, once implemented it will begin saving you money. Keep reading to get a taste of all the changes that you can initiate yourself now!

Distinct types of agility

We cannot stress enough the following fundamental principle of agility.

Agility is not just about the decision process. Business agility's magic comes alive in the anticipation, execution, and implementation of those decisions you make!

You will also quickly begin to realize that all major inhibitors of change are found in the execution of change, rather than in the decision-making process itself. Deciding is relatively easy. Transforming those good decisions into practical change, which you dare to measure, is the key. The accuracy and economy of decision-making is improving drastically with modern tools such as AI and Big Data analytics. The issue becomes your agility in the mastery of each execution.

Many types of agility are now discussed, and many definitions are given. We have chosen to focus upon the two shown below in this book, as these have provided the most obvious leverage when it comes to delivering measurable results. We have successfully used the following two types of agility to help companies navigate current turbulent waters. Most of the tools below have traits from both:

Strategic

Spotting and seizing game-changing opportunities. These tools focus on better strategic definition by describing in measurable detail the "where," "why," and "what."

Operational

Exploiting opportunities within a focused business model and helping to better define the how, who, and when.

The primary type of agility each tool below enhances is shown in the parentheses following its name. Most demonstrate a combination of Strategic and Operational properties with the one named being the dominant one for that particular tool.

PART IV

The Agility Toolbox

Below are some of the effective tools we use that are immediately available and will make your organization more *agile.* However, moving into this journey into agility will require a major shift in the mentality on behalf of management personnel. Here are some of the most challenging shifts necessary in leadership to achieve agility throughout an organization:

1. **Understanding Transformation and Agility** (Strategic)
    The ability to understand the importance of agility and the ability to implement it.

2. **Forward Decision Drivers (FDDs)** (Operational)
    Creating a project-driven organization instead of a silo-based organization.

3. **7S Framework (C7S)** (Strategic)
    Ensuring harmony among all 7 points in the 7S framework, with particular attention to systems implementation.

4. **Inclusiveness Funnel (IFS)** (Operational)
    Creating an inclusiveness in initiatives and decision-making processes to empower bold decisions.

5. **Rolling Budget System (RBS)** (Operational)
    Detaching from the yearly budget precedence to create the ability and adjust direction on queue.

6. **Marketing Responsibility Assessment (MRA)** (Strategic)
    Increasing marketing muscle to achieve greater nearness to the customer.

7. **Overhead Value Analysis (OVA)** (Operational)
    Implementing a selective approach to greater cost reduction.

8. **Leadership Assessment** (Strategic)
    Ensuring balanced right- and left-brain skill sets among leadership personnel.

9. **Carve-Outsourcing Services (CORE)** (Operational)
   Correctly defining and outsourcing opportunities in order to focus on core opportunities and strategic direction.

10. **Injecting Entrepreneurship into your Organization** (Strategic)
    Supporting leadership personnel by creating opportunities to foster growth-oriented careers rather than functional careers.

11. **Evaluating Direction with the Strategic Triangle** (Strategic)
    Ensuring a balanced view on strategy with an equal weight on the company's own resources via the customers' needs and the customers' alternatives.

12. **STA+R** (Operational)
    Utilizing the STA+R process to evaluate overhead and supporting functions in particular.

13. **Setting up a Virtual *DNS* and House it in a Physical *DNC*** (Operational)
    Using a Dynamic Navigational System to implement a mission control center for all agility initiatives.

14. **Advanced Leadership Agility Coaching**
    Leveraging experts to provide agility coaching and mastermind events.

TOOL	STRAT	OPS	PROC	SYST	ORG	CULT	GEN LED
Understanding Agility	☺					☺	☺
Forward Decision Drivers		☺	☺	☺	☺	☺	☺
7S Framework	☺	☺	☺	☺	☺	☺	☺
Inclusiveness Funnel		☺					☺
Rolling Budget System		☺	☺	☺	☺		☺
Marketing Muscle Assessment	☺	☺			☺	☺	☺
Overhead Value Analysis		☺			☺		
Leadership Assessment	☺	☺			☺	☺	☺
Carve Outsourcing Services		☺			☺		☺
Injecting Entrepreneurship	☺		☺	☺	☺	☺	☺
Dynamic Navigational Center		☺					☺
Strategic Triangle	☺						☺
STA+R		☺			☺		
Corporate Role Assessment	☺	☺	☺	☺	☺	☺	☺

Understanding Transformation and Agility

This first tool is a process of guided discussion and dialogue where the need for and benefit of business agility is thoroughly explained, discussed, and firmly anchored throughout your organization.

Recognize any of these companies, or do you remember their products?

- Digital Equipment Corporation and mini-computers
- WANG Corporation and word processors
- American Motors, Plymouth, Hudson, etc. and the auto business
- Eastern, Pan Am, TWA, Sabena and the airline business
- Nokia, Blackberry, ITT, Motorola and mobile/cell telephones

Once upon a time these were some of the best and largest companies in their field.

What happened?

One way or another, they all got stuck in business as usual. In their day, these were some of the biggest names in the Computer/Telecomm, Automotive and Travel Industries. Each had a pedigree and reputation built up and refined over a long period of time. In each case, their industry changed so drastically and so quickly, that they were forced out of business, had to reorganize or were gobbled up by a more agile competitor under stressful conditions. Resting on their laurels and prior accomplishments wasn't enough to keep them at the top of their game, especially when their market and its rules changed.

Here we have documented and measurable proof that steering from the rearview mirror is a fool's game, especially if you add a bit of hubris to the mix. Tragically, displaying hubris is how many very talented executives were trained to behave. Very often, this ends up a habit to which they become blind to and ultimately contributes consciously or (most often) not to an increased level of arrogance. In the current cult of star executives, many have actually been marketing themselves, using their achievements as bragging rights to garner bigger and bigger compensation packages, often at larger and larger firms. They often do this while nonchalantly brushing aside the fundamentals and humility that made them successful in the first place! Many appear unaware that they have unconsciously fallen into this trap and often will viciously defend their new expertise and improved behavior, especially when profits disappear. Could the intensity and expertise of their defense actually indicate how much agility they have ignored, suppressed or forgotten to learn?

"Whatever you think it is, it's not."
—Ancient Chinese proverb

How many current executives cut their teeth in a much more predictable time? A time when past performance could be used as a reliable performance measurement. As the pace of events began to accelerate, many of these current leadership icons slowly became unconscious slaves to old-fashioned tools, traditions, and behavior that could very well signal their ultimate cause of destruction.

If you are wondering what we mean, just remember one of our world's most tragic and destructive clichés is 'Our generals are still fighting the last war.' How many brave, good-hearted young men and women sacrificed their lives because these heroes were not agile enough to put down their textbooks, become present to, improvise, and adapt to their current reality in real-time?

Future success will require a whole new set of forward-looking tools to steer your company. With accelerating megatrends and increasingly bigger storms on the horizon, a whole new and more agile way of behaving is no longer an option. One thing is becoming more certain; what was true before will most probably not remain true in the future. Any effective change usually requires a process.

To help you cultivate an effective way of enrolling others in your organization to understand and begin applying agility skills, we offer the following process. This process can be done best by a savvy, third-party facilitator in a workshop format with the specific purpose of creating a more agile business atmosphere.

1. Establish urgency

Free thinking, responsible, and potentially agile people will not blindly accept yet another transformation process. They need to understand and sense that the reasoning behind identifying and replacing non-agile ones is essential. Sometimes this takes a real slap-in-the-face wake-up call that measurably threatens the company and their job. Only your organizational sheep will offer blind acceptance, and they are exactly the people that most need to understand their part in consciously employing more business agility. Remember, agility does not mean giving up your curiosity, skepticism, or your ability to express it. On the contrary, these traits need to be empowered and enhanced!

At this early point, the risks of why business agility is important for the survival of the company and (each participant's job) need to be defined, expressed, and measurably rubbed in until they hurt. Every employee needs to be made keenly aware that more business as usual at this late date is just as dangerous as making a strategic mistake. Make your message simple and make it sting!

Again, the best "aha" experience usually starts as a, pardon the expression, "Oh crap" experience. Why?

Up until this point, your listener has not felt the connection between his/her business-as-usual behavior with its aggregated and growing consequence. Bring up the megatrends; hit them over the head with perfect storm anecdotes. Do it until they get it. Once that risk is defined, refined, understood, and becomes personal, they should begin to sense the gap between their current behavior and the agility needed to change it. Only then is there the possibility for change. Just as you cannot treat an alcoholic's need for liquor until they realize the personal consequences to them specifically, neither will your crew consciously and responsibly spring into action just because you say they must. If that feeling of urgency is not expressed and experienced in a way that emotionally moves them, then your message will remain an abstraction and therefore, someone else's problem. Excuses, reasons, justifications, and explanations rather than results will continue to fester.

Once your reasoning is presented in an understandable and undeniable format, your listeners can then respond to it with a personal and conscious choice. Therefore, make sure that all your stakeholders are equipped and inspired to personally answer the question, "Why?"

The more you can provide the understanding for why the change to business agility is necessary, the faster you will get others to jump onboard. Make sure you advance beyond just dumping more knowledge on them and give them the information they need to understand and experience a personal and profound "aha" moment.

Remember, "knowledge leads to debate, understanding leads to action." So, look for the evidence that they understand and respond. It will come in the form of measurable results or more excuses. Most importantly, if they understand the gravity of the situation, yet still choose not to accept it and begin changing behavior, then it's probably time for them to sign on to another corporate boat.

2. Form a coalition of change agents

Find or create a trusted group who either inherently grasps what you are trying to accomplish or who are quick, curious, and willing learners. Look specifically toward those players who possess a strong sense of personal integrity. Arm them with your simple, emotional message, then get them out there as advocates. Have them explain to everyone affected why agility needs to be implemented. Have them read this book for instance, as we have tried to make our points as simple and as actionable as possible. Be sure each advocate can express a convincing and moving response to the question, "What's in it For Me" (WIIFM). The more quickly and powerfully this message begins to resonate throughout your company, the faster, more confident, and sustainable your collective jump to business agility will become.

3. Create a strong, simple vision and strategy for change

Ask anyone who has consciously given a successful speech; the key is the right balance of content, delivery, and confidence. The more you design a simple, interesting, and understandable story to support the change you want to affect, the faster you can powerfully convert skeptics to your new program. The simpler and easier it is to understand, the less doubt and debate you will create. The more confidence the speaker projects, the easier it will be to trust them and the message.

The simpler and more jingle-like you can make your message, the fewer handles there will be to latch onto to start a debate. One of the reasons given that many great people have used simple parables to get their message across is that it addresses and satisfies the needs of both hemispheres of your brain equally. A simple message satisfies the practical, transactional, left hemisphere of your brain, and its jingle-like, sing-song delivery will attract the more receptive, relational, and artsy, right side of your brain. This is no time to get analytical. Using your smarts to analyze and create a complex, intelligent, and often aloof argument will only succeed in confusing and shutting down your listeners' curiosity and motivation. To get things done quickly, you need both understanding and engagement. A simple, catchy, and actionable message is the most efficient way to achieve this.

The key to this whole vision conversation is to distill your message down to its essence. Discovering those critical keywords and catchy phrases needed to anchor listener understanding will encourage them to act. The clearer path your words and gestures create, the more clearly your milestones can be laid out and measured, the easier it will become to get others to sign on and support them.

4. Communicate direction/vision vigorously

Overdo it, constantly and creatively! It is better your people get tired of hearing your message than not to hear it enough. Keeping it top-of-mind with reminders will also boost its integration. Make your message visible! Put it on posters, place it on everyone's email signatures and put it on everyone's screensaver. Don't forget, if inspiration doesn't work, one of the most powerful change agents is still *nagging*. The trick is to enroll as many *co-naggers* as possible. Sooner or later with the help of a constant chorus of inspiring messages spiced occasionally with a bit of nagging, resistance usually gives way. Even those with darker intentions understand the power of repetition. For instance, Hitler, Goebbels, and even Lenin have all been credited with saying something to the effect that if you "tell a lie often enough, it becomes the truth."

We are absolutely not recommending the lying part, only the power of the repetition part.

Want more proof of the power of repetition? Just raise some children! Persistence and determination bordering on stubbornness are the keys. Become relentless in broadcasting your message as often, upbeat, and as convincingly as possible. Encourage your agents, as well as everyone else with influence, to do the same. Mix in a little heartfelt passion and child-like curiosity with your professional determination, and don't ever give up!

5. Empower others to act

Invite and encourage participation. Get everyone involved. A textbook example is Jan Carlzon's transformation of Scandinavian Airlines System. When he took over, his first task was to empower his front-line staff to service each customer better. He talked relentlessly about the SAS employee team's "fifty thousand moments of truth per day." This was an approximate number of daily contacts and opportunities the SAS team had to make a positive customer impression. The best way to get the ripple-effect going is to delegate heartfelt responsibility to others so they feel directly involved. The more you empower and encourage others, the more they will help shoulder your burden and the more this will positively ripple out into your market.

One of my first "aha" moments about service was working selling tires. For most people, buying tires rates right up there with going to the dentist. It's no fun. Yet the owner and CEO Tom Pumpelly's idea of the Crescendo Effect of a string of positive service impressions, from initial phone contact right through to leaving the mounting bay, allowed the company to grow from a local Washington, DC phenomenon to one that stretched over the Mississippi River. In the 1980s it was very common to see a "Tires by NTW" bumper sticker on cars all over the Eastern United States. Think about the kind of customer experience it would take to get *you* to put a bumper sticker on your car, advertising where you bought your tires! As everyone in the company was on board to perform this kind of service, they felt empowered to deliver. Many customers responded happily and business exploded!

Above all, the most important point in this whole empowerment process is to *make it personal*. Engagement demands a personal feeling of involvement. Otherwise, it becomes just another abstraction. There is no empowerment in abstraction. No matter how intellectual and logical your message is, if you can just sightsee without direct involvement, your message ends up being as motivating as watching TV. The moment of truth is when you and what you personally engage in are in play. It's riskier, but that's empowerment; i.e. "No guts, no glory!"

6. Create short-term wins

We have now developed a culture of all or nothing. You are either a superstar or a zero. Recognition may be making a bit of a comeback, but it is still rare enough to stand out. Use this important tool to motivate and empower!

Practice announcing small wins. Make a hero out of each winner. It does not have to be much in terms of what has happened or what is won. The main criteria are that it is measurable and indisputable. A simple mention in the company blog or in the newsletter is normally enough. A dinner or theater tickets are also inexpensive ways to get most people interested and engaged. We humans love to compete. Use this trait to further leverage the power of your message.

Break up each important process into small, measurable goals and milestones. Reward the steps in a visible way. It may just be that little mention in your company newsletter, but mark it nonetheless. People love being acknowledged. Acknowledgement encourages involvement, especially when your peers see and recognize it.

7. Consolidate/cement and broaden the effort

Implementing the above steps will both anchor the need for change and get your agility ball rolling. Once you start getting traction, turn the volume up. Yet, be very careful that you don't fall into the same old ruts from which you have just escaped. It is even better if you can get each employee to willingly and physically stand for change and sign off on it. This means getting everyone who is with to stand up and visibly show their support and/or having them sign off on an agreement or letter of intent demonstrating that they are accountable and on board.

303

Cement and acknowledge the progress you make, and then allow it to bloom throughout your company. Again, agility is not so much a process as it is a lifestyle. Therefore, until it permeates your entire organization, there is still more to do. Agility needs to become viral. The more contagious you make your agility program, the more people both within and surrounding your organization will be positively smitten. This requires constant reminding, encouraging, and acknowledging to a broader circle of listeners.

8. Institutionalize new approaches/products/services

As oxymoronic as Institutionalizing Agility sounds, your goal is to integrate these new agile wins into your company behavior. You want agility to become part of your new cultural DNA, and this is what is meant here by our use of the word institutionalize. Probably the best way to describe this process with no pun intended is to incorporate it.

Cement the changes into your Rolling Budget System, Tool Number 5, and your 7S program, Tool Number 3. Separate or distinguish new groups and create new 7s systems for them. These changes will promote and cement more organizational agility. Each group will feel superior to the static business-as-usual processes and traditional legacies that you replace. Count on those wedded to business-as-usual practices to cause some friction. Remember, friction is a sign of progress. Keep going and the friction will diminish as more hop on board. Push on until you create a new agile "standard" in your company. Keep measuring it, rewarding those who demonstrate it, and observe how what you have institutionalized begins to improve the spirit within your whole company.

Agility is about being conscious, powerful, and flexible enough to avoid potential traps as well as spotlighting potential bonanzas. It's realigning everyone's focus forward, to take advantage of the opportunities ahead of your boat. It is all about looking forward instead of groveling or grinning over those experiences now in your wake. This requires a distinct shift in everyone's behavior coupled with a broader and deeper understanding of each customer's behavior. To improve on your forward vision, you need to set your sights on fully understanding why your customer does what he/she does. This helps train you and your crew to sense and anticipate your customer's next move.

Practice makes perfect

The practicalities of looking forward should be practiced in combination with understanding what consequences new technologies will have on your business. Also, remember to pay close attention to what effect the constant bombardment of new laws and regulations will have.

Practice also developing a feel for which direction new laws are heading. For instance, are lawmakers opening up new possibilities and deregulating aspects of your business? Or are they tightening down on opportunities to protect the current TBTF players and their now well-established version of business as usual?

Currently, an important answer to this question could well be found in the interplay between geopolitical and now health-related upheavals that seem to be running amok everywhere now at an accelerating pace. For now, prepare for more regulation and control until the wind changes again. Missing just one of these important areas of agility can cause major damage to an otherwise foolproof plan. Getting them all correct will help put you and your company in a sustainable and profitable class by itself.

The growing importance of soft skills

To fully accomplish this transformation requires strong doses of curiosity, compassion, and empathy. These are three relationship qualities that have been sorely lacking in the transactional culture that developed in business over the past thirty years. In fact, until recently, soft skills were often interpreted as weaknesses on the executive floor where more robotic, cold, calculating, and often sociopathic traits were often been rewarded. "It's just business" used to be a reasonable and accepted justification to take a heartless decision. Just think about some of the popular terms used to describe successful business leaders such as calculating, sharp, and ruthless. How often have you worked for someone like that and been motivated to enjoy doing your best? Authentic respect comes from admiration, not fear.

Balancing these softer, relation-building skills with technology and all those measurable hard skills you either learned in school or acquired from experience will set you on the path toward mastering agility. Balance is key. The pressures from increasing competition, regulation, and technology are becoming relentless. This is creating an unbearable level of stress for those who have a job. For instance, overlooking the symptoms that one of your key players is at risk of overworking her/himself can cause them major health problems. It can also cause a logistical and business nightmare for you and the others who are left to pick up the pieces, or even worse, start from scratch with someone new. Adding this extra stress on the rest of your already overworked team is *not* a winning formula. Therefore, be vigilant; encourage good performance and monitor your team's well-being and workload. A rejuvenated and restructured HR department can help.

Forward Decision Drivers: Constant Monitoring (FDDs)

This tool is a powerful way to continually gain important sales, marketing, competitor, and product development information, from its source, without pestering anyone with another survey.

But first, would you please take a moment and fill in the following questionnaire?

Just kidding!

If you are also sick and tired of being badgered by ring-back customer satisfaction calls and to fill in yet another survey, do you think those with whom you do business are any different? Of course not. Current business-as-usual practices still dictate that this is the best way to gather important information. Yet look who is now promoting it. Isn't it mostly the techies and number crunchers who would rather die than talk with a real customer? What if this practice is now actually alienating you further from your customers' hard won and even harder to keep loyalty?

Most decision makers now often grudgingly agree upon research that implies when all is said and done, you and your customers will ultimately make their purchases based upon perceptions and feelings. For instance, you may have all the facts and statistics showing that a product is either the same or technically better than another. Strangely enough, research finds that you still usually decide to buy based upon your trusted friend's judgment and experience. His or her perception has now effectively become yours. Importantly, we again urge you to realize that in competitive product comparisons, the hard buying factors, which are easily measured in the form of price, delivery, terms, features, and performance are quickly becoming indistinguishable. This is the commodification factor we discussed in the first section. Whereas the soft and more perception-based attributes are becoming more important, such as personal service, trust, design, and status. We further argue that quality is also a soft-buying factor. In short, all those warm and fuzzy factors which, up to now, were usually laughed at by the good ole boys in management are increasingly winning the day. If you haven't already pivoted your marketing plan based upon this realization, when would be the best time?

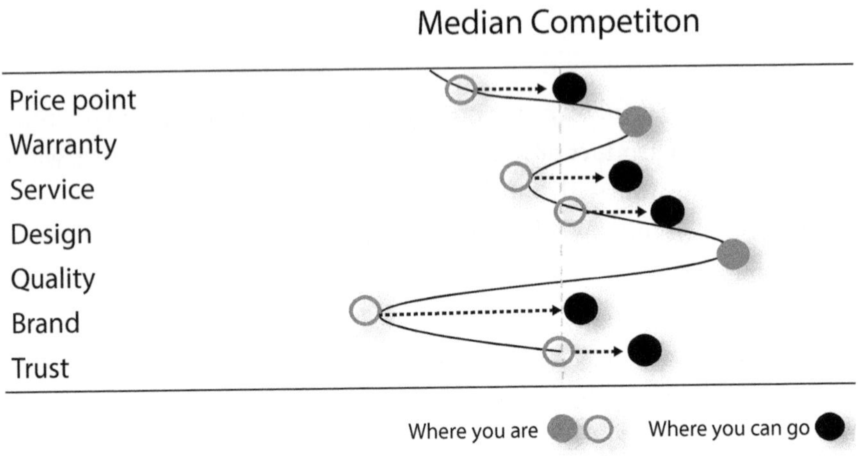

Median Competiton

Price point	
Warranty	
Service	
Design	
Quality	
Brand	
Trust	

Where you are ⚫◯   Where you can go ⚫

Figure 22. Forward Decision Drivers or FDDs

If you too agree with the concept that *in the end*, customer purchasing is mostly driven by perception, this realization opens the door to a very effective and *non-intrusive* feedback loop to determine what drives your customer's decisions. You can effectively use this loop to:

- Show customers that you care without boasting about it
- Serve them better by demonstrating your appreciation for their valuable time
- Get measurable information directly from the most qualified source
- Get a better handle on why your customers buy, *or not*
- Support and improve the perceptions of their reasons for buying
- Use it as a powerful closing tool
- Better manage and motivate your sales team
- Improve your competitive analysis and ultimately produce a better product
- Strengthen your buying trend analysis

The name of this agility tool is the Forward Decision Drivers or FDD. FDDs help you and your customer to locate and define each customer's perceptive reasons for choosing (or not choosing) your product, together while painting them a more compelling reason to buy.

Just like the powerful ocean currents hidden under your boat, perceptions are subject to constant change. Therefore, with the power they exert, you need to continually monitor them as well as build and update a database to measure changes in critical trends. The process for identifying your customers' Forward Decision Drivers is a process combining technical tools with a number of practical workshops. It works best as follows:

- **Identify the Key Buying Factors** including the all-important Hard and Soft ones. This is most effectively accomplished via an open dialogue with those directly involved. This is often done best in a workshop setting during an organized brainstorming session with your sales and service departments, plus other key players.

- **Arrange these Key Buying Factor discoveries** into an easily understood array and:
  - Create a list of questions to quickly and accurately gather this information with the minimum amount of intrusion and irritation for your customer. This implies spicing your normal conversations with some key questions.
  - Build a data capture program or app which can quickly enter new data into your database and then analyze it.

- **Ask each customer or contact in the company** to participate. This can be done either on paper or a simple app and ideally shouldn't take longer than sixty seconds to complete. It can be an excellent and non-intrusive icebreaker or precursor to the business at hand or better yet, you can weave them into your typical sales or service conversation template. Each question should be designed to easily reveal the information you seek. Our experience is that, when done correctly, it is always welcomed. It demonstrates quickly to your customer your interest in a non-intrusive and service-minded way of doing business. It also provides you with a very high yield of answers quickly, due to its brevity and that it only asks for perceptions rather than facts. Ask on a regular basis, update the data, and important trends will begin to appear.

- **Compile the data** and organize it. This can be done automatically in your back office.
- **Analyze the data** to determine your strengths and weaknesses in your market's eyes as well as from your competitors' standpoint. You can develop this system to automatically look for measurable statistical correlations and deviations.
- **Implement** the needed changes. Whether in your marketing, sales, or product development, adjust accordingly by taking the appropriate actions. Then continue to measure and update new results taken from fresh data you collect on your next visit.
- **Rinse and repeat** because this powerful tool is designed to eventually become a behavior that you and your team do automatically during each customer encounter. Your properly designed and implemented FDDs will drastically minimize the risk of sales-team mediocrity. It will be quickly and painfully obvious which salespeople strive to blame their poor performances on, for instance, bad pricing.

Expectations versus results

From the completion of your first survey, you will immediately begin building a database of those hard and soft perception factors that each of your customers *perceive* as most and least important. You will also create access to a number of other analysis opportunities such as:

A powerful, consequential selling tool

Sales people can immediately sell more in less time by using this information to better:

- Streamline your sales/service pitch by eliminating unwanted information
- Handle objections more effectively and build more value
- Focus on strengths while minimizing weaknesses
- Uncover and fix perceived weaknesses and learn to quickly neutralize them or turn them into strengths

- Float more trial closes with increasing confidence
- Deepen your competitive analysis by gathering unfiltered information about your customers' perception of your competitors
- Assess and offer sharper (instead of deeper) discounts
- Adjust quicker to objections and ask for the close again
- Create better understanding, cooperation and more loyal relationships

Marketing can use it to:

- Strengthen your marketing message by focusing on those factors that your customers say they value!
- Track trends in how changes in your message are being perceived
- Trigger and/or justify sought-after features and developments
- Discover new or rising objections and competitive threats
- Dial in more effective pricing strategies
- Choose the best, most efficient and appreciated distribution channels

Over time, valuable data will be collected and compiled. Marketing will build a very detailed picture of how the product has historically been perceived as well as its current perception. It will also provide valuable trend tracking, greater functional and qualitative information, as well as statistical correlations throughout. This will provide you with more accurate forecasting of future market trends and swings. Effective FDDs can actually do away with the need for traditional and costly marketing research! This information can now be continually updated directly from the best, most effective source available, your customer.

All of the above uses also apply to management, as well as the uses listed below.

Management can use it to:

- Reveal and eliminate excuses from salespeople who are used to blaming price
- Support, train, and encourage ineffective salespeople to be quicker and better

- Reveal and replace unmotivated or lazy salespeople
- Bring new salespeople up to speed quickly
- Create a more powerful, motivational and effective sales message, based directly upon what the current market says it; this, in turn, should motivate the salespeople even more as it is they who gathered the information in the first place
- Measure the effect of adjustments and tweaks with each new message iteration

Thus, for about sixty seconds of your customer's precious time, you will have a tool that can support sales, marketing, management, quality control, logistics, and service (to name just a few).

Keep in mind that empathy is different from market research, yet both are going to be needed in equal portions for sales success going forward. For example, knowing more about the customers than they know about themselves is the key to a powerful Forward Decision Driver (FDD) strategy. Loyalty improves further when you train your team to ask these simple questions with increased empathy and curiosity.

Creating and refining your FDD tool is a much better tactic than conducting the world's most effective interrogation or filling it with the most beautiful and well-thought-out questionnaire. It is light-years ahead of the traditional "jamming" your product down your customer's throat with so-called "sales arguments." Exactly how much loyalty have you ever created by arguing anything? Master this tool and you can start anticipating future customer needs, wants, and wishes better than they can. This kind of agility naturally leads to a successful, sustainable, and growing win-win!

The Seven S Framework

This proven tool is a process or framework with which to measure and adjust the balance, interplay, and harmony of the important hard and soft components which make up your organization. It provides a practical picture, plus tools and tips of how effectively and successfully your organization functions.

The Seven S's

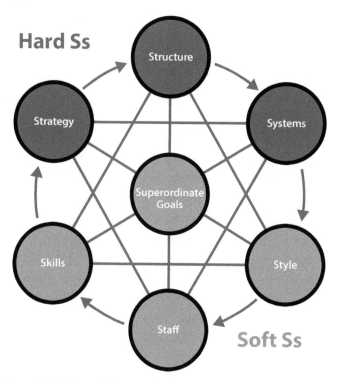

Figure 23. The Seven S Framework analysis tool

Originally conceived by former McKinsey colleagues Bob Waterman, Tom Peters and Julien Philips in a White Paper called "Structure is not organization,"[1] the Seven S's Framework presented there is the precursor to the 1982 worldwide business best seller, *In Search of Excellence*. The objective with this original analysis aims at a desire to understand why some companies seemed to be consistently more successful than others. The research done by the authors and their teams uncovered the following factors, which all conveniently started with an *S*.

The findings uncovered in the initial research indicated that in successful companies, there was always a higher degree of harmony when comparing the interaction of these seven Ss to those in a less successful company. In the thirty-plus years since it was written, we have uncovered more and more evidence that these important relationships are still constantly at work. Therefore, becoming more conscious of these factors and then deliberately balancing and harmonizing them has proven to be a valuable and on-going process. Now we have an environment of ever-shorter cycles and explosive volatility. This puts tremendous pressure on your company's organization, systems, and people. This forces you and your team to become even more agile. Paying close attention to the interaction of these seven properties that start with "S" is arguably more important now than when the book was first written.

For example, let's say that your company decides to expand aggressively. The strategy chosen is to grow its top line. This will be accomplished by increasing sales and capturing market share. In this scenario, this decision would create an obvious disharmony to continue systematically compensating the sales force based upon the bottom line. The profit numbers could increase radically, but the loss in top line revenue growth could kill not only the expansion plans, but also the entire company.

As this is being written, the word "survival" could justifiably be added to make it an eighth 7S tool. For now, increasing your team's survival skills can have a direct impact upon whether your organization indeed survives or not. Focusing on saving money and challenging loyal customers to dare to risk a bit more are two skills that can produce directly measurable returns to your bottom line and the team's motivation.

The 7S methodology, well understood and implemented, supports and helps your company work, as a metaphoric well-oiled machine, a finely tuned orchestra or why not even a well-led crew on a sailing vessel. They are meant to be stable and reliable, as well as in constant motion. This is very similar to the eastern Yin-Yang model. The more everyone is anchored in a common understanding of each S, the more they can work in a continuously evolving harmony toward well-defined and common objectives.

Another example is where a company has decided to develop a new technology. Through the 7S prism they can easily discover that they might have everything else in place but lack the appropriate skills or competencies. Armed with this insight, management can now invest in the correct staff, skills, and resources to succeed.

As a young McKinsey consultant, one of your authors had the challenge and pleasure of being in the group that provided the research from European corporations for the first 7s White Paper. What he learned about this methodology during this period he has continued to use, develop, and master throughout his entire career! Even though the business environment has changed drastically since then, he has used this tool with practically every client since he learned of it. For analysis, managerial purposes, and producing measurable results, it is truly one of the most useful and efficient tools management can ever use.

This tool is best implemented in the form of a series of workshops focusing on defining, measuring, and adjusting each S of the seven. The more the chosen group learns to measure and feel the optimal balance, the more they will be able to sense when the interplay changes. Then they can respond quickly by identifying and adjusting the culprit variables back into harmony. Thus, this is a dance or ongoing process that should be effectively taught to and mastered by each responsible decision maker on your team. The decidedly less agile alternative is creating a dependence upon outside consultation.

Inclusiveness Funnel (IFS)

This tool can be employed as a powerful lever to increase personal engagement and motivation within a project, group, or a whole organization. It is based upon that simple human behavioral fact that the more we feel included in a process or group, the more we will actively contribute and participate.

There is only so much you can do by persuasion, intimidation, and commanding people to reach a quick consensus. Not only that, but these intrusive tools are also becoming less potent as people become more educated, determined, and independent. With or without mandates, people instinctively hate being bullied. This type of behavior fosters a feeling of helplessness and no one worth hiring likes feeling helpless. The more a team feels that they have no say, the more they will actively resist whatever is being proposed or implemented, regardless of its brilliance.

On the other hand, the more they feel included, the more they will willingly participate. These basic observations are the basis of our Inclusive Funnel Process or IFS.

IFS, a summary
This consists of a simple workshop-based system containing several brainstorming sessions that eventually funnel understandable results into a well-grounded, thoroughly thought-out agreement and mutually binding document.

The steps are as follows:

- Set clear objectives
- Agree with all stakeholders
- Brainstorm 1
- Homework
- Brainstorm 2
- Consensus workshop
- Homework
- Plan
- Execute

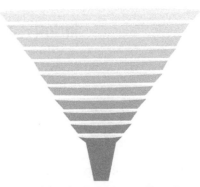

Figure 24. The Inclusiveness Funnel

The process works like this. Let's say your company has a big strategic decision to make. For example: Should we launch or not in the USA?

Your CEO openly admits that he/she doesn't have all the answers and is not yet comfortable enough to responsibly take this important decision. Instead of going with his/her usual small group of trusted and often "HPPO" based advisers, he/she instead deliberately seeks input from a broader group by conducting an IFS process.

Note: To ensure objectivity and efficiency our experience shows that the IFS system is best run using external and therefore neutral third-party facilitators and report writers.

The IFS process

1. **A list of relevant knowledge, opinions, and ideas is compiled.**
   These come from the direct stakeholders whose judgment is already trusted, plus other important people involved in the process. In this first round a big group is sought, with varied but relevant backgrounds, taken from different levels of your entire organization.

2. **One or a series of workshops is/are initiated.**
   All participants are encouraged to actively participate and the objective of each exercise is clearly defined and disclosed. The more everyone is comfortably on board with the task at hand, the more decisive the results will be. Each workshop ends with a blind brainstorming session where each participant is encouraged to anonymously write down his or her best ideas.

3. **First Round Analysis begins**

   The participants are sent home and the workshop leaders compile and analyze the ideas. They then prepare a report of their findings. They organize them, sift through the commonalities uncovered, and compile statistics. The result should be a simple three- or four-page report with a concise summary.

4. **The Second Level of workshops is initiated**

   The most opinionated five participants from the original group, plus future project leader candidates and senior advisors, are all invited back. Another round of brainstorming is initiated, but this time from the leadership perspective and from the risks and opportunities of the issues generated from the first report. Everyone will have prepared by studying the results of the first report.

   A new report is then produced from this session. This report concentrates on the potential risks and opportunities. Each is identified, analyzed, and weighted.

5. **The Third Level of the funnel**

   This latest report is distributed to the selected project leader candidates, one of whom will later be chosen to champion the final decision.

   A new, even more intensive meeting is scheduled with these potential leaders. This meeting is facilitated all the way through to consensus. This simply means that no one can leave until consensus is reached.

   The focus here is purely on business issues. Personal concerns are deliberately omitted. The result of this meeting will be the creation and mutual agreement of a simple business plan.

   The process is thus anchored broadly throughout the organization, providing a sense of attachment and inclusion for all. Then it is further narrowed down and polished until consensus is finally reached on how to implement it. The process can usually be accomplished within a month or two. Everybody feels attached and your CEO can sleep slightly better, as he or she has now collaborated with and included the rest of the company in this important decision.

The Rolling Budget System (RBS)

This tool eliminates the frustrating "ketchup effect" of the traditional end-of-the-year "budget crunch" by finally disconnecting the process from its agricultural origins and spreading it out over the life of the different products or services it serves.

"Can I call you back after we finish the budget?"

How many times have you heard this reply when contacting a decision-maker at the end of the fiscal year? If you think you are frustrated, listen closely to sense the frustration in their voices.

Creating more harmony and flow in your organization's financial process will not only ease tensions and tempers, it can also make it easier to quickly aim that flow away from financial traps and toward important and emerging opportunities.

The annual budget (most loved by accountants and Wall Street promoters) is actually an ancient anachronism, a relic from our agricultural past! It is possibly the most obvious part of this stubborn business-as-usual attitude that the world has accepted and has unconsciously taken for granted. It actually may be one of the greatest remaining financial flaws in modern business. It truly is a holdover from a more rural society, where the weather and seasons steered our activities. The simplest, most agreeable cycle of comprehension was the yearly seasonal variations and their recurring weather patterns. The seasons thus became the basis for all major planning, first for farmers and then for everyone else.

Think about it, the agricultural society has its basis in nature and is ruled by weather. Regardless of where you live, you have a natural cycle of seasonal activities to contend with. This in turn has had a profound impact on our calendar. We not only have the four seasons, but many holidays such as the American Thanksgiving, the Thai Water Festival, the Swedish Mid-Summer, and the chosen dates for Christian Christmas and

Jewish Hanukkah celebrations can arguably be traced back to the growing cycle. Many of the activities critical to our agricultural past were directly based upon the seasons. Therefore, major celebrations usually had to wait until all necessary farm work was complete.

Since Industrialization, we have increasingly learned to live using other cycles. For instance, products and services are now much more dependent upon their own cycles than upon the seasons of the year. Despite this, almost all companies have doggedly maintained planning, reporting, and compensation cycles based upon agricultural planting and harvesting cycles. Why? Now, that basis doesn't stand up to scrutiny, as we increasingly import seasonal foodstuffs from all over the world, year-round. Even though the origins are now totally irrelevant, the growing cycle still unconsciously and comprehensively influences the governance of corporate life. This anthropological fact now makes the annual budget a giant inhibitor of change and business agility. For the biggest and most tragic example of this, look no further than your own annual budget process.

From roughly mid-October to the last day in December it is not uncommon for many large corporations (like yours perhaps?) to act like the approaching winter season and freeze up. Try calling a decision maker during this period and you will very often get that polite, but stressed and sometimes irritated, "call me back after the budget is done." During this time a disproportionate amount of time, energy and resources are spent on calculating and haggling over next year's budget. Tragically, even the concerns of your customers often take a back seat to this internal number crunching.

What happens when this agonizing process is finally complete? All your other company systems hook up to what is handed down. Financial decisions are now cemented in place for at least one year forward. Critical departments such as Marketing, Selling, Production, HR, and the supporting compensation plans are now all firmly anchored into it. Although quarterly tweaks can and often do take place, for the most part from now until the next budget crunch, anything that could change this budget, for better or worse, usually has to wait. Even desperately needed course changes caused by a major disruptive event, such as leap-frogging technology that your competitor unexpectedly launches, or a surprising, game-changing geopolitical event *or virus* will often be dangerously delayed while waiting for the new cycle. The best-ever example of this unfolded in 2020 during coronavirus lockdowns. Companies that couldn't adapt quickly enough to the new draconian rules bled to death financially. Up to now, you and your team may have been comfortably able to take credit for any unexpected windfall or to blame any subsequent loss on unexpected circumstances. If so, how long will you continue to have this luxury instead of being agile and responsible enough to do something about it before it's too late?

From the first day of a new budget cycle, executives and their wannabes furiously focus their time and energy on meeting or surpassing the agreed-upon figures. They become heroes if they meet the budget and devils if they don't. The problem is that the very moment the new budget is finished, this hallowed document becomes an abstraction. The stated figures are now extracted from the reality of your market and rapidly changing world events, and changes in both of these dimensions continue to accelerate. Volatility and uncertainty are increasing drastically. Despite this, most decision makers practice politely side-stepping critical budget issues, instead preferring to focus on the usual brush fires that litter their desks. This may be better known as busy-ness. Meanwhile, discrepancies between the plan and reality inevitably begin to widen. If asked, many decision makers will discreetly admit that they politely agreed to the proposal, but felt and even feared the figures were optimistic, or just plain wrong. "Hockey stick" reporting, based upon rosy "guesstimates," are becoming more common in this new era too. Whether they are based upon the swings of greater volatility with bigger, shorter cycles of new products and services or that personal responsibility is getting harder to prove, the result is flawed figures upon which the business continues to be conducted.

As long as the economy is growing, this agricultural-based problem generates little concern. This is because budget goals are usually, easily met and surpassed and mistakes can easily be hidden. This often makes those responsible look like gods. What we often forget is that when things begin heading in the opposite direction, yesterday's corporate gods become slaves, handcuffed to the consequences of that same plan and risk becoming management pariahs overnight. Their only respite is providing excuses and blaming the circumstances convincingly enough to survive until the next budget go-round. Then they have that once-a-year chance to change it.

Seasons or cycles?

The vast majority of today's products and services have little or no direct connections to seasonal growing cycles or the calendar year. Yet to change this ingrained yearly cycle behavior to something new will take a MAJOR effort. Remember, once the budget is decided upon, all other departments, especially support functions like HR and service, lock in to it and make any subsequent budget adjustments even harder to change. Count on any attempt to change the figures before the next cycle to be met with blind and unrelenting resistance from both systems and culture.

Even so, the benefits of this large, but one time change in behavior may be very much worth the effort. For instance, you will quickly begin to realize:

- Inefficient decisions can be adjusted quickly, saving months of time and freeing up idle, often wasted resources for accelerating or promising projects.
- Cycles can be given more time to mature. They can now stretch over the hereto-sacred one-year boundary. This can prevent a premature decision to stop a promising project that has not yet blossomed into its long-term promise.
- Biting off smaller bits of the overall budget, over the entire year, eliminates the typical corporate year-end "budget crunch" that currently handicaps your crew's decision-making behavior, customer service and team-spirit for months.
- Focusing on the customer and generating more business can again take precedence, even in the cold winter months when there is nothing else to do but spend, spend, spend.

For example, if you know that the natural cycle length of your product or service is one and one-half years and you acknowledge your company's reaction time is three months, establishing a one and one-half year cycle, with regular quarterly reviews, will be a much more efficient alternative. This means that every quarter you now force your team to look a full six quarters forward. They can also adjust or tweak the current direction every three months. This means you gain at least three quarters' time when compared to the traditional annual budgeting process. What would that extra time mean for your company's agility and bottom line?

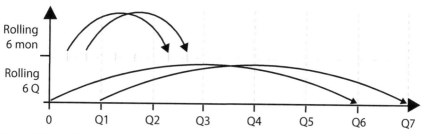

Figure 25. The Rolling Budget Process or RBS

The Rolling Budget is a major tool that will help you adjust your firm to each of your product's natural business cycles and assist everyone in understanding and mastering your firm's financial reality. Moreover, implementing a rolling budget may really be cause for Thanksgiving! When November rolls around, it will feel more like a normal month, as you will already have next year's budget well under control.

The Rolling Budget process steps

Step One: Define the cycles

Assemble the responsible people to discuss and calculate the natural cycles for each product, group of products, and/or services. Be sure to respect that different products have different life cycles and revenue streams. Discuss, acknowledge, understand, and agree to each on its own terms.

Step Two: Plan

Create a holistic planning model that divides your product categories into distinct time cycles. For instance, Honeywell has products and categories ranging from home security to nuclear plant steering systems. Each one of these products has a different timeline and business cycle. You need to adjust and service each on its own merits. Remember that, although all products are not the same, this also includes their business cycles. Now is the time to recognize them as each having separate and unique cycles.

Step Three: Establish routines

Having budgets expire and renew at different times during the entire year will put increased strain on keeping track of them. This has to be consciously and firmly taken care of by finance and accounting. To help anchor these now individual processes, it is important to have your IT gurus create systems to monitor each and then create simple, graphical, holistic representations of all the varying budget cycles. Finally, place them where everyone in a decision-making role can easily see them. This is further discussed in the Dynamic Navigational Center (DNC) section.

It is also advisable to create a hybrid model for defining responsibilities between marketing and finance. These financial cycles must be decided upon with the help of the eyes, ears, and intuition of your marketing and even sales teams for them to remain correct. If you truly want the complete picture, internal and departmental factors, as well as industry and global factors, must be taken into consideration. Can you name a group of people who can contribute this type of up-to-date input better than marketing? If you can, then it may be wise to quickly take a closer look at what responsibilities and functions your marketing department currently has. Marketing's power and contribution to the RBS Process will be further enhanced if they have already instituted a Forward Decision Driver (FDD) program, as described above in Tool Number 2.

Step Four: Align compensation

In the final analysis, a successful business is still based upon a satisfied team. Therefore, your bonus and compensation systems need to be updated to reflect these new rolling changes in a way that is acceptable to your employees. As Geoff Colvin writes in the November 1, 2015 issue of Fortune Magazine, "In the twenty-first century corporation, whether it is acknowledged or not, employees own most of the company assets because they are the assets[1]. Should you forget or avoid this crucial step, you may turn around and find your best and brightest people and assets working for the competition."

Step Five: Adjust all other systems

All elements of your entire business system, per category, including your personnel and planning systems will also have to be realigned. To really cement this, close cooperation with your HR people is highly recommended. This is so that workflow, including those actual seasonal adjustments that do remain, can also be dealt with on a rolling basis. A good way to analyze and harmonize this whole process is doing it through the lens of your 7S system. The result will be more cooperation and less hiccups once you are up and running. Review the impact and implement all potential actions for each 7S step every time the plan is updated.

A big help to anchor this change process will be to increase your use of automation. Use available technology and now especially AI to automate and accelerate accounting all processes necessary to enable closing your books more frequently. For instance, create or acquire a "Virtual Close" process.

Once all these systems are rolling along, they should also be graphically represented in your new Dynamic Navigational Center. Building your own DNC is described in more detail later on in Tool 14.

Count on that installing your Rolling Budget System will take more time than you think. Start with the understanding that the full implementation of your rolling budget will take at least one year to complete. As this is such a big project, the greater the support for it, the faster and smoother the change will become.

Therefore, make sure to mandate and motivate key players to spread the word. You want them to become your trusted agents of change. Delegate responsibility and get the action going. Create a story with your chosen team and make sure each player can easily verbalize it in a way that all their listeners can understand and can begin implementing. Your agents must be able to empower others to create and announce progress, especially on short-term wins. Make sure that this important change in course is observed and recognized by everyone.

Changing to a rolling system is a big change, but the end result is worth it!

Although the overall amount of energy will likely remain similar, spreading your budget process out over the entire year will help avoid all the pent-up frustration brought on by the shutting down of critical functions, sometimes for months at a time. Most important of all is that you and your company will definitely become more connected to your market's specific reality.

The implementation of the rolling budget process usually takes the form of a series of workshops with the assistance of consultation and coaching, plus technical support.

You will also become far more nimble and agile in running a profitable ship. Some agile corporations have already started this. For instance, here is what one of *Business Week's* "World's Top 25 Executives" and former chairman of EMC, Michael Ruettgers, had to say about Rolling Budgets:

"You have to be nimble enough to respond quickly to unexpected changes. For example, our new six-quarter rolling budget process allows us to constantly adjust our budget allocations to meet changes in the market [and] . . . the regular and detailed sharing of information allows us to effectively look at our P&Ls on a monthly basis and make business decisions on the fly."

Marketing Responsibility Assessment (MRA)

This tool literally refocuses your corporate ship toward the horizon and success by re-invigorating your marketing people to work with what they were trained to and love to do.

With the focus on sales and finance during the last few decades, the power of pure, old-fashioned marketing has been diluted to become a step-child of sales. In today's turbulent environment, this makes total sense; especially lately, when so much money has been sloshing around that many well-off people buy almost by habit. After a quick Google search, we are off to the store or into our favorite bookmarked web-shop. Then, the shopping carts start filling up. Who needs powerful marketing in this environment?

To answer this, just put your ship's helm in the boiler room. Notice how easy it becomes to avoid the larger icebergs of today's increased global competition. How easy is it to see the rocks making up The Next Big Things and the storms of sudden, drastic global financial updrafts and downdrafts? Sadly, our experience confirms this trend of weak and undefined marketing as being an increasing problem for companies striving toward better and more agile navigation.

For the agile among you, this also opens up an opportunity! An opportunity which most companies have forgotten about or have chosen to avoid. Marketing is one of the best and most critical functions for increased agility. Just like HR, it is currently misunderstood, mistreated or positioned tragically wrong. This is most obvious in industrial companies, but to a lesser extent even shows up in the Fast-Moving Goods or FMG sector.

In a recent C-Level survey performed in medium to heavy industrial companies, it was discovered that 80 percent of the CEOs who were interviewed could not even correctly define what marketing was! Most definitions explained it as, "marketing was equal to sales plus advertising." Again, if everything is going according to plan and your corporate boat is also rising in a sea of newly borrowed and printed money, this kind of definition is good enough. You are also warmly reminded again of what the mythical person jumping out of the Empire State building was heard to say as he passed the fifth floor toward the rapidly approaching pavement: "Everything is just fine, so far." With the trends and storm warnings we have discussed that are whipping up an already uncertain sea, it may be worthwhile taking out your Marketing 101 book and giving it one more, fresher, and closer read. There is no better way to ground yourself and your business than with fundamentals.

This book is written as a cheeky but serious reminder that your marketing department, as well as the entire C-Level team, should spend its time and resources observing, understanding, and preparing for what lies ahead, rather than behind it. Your marketing people should thoroughly understand their customers as well as the current and future competitive environment, or quickly find another profession.

Sales is not marketing!

Correctly defined, your marketing organization has very little to do with sales. To be truly agile, marketing's true focus, interest, and responsibility must be firmly fixed on the classic 4 Ps. The job of selling gets much easier when this is successfully accomplished!

As a reminder, the traditional 4 Ps are:

- Price
- Place
- Promotion
- Product

Out of these four, most respondents in the above-mentioned survey usually managed to get only one area out of four correct. The conclusion here is that many industrial multinationals are handicapped by not understanding nor appreciating marketing's capabilities or its real responsibility. In a truly agile environment, there should be heightened marketing input and influence rather than less. When used correctly, marketing is the center of your organization's sensory mechanism. A well-defined marketing department with a strong Chief Marketing Officer (CMO) is, or shortly will be, the natural navigational hub in an agile, sustainable, and profitable company.

In well-developed, marketing-centric corporations such as Procter & Gamble (P&G), the establishment of a strong program management team that is fully line-responsible for all four Ps is standard practice. Compare this to other more industry-centric corporations, and there you will see that make/buy, pricing, and launch decisions can often be the responsibility of everyone from R&D to sales, production, and even finance. Take a step back and ask yourself, "What are these departments doing making marketing decisions?"

When these critical marketing functions are diluted and parceled out to other groups, your marketing people are tacitly robbed of their dignity and ultimately, their reason for existing. To add insult to injury, the general attitude often expressed by those inappropriately charged with these important decisions is something like, "Well, we price it at what the market can bear." Try to get a sense of how capricious this seat-of-the-pants attitude sounds! This usually shuts down any budding ability or will for good marketing people to engage in the details and look forward. Get a sense also of how helpless it sounds. If you get any sense of this being the situation onboard your corporate ship, consider yourself blind to what is now rapidly approaching on your horizon.

Inefficient marketing = inefficient business

This nonchalant attitude creates a dangerous add-on effect. It can weaken your sales effort by allowing some much too comfortable sales people to ride around on their high horses and blame bad pricing decisions for everything, especially their missed sales numbers. Ironically, there may be some twisted truth to this claim, especially if your marketing people have unwittingly been stripped of their ability to do their job. Wouldn't this also further disrupt and inhibit marketing's ability and motivation to help fix the situation?

Leaders, who buy into believing that bad pricing is indeed the problem, often irritate the problem by spending a disproportional and unnecessary amount of precious energy and resources on even more cost-cutting efficiencies. This is instead of improving pricing, where the benefit would be most efficient. Revenues usually fall, as ineffective salespeople feel further justified in their poor performances. Ironically, marketing may also suffer from further budget and personnel cuts due to this totally misguided exercise!

Anyone that understands the power and simplicity of basic marketing, as it was meant to be implemented, will also understand that effective pricing models will *always* have a vastly higher impact on the bottom line than cost models. Why?

If you have allowed your marketing people to do their homework on cost and have a competitive product, every price increase—and every extra penny generated—contributes directly to a stronger company bottom line.

The 4 Ps, a review

A simple solution is to prepare a Four P Marketing Review, based upon the suggestions below and assess your current marketing muscle. This can easily take the form of a simple internal survey-based analysis. The analysis can be enhanced by some personal, objective interviews. Done effectively, this whole process should take only one day to execute.

Price

Pricing creates much more positive leverage than cost cutting does. Why? Again, because each extra penny goes directly to the bottom line! Unfortunately, that power often goes unnoticed. Company focus is normally put on cost cutting. More often than not, the marketing department is not even responsible for pricing! This is plain wrong.

Question One: *Who is responsible for pricing decisions in your company, and why?*

Place

Distribution channels and all clusters of employment and contracting must be regarded vis-à-vis current and future customer needs, wants, and wishes. The process of bringing a product or service to the marketplace, as quickly and efficiently as possible, is central to any true marketing department. This is, more often than not, handled on an ad-hoc basis, often triggered by the sales manager and all too often to stop inexperienced salespeople from whining that they can't sell what they have. *This is also wrong!*

Question Two: *Who is in charge of the process of bringing a new product or service to market in your company?*

Promotion

Possibly the best understood part of marketing is promotion. But even here this understanding is curtailed by marketing only being fully responsible for external promotion and advertising issues. Effective internal communication is often forgotten.

We have further argued that both external and internal corporate training should also be part of the marketing department rather than the HR department, where it often resides. The skills needed for effective behavioral change are much more akin to the skills in market communication rather than the typical personnel skills used in HR, such as hiring and firing, personnel evaluations, payroll, pensions, etc. As product cycles continue to shorten, corporate training is increasingly becoming a bottleneck for new launches. Efficient training functions need to be incorporated into the eyes and ears of your front-line employees more effectively. The internal training offered must strengthen and complement the anticipated needs for success. It all goes back to understanding and sensing what your customers need, want, and wish.

Effective promotion requires communicating effectively to the listening that already exists or the often expensive new listening you choose to promote in the market. Obviously, the department responsible for seeing, hearing, and feeling the market pulse for your products can only function effectively by sensing proper and timely forward-looking input.

Therefore, all internal and external communication should flow through marketing. This gives those who are specifically trained to understand and communicate the interaction between your market and your message the best chance to function effectively. Optimally, marketing should have all internal and external communications, including corporate training, reporting into its function.

Question Three: *Where does the responsibility for each of your different company communication and training functions lie?*

Product

All aspects of product features, benefits, and new product development must be accepted and triggered by a marketing decision. In an agile company it is marketing that triggers R&D. Our experience has shown that most often R&D triggers R&D. When this is the case, R&D becomes more of an insulated and costly playground for pampered geniuses rather than your company's responsive and creative arm. This further disconnects marketing's eyes, ears, nose, touch, and intuition from what is being created in the mind of R&D. R&D disconnected from marketing's keen senses is wrong! R&D and marketing should cooperate, absolutely, but the most effective way is for marketing to provide R&D with fresh, real-time input first, rather than vice versa.

Question Four: *Who is responsible for and triggers R&D decisions in your company?*

Up the down R&D escalator revisited

Let's take another look at the metaphor for the current challenge facing your research and development department; climbing up the downward R&D Escalator. This metaphor is used by, among others, the Swedish telecom giant, Ericsson AB. Compare the inevitable forward progress of new inventions and products to the downward set of escalator stairs. Picture your R&D people walking up those downward going steps, just like we did when we were kids. The faster they work to climb those steps with exciting innovations, the more competitive they and your company become. What happens, though, if they stop, even for a moment's rest?

Just to keep up with the market changes they have to keep climbing. To get further ahead, they have to climb up those downward moving escalator steps at an even faster rate. Now what happens when more competitors from all over the world enter your market?

That escalator begins to move faster and there are more people, bags, and obstacles to avoid during their ever more frantic and exhausting climb.

What if this is metaphorically the situation facing you and your R&D crew today? If they are now focusing on carrying their latest developments up that escalator, do you think they would appreciate a bit of help from their Marketing colleagues' finely tuned senses to find the most efficient path up that cluttered and moving staircase?

Time to let your more agile and 4P-focused marketing department lead the way!

World-class agility will transform research and development

Another related situation is that, for too long a time, tradition has dictated that R&D needed to be done by highly trained and responsible people in the developed western countries. Once upon a time, only after a high-end version of your new product was ready, a watered down and cheaper version would then be synthesized for smaller, developing markets. The selling to these inferior markets with the cheaper version would then commence. What has now happened to this time honored, traditional way of handling product development, and what does this twist have to do with agility?

For anyone who has traveled to most developing countries before the lockdowns, you could not miss that there are now very many well-educated, relatively well-paid, and communicative people virtually everywhere you go. Many are as good, if not better, engineers and technicians than those back at your own headquarters. More importantly, they are also still more cost effective to use.

This development has opened a brand-new door for the agile. You can now literally turn your insulated and comfortable R&D team and their traditional processes upside down. From this point on, instead of developing a high-end product in a high-cost location first and then taking the bells and whistles off to sell it in a lower cost market, it is now possible and much more profitable to do the exact opposite.

Right NOW, by developing a low-cost alternative of your product in a highly qualified, but low-cost location first, you immediately shorten and cheapen the traditional development cycle. With this new approach there is obviously less time, energy, and investment needed to research and develop! You lower the cost of the work performed by an order of magnitude directly, since those local labor costs sink dramatically compared to your "normal" process. Not only that, but you can also now begin recouping your costs faster by releasing the new product directly into these local markets, long before you normally would. Then, you take this simplified and now tested model back home. There you finish the development process in the high-cost location. Now you can even afford to develop more high-end, high-margin gizmos, as you can finance them from a present and growing, rather than future, revenue stream! This will help you maintain and enhance your competitive lead while maintaining or even enhancing your cash-flow.

Agile marketing generates agile business

In a truly agile organization, your Chief Marketing Officer (CMO) should enjoy the same listening and respect as the Chief Financial Officer (CFO).

When this first critical step in balancing corporate influence is complete, then a powerful and agile triangle of CMO, CFO, and Chief Human Resources Officer (CHRO) can begin to function as a well-oiled team. Your forward-looking team, the one needed to run your Dynamic Navigational System (DNS), will now be in place. As you will soon see, this DNS Troika is enormously important for future success.

First, make sure you install some marketing muscle. Reintroduce true marketing, based upon the 4Ps, into all your companies and segments. Then let Marketing, HR, and Finance eventually "run" your Dynamic Navigational Center or DNC together as described below.

The very first thing to do when addressing marketing is to understand the current state of affairs by analyzing the marketing muscle in the group. The four simple marketing questions above will be a powerful start to this process. There are, of course, much more specialized methodologies available to accomplish this analysis. Remember to let both sales and marketing constantly nag you that your customer comes first, last, and always.

Overhead Value Analysis (OVA)

This is a powerful and very objective analysis tool that can help you to evaluate where there may still be extra fat to trim from your organization. This tool functions without the complication of human emotion. Although this sounds counter to our book's overall message of bringing humanity and emotion back into your organization, there are, nevertheless, some places that these important qualities remain counterproductive to corporate survival and reaching agreed-upon goals. Eliminating overhead is such an area.

Cost cutting is always inferior to efficient pricing

With the risk of us nagging, one of the most dominant beliefs governing today's business-as-usual mindset is that improving efficiency by cutting costs is the most reliable way to increase profits. This thinking is especially true in an environment where market requirements change only gradually; one where companies have the luxury of plenty of time to minimize existing product production costs. When was the last time your market looked like that?

Today of course, constant cost-efficiency improvements are a prerequisite for a healthy and sustainable bottom line. Yet now they have become a requirement. Even so, they're no longer sufficient by themselves. To be agile you need tools for both sides of the coin. Only then can you use them all to go deeper into the entire valuation process.

OVA is also a proven McKinsey cost cutting methodology that is simple and brilliant, as well as effective. This tool was invented by Jon L. Neuman from the New York Office of McKinsey in 1975 and subsequently published in the Harvard Business Review[1]. The ideal organization, department, or group with which to perform this process contains 10 to

200 people. In our experience, overhead organizations such as human resources, finance, accounting, reporting, and other support functions represent your first, best candidates. Surprisingly, these particular support functions have so far escaped many previous downsizing efforts. Could this have to do with that they were often the ones usually charged with performing the downsizing on the other departments? Regardless, we find these groups can have considerable fat left when put under your sharp OVA microscope.

Absent this methodology, companies still routinely take a 20 percent chop right across the organizational chart. The natural consequence of this slash and burn policy is that cuts are made in areas that currently show promise, thus inhibiting areas that are currently being promoted and invested in for the future. In contrast, relatively little is cut in groups where there is still massive waste and redundancy.

> "Don't go away mad, just go away."
> —**Charles Schultz,** *Peanuts*

The reason OVA is so effective is that it is extraordinarily objective and selective. Therefore, it can be used with surgically selective efficiency. When performing an efficient overhead value analysis, emotions dare not cloud the issue. They will influence your view of that which needs to be objectively addressed to maintain forward motion. It literally boils down to this: face a smaller amount of emotional blowback now or face organization-wide blowback in a rapidly approaching, increasingly uncertain future.

Your choice, Captain . . . again, a good amount of the inevitable, emotional damage you will unleash can be dampened exercising a bit of empathy for those loyal, but inefficient individuals this process will uncover. Have your crew practice listening with all their senses to get a real feeling of how their message is received and digested. Also, have them practice being more conscious of the content and delivery of these potentially career-threatening messages. This process includes your own presentations and conversations.

Overhead value analysis in practice

Once again, OVA works best on support functions. This methodology is not as effective on forward-looking departments such as sales and marketing. Forward-looking groups can also be potential candidates for this analysis, but they must be subject to special treatment since they are, directly or indirectly, revenue-producing entities. Their leveraging effect on your bottom line is the key issue. Get it right and it will work. Get it wrong and it will not only wreck your bottom line, it will also directly crush any team-spirit you have previously built up.

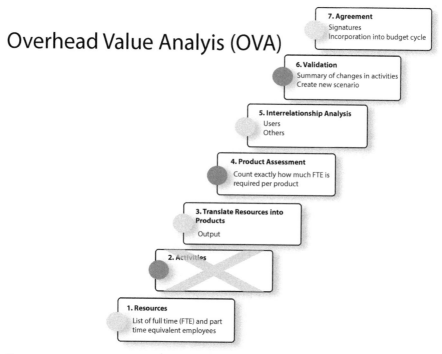

Figure 26. Overhead Value Analysis or OVA, originally from McKinsey

The OVA process is fairly simple and effective. It can be done as a project, implemented from inside, but usually better using external resources, or by using workshops with key internal people, guided by external ones. To maintain strict objectivity, we again strongly recommend facilitation from a third party. The key points are:

1. **List all functions**

   The responsible people and all other non-personnel resources should be listed. Redefine them in terms of Full Time Equivalent Units (FTEs).

2. **Translate output**

   All outputs (services, reports, etc.) should be translated into Product/Service FTE units.

3. **Skip defining and evaluating each activity**

   Focus on the results produced. Who does what is not important here, only accurately and objectively measuring the resulting output of those efforts.

4. **Define and analyze the output**

   Where does it come from? What is its frequency? How many FTEs does each output require?

5. **Assess the output**

   Where do these results end up, who uses them, and how much are they used?

6. **Interrelationship Analysis**

   How much is each specific output valued and used? Can this information be sourced elsewhere, or combined with something else? Can certain groups share the output more efficiently? If we stop sourcing it, will it pop up somewhere else?

7. **Validation**

   Perform a comprehensive "What if?" analysis on the output.

8. **Summary and agreement**

   Get all stakeholders to sign off on the findings and then integrate the changes within the next budget cycle.

Selectiveness is key

Start with well-defined overhead cost centers. This is irrespective of whether or not they have been affected in previous downsizing attempts. Who does what, and for how long they have been doing it, is becoming precariously inconsequential. This may sound very cold in its execution, but what if

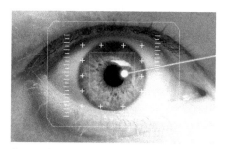

Figure 27. Be as selective as a laser surgeon!

it may increasingly be the key to your organization's survival and subsequent success? This is again where your redefined HR angels will play an increasingly vital and empathic role in motivating everyone affected, by:

- Encouraging and training them to increase their measurable value to the group
- Effectively expressing the value with conversational and presentational mastery
- Better handling finding other employment or income sources, should this OVA analysis affect them personally and precariously

On the brighter side, you may become keenly aware that some departments may actually need to be boosted rather than cut.

Objectivity is crucial! With the possible exception of the first step, the rest of the OVA process is focused upon the effectiveness and measurable value of each specific output. This literally means focusing closely on the utility of the following:

- Who reads which reports?
- How powerfully does what they contain affect the reader's ability to perform?
- How can this information be shared more effectively?
- Is there better information available faster, from other sources, and at a cheaper price?

Other streamlining tips

In today's rapidly changing markets, many products become obsolete before they have been "leaned out," so managers get less time to optimize their production processes fully. Companies are now implementing two new strategies:

- Increasing flexibility and embedded intelligence going directly into the production process
- Integrating research and development with operations creating what is now called DevOps

Building flexibility and embedding intelligence

Embedded intelligence can, over time, help companies to improve both the performance and the value-in-use of products and services, thus improving their pricing efficiency. In a sense, digitalization is empowering businesses to go beyond efficiency, to create effective learning systems that work harder and smarter. Doing this helps to adapt even quicker to changing conditions and needs.

For instance, a certain web-based global hotel-booking platform began using quicker feedback cycles to reframe the focus of its business model from the standard one at the time, to a new user-based satisfaction model. By pioneering this innovative model, they succeeded in creating brand new revenue opportunities. Until this particular project was undertaken, the hotel-booking industry's central belief had been that online success depended on two things: negotiating power with hotels through measurable traffic statistics and a reliable web interface for customers.

One company was one of the first to rethink the established belief that when customers booked a hotel room they were only interested in convenience, speed, and cost. They tested different, so-called, A-B web design models with small improvements over a longer time. For instance, they tested warmer and cooler tones on website graphics. They added testimonials from satisfied customers. Their testing confirmed that their site had transformed into more than just a typical hotel booking service; it now engaged the customer's interest, more often emotionally moving them into action. They also integrated feedback effectively and began testing experiments into key activities on a daily basis. They ended up creating a true online learning organization. They were learning and adjusting as they went. Just like Amazon, it now adjusts and tweaks its site daily to boost customer engagement and increase revenue. For anyone who has booked a hotel online recently, this type of online experience approach has now been adapted by agile competitors as the prevalent one.

Creating DevOps

In the same vein and also to develop more of an edge in software development, successful companies as diverse as Red Hat, IBM, and Amazon are speeding things up by integrating their R&D department with operations. As we previously mentioned, Amazon is rumored to have, on average, one hundred development projects deployed on their site at any given moment. This allows them to get real-time performance measurements and feedback, *directly from customers* who are actively shopping in real-time. They then tweak these developments to improve their customer experiences.

As this goes to print, we came across another wonderful, out-of-the-box application of technology. According to *Fortune Magazine's* November 1, 2015 article "Burning cars are never a good thing," Tesla had a problem with its batteries bursting into flames. The cause was finally identified as stemming from the batteries being mounted too close to the ground. According to this incredible article, instead of a massive recall, "Tesla beamed an update of the software to the affected cars, raising their ground clearance at highway speed by one inch. The problem went away." Simple? Maybe. Agile? Definitely!

Simple, Effective Leadership Assessment

This tool simplifies and lowers the cost of leadership recruitment with virtually no compromise in quality. This is accomplished simply by focusing more on the traditionally immeasurable soft skills that a leader (as distinct from a manager) needs to succeed.

A lot of effort and huge amounts of money go into analyzing and choosing organizational leaders. In the last few decades, the Evaluation and Headhunting Professions have become big business. Many headhunters charge enormous amounts for evaluating candidates. Now, what if their primary analytical methods still gloss over the most important points of leadership?

Managing is usually about measuring and allocation, whereas leadership is about passion. Express your passion in a way that (emotionally) "moves" people to action and watch them become inspired to cooperate and succeed. To paraphrase Rear Admiral Grace Hopper, you manage finance, products, and even services, but you lead people! If you want a good manager, then by all means use all those expensive evaluation options; or better yet buy a software program. If you want a leader whom people want to follow, you may want to read further and begin using our simple four-point test. A major difference is that in our version of the process, you will save a huge amount of time and money.

Unfortunately, we often see that with the current academic approach to leadership testing, the important and emotionally based leadership soft skills often get lost in the evaluation process. Millions are spent on all kinds of behavioral profiles and leadership assessments. Popular examples include 360, Myers-Briggs, and DISC, to name a few. They absolutely do produce important profile information that can be used in many creative ways. Yet they all have two things in common:

1. They all rely upon measuring from a strict battery of questions.
2. They often cost enormous amounts of money, especially when an executive position is in question.

Our experience is that when judging current management teams, we see a lot of unfortunate hiring, firing, and promotions that took place, didn't take place, or which shouldn't have taken place. These are all partly due to trying hard to put a hard, square management peg into a soft, round leadership hole.

Remember, there are *at least two* distinct ways you can use the word *sense*. One is to measure various degrees: as in hot/cold, hard/soft, dark/light, on/off, etc. More to the point is the expression, "If you can measure it, then you can manage it" or at least decide, regarding it. The other is sensing as in feeling. This is where you practice using your senses to feel what is happening around you. You can also practice emoting a certain sense of your feelings in order to inspire and engage others. Which of these descriptions of the word sense do you think works better when your goal is to inspire and lead others to follow?

More importantly, how does it feel when you are forced to take a battery of tests with questions that you sense were written, "long ago in a universe far, far away"? While completing what often feels like a long and totally irrelevant questionnaire, you discover that what you really burn for was either reduced to one multiple-choice question, or forgotten completely!

To assess leadership potential correctly and distinguish it from common management skills, the following properties, qualities, and your relationship to them need to be addressed:

- People/Partners
- Customers
- Competitors
- Product/Services
- Economics, Mathematics, and Analysis
- Strategy/Tactics/Structure

Strategy/Tactics/Structure are addressed throughout this book. So, let's spend a few minutes on some softer skills. Let's discuss them from the prospect of being a more agile leader, capable of using your senses to express your message effectively and guide your crew or company through uncertain waters. To do this you must be fairly balanced in four critical areas, three of which involve further soft-skill development. We strongly suggest you evaluate potential leadership candidates in the following four areas of human passion. See if you can get a sense of the power, simplicity, and beauty in how the following areas can be focused upon and how they can contribute to being a respected leader.

- **Passion for People:** How can you be a good leader if you don't like people?

  To lead others, you must come across as empathetic, trustworthy, and likeable. These traits will make you seem more authentic and attractive for others to follow your lead. There are many good analytical types out there, but what if they only have it half right? Remember the key to success is good content and actionable delivery. Leaders must have a high degree of passion and emotion with regard to relating to people as in the end, it is always and only about people.

  o Are you attracted to this candidate? If so, detail why.

- **Compassion for Customers:** How can you be a good leader without being compassionate, curious, and empathetic to each customer's individual situation?

  You need to be interested both technically and emotionally in the people who are buying your services and products, in a positively contagious way. As a leader, the more your compassion ripples out to those who need to hear and feel it most, the more they will be attracted to doing business with you and your company.

  o Do you feel that this candidate sees, hears, and understands you? If so, describe how.

- **Product/Service Fanatic:** How can you be a good leader if you don't know your products and services inside and out?

  A powerful leader must be curious, interested, and passionate about the products and/or services your customers are buying, as well as knowledgeable about those your competitors are offering. You need to be continuously curious, ask about, and engage in the following:

  o What are the future substitutes and/or technologies for your products and services?
  o How can you improve on what is provided?

- **Math Competence:** How can you even consider yourself a leader if you cannot calculate whether or not or when your products will pay off?

  Being a good leader means you can count. Being good at math is one thing. Expressing excitement when analyzing those numbers is even better. Leaders are employed to get a team to produce measurable results. To do this effectively, you must also enjoy being able to connect the numerical dots. How can you expect to navigate effectively unless you can sense, calculate, and feel the consequences of your decisions and actions? It will be even easier to accomplish, and you will produce better results if you also enjoy the ride. Testing this can be as simple as putting an income statement and balance sheet in front of the candidate and asking them what they see.

In short, costly management assessment and analysis systems may be missing the leadership point. Assessments and evaluations cost both time and money. At this late date, even the most effective ones do not capture these four simple, soft, but critical leadership traits. These traits can be effectively qualified by one person, well versed in them, who asks appropriate questions and senses (again using a balance of both definitions) the candidate's responses. Furthermore, to make this shift effective, those already in leadership positions in your company must all start singing authentically from the same hymnal, by also praising and applying these four traits. Otherwise, forget about becoming more agile. Your efforts will wind up looking like more inconsequential bling. To get this whole process going takes a measurable and sincere effort to train everyone's power and effectiveness in oral, written, and body language, especially the listening with all the senses part. This, of course, means everyone, including you, needs to be more conscious of, and be able to adjust, their own message for maximum efficiency, understanding, and action.

In our fast-moving, exciting, and volatile world, it is natural that younger and inexperienced (as well as normal hardworking) employees are forced to observe and respect the behavior of their leaders. As it is getting wilder out there every day, many "worker bees" either put their blind trust in their skippers, or jump ship when they get scared. Unfortunately, there is precious little time for conscious reflection or thinking for yourself, unless you deliberately take it. Therefore, your Captain better know how to navigate the ship and inspire the crew or, by the time the crew does begin questioning the skipper's behavior, everyone on board will risk going down with the ship!

This book is about the tools and methods needed to create an agile organization. What sets us and this book apart from a standard business book is that your authors heartily agree that, without being able to consciously experience and genuinely express human emotion, you will become increasingly disadvantaged.

Just like climbing up that down escalator, without constant development and improvement of your soft skills, you and your team will lose your ability to engage others and get the results you desire. The days of command and control are rapidly coming to an end! Again, it is always and only about people. The more you practice understanding individuals, develop your respect and compassion for an individual's emotions and behaviors, and not just on an intellectual level, the more powerful, agile, and attractive you and your organization will become.

Al provides one of the best examples we have come across of applying the above type of leadership thinking. Their passenger safety success is now reflected in the long and enjoyably uneventful flight record of Israel's national airline. With a tragic and bloody past, filled with too many hijacking attempts and terrorist attacks, they were forced to think outside the box. They instituted a series of simple questions, which enable their specially trained and very body language conscious security people to quickly and (as evidence suggests) effectively sense each individual passenger's behavior. Since they started this program, they have not had another tragic incident. This is the power and success of leadership by sensing, using both measurement and feeling.

Carve-Outsourcing Services (CORE) for Specialized Functions

This tool is a high-level, corporate surgical tool that can be used to gain heightened efficiency through identifying and redeploying non-core operations. This is accomplished by sourcing them to more powerful, pure-play business allies. The result is a higher quality operation and product, with more satisfied and motivated workers, at a lower cost.

One widespread premise in modern business has long been that companies increase their competitiveness by owning the assets that matter most, in their chosen strategy. Competitive advantage, according to this belief, comes directly from owning and controlling these valuable assets/ resources. Historically, these resources have tended to be scarce and needed to be utilized efficiently over long periods of time. They normally used to be company and location specific. Ownership (rather than leasing, renting or outsourcing) frequently appeared (and often still does) to be the best way to ensure exclusivity and control. But what if now these costly assets are used infrequently or inconsistently?

The decreasing effectiveness of ownership

A powerful and timely discussion has arisen especially since the 2007 American real estate collapse. Is it still better to own?

Let's start with a house. You may have the title to it, but what good is that if you also have it mortgaged to the hilt and fall behind on your payments? What about if you fall behind in your property taxes? So, paper and ego aside, who really owns your house?

From a business standpoint, if you add together the accrued interest you pay on your mortgage plus what it costs in taxes and upkeep, how much does that house really cost to own compared to the value of its utility for you and your family?

Could not owning it actually be a better deal?

The same holds true for most of the services you can now outsource. If we just focus on marketing, you can now get good advertising copy, SEO optimizing, and a professional layout starting from a bare-bones five dollars each on for example, Fiverr.com. Compare that to paying a full-time staff and keeping their tools and resources up to date, and is it still better to have all of these functions in house?

By increasing transparency and reducing search and transaction costs, digital technology is enabling new and better value-creating consumer models. As a result of this, ownership may have already become an inferior and increasingly unprofitable way to access and service key assets; and this doesn't include steadily increasing tax burdens. The traditional way of doing business is increasingly being replaced by flexible win-win commercial arrangements using partners with better, up-to-date, laser-specific skills and competence.

One of the most controversial examples of building a huge, multi-billion-dollar business without owning the assets is Uber. It is basically a skeleton staff and some nifty software that controls a multitude of rolling assets and people, namely independent cab drivers. Its per-employee valuation is currently astronomical.

With all the opportunities to minimize cost in all of these areas, one of the most common and accepted solutions is to outsource. Surprisingly, this has become an almost catch-all solution. Yet all too often, it later fails.

From our experience, the most common reasons given for why a chosen outsourcing company ends up being fired always seems to focus on one or more of the following:

- "They didn't understand the ..."
  o Customers
  o Technology
  o Products
  o Work Culture
  o Systems

- "Their established routines took longer than our norms"
- "Cost analyses proved that we really could do it ourselves just as cheaply"

Regardless of the reason for failure, statistics point to up to 40 percent of all outsourcing deals currently wind up failing and costing enormous amounts of time, frustration, and money. The unhappy client often decides to take a step backwards and insource the process again. The whole thing becomes at best, a costly embarrassment or at worst, the death of the company. Does this sound like an agile solution to you?

You become the risk

Most companies involved in the outsourcing business normally force their clients to use their proprietary systems and their own 'qualified personnel' to ensure that proven and well-defined procedures are precisely followed. Examples of this are SAP, IBM, and Accenture. This is fully understandable, as requiring strict adherence to the system is believed to ensure the project's success. Yet this obvious covering of your 'assets' approach also offers your chosen outsourcer a juicy opportunity. They can now easily blame any subsequent failures upon your firm's inability to grasp the brilliance and effectiveness of their system. In other words, you didn't follow their instructions correctly.

Your outsourcer is the hands-down expert at using their own system, but what about their ability to tailor it to meet your and your customer's specific needs? Should your way of doing things be found to be at odds with theirs, each point in every one of their suggested guidelines and procedures could possibly represent an additional point of failure. Also, can you think of any incentive for them to adjust their system to your needs compared to you being forced to adjust your needs to their system? Will these costs be equally divided? Tragically, most of these points of friction do not show up until long after the contract has been signed and your payments have started.

To effectively handle these concerns and create a win-win collaboration, our trademarked methodology called Carve-Outsourcing™ or CORE™ was developed at Catalyst Acquisition Group LLC and is now available through CAG International AG and The Minerva Group. Its basic structure is easy to understand and the following explanation may help prevent you from choosing to outsource with the wrong partner or not fully appreciating the risks if you do.

CORE is particularly efficient in many specialized overhead service functions such as training, event management, conference management, training administration, etc. Companies like Cognizant, CAG and Minerva will take on your existing department or parts of it, as well as existing staff, system and products, *as is!* Then, as part of the service, they will upgrade their effectiveness and lease or sell this upgraded service back to you, at *or below* your current cost level. This ensures that your company can save money, get a much better service *and feel safer during the entire transition.* This also *eliminates much of the precariousness and worry* for those employees in the outsourced department. Also, you can now rest assured that your way of doing business will remain fully understood and production can continue as usual, from day one. Finally, you will be guaranteed that the performance and result will never be worse or more expensive than it has been historically as the same trusted people are still doing what they do best. Only now with better resources, training and at a lower price point. This is the methodology behind Carve-Outsourcing™ or CORE™.

A hybrid of the best

CORE™ can be further described as an *optimized hybrid* of three different concepts:

- **Mergers and Acquisitions** which are where you merge or purchase a company or group to expand into new territory or enhance what you already do well.
- **Outsourcing** where you farm out an existing task or process to another firm. They handle that responsibility more efficiently and usually cheaper, because that is where their competence excels.
- **Spin-Off** which is where you create a specialized subsidiary that now has more freedom to excel at what it does best. There is also the enhanced opportunity for your former colleagues to test and evaluate new ideas and methods—learned from their new colleagues—than they ever could have when they were part of your company.

To increase agility, constant focus needs to be put upon the question of who can do each task, product and/or process faster, better and cheaper. Anchoring this concept in reality, it is important to understand the gravity of the following statement.

Everything we do by ourselves will be anchored in and influenced by our own inhibitors.

These consist again of our own internal behaviors, systems, culture, organization, and processes. These concerns naturally begin to fade as you enter into your own CORE™ process.

Here's a quick lesson in how the process works.

Step One: The audit

To assure absolute success, you should first perform a specialized audit procedure in each area of interest. We, *of course*, recommend one based upon our Trade Marked STA+R™ methodology. Skip to Tool 13 for details.

Step Two: Defining your company's primary role

It is critical to understand what your company's essential role is in the world. In this step, you will become very clear as to whether your role is to build, implement, market, or develop a product or service. Regardless of whether it is producing ball bearings, installing communication equipment, manufacturing bowling pins, or serving fast food, this process will get you and your team crystal clear on a powerful, agreed-upon, and useable definition of your core business.

Step Three: Efficiencies

Once defining your role is complete, everything that is not directly related to your core skills and business becomes a candidate to outsource. Objectively, all of these non-essential roles now become potential areas for outsourcing, but due to their more general nature, and the fact that most other roles have probably by now already been optimized, most overhead functions are in focus as the prime candidates.

The result: CORE™ increases your agility in the following ways:

- **Pure-Play**

  It means increased competence. Your old department has now become part of a group that has its core competence as its own specialized business model. It now becomes a congruent Pure-Play company. Everyone involved will now get to develop their expertise in their chosen field. This model thus offers a more relevant, challenging, and exciting home for your effective and responsible former employees.

- **World-class tools**

  You can now be more certain of being supplied with up-to-date Best Practices and quicker implementation of next generation methodologies and technologies. They will also share their knowledge with their new colleagues and brainstorm with them on new ways to more effectively solve old challenges. This is an immediate requirement, as your former colleagues will now also sense their own burning need to get agile or die. They are no longer in a company backwater. They are now in the spotlight and need to actively compete for your business against best-in-class competition, or die trying.

- **Traditional ways**

  Old ways of doing things are augmented with best practices from industry leaders. Petty internal politics and bottlenecks that used to gum up the process have to be wiped away. The result is world-class efficiency, yet with a warm, familiar, even friendly, touch.

- **Conflicts of interest are reduced/eliminated**

  There can no longer be any question of a bureaucratic department head needing to protect pet projects or cover his or her assets. Now there is no more dreaming up reasons, justifications, and excuses for the failure of his/her own decisions.

- **Less overhead and more flexibility**

  The entire department now becomes a recurring expense from an independent company. You should immediately begin to see cost savings in the neighborhood of twenty to twenty-five percent. Should times get rough, you can scale down your costs or metaphorically "trim the fat" without carving into the bone. As your former supplier is now strengthened with business from other sources, should business slow across the board, you both can scale back more easily to survive and prosper another day. This is agility. This is Win/Win business.

- **Increased ability to switch outsourcers**
  You can now switch or, alternatively, shut down the whole department or parts thereof, should this separate (and now independent) entity fail to satisfy. When things are going well, response time to your requests should be much quicker.

Outsourcing still demands responsibility

It is very important to keep in mind that outsourcing does not remove your responsibility for making sure that each outsourced job gets done. For example, should you outsource your IT department to IBM, Cognizant, or even Minerva, you would be well advised and encouraged to retain an internal manager. It is a big plus to have a homegrown champion who can monitor and manage ongoing events and activities. This is important in order to guard your organization's ongoing and possibly changing interests.

Some outsourcing examples

Siemens jumped early into the outsourcing boom by moving much of its software development to India. In the early days, this information was then transmitted by satellite at the end of each business day, back to Germany or in many cases directly out to the specific project site. This allowed the company to charge local rates for development services that actually cost them much less. This process drastically improved their profits.

In recent software examples, Microsoft's Office 360 is a subscription-based application of its popular smorgasbord office suite of products such as Word, Excel, Publisher, and PowerPoint, with a dessert of Skype usage. Adobe now offers its products such as Acrobat and Photoshop in a similar fashion. With your subscription, you will get the latest upgrades from these giants directly to your computer as soon as they are available. Google has a similar suite of products, but their price is even better. Many are free!

Call into many large service desks, such as Dell Computer and you will probably be talking with someone with a distinct Indian accent. Due to the increase in education, coupled with the almost free cost of telephone and internet service, placing your call center in India can be a very profitable choice. Even non-English speaking service desks have moved there and hired someone to teach the local operators to speak the necessary languages. As many in India are very good with technical issues, sometimes the level of help can actually be better than local technicians located in the market where the product or service was purchased. This is not only happening in India. A Swedish taxi cab company placed its call desk in Estonia. It was much cheaper to operate from there and there were enough Swedish-speaking Estonians who were eager for the job. Of course, there are the inevitable complaints of not being able to understand the operator's strange dialect, but even these complaints disappear as soon as they practice and master their new language.

More practically, in most every office, you now have a cleaning company that comes in to keep your office looking fresh and to replenish various consumables in the bathroom and pantry. Most coffee services and many other refreshment, fresh fruit, and snack services are delivered on a regular basis from a growing list of chosen outsourcers.

Many companies, both large and small, use services like Dropbox and various secure, cloud-based services to handle their data. Basic bookkeeping to full blown cloud-based business systems can make keeping track of your money easier than ever. Computer-based services, from having a SPOC or Single Point of Contact PC technician to managing your entire data department, are now available. Need some office help and can't afford to hire someone? No problem. Google the phrase "virtual assistant" and you will be able to find the exact service you are looking for, often with both reviews, testimonials, and a great price. Fiverr.com is a prime example of a site to find just about anything regarding getting your online message out in a fast, professional way.

Even in shipping, a great example is offered from a June 2015 McKinsey article called, "Disrupting beliefs: A new approach to business-model innovation[1]" by Marc De Jong and Menno van Dijk. "Consider how a big European maritime port embarked on a large-scale land management program. The industry belief reframed by the port was that large liquid-bulk-load ships valued private access to storage tanks. The underlying assumption was that shipping companies wanted the ability to deliver their bulk loads anytime and therefore required entry to their tanks at close range."

"In response to this perceived need, most maritime ports have developed jetties to which they provide individual shipping companies private access—essentially the equivalent of 'ownership.' As a result of each company's varying schedules and traffic, many jetties ended up being mostly unused, but others weren't sufficient for peak times. Seeing this problem, the port's management reframed the industry belief by asking if customers cared more about access on demand than exclusivity. The port now intends to help all customers use any jetty to access any fuel tank, by developing a common-carrier pipe connecting them."

These stories do not even touch the new and exciting world of blockchain. Many projects are now in the works to outsource financial services (so-called Defi), payment services, and even secure voting services. With recent events these projects are gaining traction as their distributed ledger, transparency, and secure encryption advantages are proving to be more trustworthy and reliable than their human public servants. As they say in crypto, "as long as you trust mathematics, it works!"

Outsourcing is clearly a trend that is just getting started. Finding the correct outsourcer for you first project depends upon getting clear upon what you want. Accomplishing only this first, simple step, to get clear on your needs, will give you much more control over the rest of the process and produce a better, more efficient final result.

Injecting Entrepreneurship

This tool will help you nurture a young, daring spirit of creativity and development even in a large, established, and often cautious company.

First, a very important disclaimer and red flag!

Many executives and "talking heads" argue that the entrepreneurial spirit is the one and only key to making your company more agile. This could not be further from the truth!

Just trying to define entrepreneurship correctly can make you dizzy. Some common denominators are risking your own money, starting up something new, aggressive leadership, and vision into action.

Wikipedia states: "Entrepreneurship is the process of starting a business, typically a startup company offering an innovative product, process or service.[1] The entrepreneur perceives an opportunity and often exhibits biases in taking the decision to exploit the opportunity. The exploitation of entrepreneurial opportunities includes design actions to develop a business plan, acquire the human, financial and other required resources, and to be responsible for its success or failure. Entrepreneurship may operate within an entrepreneurship ecosystem which includes government programs and services that support entrepreneurs, entrepreneurship resources (e.g., business incubators and seed accelerators), entrepreneurship education and training and financing (e.g., loans, venture capital financing, and grants)."

Does that simplify things for you?

However you define it, entrepreneurship is a powerful, creative force, if directed correctly. A brilliant application of entrepreneurship is, for example, launching a new product or service. Yet, it is not uncommon that an entrepreneur might also turn out to be the most single-minded, money-driven, and inflexible person in the company! Many are later shown to have no willingness whatsoever, to move, adjust, or accept any agility at all.

Let's define and distinguish the following terms more clearly:

1. An entrepreneurial company is a company without legacy to hinder it in its quest for success
2. Business agility is the ability to change or adjust direction quickly and effectively, whether you are an entrepreneurial company or not

As the skipper, injecting entrepreneurship back into your established corporate structure may be one of your greatest challenges. It is also no wonder that most successful entrepreneurial leaders ultimately sell out or hire an agile leader to take over their successful enterprise, once it is up and running. This is usually a wise choice because the personality type that makes a good entrepreneur, more often than not, usually displays the exact opposite behavior needed to maintain growth and stability. At some point, the freedom in unfettered entrepreneurship naturally begins to complicate and conflict with the systems necessary to continue growing. That freedom to think outside the box is what often ignited the company's initial success. Consider the famous battle for control over Apple's future between founder-entrepreneur Steve Jobs and John Scully, Job's own pick for a hired-in manager. Their battle reminds us there are exceptions to the rule and timing does matter. Ultimately, without a continuous, fresh stream of entrepreneurship, emphasis ends up being focused upon caution and maintaining a business-as-usual or survival stance. The word survival may not come up in discussion, but if you are more concerned about protecting your present level of business instead of expanding it, what would you call it? Regardless of what you call it, if your goal is survival, the most you can ever expect to accomplish is to survive. Once in place, a survival mentality can persist until the forces of legacy and bureaucratic momentum simply overwhelm yet another once-successful company.

Usually, the bigger the company is, the larger the entrepreneurial challenge. Large corporations have been struggling for decades to inject entrepreneurship into their organizations. This problem is recognized and is nothing new. Still, many have experienced the hard way that newcomers to their market are more agile and much faster with innovation. Take the automotive business for instance. Many years ago it was estimated that

General Motors was saddled with approximately $1,400 per produced car just to pay for the benefits of all their already retired workers. That's $1,400 per car before production even starts! Korea and China had no such burden. The result has been that these wide-eyed newbies can (and obviously did) take big chunks of market share and attention quickly; think Kia. They can introduce faster, better and cheaper products often before established companies even sense a threat. What if other established industry leaders have so far just been lucky to avoid Schumpeter's ongoing process of creative destruction?

We have already talked about established and successful companies and their valiant efforts to become more flexible, many of which failed horribly. Their failures are usually due to ingrained traditions, legacy systems, cultures of mediocrity and processes that all support the four big inhibitors of change: Systems and processes, Organization, IT, and (not least) Culture.

For anyone used to working in a large company, it is no secret that entrepreneurs find it difficult to work within the strict, monitored confines of a contemporary corporate structure. Just having to wear an ID badge drives many pure entrepreneurs mad! Yet aren't shorter and shorter cycles now screaming for a more entrepreneurial approach? How can this dichotomy be resolved?

An entrepreneurial solution?

Many companies have chosen to create distinct groups, projects, and divisions that function separately, at arm's length. This deliberately puts distance between company imposed legacy systems, and these new cowboys are now tasked by the "Suits" to achieve greatness. Sometimes totally separate subsidiaries and entities are created to actually wall off what, in the worst case, could be called corporate rot. These rebellious, yet productive groups have been called Intrapreneurs or Skunk Works.

The pitfalls of structured entrepreneurship

Having worked with a project orientation all our lives, we see this selection and unshackling of appropriate individuals, who seem to have the Right

Stuff, as your key to success. Giving them room to run, directly, contributes to creating profitable entrepreneurship or intrapreneurship.

Having made this point, the question then naturally arises, "Is entrepreneurship a gift with which you are born, or a trait that you can develop through training?" Our observations suggest that with practice, determination, and the right environment, anything is possible. What we have discovered though is that it is much more effective to find those special people who already have that free-thinking entrepreneurial spirit. They can usually get up and running in these companies and subsidiaries to produce miracles at a much quicker pace. In other words, practice noticing those who are naturally agile. The real trick then becomes "riding herd" over them to keep them happy and pointed in the right direction.

We have also observed that countries, cultures and organizations blessed with high levels of entitlement are often cursed when it comes to entrepreneurship. In these cultures, those naturally gifted entrepreneurs can quickly become uncomfortable, indignant, and even protest and resist being unleashed! One of your authors experienced just that in a very well-established electronics company. Our boss gave us the responsibility and free reign to produce as we wished according to agreed-upon goals. Yet, a formal complaint from the staff, lodged by their union representative quickly crushed all entrepreneurial hopes that management had tried so hard to cultivate. It was too much freedom too soon as the staff was very accustomed to being managed, also known as babysitting. Many of these people were thirty-five-plus and very professional! Acceptance by the crowd usually overwhelms most everyone's spirit for adventure, except for those with the most obsessive and compulsive entrepreneurial behavior. Due to the gravity inherent in oppressive peer pressure, the average employee usually will try to avoid letting go of structure and inhibit the qualities necessary for real entrepreneurship. They seem to prefer comfort and safety over growth, excitement, and results.

This reality can further aggravate any future hopes of being both agile and entrepreneurial. How? Easy, the only entrepreneurs who make it through this gauntlet of conformity often become fanatics with tough skin and hardened views of how entrepreneurship *"should be."* Once they make it into a position of power, they have usually trained or been forced to become less agile just to survive without going crazy. Think about it.

If you constantly had to argue that your way was the right one, how agile would you still be? This is the best case. Worst case? Having reached a position of power, they now want revenge.

We have mentioned entitlement in a number of situations, but there is still one more. What if it can take the form of a highly unionized environment? France and Sweden are good examples. What about highly structured or hierarchical cultures such as Finland and Japan? If everyone in a culture has been brought up doing everything equally or knowing and sticking to their assigned place, how much of a spirit still exists for free thinking or acting creatively?

Yes, there are always exceptional examples of people who come from these places and thrive on going directly against their societal grain. For instance, some Swedish rebels like Alfred Nobel and one of Skype's founders Niklas Zennstrom became fabulously rich and successful in spite of their environment. Keep in mind though that their entrepreneurial behavior is far from that of the normal Swedish worker attitude. Even recently, over 80 percent of working Swedes still felt the need to belong to a union. Yet even this well-established norm of mediocrity could be changing again. Keep in mind one quarter of the Swedish population followed a good many other Europeans and immigrated to North America between 1850 and 1920. Their mission was to escape the peer pressure of living in a very structured society and be free to create something of their own. What does this also say about those who remained?

Younger Swedes are beginning to sense how precarious their chances actually are of getting and holding a "real job." They are beginning to sense that they will probably not be benefiting from the established (and deteriorating) welfare system in a way that equals to what they are currently forced to contribute. In fact, a growing number see no sense nor future in getting and keeping a "regular job." This trend has now been compounded and accelerated by getting paid not to work due to the pandemic.

Entrepreneurship in these rigid or traditional environments is often viewed as a threat to the status quo and quite rightly so! Sweden's social cost structure is still primarily set up to handle the ever-decreasing Salariat. For instance, one of your authors has learned the hard way that an entrepreneur that has a run of bad luck for more than one year can be ostracized from standard unemployment and sick leave benefits. In this case, both Swedish Unemployment and Sick Leave System payments are directly based upon what you made in the past year. If you have a rough year and one day after that year is over you realize your situation, your benefits will now be calculated on your new year's results. You can wind up having paid into a pool of funds that you will now find impossible to access. Even in the most effective welfare system on the planet, you can still fall through the cracks, especially if you have an entrepreneurial bent. This anecdote is from personal experience.

Therefore, it often takes either lots of guts, blind luck, a bit of stubborn stupidity, or a mixture thereof to dare to start your own company. This can be especially foolish if you have a weak business plan or find it tough to articulate why people should buy you or your product. Still, for an increasing number of us, the taste of freedom that entrepreneurship provides is still too tempting to go back to a standard nine-to-five job, while many (who have been laid off or unemployed for a while) simply have no other choice. Yet if you are a closet entrepreneur and lucky enough to be employed in a company that appreciates entrepreneurship enough to nurture it you may still hit the jackpot.

Brainstorming the intrapreneurial process

Starting this process is best accomplished through a series of workshops followed by an action plan, implementation, and follow up, which includes coaching or mentoring to make sure your plan sticks.

Workshop 1. *Uncovering Entrepreneurial Potential*

This is a workshop designed to uncover entrepreneurial talents, brainstorm on how to optimize them, to further open up and allow for entrepreneurial practices into your organization. This is a brainstorming free-for-all, where everyone can contribute to a "Christmas wish list" of:

- what is needed
- what they are able to contribute
- what they would like to do
- what they see as possible/impossible and why

Workshop 2. *Identify, Agree, and Implement*

This second workshop takes the next practical step. Its purpose is to identify candidate areas, to agree upon which of them offers the most potential and would be easiest to implement into this new way of working. The workshop then winds up with participants mapping out the steps of a realistic implementation plan.

Once you have decided and agreed upon where entrepreneurial practices would be most effective and welcome, it is time to create your action plan. This is where you specify what the real goals will look like. You will now endeavor to find someone who will not only be personally responsible for this achievement but burns to champion the process. The final piece of the puzzle is setting up and agreeing upon clear, measurable and manageable deadlines with this champion.

Its implementation

Implementing a solid strategic, entrepreneurial plan can help energize and optimize those newly discovered people and resources. It will point them directly toward your customers' needs, wants and wishes, as well as how to better highlight deficiencies in the organization. Once an action plan is agreed upon it is time to break the deadlines down into a timetable and assign a tight budget to these 'Intrapreneurs' and 'Skunk Workers.' Then and most importantly take the conscious and visible leadership step back and allow these now officially sanctioned rebels the freedom to do what they love.

Coaching entrepreneurship to success

> "You manage things and you lead people."
> **—Grace Hopper**

Good leadership often has as much to do with being the silent space where others can boldly create as it does encouraging, most often badgering, others with what to do. Although there is a critical need for a clear strategy and measurable objectives, once they are established it is time to let go and trust these creative individuals. Dare yourself to allow their process to unfold in their chosen way. Keep your eye on agreed-upon goals and their timetables. If you absolutely have to, suggest and invite rather than order or command.

Trying to babysit this group of unleashed entrepreneurial cowboys will compress that freedom that you have just committed to sanctioning. This will be seen as raw betrayal and will succeed in killing any future trust in the value of your or the company's word. To help anchor and cultivate this new, entrepreneurial way of thinking you now need to back off and, at most, coach them instead. The more you give them the trust, responsibility, and freedom they desire, the quicker you will enjoy the result everyone wants.

Learn to coach:

- Focus on the "What," NOT the "How"
- Practice asking reflective and insightful questions
- Listen with all your senses to the complete answer of what is said and not said
- Encourage them to think for themselves
- Compliment good ideas
- Openly acknowledge all milestones that are achieved
- Reward good results

Then watch your team become more self-inspired and engaged to achieve greatness!

A sneaky, but effective tip in the accompanying managerial process to minimize internal resistance is to call these entrepreneurial undertakings projects. This can be used in lieu of going full out and starting other departments or creating separate companies. Calling them projects makes it much easier for those cautious people in your organization (who have invested a lot of their career in your company's traditions and legacies) to more easily swallow this new way of working.

Using this little trick, these dedicated yet conservative team members can then relax their guard and let these new projects—and those restless people assigned to them—do their thing, on a longer but still visible leash. The trick here is that it is often easier for those in your organization, who are used to structure and limits, to accept a project instead of just letting go of it completely. By definition, time and resources are always limited in a project. Therefore, these cautious decision makers can now feel a bit more comfortable due to these measurable limits. This way they still feel they retain some practical means to pull the plug, if needed. Chances are though, these are the same, structured people in your organization who probably won't dare.

The pitfalls of entrepreneurship/intrapreneurship

Beware! Should your company try populating these new, faster, more creative ventures with legacy prone employees, they can quickly strangle any entrepreneurial spirit that may just have begun to blossom. Experience teaches that freedom, combined with responsibility, encourages powerful entrepreneurship. The more you try to shackle your workers, even with accepted and popular programs such as TQM or Lean, the more you will ultimately force them into process that they consider constraining, irrelevant and sometimes plain silly. If you do, count on them leaving!

Entrepreneurial success

Look no further again than Google to see a brilliant implementation of intrapreneurship. Somehow, they have managed to grow into a major corporation without losing their corporate ability to think like entrepreneurs. Hewlett Packard was another success story, which was started in a garage by two entrepreneurs. Over time, this once great company seems to have lost touch with its entrepreneurial roots.

Apple is a microcosm of the pluses and minuses of this whole discussion. This company started as an entrepreneurial success story with Steve Jobs and Steve Wozniak at the helm. It began to grow faster than they could "manage." To their initial credit, a successful and traditional manager, John Scully from Pepsi was then called in to run it. A titanic clash of cultures and egos developed, pitting entrepreneurship against business as usual. It almost crushed the company. Business as usual won out for a time, when Scully successfully engineered a coup and threw Jobs out. Just a few years later, Scully's strategy was found wanting, then it faltered completely. A now older and more experienced Jobs was then called back in.

With his entrepreneurial genius now seasoned with better management skills, the rush to current Apple greatness began. And at the same time, Mr. Job's reputation for stubbornness and outbursts demonstrates a passionate rigidity to his vision, alone. It will be interesting to see how Tim Rice fares in Apple's next chapter, which is unfolding.

These stories are not as unique as you would think. An entrepreneurial visionary has started many successful companies. The biggest difference between Hewlett and Packard, Jobs and Wozniak and today's entrepreneurs is the pace of their success. Zuckerberg's Facebook and Zennerstrom's Skype achieved billion-dollar success and these individuals achieved heroic celebrity in less than ten years. Even that blistering pace is on track to increase even more quickly, going forward. Just look at the ridiculous fortunes now being minted in the blockchain space. It must be sweet revenge that Cameron and Tyler Winklevoss, the twins who left Facebook and Mark Zuckerberg, have now created the Gemini Crypto exchange in the process of becoming the first recognized crypto billionaires.

Entrepreneurship's missing link: Passion

The most important lubricant in creating a well-oiled and outstanding team of Entre- or Intrapreneurs is passion. The ability to express and bring alive that for which you burn. The more you encourage them to let their passion loose, the more they can put that exciting and contagious feeling into their work. The best way to encourage others to unleash their passion is to relax, then constantly and contagiously practice unleashing your own.

Expansion versus compression

An important key to uncovering how much of this entrepreneurial lubricant can be found is by observing behavior. Is your team's behavior relaxed and expansive or tense and compressed? The freer and more expansively the team moves and communicates, the more room they usually sense to express themselves. The more room they have to express themselves, the more fun they can have while successfully solving the challenges at hand.

The opposite is true also. If you observe your team of entrepreneurs looking tense or you sense a feeling of politeness and compression, it is high time to act. If you notice them just doing their jobs, with little or no self-expression or walking around with their heads down, locate the source of their resignation immediately. Be aware, it can be and often is you. Hesitate, even for a moment, and you may end up with sub-par results, lose your best cowboys to the competition, and often both. Remember, polite also means 'pissed-off, lightly.'

Entrepreneurial mergers and acquisitions

As we mentioned in part two, we see a rise in mergers and acquisitions going forward, but not in the traditional sense. The new M&A model will be much quicker and more entrepreneurial. Many enabling tools have been developed to enhance agility such as Digital Data Rooms (DDR). Another good example of such a service is DataSite[2], which provides real-time information about companies and deals going down in the M&A sphere.

Motivations for quick M&A

This new era of agility will push corporations and institutions to further consider M&A as a primary area for growth. This trend actually started long ago. For instance, do you know that most of Microsoft's incredible growth has been made via M&A? Their strategy, sometimes referred to as embrace and devour, is a very descriptive metaphor for their process of finding something good and acquiring it. In Sweden, the Electrolux Group was more or less re-created by Hans Werthen as an M&A growth machine. In the future, many companies will look to an M&A solution instead of trying to be agile enough in their own so-called core business. In its extreme, this strategy will make many corporations look more like some agile and effective Private Equity (PE) firms like Platinum Equity Holdings[3]. They may even come to resemble traditional conglomerates. Many will focus on synergies in distribution and branding rather than in the more traditional cost areas of scale, technology, and production. This, in turn, will also require practicing business agility to identify and divest of slow-moving companies in the portfolio. These stragglers can and often do drag down the average growth of the whole group.

As with all other non-core functions, internal M&A departments are also the victims of the Big Four inhibitors of change. We therefore envision an increased move toward outsourcing even for these internal M&A departments to specialized providers. There they can be much more cost and time effective. For companies faced with M&A opportunities, new factors need to be considered, including:

- Finding candidates with adequate compatibility to merge with or acquire
- The global impact of the arrangement
- The likelihood of a quick, painless, and friendly negotiation process

The dealmakers—those entrepreneurial front-line workers, who spearhead these deals—must address traditional factors plus these and other new factors in order to successfully broker future M&As; and they will need to do it quicker than yesterday's deal.

Decision makers, prospective investors, and investment banks currently have a very few tools to provide a quick assessment of a proposed deal. That is without spending (or wasting) too much time and energy on small details. To help, we offer the accretion/dilution analysis.

What is accretion/dilution analysis? What is its value?

The answer to these questions is the following question: "Does the proposed deal increase or decrease the post-transaction earnings per share (EPS)?"

This fairly simple analysis determines the justification for the deal. The steps are:

- Estimate a pro forma net income for the combined entities
- Calculate the combined company's new share count
- Divide pro forma net income by pro forma shares to arrive at a pro forma Earnings Per Share or EPS
- Double-check the accuracy of your numbers

Is the calculated pro forma EPS higher than the original EPS?

An increase to EPS is regarded as accretion, while a decrease is regarded as dilution. Many on Wall Street typically frown at dilutive transactions. If the deal has a reasonable likelihood of turning accretive from the second year onwards, the proposed business combination may be more palatable.

Accretion/dilution analysis is often seen as a proxy for whether or not a contemplated deal creates or destroys shareholder value. It is a very simple but practical tool to have handy.

Is there vulnerability in agility?

In western culture the word "vulnerability" is often associated with being weak. Many also see it as a negative personality trait. We have sometimes even used this generally accepted interpretation of it in this very book!

What if this is not the whole story? What if vulnerability actually demonstrates your capacity to confidently relax and be ready for everything? What if it defines your ability to have all your physical and mental resources ready, willing, and able to handle whatever threat or opportunity presents itself, right here and now?

This is how a true master of martial arts treats vulnerability. Just as you can catch more money in an open and relaxed palm compared to a tight and straining fist, so can you increase your chances to be agile, if you stay relaxed and vulnerable and by keeping all your resources and energy at the ready! How many more threats and opportunities will you be able to see and respond to with increased agility if you practice mastering vulnerability?

Why is this fuzzy-sounding soft skill so important in this age of agility?

Because the more energy you use, straining to anticipate, prevent or defend against threats, the higher the risk becomes that you may get stressed, tired, and also miss the chance to act on an important opportunity. Sometimes, you also need to be able to focus on, prioritize, or avoid the less important ones. Yet these have to be balanced and in perspective with the Big Picture. Keeping a relaxed and vulnerable demeanor will help. Challenges can be on a personal as well as corporate level, or both. One wise man who also happened to be my father, Birger Amell, once said, "The size of a man is often shown by the size of the things that upset him." The point he was making was that too much energy is spent getting upset over or worrying about the wrong or petty things.

The Strategic Triangle

This is another simple balancing tool, which is an easy and effective reminder to focus forward, toward the horizon, instead of in the rear-view mirror as you sail into the future.

Strategic plans are very often overdeveloped in some areas and underdeveloped in others. This phenomenon can easily be traced to Globalization. Globalization increases the pressures resulting from greater competition and thus increases the subsequent knee-jerk reaction to focus on cutting more costs. This phenomenon has drastically expanded over the last few decades in lock-step with the explosion of global competition. Again, costs have already been cut way past the fat, through the muscle and deep into the structural bones of many companies. This directly limits their capacity, resources and ability to plan ahead at all. How can you expect a company to become or remain agile in this stressed, weakened, and emaciated situation?

To regain a balanced planning perspective, we offer you our Strategic Triangle. From the three rings of customer, company, and competitors you can create a clearer and more balanced path toward your stated objectives.

From now on, your strategy should equal the harmony of your own:

Optimized company resources
to efficiently meet . . .
Customer demand
vis-à-vis attractive customer alternatives
and then, handle the **Competition** using . . .
Strategy and tactics,
to clearly describe *how* to handle it

When this formula is accepted and implemented, you can begin placing relatively equal amounts of energy into these three distinct areas. Once again it is our experience, drawn from decades of analyzing strategic reports and plans offered from most of our clients, that there is a chronic imbalance between these factors. In fact, it is not uncommon to see 80 percent of management's time, energy, and resources spent on internal issues, 10 percent customer concerns, 1 percent on the competitive environment, and the remaining 9 percent on directional or strategic decisions.

Our experience suggests that optimal agility is attained when this situation is rebalanced closer to a 30, 30, 30 and 10 percent split. Metaphorically, this is in terms of total calories burnt operating in these different areas. (See figure below)

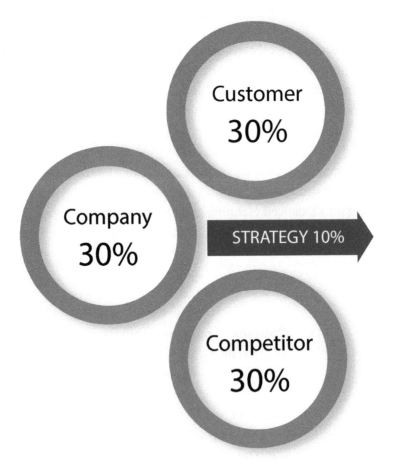

Figure 28. The Strategic Triangle

The test

The quickest and most effective test to measure the weighting of these areas in your current plan is easy. Simply take a printed copy of your current business plan and separate these three sections from each other. Then weigh the paper contents of each. Each section's comparative physical weight will provide a quick, but reliable indication of the weighting you have placed on each of these important strategic components in your current plan. In fact, most CEOs find this simple test both refreshing and appreciated. It demonstrates a classic, visible case of "not seeing the trees because of the forest."

This simple test makes it obvious, even to the Highest Paid People's Opinions, that unless you have a balanced plan, it is virtually impossible to focus on thinking forward. It is also important to note that once this rebalancing is complete, up to 70 percent of company energy will now be aimed toward making your strategic report more forward looking. In the uncertain business environment we currently find ourselves in, could anything be more useful?

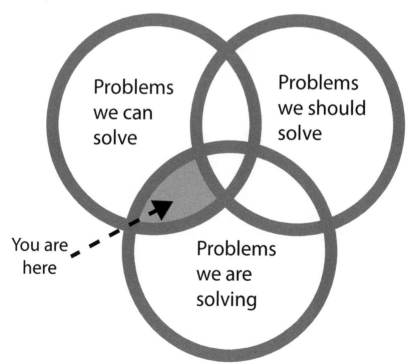

Figure 29. Problems to solve, such as transforming bureaucratic traits to agile traits

Ample examples exist of misguided strategies impeding and even crushing companies. Dig deep enough and rest assured that every company has a horror story about some misguided strategy, based upon looking backward while trying to plan forward. The eventual outcome is that these plans almost always fail during their execution.

One classic story is a short-lived company named Osborne Computer. In the Wild West environment of the PC's introduction in the early 1980s, Adam Osborne produced one of the first success stories in the blossoming portable computer business called (can you guess?) the Osborne. Flushed with success and while still producing this Osborne One in quantity, the company couldn't wait to boast of its new and improved version. Osborne then made the strategic and now classic blunder of announcing, with overwhelming fanfare, their new Osborne Two model. Predictably (except for management?) potential Osborne One customers *wisely* decided to wait and buy the new and improved Osborne Two. This quickly drove the company out of business before the large inventory of Osborne Ones could be sold. From start to finish, this whole process lasted only thirty months and destroyed one of the most promising new companies in Silicon Valley. This fiasco is now actually referred to as "The Osborne Effect"[1] and is the painful reason that Apple and others never preannounce new products.

Benefits of a strong DNS and consequences of a weak DNS

It is not only Osborne. Below are some other fun facts about agile organizations:

- Forty-seven percent of the pre-2000 leaders (ranked in the top twenty percent of hi-tech industry) lost their leadership positions during the 2000–2002 recession.
- New leaders emerged after the recession. They were the agile firms that quickly reacted to economic and industry shifts, cutting costs quickly and smartly. Former industry leaders lost their placement by blindly cutting costs, delaying important product improvements, and cutting important marketing investments.
- Decisive and agile management teams moved early, which led to improvement in their competitive standing. Some research we

found pointed to that new, post-recession leaders were 30 percent more likely to make acquisitions in the heart of the recession and their deals were 37 percent larger than the post-recession laggards. Even if these numbers were off by a considerable margin, we include them as worthy of food for thought.

STA+R Training Analysis

Note: The STA+R Analysis tool can be used for many other applications than those described below, but since we ourselves have used it with great success in training, we have chosen to focus on this area for our example in this book.

Our Systematic Training Audit plus Recommendations tool is a powerful auditing process that provides you a clear, measurable handle for what a specific department or function delivers in value, compared to best practices, plus it suggests recommendations to improve.

Again, your internal training department is probably not part of your company's core product unless your core product is training. Regardless of whether you make ball bearings, planes, books, or software, you are probably very good at that and most all of your resources, money, and energy should be focused on that. This necessarily means that with the resources, money and energy you have left, you can only be marginally good at planning, executing and improving non-core areas such as training. Education is its own craft. Educational resources are now readily available from many external sources and are offered on an enormous variety of delivery platforms to suit your organization's needs, wants, and wishes. Doesn't it make economical- and even common-sense to use them instead?

To recap for this important tool, in today's extremely uncertain business environment, combined with increasingly shorter lifecycles of new products and services, training, especially product specific training, is now becoming a dangerous bottleneck. The current mindset that clouds the effectiveness of this type of training is that you cannot develop or start training until what you want to sell is developed and ready for market. How can it any longer be acceptable to develop and distribute training only after the product is complete? This is especially relevant when the product cycle you are training for may only survive for one or two iterations. Even so, tradition still screams that you have to develop the product or service first, in order to even know what you need to train. Only then can you train. Isn't that right?

Being right or wrong about this has now become a moot point. Waiting for the training until afterward is no longer an option. Development and production cycles are getting squeezed to shorter and shorter lengths, forcing new, timely solutions. Current business practices now demand that your training cycle be quickened, or your edge will be lost. This situation is not helped by the usual coziness (dare we say irrelevance?) of an internal training department nestled snugly, deep within HR. In this configuration, training remains more of an administrative function than the precision marketing tool it now absolutely needs to be.

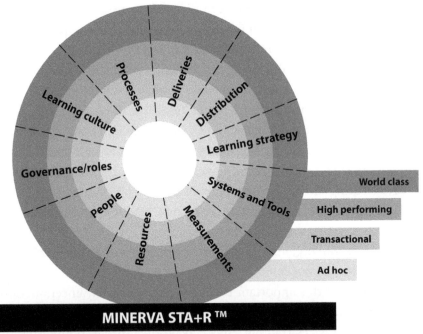

Figure 30. STA+R diagram

What to do?

To facilitate getting a handle on this training challenge, we would like to offer you a peek into a unique process we have developed called Systematic Training Audit and Recommendations or STA+R for short. It is a fairly complex process, while being one of our most effective tools, yet the fundamental components we list below can help you to get a clearer head start on your training challenges and how to tackle them.

First of all, it is important to distinguish the different types of training that are currently offered in the corporate sphere. The following list may help to highlight some forms that your current program may not yet address.

- **Introductory training**
  This is offered internally for new company employees in order to ramp them up as quickly as possible. It provides rules, guidelines, tips, and tricks to get going quickly. Good introductory training also provides tips on how to avoid making predictable, costly mistakes.

- **General basic internal training**
  Once you are in and settled at your workstation, the next step is to get efficient. This is used to get everyone on the same page in your organization. Internal training goes into depth as to what is now expected of you. Written and unwritten cultural issues should be included to help familiarize everyone and to help dispel persistent myths and rumors both within the organization as well as within your industry or branch. How to use the internal network, the dos and don'ts of company and personal security, company communication channels, and the handling or avoidance of other communication systems (as well as social media platforms) should also be addressed.

- **Compliance training**
  These training programs are broader in nature and provide required information needed for dealing with applicable laws, global rules, and accepted universal standards.

- **Open, generic programs**
  These are generic content programs to get you up and running on specific software or equipment used in your office. The most common would be training for standard software packages such as Outlook, Oracle, Word, Adobe, etc.

- **Company specific training**
  These courses are specific, not generic in their format. They are tailored or specially developed to support and promote efficiency on

products and services, specifically designed or customized for use by for instance, your production staff, your sales force, or back-office personnel.

- **Customer specific programs**
  These better fuse your customers with your products, services, and/or company. They are designed to not only make your customers' lives easier but should also encourage them to cooperate and collaborate more with you. Executed correctly, this training will help you communicate better while creating and enhancing each customers' loyalty. Done with a combination of excellence and passion, what your customers experience will then naturally ripple out via their word of mouth while it boosts your marketing message handily and cheaply.

With the exception of open, generic, off-the-shelf training and possibly compliance training, typically offered by the governing body of those standards, each one of these areas can be developed into an important communication channel to improve your company's success. Training is an avenue of growing importance for communication and marketing. It is a direct avenue that can go straight into your customers' thoughts, actions, and behavior.

On the other hand, think of how easily training can become a bottleneck if it is not fresh, exciting, free-flowing, and of the highest quality. Think of the damage possible if it becomes some corporate bureaucrat's political claim to fame. With all the other issues we have talked about on your plate, how can you handle this effectively also?

If you are looking for increased agility, you will probably need some sort of process, function, or reliable group with which to feel safe and comfortable. An effective alternative may be to outsource your training. Before you can tackle this question internally or even think of outsourcing this too, you need to familiarize yourself with what to look for.

Below are some general suggestions on how to proceed.

Systematic training audit and recommendations

This is done most effectively as a project consisting of interviews, workshops, coaching and analysis. A neutral third party is highly recommended to perform the process.

- **Clarify Company Goals and Objectives**

  Is this beginning to sound familiar? Obviously, before you start out on any trip you need to decide your destination. Sit down with those responsible and define your goal in a specific and measurable way. Describe what each core program is meant to achieve. Those responsible should definitely include representatives from other disciplines throughout your company. More specifically, this means people from outside of your Training and/or HR department.

- **Discovery**

  This is where you roll up your sleeves and look at the nuts and bolts of each program. You uncover the input and follow its development all the way from its source to the results produced. You play the role of detective to discover differences and gaps between the amounts of calories invested in each training routine compared to those returned. This can be done by gathering relevant data and conducting appropriate interviews to provide objective statistics as well as a subjective feel.

- **Current State Analysis**

  Now it is time to get to work and create an effective gap analysis between what is actually happening and the results being produced and then compare it to the best practices within your industry. This can be rather a complex task, but even a relatively rough analysis can be both worthwhile and created quickly, even by you and your internal group. Google is an incredible source of information. Results from Google taken with a grain of salt and mixed with the experience of those responsible can produce a quick and often accurate enough assessment.

- **Recommendations**

  Then it is time to present your findings. The purpose is to repair any imbalances or weaknesses uncovered. From all you have read so far, the size and scope of the role your marketing department can and should play a drastically bigger role in this development

385

process. The current compared to the optimal effect of marketing should become fairly apparent. Keep in mind that the best "aha" experience usually starts as an "Oh No!" or "Is that why?" experience. This is progress too, as before this you were not even aware of what you were missing. This step ends when everyone agrees with the weaknesses and blind spots identified. Then an action plan is agreed upon and drawn up.

- **Implementation and Follow-Up**
  Then it is time for the responsible people to act. Their focus should be to hit specified and agreed-upon milestones in your action plan, by a specific deadline date/time. The progress made here should also be easy to graphically depict and display in your Dynamic Navigational Center (DNC). (See the next tool.) The same rules and need for simple and clearly understandable displays of output apply for this project as all others in your DNC Pilothouse.

If this entire process sounds a bit challenging, that is probably because it is. The program that we created is complex on many different levels and has taken years to refine. Why?

Because creating and maintaining a world-class training offering, encompassing all the different categories of training necessary to compete globally, requires an increasing amount of time, energy, and money. Take another look at figure 29. Just some of the areas that need to be addressed are your learning culture, strategies, distribution, and measurements. Think of the egos and kingdoms this can disturb! The key to get even slightly better results is objectively following the above steps. To get world-class results, count on using the help of specialists, professionals who are totally detached from the process and personalities involved, while remaining laser-focused upon the desired outcome.

Indeed, getting a good grip on just these internal areas first will give you more control of your situation. It will also provide a powerful and agile leg up on your competition. Once done, you will probably want to sharpen your edge further by continuing this process on a regular basis. This is especially true if you are serious about understanding the power of training, communication and mastering your organization's path to education agility.

Dynamic Navigational System DNS/DNC

One of, if not the most, powerful parts of becoming and remaining agile is constantly practicing with the tools and methods described here. As they say, "Practice makes perfect." The more you use them the more agile you will become. Not using them, especially after being introduced to them, will create consequences. If you are now beginning to see the value in applying these tools, then what's the best way to continue?

> "Being reasonable leaves you with reasons, not results."
> **—W. Erhard**

By constantly keeping a simple, understandable and graphical representation of your progress in your crew's face. The simpler and more understandable you make each graphic representation, the less room for justification, reasons, excuses, resistance, and debate and/or argument there will be. How much time will this save you?

This is done by building your own Dynamic Navigational Center/ pilothouse or DNC for short. This is a great way to visibly keep these powerful tools from collecting dust. Just as on a ship, the DNC is your command center, your virtual pilothouse. What you and your team observe in your DNC is the real-time graphical depiction of all your agility projects and initiatives, important for your organization's success. All the current, relevant information you need to run an agile organization should be clearly found here. This information will give you a clear view not only on your past results, but in all directions, especially for what lies ahead.

It is from this physical room where you, as the responsible captain, and your trusted crew will guide your ship toward its destination. Just as with a car or your beloved sailing yacht, the vast majority of instruments and tools located here are focused upon the present situation, yet are designed to go further, to look forward. Looking forward makes just as much practical sense when steering a company as it does when steering your car or ship.

Normally, a typical corporate dashboard configuration will contain anywhere between 60 percent to 85 percent historical backward-looking indicators. They measure the wake behind your boat, but say little to nothing about the iceberg, storm, or smooth sailing dead ahead. How could you, as captain, honestly expect to maintain control of a large sailing ship or company if you are looking backwards sixty to 85 percent of the time? If you naively believe you are in control, you are, consciously or not, fooling yourself, while endangering your crew, your organization, and your customers.

Almost all Key Performance Indicators (KPIs)fall neatly into this very common and accepted trap. Just like an athlete's statistics, KPIs measure what has been, instead of looking forward toward what could be. Yes, looking back is very human, as looking back is quantifiable history, and yes, we should consciously strive to learn from the past.

By adding to this current information from your horizon can often make this process anything from overwhelming to scary. This is why both you and your crew have, consciously or not, created a slew of habits, reactions, justifications, and reasons not to monitor it. Today's CEO is increasingly bombarded with internal politics, corporate politeness, and energy-draining bureaucracy. All of these and more have morphed into tools to maintain a safe, comfortable, blind, and unwavering course of business as usual.

The reality is that they chew up enormous amounts of company time, energy, and money without measurably contributing to any forward progress! In short and blunt terms, your very own DNC pilothouse will directly eliminate all the corporate bullshit that can and often does thwart the ultimate success of your enterprise.

Therefore, placing the results of your Dynamic Navigational System (DNS) in an easily understood format, where those directly responsible can see them, will be a constant and in-your-face reminder of your collective commitment to mastering business agility. By making these tools and their results visible and then keeping them updated in real time, you directly transform these agile management tools into a Dynamic

Navigational Center or Pilothouse. Below are the steps to setting one up in your headquarters.

Setting up your virtual or physical DNC

This is not a tool, so much as it is graphically clear, simple, and measurable evidence that your plan to master business agility is physically being implemented, practiced, and by whom. Your DNC provides undeniable and measurable proof as to where your plan is working and where it needs to be acted upon or updated, immediately.

- **Step One:** Choose the relevant tools you want to use from the selection of DNS tools in this book. We invite and encourage you to use or invent other forward-looking tools that you find effective. We would be very thankful to learn of and share any tools you find effective and agile. Please let us know by contacting us at www.caginternationalag.com!

- **Step Two:** Find a small, secure, empty office or room, as close to management and the CEO's office as possible. Go ahead and actually rename it "The Pilothouse."

- **Step Three:** Populate your pilothouse with visual, graphical displays and/or charts that clearly, simply, and understandably depict the output from those tools. Again, the simpler and easier these visualizations are to read and comprehend, the harder they become to avoid or downplay their raw and graphical truth.

- **Step Four:** Find a reliable, committed, up-and-coming junior-manager from each relevant department. These departments will include marketing, sales, finance, production, and HR and will vary depending upon the tools selected. Charge each of these people as designated champions. Have them consistently update the information provided by their departments, in the desired and agreed-upon format. Take the necessary steps to make sure they and all of their department superiors understand the importance of delivering unedited or non-massaged data. In some cases, it may be necessary to provide incentives to these juniors to report any behind-the-scenes suggestions, commands, and even threats to "massage" the information provided. Until everyone understands and is committed to this new way of working, the possibility of interception and tampering with the input to mask or hide a real or perceived problem needs to be expected, prepared for, and guarded against.

- **Step Five:** Place a conference table in your pilothouse and begin holding formal and informal meetings directly under these graphical displays as often as possible. Encourage other senior decision makers to conduct more meetings there too. Here, all participants will have instant, understandable, and undeniable access to the latest information. All will be able to see how the situation looks historically, here and now, as well as going forward, from relevant perspectives. Providing this information will automatically force your team to become more agile. How?

  Your managers will no longer be able to waste precious time hiding behind, "I'll get back to you with that information," because it is now clearly and sometimes annoyingly in front of theirs and everyone else's noses. Any decision maker not properly prepared with their next step suggestion will be painfully evident to everyone in attendance.

Value gained from your Pilothouse

- You and your management team are now the skipper and crew of your organization's future, not just its historian.
- You now have active control of your ship's helm, not just its logbook. You and your crew now have all the current, graphical information necessary to effectively run the ship, spread clearly out before you.
- Starting here and now, you and your crew will be able to directly respond to threats and opportunities, in real time. Remember, responsible means the ability to respond and now you can respond directly.
- In-your-face information. No longer is there anywhere to hide for those responsible. The information on the charts that surround you tells the simple, unedited, non-political, and current truth. Either the person responsible for the data can interpret it, explain

it, and present a plan to fix or improve it, or it is high time to replace him/her with someone who burns for this type of decisive, agile, and active leadership.

- An increased level of responsibility. Having an ambitious person from each department responsible for regularly updating the displayed information will light a real fire under their managers to act now! No leader likes to look inadequate, especially in front of a subordinate charged by the CEO with providing reliable information. This will usually encourage even laggards to either shape up or wash out quickly. This will strengthen your leadership bench!

- Meeting times will diminish, as most personal opinions especially those from your HPPO's can now be quickly neutralized. Clear, simple, and easy to understand information will negate the need for endless discussion, justification, positioning, excuses, and politics. Precious minutes will be used instead of hours to decide, act, and start measuring anew. The time saved will be massive and cumulative, as decisions and course changes can now be taken in real-time. Already at the next meeting changes in the charts will either support the change or reveal the need for even more drastic adjustments.

- The transformational effect upon the agility of your crew should quickly become visible. Decision makers will have to practice and master thinking on their feet. They must practice learning to make changes directly and to be directly responsible for their actions or suffer the consequences for not changing. So, you look at the information and realize, for example, that:

    o The competition is eating our lunch
    o Sales margins are rapidly decreasing
    o Training costs are increasing while customer satisfaction is decreasing

- You can now go instantly to the source to call on those responsible for direct answers and get briefed directly on what steps are planned and what date and time you can expect the problems to be corrected. Then you are all free to leave and follow up at the appointed time.

- Confidence in management will increase as visible decisions and actions will replace rumors and speculation. People can comfortably and efficiently focus on their tasks, rather than just the latest water cooler chatter.

- Also, when all agree that the charts depict smooth sailing ahead, the second in command can calmly replace the skipper, who can then practice mastering the art of a well-deserved break.

- An effective tip: The DNC can also be operated as a project. This will make the changes easier to swallow for the obvious and even covert bureaucrats in your management team. Reactions to this decision and resistance (often from the usual suspects) to it will also send an early flag up to monitor those whose behaviors still seem to inhibit agility, rather than promote it.

- This tool is also particularly effective and adds value in mergers and major transformations, as all mission-critical projects are now monitored and managed from your DNC, in real time.

- An important final note, make sure to have a secure lock on the door. This is not only the intelligence of your operation, but is now literally your organization's heart. The CEO and management can actively help increase security by frequently using this room.

Advanced Leadership Agility Coaching

If you have come this far in this book, then your path to mastering business agility probably includes the practice of putting people and their subjective needs, wants and wishes over objective system demands. Count on that your people, who include customers, prospective customers, your employees, your alliances, partners, suppliers, and just about everyone else, are your most important asset going forward. Should you forget this important point be prepared that they will remind you, often, at the most inconvenient times. That is why the art and practice of agile leadership is so important to practice and master. We would love to talk to you[1] if you are also committed to the path of mastering business agility on a personal level and are interested in, among other things:

- **Consciously placing people over processes and tools**
  Learn to walk the talk. It's one thing to say you do this. It is often experienced quite differently by those you lead. Practice closing this gap and, in the process, empower everyone involved into an easier, more efficient and enjoyable environment in which to succeed.

- **Responding to change over plans**
  Agility means being able to improvise, adapt and overcome when the situation and circumstances shift right before your eyes. Become consciously aware of all those hidden inhibitors lurking deep in your own behavior. Discover tools and methods to handle them quickly and efficiently.

- **Prioritizing soft factors over hard factors**
  Or at least learn to use them in balance and appropriately. The more you practice listening with all your senses, to empathize with others and understand their points of view, the better the chance you have of creating and honoring profitable and sustainable agreements that stick.

- **Anticipating what is to be expected going forward**
  This is primarily a soft factor, a skill that develops with both experience as well as being open and sensitive to what is happening all around you. The more stressed you become, the less sensitive you also become as you are using your energy to defend rather than receive. Training to relax and open up your senses as well as comparing new cues to what you have already experienced will go far to increase your agility.

- **Flexible collaboration with customers and vendors**
  Any agreement needs to be fluid over time. Practice the art of mutually increasing the breathing room in every agreement and contract you create and sign. It is critical to create the trust necessary to come to new agreements when the situation drastically shifts on its schedule rather than what the contract originally spelled out.

- **Anchoring and implementing your DNC within your C-Suite**
  Count on those managers who, either obviously or stealthily, subscribe to business as usual and, in their unique way, resist the responsibility and accountability needed to establish your *Dynamic Navigational Center*. Use the tools and methods available to either get them on board quickly or those which help them ease out of their position and into a new one, in a win/win way.

- **Resolving conflicts at their core**
  There are many methods to solve conflicts, but very few that erase the underlying principles or opinions that caused them from the start. Make it your priority to objectively source a conflict directly back to its core. Only then can you proceed to resolve it so that all the behaviors involved can move forward together as a team.

There are of course a multitude of other tools, methods, and tips which can be used to distinguish your agile leadership style from that of a manager. Learning them is only part of the adventure. Continuously practicing their application with the appropriate amount of energy, force and attitude puts you and keeps you square on the path of mastery. We are looking to contact you who also see this as a key component to mastering business agility. Don't be shy!

Additional Tools and Methods

Lean startup

What is lean startup?

Below is another angle to encourage agility and entrepreneurship and is penned by friend and colleague, Andy Cars, founder of Lean Ventures and Seedcap.

"As a term, lean startup was first used in 2008. It was coined by Eric Ries on his blog Startup Lessons Learned in a post titled 'The Lean Startup.' It has its roots among high-tech start-ups in Silicon Valley, but has since been adopted by start-ups worldwide, and has also won great acclaim among large established companies and organizations such as General Electric, Telefonica, BBC, and even the United States Government, to name a few.

But before we get ahead of ourselves, let us start by defining the meaning of lean and startup. All too often we talk past each other without understanding the meaning of the words we use. For example, have you ever stopped to ask yourself and your colleagues how they interpret the words lean, startup, or innovation, terminology that is often used but seldom understood?

Traditionally, lean is associated with the Toyota Production System, Total Quality Control, and Six Sigma where the focus is on reducing waste and the number of errors that occur during manufacturing. However, in lean startup, being lean means to use the least amount of resources while inching toward a solution that addresses the customer's most pressing problems significantly better than competing alternatives. It is not about streamlining or incrementally improving the existing production system; it is about finding out what to build in the first place.

When it comes to the often-misused word startup, the accepted definition in the startup community comes from Stanford Professor Steve Blank, and reads as follows:

"A startup is a temporary organization designed to search for a scalable and repeatable business model."

What this means is that a startup does not know who the customer will be, what the final product or service will look like, how to price the offering, or how to best reach their customers. What startups have are a bunch of assumptions.

While a startup is searching for a business model that works, an established company is fully occupied with executing on a finely tuned business model that figuratively speaking generates $2 for every $1 that is put in. Yes, we are talking about the golden cash cow that established companies tend to protect until their dying days.

The differences between searching for a business model and executing on a business model are as significant as night and day and affect everything from metrics, methods, and tools to recruitment, incentives, leadership, and definition of risk. And this is where lean startup comes into the picture. Lean startup is both a methodology or set of methods and a mindset that fundamentally differs from business as usual.

The overall process is often illustrated in its most basic form as shown here, which first appeared in Eric Ries's book *The Lean Startup*, published in September of 2011.

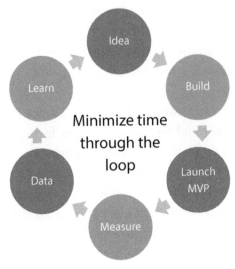

Lean startup is data and experiments driven, where the aim is to turn assumptions into validated learnings as fast and efficiently as possible.

Lean startup advocates a fail fast, fail often mindset in order to gradually learn and understand more about the pain points and constraints that the customer is experiencing.

The goal is to achieve a problem/solution fit, which simply means we have something that the customer is willing to pay for and where the cost of recruiting a new customer is significantly lower than what we can earn from that customer. Or put differently, to build a sustainable business, Customer Acquisition Costs (CAC) have to be significantly lower than Customer Lifetime Value (CLV) (CAC < CLV).

The key is to learn what works and what does not, as opposed to prematurely executing on the wrong business model. According to the data scientists at The Startup Genome Project[1], the number one reason why start-ups fail is because they scale-up too early. Since scaling burns money like nothing else, scaling before reaching product/market fit only results in a deeper hole in someone's pocket. While sales may very well increase, profitability will remain elusive.

Fundraising to promote something that the market does not want is a sure recipe for disaster. Boo.com, Webvan, Better Place and Pets.com[2] are only a few examples of failed start-ups that chose scaling to capture market share over providing customer value. They ended up burning hundreds of millions of dollars of other people's money in the process.

As always, the devil is in the details. Doing customer interviews in a way that introduces large amounts of biased data, or only relying on quantitative data while ignoring qualitative data, will only cloud judgment and increase the chance of failure. Since the most likely scenario is for the initial business idea or model not to rhyme with the market, *lean startup* practitioners *do not* spend valuable time writing thirty-page business plans with five-year Excel projections to boot.

Instead, we quickly list our assumptions about the market on a business model canvas[3]. Then we identify the riskiest assumption that, if it were not to hold true, would kill the business idea. Next, the focus shifts to turning the assumption to be tested into a measurable hypothesis. We design our experiment and set a target for what we hope to achieve. Then we 'get out of the building' and run the experiment. Based on what we learn, we update our business model canvas. All of which can be done within one week. Compare that to most large companies that take several weeks just to call a meeting in which the Highest Paid Person's Opinion (HPPO) often prevails over this data-driven approach.

If the assumption is not verified, which is the most likely scenario, we start from scratch with a new experiment and keep at it until slowly but surely or as long as the funding will take us we crawl toward something that the market wants and is prepared to pay for.

The experiments are often referred to as Minimum Viable Products (MVPs) or Minimum Viable Experiments (MVEs). MVPs are used to test for user engagement and MVEs for initial user interest. Similarly, prototypes are used to answer the question, "Can we build it?" while pretotypes[4] are used to answer the question, "Should we build it?" By putting a pretotype in front of customers, such as paper sketches, explainer videos, or landing pages that communicate the value proposition, we can test for and measure initial user interest. Since the aim is to use the minimum number of resources possible to maximize learning about the riskiest assumptions, the pecking order should be pretotypes and MVEs followed by prototypes and MVPs.

There are many who have helped to develop lean startup to where it is today. The Business Model Canvas, which has become a key element of lean startup, was first presented by Alexander Osterwalder and Yves Pigneur in their book *Business Model Generation*, published in 2010.

Ash Maurya introduced his own version of the Business Model Canvas, which he calls the Lean Canvas in his book *Running Lean*, published in 2012. Another Business Model Canvas variation is the so-called Javelin, also known as the Validation or Experiment board, developed by Trevor Owens, founder of the Lean Startup Machine.

On the metrics side, Dave McClure, founder of the 500 Startups accelerator program has contributed to the ever-growing lean startup toolbox with his Startup Metrics for Pirates, which Alistair Croll and Benjamin Yoskovitz then elaborated on in their book *Lean Analytics*, published in 2013.

The above examples show that lean startup is a set of methods and tools under constant development, but with the distinction that they all share one common mindset, namely that of disciplined data-driven experimentation in direct contact with the customer to quickly and economically find a business model worth scaling.

Those who are the most creative in designing and running experiments to obtain validated learning will be those who are the most likely to succeed. Remember, everything is an experiment.[5]

What Andy seems to be confirming is what we have been promoting also. Data-driven testing and research to discover and learn from the most business agile path forward.

E-Learning and blended learning and LMS

We have saved the best for last when it comes to one of the biggest forces of change currently rushing through company after company. All you need to know and find out is already available at your fingertips, with help of your smartphone or smart pad. Even before COVID-19, most users had already begun to expect an individualized learning experience, on demand, wherever and whenever needed, twenty-four seven .

Using simple e-learning/online techniques and then blending them together with traditional, live face-to-face courses or workshop training has been confirmed to produce drastically better results and massively boost business agility within organizations. This will also create a side effect of increased customer loyalty, while profiting from and enjoying massive cost reductions! Today's workforce now expects the same, seamless online experience, when it comes to training as they enjoy in most other parts of their lives. Add to this the current situation where many are either forced to or choose to work from home and you have the perfect atmosphere to innovate, customize, and improve the individual online training experience.

To get people excited about continuing their education and truly become a learning organization, we need to consider how people really learn. From our own research we now understand that people gain knowledge according to the generally accepted 70-20-10 rule.

- Ten percent is the average gain by formal learning. Today, formal classroom/lecture-style learning can be done effectively by using a powerful combination of tailor-made courses and universal off-the-shelf courses.

- Twenty percent is the average gain realized when colleagues and peers share their knowledge and experience. This can now be accomplished more effectively by utilizing a modern Learning Management System (LMS) enhanced with social learning capabilities.

- Seventy percent is the remainder that occurs when learners search for knowledge on demand and solve a specific problem or challenge, in real-time, when the need is identified. This is kinesthetic learning, which is what people typically do when they are searching for more knowledge on, for example Google, social media networks, etc.

A modern, competitive company must be able to provide access to, a blend of, and support for all of three of these different learning styles within this growing, online arena. Here is where a modern Learning Management System (LMS) is utilized to become the backbone for boosting your capacity for on-demand learning.

In his book, *The Fifth Discipline*, author Peter Senge defined a learning organization as, "An organization that constantly increases its capacity for success." Your chances for success will increase and your own effective learning organization will develop when you have effectively implemented this mindset and blended these three types of learning styles within your training program, throughout your organization.

Call it online learning, digital learning, blended learning, or whatever you choose, increased learning and the measurable improvement of your skill set is becoming the best way to maintain your relevancy and value when it comes to making a good living. As we become more technically oriented and the information flow continues to accelerate it is important to keep up with important trends, otherwise you and your team can easily ride that escalator of development right back down to the first floor.

The good news is that the task of learning and developing your employees has never been easier to accomplish! With all the modern techniques and methods available, and since your future success depends upon staying current and agile, what are you waiting for?

Conclusion

The governing institutions, the corporations, and private individuals who choose to continue with their version of business as usual into this new era of colossal and rapid transformation we are now firmly in will inevitably vanish or be left on the sideline as bystanders. At best, they will end up being forced to be reactive to all the new and exciting challenges and chaotic, exponential growth caused by new developments introduced by more business agile competitors.

Think ahead just a few years from now. Some of us may then have children graduating from college. Some may be just starting a family, while still others will be heading into retirement. Regardless, all of us will be living in a world where we have either fought to solve the incredible challenges outlined in this book, or failed trying. Although newer challenges will still be bombarding us, do we have any other option than to keep trying? This constant development process is sometimes called *life*.

You have now been introduced to the wonders of our sailing metaphor into the treacherous and sometimes towering seas that are now constantly building in today's business climate. We have used a sleek sailboat handled by a competent team of sailors as our metaphor for your management group, with you as El Capitan (the Skipper) or CEO.

It should now be painfully obvious that these seas are getting progressively, even exponentially rougher, more uncertain and even less forgiving. There is no sign yet of any measurable change in this process. Our collective sin has been that we have been much too complacent with regards to honing our ability to get consciously agile. We got fat and happy, taking the good times for granted. We now need to practice the art of looking forward more and master acting decisively instead of just relaxing into another round of business as usual.

We desperately need a new and enhanced toolbox stuffed full of agility tools and skills to confidently move into this turbulent weather system and this new era of colossal transformation. Explosive growth and new developments are making all product and service cycles increasingly shorter. Massive megatrends set against the background of unpredictable, volatile economic, environmental, and geopolitical storm squalls have now generated an environment for a major perfect storm. This increasingly turbulent and uncertain environment will force corporations and institutions that wish to survive and thrive to become extremely vigilant, more trustworthy, and most of all, very agile! In our opinion, corporate agility will be so vital going forward that if leaders disregard incorporating it into their every action, it will be equal to abdicating their role as responsible and trustworthy leaders.

For a good sailor, agility is second nature. For leaders of organizations, this quality has been and remains a struggle to take on. The problem is not so much in identifying the problem or taking a decision; it is usually in the execution and follow up of what was decided! The tools for seeing the icebergs around us are getting more accurate, but ironically getting individuals in our organization to act, change, or adjust direction is becoming increasingly more difficult. In the good old days, we enjoyed longer cycles, less competition and a more forgiving environment. Once upon a time the answer was to put finance and accounting in charge of squeezing every last penny out of one reorganization after another. Look around your organization; how much is still left to squeeze?

The answer going forward is proving to be the opposite of dumping the challenging and exciting task of leadership on your accountants, legal, and other masters of administration. It is also not to prioritize actions that try to meet the increasingly disconnected or selfish demands from insulated, often isolated boards and investors. Tomorrow's successful leaders have to actively and consciously keep their hand firmly on the tiller and relearn their forgotten ability to execute change quickly and decisively.

Choosing to master agility, you will ultimately have to face all of the largest inhibitors of change and growth. One of the primary bottlenecks that encompass all four of these inhibitors is the decision and process of doing or making it yourself. This critical question pops up in virtually all of those following four areas:

- Systems and processes
- Organizational structure
- IT
- Company culture

You will need special tools and ability to responsibly master them to help you navigate all the internal challenges you are bound to face.

Furthermore, your agility challenge is seldom just in decision-making. That process was streamlined to a point beyond efficiency long ago. Rather, we see the execution, implementation, and adjustment of agile change as the BIG issue here and now. In order to be effective, you must have clearer forward vision and accurate, up-to-the-minute information about all current variables, issues and situations. Relying mostly on past performance will crush you! Practicing "The older I get, the better I was," is now a recipe for disaster. Going forward, the responsible CEO also needs a conscious, well-trained, and agile crew. Your crew must be armed with simple and effective tools to rapidly execute course changes or adjustments that you, El Capitan, have ordered, usually based upon their accurate input.

Yes, your challenge to run a well-organized ship has increased, but there is absolutely no need for despair. Rather, there are many things you can do immediately to mitigate the biggest inhibitors of change, while mastering your path to business agility. To review, the worst inhibiting culprits once again are Systems and processes, Organization, IT, and Culture, all of which can be handled to encourage more agility instead of choking it off. In these pages we have mentioned just a few of our favorite effective tools that have proven time and again to be helpful. In the end, all of these tools and suggestions listed in section four have one objective in common. That objective is to keep your customers happy and satisfied enough to buy more, while they eagerly spread the word further about your products and services. Continue with business as usual and expect your customers to move to more agile and competitive alternatives.

We sincerely hope this book has been a valuable read and that you have been inspired to join us on the path of mastering business agility. With any luck, you also see a possibility to use this as a handbook. Then you can practice using these tools to inspire your crew into action in real life. Let's move forward together in a joint quest of making your organization or institution more responsive to the changes and challenges that lie ahead. We also hope that you now have a heightened awareness of the uncertainty that lies before us all, but now feel as excited about the future as we do. You are also invited to participate and contribute to this conversation about agility by visiting our blog at www.masteringagilityblog.com.

Finally, if you think the past thirty years of development have been epic, just wait for the next thirty!

They will be yielding colossal transformation in all areas of well-being, human interaction, and enterprise; only now *you* will be successfully navigating this uncertainty, together with us, on the path of mastering agility in all we do.

Welcome aboard and prepare to cast off!

Works Cited

Preface

1. The impact of agility: How to shape your organization to compete. (2021). *McKinsey & Company*. https://www.mckinsey.com/business-functions/organization/our-insights/the-impact-of-agility-how-to-shape-your-organization-to-compete
2. Ibid.
3. Lipton, B. (2008). *The Biology of Belief*. Hay House.
4. The impact of agility: How to shape your organization to compete. (2021). *McKinsey & Company*. https://www.mckinsey.com/business-functions/organization/our-insights/the-impact-of-agility-how-to-shape-your-organization-to-compete

Chapter 1

1. Vinge, Vernor. (1993). Technological Singularity. *Whole Earth Review.* . https://frc.ri.cmu.edu/~hpm/book98/com.ch1/vinge.singularity.html
2. *New lecture: Hybrid work*. (2021). Future Wise. http://futurewise.se
3. Pogue, David. (2015). Robots Rising. *Scientific American, Volume 313*.
4. Yasada, Y. (1990). *40 Years, 20 Million Ideas: The Toyota Suggestion System*. Productivity Pr.
5. Halberstam, D. (1986). *The Reckoning*. William Morrow & Co.
6. Kageyama, Yuri. (2015). Toyota at top in global vehicle sales for first 9 months. *AP News*. https://apnews.com/article/58b018936635489ea35c9902af0ef929
7. Aghina, W., Handscomb, C., Ludolph, J., Róna, D., & West, D. (2020). Enterprise agility: Buzz or business impact? *McKinsey & Company*. https://www.mckinsey.com/business-functions/organization/our-insights/enterprise-agility-buzz-or-business-impact
8. Ibid.

Chapter 2

1. Dobbs, R., Remes, J., Smit, S., Manyika, J., Woetzel, J., & Agyenim-Boateng, Y. (2013). Urban world: The shifting global business landscape. *McKinsey & Company*. https://www.mckinsey.com/featured-insights/urbanization/urban-world-the-shifting- global-business-landscape

Chapter 3

1. Disruptive technologies: Advances that will transform life, business, and the global economy. (2013). *McKinsey & Company*. https://www.mckinsey.com/~/media/mckinsey/business%20functions/mckinsey%20digital/our%20insights/disruptive%20technologies/mgi_disruptive_technologies_full_repor t_may2013.ashx
2. McKinsey & Company. (2013). *McKinsey & Company Quarterly*.

3. Marr, Bernard. (2018). The key definitions of artificial intelligence (AI) that explain its importance. *Forbes.* https://www.forbes.com/sites/bernardmarr/2018/02/14/the-key-definitions-of-artificial-intelligence-ai-that-explain-its-importance/#454befca4f5d

4. Britannica, T. Editors of Encyclopaedia. (2020). Mississippi Bubble. *Encyclopedia Britannica.* https://www.britannica.com/event/Mississippi-Bubble

5. *Free online courses by Harvard, MIT, & more.* (2021). EdX. http://www.edx.org

6. Manchester, W. (1993). *A World Lit Only by Fire: The Medieval Mind and the Renaissance: Portrait of an Age.* Little, Brown and Company.

7. *Free online course, lessons, and practice.* (2021). Khan Academy. https://www.khanacademy.org

8. North, Gary. (2015). How Salman Khan has smashed 3,000 years of classroom education mythology. http://www.garynorth.com/public/14327.cfm

9. *A college alternative that leads to a full-time job.* (2021). Praxis. http://www.discoverpraxis.com

10. Moore's Law: Transistor number's trend chart. (2011). Wikimedia Commons. https://commons.wikimedia.org/wiki/Category:Moore%27s_law#/media/File:Moores_law_(1970-2011).PNG

Chapter 4

1. Malthus, Thomas Robert. (2018). An essay on the principle of population. *Econlib.* http://www.econlib.org/library/Malthus/malPop.html

2. Brandon, Emily. (2013). The baby boomer retirement crunch begins. *U.S. News.* http://money.usnews.com/money/retirement/articles/2013/05/13/the-baby-boomer-retirement-crunch-begins

3. Dychtwald, K., & Kadlec, D. (2010). *A New Purpose: Redefining Money, Family, Work, Retirement, and Success.* Harper Collins. https://books.google.se/books?id=6NRDqtmcLZ8C&redir_esc=y

4. Brandon, Emily. (2013). The baby boomer retirement crunch begins. *U.S. News.* http://money.usnews.com/money/retirement/articles/2013/05/13/the-baby-boomer-retirement-crunch-begins

5. Schubart, Bill. (2013). Curling parents and middle-aged children. https://schubart.com/curling-parents-and-middle-age-children/

6. Taylor, Charles. (2019). Why Gillette's new ad campaign is toxic. *Forbes.* https://www.forbes.com/sites/charlesrtaylor/2019/01/15/why-gillettes-new-ad-campaign-is-toxic/#2d335d0c5bc9

7. Merriam-Webster. (n.d.). Sheeple. *Merriam-Webster.com dictionary.* https://www.merriam-webster.com/dictionary/sheeple

Chapter 5

1. *Build your business.* (n.d.). Amazing Selling Machine. http://amazingsellingmachine.com

Part Two

1. Office of Public Health Preparedness. (2015). [Three category 4 hurricanes in the Central Pacific region]. [Photograph]. State of Hawaii Department of Health. https://health.hawaii.gov/prepare/advisories/hurricane-season/

Chapter 7

1. *Bill Bonner.* (2021). Rogue Economics. https://www.rogueeconomics.com/authors/bill-bonner/
2. *History before it happens.* (2021). Trends Research. *The Trends Journal.* http://trends-research.com
3. Merriam-Webster. (n.d.). Quant. *Merriam-Webster.com dictionary.* https://www.mer-riam-webster.com/dictionary/quant
4. Aghina, W., Handscomb, C., Ludolph, J., Róna, D., & West, D. (2020). Enterprise agility: Buzz or business impact? *McKinsey & Company.* https://www.mckinsey.com/business-functions/organization/our-insights/enterprise-agility-buzz-or-business-impact
5. McClelland, Rob. (2013). Differences between the traditional CPI and the chained CPI. *Congressional Budget Office.* https://www.cbo.gov/publication/44088
6. Maverick, J.B. (2020). How big is the derivatives market? *Investopedia.* https://www.investopedia.com/ask/answers/052715/how-big-derivatives-market.asp
7. Standing, G. (2016). *The Precariat: The New Dangerous Class.* Bloomsbury Academic.
8. Getchell, Dr. Michelle. (n.d.). The Progressive Era. *Khan Academy.* https://www.khanacademy.org/humanities/us-history/rise-to-world-power/age-of-empire/a/the-progressive-era
9. Benedikt Frey, C., & Osborne, M. (2013). The future of employment: How suscep-tible are jobs to computerization? *University of Oxford.* https://www.oxfordmartin.ox.ac.uk/downloads/academic/The_Future_of_Employment. pdf
10. CBRE. (2014). Genesis research report. Fast forward 2030: The future of work and the workplace. https://www.genesiscommunity.cn/file/CBRE%20Genesis%20Report_Workplace2030_E NG_Full%20Report_1203.pdf
11. Gorman, China. (2015). The global workplace of 2030. *Great Place to Work.* https://www.greatplacetowork.com/resources/blog/the-global-workplace-of-2030
12. *History before it happens.* (2021). Trends Research. *The Trends Journal.* http://trends-research.com
13. *Home page.* (2021). Creator, San Francisco CA. https://www.creator.rest/
14. Love, Dylan. (2014). Here's the burger-flipping robot that could put fast-food workers out of a job. *Yahoo! Finance.* https://finance.yahoo.com/news/theres-burg-er-flippin-robot- designed-140524287.html
15. Andrews, Evan. (2019). Who were the Luddites? *History.* https://www.history.com/news/who- were-the-luddites
16. Bernays, E. (2004). *Propaganda.* Ig Publishing.
17. Bloomberg. (2021). BDI Baltic Exchange Dry Index. https://www.bloomberg.com/quote/BDIY:IND
18. *Fred economic data.* (n.d.). Economic research. Federal Reserve Bank of St. Louis. https://fred.stlouisfed.org/

19. Williams, John. (2021). Analysis behind and beyond government economic reporting. *Shadow Government Statistics*. http://www.shadowstats.com/

Chapter 8

1. Hadavi, Tala. (2020). Lobbying in Q1 topped a record $938 million, but lobbyists say their profession is misunderstood. *CNBC*. https://www.cnbc.com/2020/10/05/q1-lobbying- spend-was-record-938-million-but-lobbyists-decry-stereotype.html
2. Breyer, Melissa. (2013). What a grocery store without bees looks like. *Mother Nature Network*. https://miarbordayalliance.wordpress.com/tag/xerces-society/
3. Gray, Jennifer. (2015). Report: Marine life has taken devastating hit over 40 years. *CNN*. http://edition.cnn.com/2015/09/17/world/oceans-report/
4. Greshko, Michael. (2019). What are mass extinctions, and what causes them? *National Geographic*. https://www.nationalgeographic.com/science/article/mass-extinction
5. Lyons, Oren. (1996). Speech. Council member of Onondaga Tribe.
6. Marks, Jay W. (2021). Medical definition of Hippocratic oath. *MedicineNet*. http://www.medicinenet.com/script/main/art.asp?articlekey=20909
7. *History before it happens.* (2021). Trends Research. *The Trends Journal*. http://trends-research.com
8. Armstrong, Martin. (2016). Is the Supreme Court acting unconstitutional? *Armstrong Economics*.

Chapter 9

1. PoliJam. (2010, March 9). Pelosi: "We have to pass the bill so you can find out what is in it." YouTube. https://www.youtube.com/watch?v=hV-05TLiiLU

Chapter 10

1. Alfred, L. T. (1854). "The Charge of the Light Brigade."
2. Latdict. (n.d.). Agilis. *Latin Dictionary and Grammar Resources*. https://latin- dictionary.net/definition/2296/agilis-agile-agilior
3. Aghina, W., De Smet, A., & Weerda, K. (2015). Agility: It rhymes with stability. *McKinsey & Company*. https://www.mckinsey.com/business-functions/organization/our- insights/agility-it-rhymes-with-stability
4. Ingram, Nick. (2015). To make a real decision you have to kill options. *Nick Ingram Consulting*. https://clearthinking.co/to-make-a-real-decision-you-have-to-kill-options/
5. *The Official Website of Dr. Joe Dispenza.* (2021). Unlimited: Dr. Joe Dispenza. https://drjoedispenza.com/

Chapter 11

1. Harvard Business Review. (2015). (pp. 20). *Harvard Business Publishing*.
2. Lane, Oliver J.J. (2021). Loneliness epidemic: Third of UK adults haven't been hugged in six months, over half haven't made a new friend. Breitbart. https://www.breitbart.com/europe/2021/07/28/loneliness-epidemic-third-

of-uk-adults-havent-been-hugged-in-six-months-over-half-havent-made-a-new-friend/

3. Standing, G. (2016). *The Precariat: The New Dangerous Class*. Bloomsbury Academic.
4. Larsson, K. (2014). Sensational Presentation Skills. CreateSpace Independent Publishing Platform.

Chapter 12

1. *E-learning*. (n.d.). E-learning. https://www.minervagroup.se/

Tool Three

1. Peters, T., Phillips, J., & Waterman, R. (1980). Structure is not organization. *Business Horizons*. https://tompeters.com/docs/Structure_Is_Not_Organization.pdf

Tool Five

1. Colvin, Geoff. (2015). Why every aspect of your business is about to change. *Fortune Magazine*. https://fortune.com/2015/10/22/the-21st-century-corporation-new-business-models/

Tool Seven

1. Neuman, John L. (1975). Make overhead cuts that last. *Harvard Business Review*. https://hbr.org/1975/05/make-overhead-cuts-that-last

Tool Nine

1. Jong, M., & Van Dijk, M. (2015). Disrupting beliefs: A new approach to business-model innovation. *McKinsey & Company*. https://www.mckinsey.com/business- functions/strategy-and- corporate-finance/our-insights/disrupting-beliefs-a-new- approach-to-business-model-innovation

Tool Ten

1. *Entrepreneurship*. (2021). Wikipedia. https://en.wikipedia.org/wiki/Entrepreneurship
2. *Premier SaaS solutions for M & A*. (2021). Datasite. https://www.datasite.com/us/en.html
3. *Mergers, Acquisitions, and Operations*. (2021). Platinum Equity. Platinum Equity Advisors, LLC. https://www.platinumequity.com/

Tool Eleven

1. McCracken, Harry. (2011). Osborne! The machine, the man, and the dawn of the portable computing revolution. *Technologizer*. http://www.technologizer.com/2011/04/01/osborne-computer/

Tool Fourteen

1. *Get in touch with our experts.* (2021). CAG International AG. https://www.caginter-nationalag.com/#map_and_contact

Additional Tools and Methods

1. Empson, Rip. (2013). Backed by Steve Blank and more, Startup Genome founders launch next- gen benchmarking tool for startups. *Tech Crunch*. http://techcrunch.com/2013/12/20/backed-by-steve-blank-more-startup-genome- founders-launch-next-gen-benchmarking-tool-for-startups/
2. 210 of the biggest, costliest startup failures of all time. (2021). *CB Insights*. https://www.cbinsights.com/blog/biggest-startup-failures/
3. *Business model canvas.* (2021). Wikipedia. https://en.wikipedia.org/wiki/Business_Model_Canvas
4. Savoia, A. (2019) *The Right It: Why So Many Ideas Fail and How to Make Sure Yours Succeed.* HarperCollins.
5. *About us: Team.* (n.d.). Lean Ventures. Lean Ventures International AB. https://lean-ventures.se/about-us/team/

Index

About the Authors

Hans Amell is a Harvard-trained Swede who has lived in the USA since 1987. He is a McKinsey alumnus and former executive officer in leading global corporations such as Dun and Bradstreet Group, Cognizant Corp, Ericsson, and others. He is called upon to execute major change in corporations and institutions via board memberships or via his company, Catalyst Acquisition Group. Mr. Amell is also the founding partner in the Minerva Group and its parent CAG International AG. He is a leading player in the cutting edge of agile consulting services with his *Dynamic Navigational System* products and in the application of efficient blended learning solutions for large organizations. He was also the lead founder and Executive Chairman of Intrepid Learning Systems and created Gartner Custom Research after acquiring the GCR unit from Gartner. His passion is creating and applying agility within organizations that understand the need for quicker implementation of change, but very wisely recognize they will need assistance to accomplish this.

Kurt Larsson is an American who has been living in Sweden since the late 1980s. He has sold everything from automobile tires in Houston, Texas to retail banking delivery systems in over twenty countries. He has driven his own educational consulting company, Expanding Understanding, for more than twenty years. His niche is transforming *consultative* business teams into *collaborative* ones to maximize customer loyalty and profit. To do this he specializes in effective selling, leadership, and customer service practices. These practices focus on more conscious and efficient use of all forms of human communication. His passion is educating people to the power and leverage available from the conscious reading of and deliberate use of body language. His skills work perfectly in line with transforming management, sales, and customer service teams from a transactional to a collaborative business model where strengthening customer loyalty is the prime goal. He has now become an active member on both Catalyst's and Minerva's Board of directors.

For more information about the authors or to come in contact with them, you are welcome to contact us via our webpage located at www.caginternationalag.com and follow our blog at www.masteringagilityblog.com.

Contact information:
Hans Amell: hamell@catalystacquisition.com,
Tel: US, +1 973 903 0100

Kurt Larsson: klarsson@catalystacquisition.com
Tel: Sweden, +46 708 736 375

CPSIA information can be obtained
at www.ICGtesting.com
Printed in the USA
BVHW042331240222
629844BV00004B/16/J